PHILIP'S

STRE...AS

Cornwall

Falmouth, Newquay, Penzance, Plymouth, St Austell, Truro

www.philips-maps.co.uk
First published in 2003 by
Philip's, a division of
Octopus Publishing Group Ltd
www.octopusbooks.co.uk
Endeavour House, 189 Shaftesbury Avenue
London WC2H 8JY
An Hachette UK Company
www.hachette.co.uk

Third edition 2010
First impression 2010
CORCA

978-1-84907-085-0 (spiral)

© Philip's 2010

Ordnance Survey®

This product includes mapping data licensed
from Ordnance Survey® with the permission
of the Controller of Her Majesty's Stationery
Office. © Crown copyright 2010. All rights
reserved. Licence number 100011710.

Speed camera data provided by
PocketGPSWorld.com Ltd

Post Office is a trade mark of Post Office Ltd in
the UK and other countries.

Printed in China

Contents

Digital Data

The exceptionally high-quality mapping found in this atlas is available as digital data in TIFF format,
which is easily convertible to other bitmapped (raster) image formats.

The index is also available in digital form as a standard database table. It contains all the details
found in the printed index together with the National Grid reference for the map square in which each
entry is named.

For further information and to discuss your requirements, please contact
philips@mapsinternational.co.uk

Mobile safety cameras

For locations of mobile safety camera sites, please check the safety camera partnership websites for the latest 'located' mobile sites on your route prior to every journey.

Some safety camera partnerships post a weekly list of the locations in which they will be operating mobile speed cameras. Others have a general list of those places where mobile cameras will be used.

Please note, however, that local authorities can now place mobile cameras at different locations which may not be listed on the partnership website. Always drive within the speed limit.

Mike Harrington / Alamy

Useful websites

Devon and Cornwall Safety Camera Partnership
www.dcsafetycameras.org

Further information
www.dvla.gov.uk
www.thinkroadsafety.gov.uk
www.dft.gov.uk
www.road-safe.org

Key to map pages

80	**Map pages at** **1¾ inches to 1 mile**
112	**Map pages at** **3½ inches to 1 mile**
148	**Map pages at** **7 inches to 1 mile**

20 Trebetherick **21**

Trevone

Trevone **107** Padstow

A389

St Merryn

31 St Eval Rumford **32**

Trenance

43 **44** Newquay Airport **45**

Newquay

Crantock **110** **111** St Columb Major

Holywell Indian Queens

Cubert St Newlyn East

54 **55** Mitchell **56** **57**

Perranporth A3075 A30 Ladock St Stephen

St Agnes Grampound

Shortlanesend A390

68 **69** A390 **137** **70** **71**

Threemilestone Truro Tregony

Portreath Redruth Malpas

66 **67** **140**

138 **139** A39

Camborne Perranarworthal Feock Veryan

80 A363 **81** **82** **83** **84**

Troon Stithians Mylor Bridge A3078

Isles of Scilly **75** Zennor St Ives Hayle

141 Penryn Flushing

Carbis Bay A30 Troon

76 **77** **142** **78** **79** Leedstown Porkellis **144** **145** St Mawes

74 Morvah Canonstown Nancegollan **Falmouth**

Pendeen Penzance Heliport **90** **91** **92** **93** **94** **95**

Botallack St Just A3071 Goldsithney Praa Sands Constantine Mawnan Smith

86 **87** Penzance **143** Marazion A394 Helston

Land's End Airport Sancreed A30 **89** **146**

Sennen Cove Newlyn **88** Porthleven Mawgan Helford

St Buryan **98** **99** **100** **101**

A30 Porthcurno **96** **97** Mullion Penhale Trelan St Keverne

Mullion Cove Coverack

102 A3083 **103**

Ruan Minor

Lizard

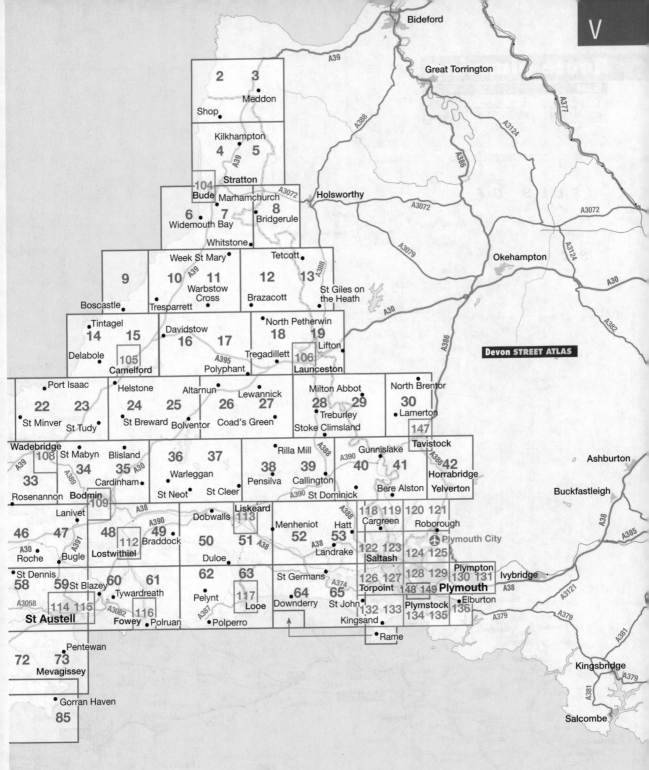

Bideford

Great Torrington

A39

A388

A3124

Holsworthy

A3072

A3072

A377

A30

Okehampton

A3079

A3124

A382

A3072

A386

Devon STREET ATLAS

A30

Ashburton

Buckfastleigh

A38

A385

A30

A3121

Ivybridge

A38

A379

Kingsbridge

A379

A381

Salcombe

| 2 | 3 |
Meddon
Shop

Kilkhampton

| 4 | 5 |
A39

104
Bude
Stratton
Marhamchurch
A3072

| 6 | 7 | 8 |
Widemouth Bay
Bridgerule
Whitstone

Week St Mary
Tetcott

| 9 | 10 | 11 | 12 | 13 |
A39
Warbstow Cross
Brazacott
St Giles on the Heath
A388

Tresparrett
Boscastle

North Petherwin
Tintagel
Davidstow
| 14 | 15 | 16 | 17 | 18 | 19 |
Lifton
105
Delabole
Camelford
A395
Tregadillett
Polyphant
106
Launceston

Port Isaac
Helstone
Altarnun
Lewannick
Milton Abbot
North Brentor
| 22 | 23 | 24 | 25 | 26 | 27 | 28 | 29 | 30 |
St Minver
St Tudy
St Breward
Bolventor
Coad's Green
Treburley
Lamerton
Stoke Climsland
Lamerton

Wadebridge
Rilla Mill
Gunnislake
Tavistock
| 108 | | | 36 | 37 | 38 | 39 | 40 | 41 | 42 |
St Mabyn
Blisland
A30
Warleggan
Pensilva
Callington
A388
Bere Alston
147
A39
A389
34
35
St Neot
St Cleer
A390
Horrabridge
33
Cardinham
A390
St Dominick
Yelverton
Rosenannon
Bodmin
A386

Liskeard
| 118 | 119 | 120 | 121 |
Lanivet
109
Dobwalls
113
Cargreen
Roborough
A38
Menheniot
Hatt
Plymouth City
| 46 | 47 | 48 | 49 | 50 | 51 | 52 | 53 | 122 | 123 |
A30
A390
Braddock
A38
Landrake
Saltash
| 124 | 125 |
Roche
Bugle
112
Lostwithiel
Duloe
A38
A388

St Dennis
St Germans
A374
| 126 | 127 | 128 | 129 | Plympton |
| 58 | 59 | 60 | 61 | 62 | 63 | | | | |
St Blazey
Tywardreath
Pelynt
117
Torpoint
148 149 Plymouth
Elburton
| 114 | 115 | | | Looe | 64 | 65 | | 130 | 131 |
St Austell
A3058
A3082
116
Downderry
St John
Plymstock
136
Fowey
Polruan
A387
Polperro
Kingsand
| 132 | 133 |
| | | | 134 | 135 |
A379

Pentewan
Rame

| 72 | 73 |
Mevagissey

Gorran Haven

| 85 |

Scale

0 ... 5 ... 10 ... 15 ... 20 ... 25 km

0 ... 5 ... 10 ... 15 miles

Route planning

Scale

0			5		10 km

0	1	2	3	4	5	6 miles

ISLES OF

SCILLY

White Island
St Helens
St Martin's
Bryher
New Grimsby
Higher Town
Bryher
Tresco
Eastern Isles
Samson
Crow Sound
The Road
North West Passage
Newford
Maypole
St Mary's
Crim Rocks
Hugh Town
Old Town
ST MARY'S
Broad Sound
St Mary's Sound
PENZANCE 2:40 (Apr-Nov)
Annet
Gugh
St Agnes
Smith Sound
St Agnes
Bishop Rock

Porthtowan
St Agnes
Portreath
B3301
Mawla
St Da
Godrevy Island
Illogan
Roscroggan
Redrut
Kehelland
Pool
Cambrai
St Ives Bay
Gwithian
Tuckingmill
Carnkie
Lanr
St Ives
Roseworthy
CAMBORNE
Carbis Bay
Phillack
Connor Downs
Four Lanes
Zennor
Halsetown
Copperhouse
Barripper
Penhalvaen
Porthmeor
Towednack
Cripplesease
Lelant
Hayle
Carnhell Green
Troon
Stith
Morvah
Nancledra
Canon's Town
Praze-an-Beeble
Burras
Res.
Bojewyan
Newmill
Fraddam
Crowan
Carnkie
Pendeen
Higher Boscaswell
St Erth
Leedstown
Drym
Releath
Porkellis
Trewellard
Townshend
Nancegollan
Carnkie
Botallack
Carnyorth
Ludgvan
Relubbus
Seworg
St Just
Newbridge
PENZANCE HELIPORT
Crowlas
Godolphin Cross
Wendron
Madron
Gulval
Trescowe
Crowntown
The Bisons
Heamoor
Chyandour
St Hilary
Goldsithney
Bosavern
Marazion
Germoe
Helston
Kelynack
Sancreed
Tredavoe
PENZANCE
Perranuthnoe
Ashton
Sithney
Breage
Trewennack
LAND'S END
Brane
Lower Drift
Newlyn
Praa Sands
Gweek
Whitesand Bay
Crows-an-wra
Catchall
Paul
Rinsey
Sennen Cove
Kerris
Mousehole
Porthleven
The Loe
St Buryan
Trewoofe
MOUNT'S BAY
Garras
Sennen
Lamorna
Berepper
Polgigga
Boskenna
Lamorna Cove
Gunwalloe
Cross Lanes
Porthcurno
Treen
St Levan
Kynance Cove
Mullion
Penhale
Mullion Cove
Predannack Wollas
St Ruan
Grade
Lizard

ISLES OF SCILLY 2:40 (Apr-Nov)

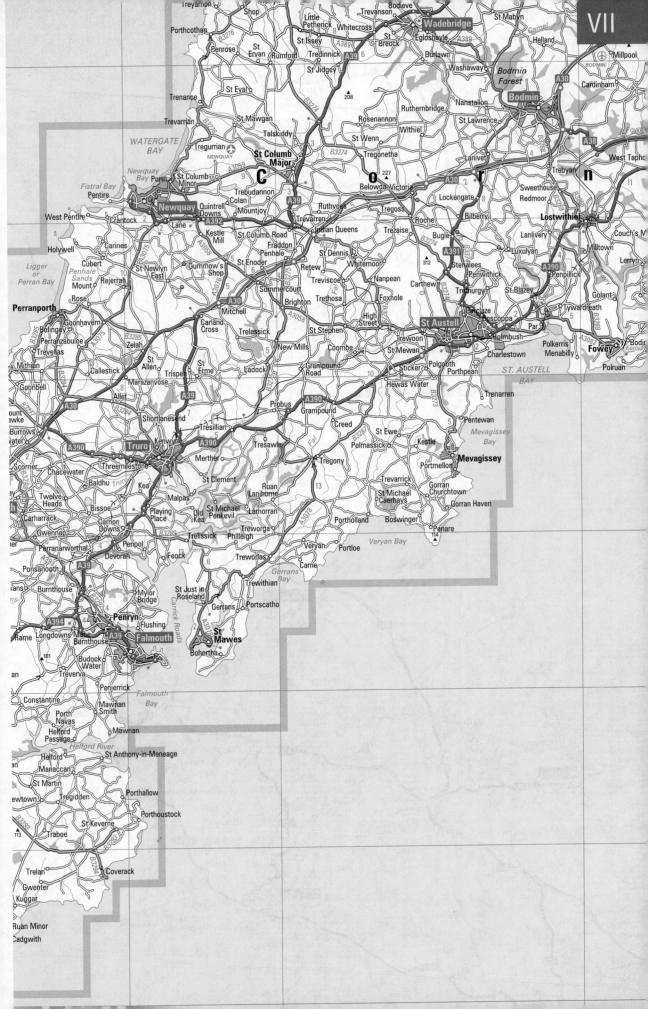

Scale

0			5			10 km
0	1	2	3	4	5	6 miles

Hartland · Philham · Higher Clovelly · Mills · Buck's C.
Milford · Eddistone · Tosberry · Woolfardisworthy · Park As
Elmscott · Hartland Forest · Alminstone Cross
South Hole · Welcombe · 235 · Meddon · Ashmansworthy
Gooseham · Woolley · West Putford
156 · Eastcott · Youlstone · Dinworthy
Morwenstow · Shop · A39 · Bradworthy
Woodford · Bradworthy Cross · Sutcombe · Venn Gre
Coombe · Kilkhampton · Alfardisworthy · Soldon Cross
Stibb · Holsworthy Beacon · Chilsworthy
Flexbury · Poughill · Hersham · Grimscott
Bude Haven · **Stratton** · Pancrasweek
Bude · Launcells · A3072 · Launceston

BUDE BAY · Bude Haven · B
Widemouth Bay · Mill · Poundst
Tregole · Tregole · St Genny's · Trewint · Rosecare
Crackington Haven · Wain Corne
Tresparrett Posts · 260 · B3263 · Marshgate
Beeny · 6 · Tresparrett · Lesnewth · Otterham · 25
Trevalga · Boscastle · Trelash
Bossiney · Tintagel · Davidstow · Tremail
Treknow · Trewarmett · 308 · 8 · Trewassa · Tremail · 13
Trebarwith · B3263 · B3262
Treligga · Delabole · Valley Truckle · **Camelford** · Crowdy Res.
St Teath · Helstone · 400 ROUGH TOR · 420 BROWN WILLY
Port Isaac Bay · Port Gaverne · Treveighan · Michaelstow · 331 GARROW TOR
Port Quin Bay · Port Quin · Pendoggett · A39 · 10 · St Breward · Codda
New Polzeath · Trelights · St Endellion · Trelill · Row · Bolv
Padstow Bay · Polzeath · Trewethern · St Tudy · Bradford · 18
Trebetherick · St Minver · Chapel Amble · St Kew · Wenfordbridge · A30
Crugmeer · Pityme · St Kew Highway · Blisland · Temple · Colliford Lake
Trevone · Rock · Camel · St Mabyn · 268
Constantine Bay · St Merryn · Bodieve · Helland · Maidenwell
Constantine Bay · **Padstow** · Trevanson · **Wadebridge** · Camel · Millpool
Treyarnon · Shop · Little Petherick · Egloshayle · A389 · Helland · Warleggan
Porthcothan · Whitecross · St Breock · Burlawn · BODMIN · St Neot
Penrose · St Issey · Washaway · Bodmin Forest · Cardinham · Mount · Ley
Trenance · St Ervan · Rumford · Tredinnick · A39 · 6 · Bodmin Forest · **Bodmin**
Trevarrian · St Jidgey · 208 · Nanstallon · A30 · Fowey
St Mawgan · Rosenannon · Ruthernbridge · St Lawrence · 11
WATERGATE BAY · Tregurrian · Talskiddy · Withiel · A38
Treguddick · St Wenn · Lanivet · West Taphouse · East Taphouse · A390
NEWQUAY · **St Columb Major** · Tregonetha · Trebyan · W
Newquay Bay · Porth · St Columb Minor · 227 · Belowda · Victoria · Braddock
ntre · **Newquay** · Quintrell Downs · Trebudannon · A30 · Sweethouse · Redmoor
Crantock · Lane · Colan · Mountjoy · A39 · Roche · Lockengate · 8 · **Lostwithiel**
Carines · Kestle Mill · Trevarren · Ruthvoes · Tregoss · Bilberry · Lanlivery · Couch's Mill
Indian Queens · Trezaise · Bugle · Luxulyan · Milltown · Bocaddon
St Newlyn East · Gummow's Shop · Fraddon · Penhale · St Dennis · Nanpean · Stenalees · Penwithick · Lerryn · Lanreath
Rejerrah · St Enoder · 6 · Retew · Whitemoor · Carthew · Trethurgy · A391 · Penpillick · Golant · St Veep Penpoll
Mitchell · Summercourt · Treviscoe · 312 · Foxhole · Treneague · St Blazey · Tywardreath · Langtos Highway
Brighton · Trethosa · High Street · Carclaze · Boscoppa · Trenewa
Carland Cross · Trelassick · St Stephen · Trewoon · **St Austell** · Holmbush · Par · Polkerris Menabilly · **Fowey** · Bodinnick
Zelah · New Mills · Coombe · St Mewan · Charlestown · Polruan · Lansallos
St Allen · St Erme · Ladock · Grampound Road · Polgooth · Sticker · Porthpean · ST AUSTELL BAY
Marazanvose · Trispen · Creed · Hewas Water · Trenarren
Allet · A39 · Probus · A390 · Grampound · Pentewan
Shortlanesend · Tresillian · Creed · St Ewe · Mevagissey

Major administrative and Postcode boundaries

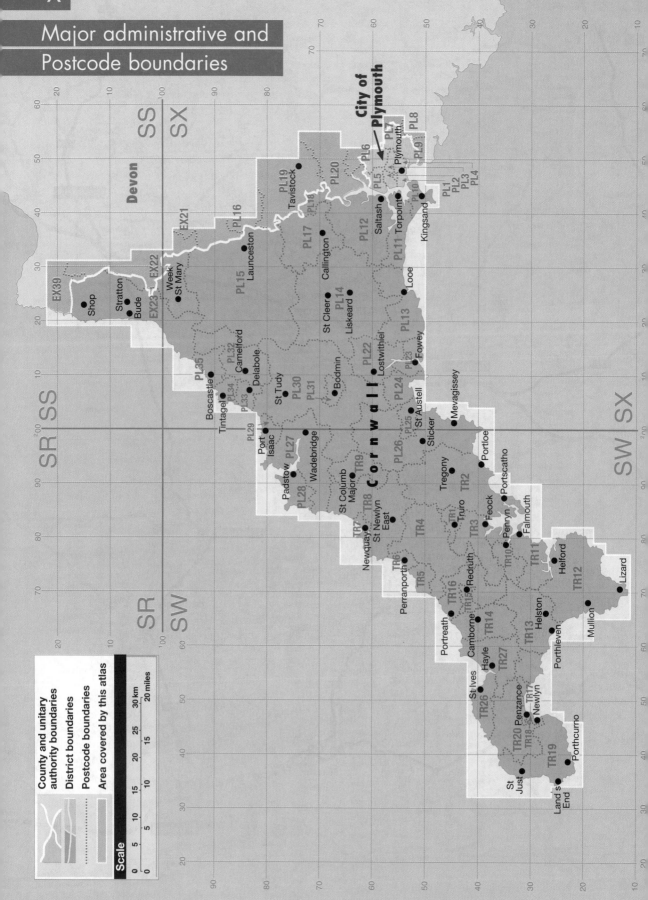

Scale

County and unitary authority boundaries

District boundaries

Postcode boundaries

Area covered by this atlas

0	5	10	15	20	25	30 km
0	5	10	15	20 miles		

Devon

City of Plymouth

Cornwall

Key to map symbols

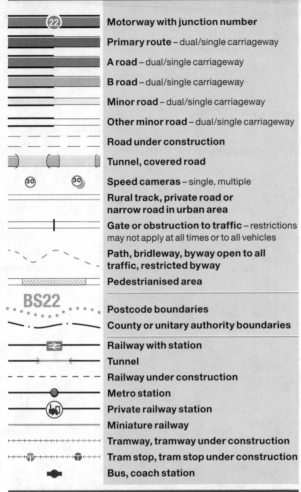

(22) Motorway with junction number

Primary route – dual/single carriageway

A road – dual/single carriageway

B road – dual/single carriageway

Minor road – dual/single carriageway

Other minor road – dual/single carriageway

Road under construction

Tunnel, covered road

(30) **(30)** Speed cameras – single, multiple

Rural track, private road or narrow road in urban area

Gate or obstruction to traffic – restrictions may not apply at all times or to all vehicles

Path, bridleway, byway open to all traffic, restricted byway

Pedestrianised area

BS22 Postcode boundaries

County or unitary authority boundaries

Railway with station

Tunnel

Railway under construction

Metro station

Private railway station

Miniature railway

Tramway, tramway under construction

Tram stop, tram stop under construction

Bus, coach station

◆ Ambulance station

◆ Coastguard station

◆ Fire station

◆ Police station

✚ Accident and Emergency entrance to hospital

H Hospital

✛ Place of worship

i Information centre – open all year

🛒 **P** Shopping centre, parking

P&R **PO** Park and Ride, Post Office

⛺ Camping site, caravan site

▶ Golf course, picnic site

Church ROMAN FORT Non-Roman antiquity, Roman antiquity

Univ Important buildings, schools, colleges, universities and hospitals

Woods, built-up area

River Medway Water name

River, weir

Stream

Canal, lock, tunnel

Water

Tidal water

58 **87** **246** Adjoining page indicators and overlap bands – the colour of the arrow and band indicates the scale of the adjoining or overlapping page (see scales below)

The dark grey border on the inside edge of some pages indicates that the mapping does not continue onto the adjacent page

The small numbers around the edges of the maps identify the 1-kilometre National Grid lines

Abbreviations

Acad	**Academy**	Meml	**Memorial**
Allot Gdns	**Allotments**	Mon	**Monument**
Cemy	**Cemetery**	Mus	**Museum**
C Ctr	**Civic centre**	Obsy	**Observatory**
CH	**Club house**	Pal	**Royal palace**
Coll	**College**	PH	**Public house**
Crem	**Crematorium**	Recn Gd	**Recreation ground**
Ent	**Enterprise**		
Ex H	**Exhibition hall**	Resr	**Reservoir**
Ind Est	**Industrial Estate**	Ret Pk	**Retail park**
IRB Sta	**Inshore rescue boat station**	Sch	**School**
		Sh Ctr	**Shopping centre**
Inst	**Institute**	TH	**Town hall / house**
Ct	**Law court**	Trad Est	**Trading estate**
L Ctr	**Leisure centre**	Univ	**University**
LC	**Level crossing**	W Twr	**Water tower**
Liby	**Library**	Wks	**Works**
Mkt	**Market**	YH	**Youth hostel**

Enlarged maps only

Railway or bus station building

Place of interest

Parkland

The map scale on the pages numbered in green is 1¾ inches to 1 mile
2.76 cm to 1 km • 1:36206

0	½ mile	1 mile	1½ miles	2 miles
0	500m	1 km	1½ km	2km

The map scale on the pages numbered in blue is 3½ inches to 1 mile
5.52 cm to 1 km • 1:18103

0	¼ mile	½ mile	¾ mile	1 mile
0	250m	500m	750m	1km

The map scale on the pages numbered in red is 7 inches to 1 mile
11.04 cm to 1 km • 1:9051

0	220yds	440yds	660yds	½ mile
0	125m	250m	375m	500m

2

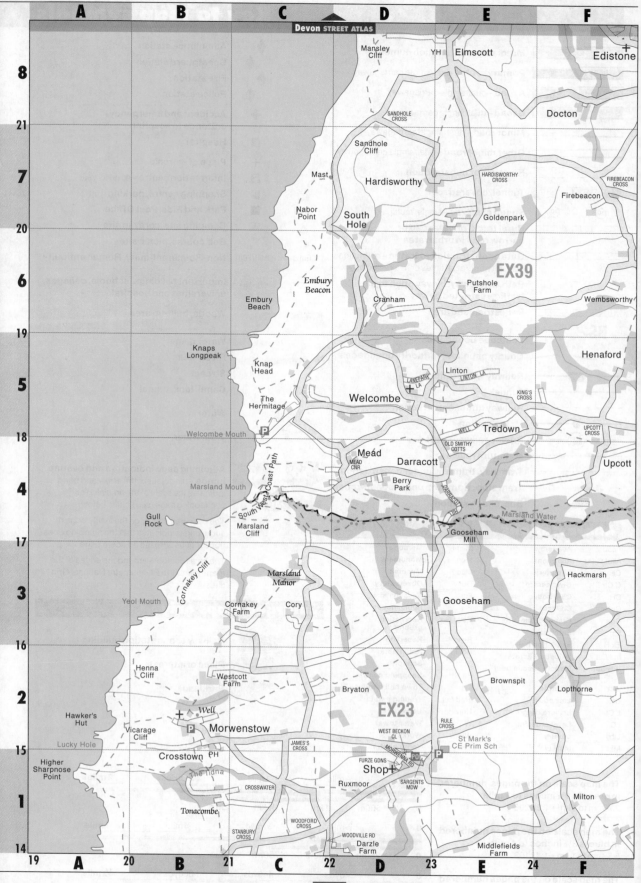

Scale: 1 ¾ inches to 1 mile

0 ¼ ½ mile
0 250m 500m 750m 1 km

A B C D E F

8
21
7
20
6
19
5
18
4
17
3
16
2
15
1
14

19 A 20 B 21 C 22 D 23 E 24 F

Mansley Cliff
YH Elmscott
Edistone
Docton
Sandhole Cross
Sandhole Cliff
Mast
Hardisworthy
HARDISWORTHY CROSS
Firebeacon
FIREBEACON CROSS
Nabor Point
South Hole
Goldenpark
EX39
Embury Beacon
Cranham
Putshole Farm
Wembsworthy
Embury Beach
Knaps Longpeak
Henaford
Knap Head
Linton
LINTON LA
LANEPARK LA
KING'S CROSS
The Hermitage
Welcombe
WELL LA
Tredown
UPCOTT CROSS
Welcombe Mouth
Mead
Darracott
Upcott
MEAD CNR
OLD SMITHY COTTS
Marsland Mouth
Berry Park
DARRACOTT
Gull Rock
Marsland Cliff
Goosham Mill
Marsland Water
Cornakey Cliff
Marsland Manor
Hackmarsh
Yeol Mouth
Cornakey Farm
Cory
Gooseham
Henna Cliff
Westcott Farm
Brownspit
Bryaton
Lopthorne
Hawker's Hut
Well
EX23
RULE CROSS
Vicarage Cliff
Morwenstow
WEST BECKON CL
St Mark's CE Prim Sch
Lucky Hole
JAMES'S CROSS
MORWENNA RD
Crosstown PH
Shop
Higher Sharpnose Point
The Ridna
FURZE GDNS
SARGENTS MDW
Milton
Crosswater
Ruxmoor
Tonacombe
WOODFORD CROSS
STANBURY CROSS
WOODVILLE RD
Darzle Farm
Middlefields Farm
South West Coast Path

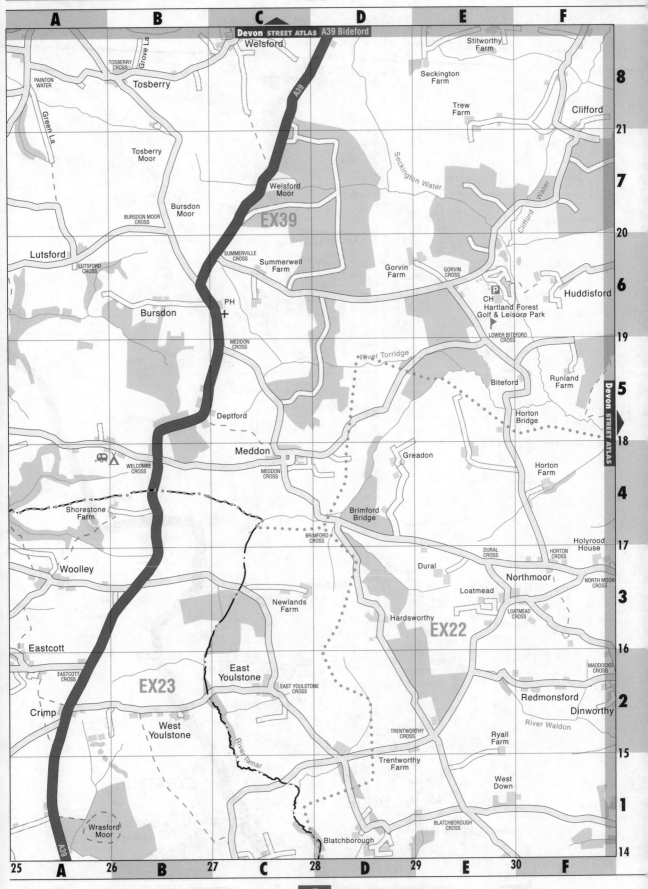

Scale: 1¾ inches to 1 mile

0   ¼   ½ mile
0 250m 500m 750m 1 km

Welsford

Tosberry Cross
Grove La
Tosberry
Painton Water
Green La
Tosberry Moor
Bursdon Moor
Bursdon Moor Cross
Welsford Moor
EX39
Stitworthy Farm
Seckington Farm
Trew Farm
Clifford
Seckington Water
Clifford Water
Lutsford
Lutsford Cross
Summerville Cross
Summerwell Farm
Gorvin Farm
Gorvin Cross
Huddisford
Bursdon
PH
Meddon Cross
Hartland Forest Golf & Leisure Park
CH
Lower Biteford Cross
Deptford
River Torridge
Biteford
Runland Farm
Meddon
Welcombe Cross
Meddon Cross
Greadon
Horton Bridge
Horton Farm
Shorestone Farm
Brimford Bridge
Brimford Cross
Dural
Dural Cross
Horton Cross
Holyrood House
Woolley
Newlands Farm
Hardsworthy
Loatmead
Northmoor
North Moor Cross
EX22
Eastcott
Eastcott Cross
EX23
East Youlstone
East Youlstone Cross
Loatmead Cross
Maddocks Cross
Crimp
West Youlstone
River Tamar
Trentworthy Cross
Redmonsford
Dinworthy
River Waldon
Ryall Farm
Trentworthy Farm
West Down
Wrasford Moor
Blatchborough Cross
Blatchborough
A39

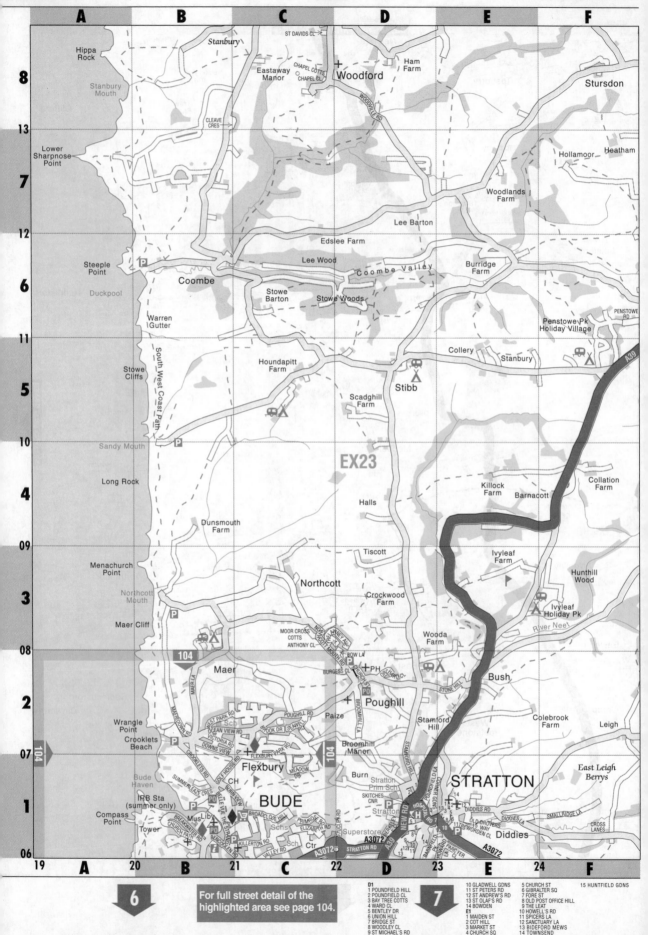

4

2

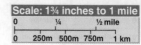

Scale: 1¾ inches to 1 mile

0   ¼   ½ mile
0   250m 500m 750m 1 km

Map labels:

Hippa Rock
Stanbury
ST DAVIDS CL
Eastaway Manor
CHAPEL COTTS
CHAPEL CL
Woodford
Ham Farm
Stursdon
Stanbury Mouth
CLEAVE CRES
WOODVILLE RD
Lower Sharpnose Point
Hollamoor
Heatham
Woodlands Farm
Steeple Point
Coombe
Lee Barton
Edslee Farm
Lee Wood
Coombe Valley
Burridge Farm
Duckpool
Stowe Barton
Stowe Woods
Penstowe Pk Holiday Village
PENSTOWE RD
Warren Gutter
South West Coast Path
Houndapitt Farm
Collery
Stanbury
Stowe Cliffs
Scadghill Farm
Stibb
A39
Sandy Mouth
EX23
Long Rock
Killock Farm
Barnacott
Collation Farm
Halls
Tiscott
Ivyleaf Farm
Hunthill Wood
Menachurch Point
Northcott Mouth
Northcott
Crockwood Farm
Ivyleaf Holiday Pk
River Neet
Maer Cliff
MOOR CROSS COTTS
ANTHONY CL
BOW LA
BURGESS CL
Wooda Farm
Bush
NORTHCOTT MOUNT RD
MANLEY AVE
CHURCH RD
ORCHARD CL
Maer
Poughill
PH
Stamford Hill
Colebrook Farm
Leigh
MAER LA
Paize
POUGHILL RD
BROOMHILL LA
STONE HILL
STAMFORD HILL
MEADOW RD
Broomhill Manor
Wrangle Point
WEST PARK RD
OCEAN VIEW RD
BROOK DR
IDLEWELL RD
DOWNS VIEW
VICTORIA RD
FLEXBURY
PARK RD
Burn
East Leigh Berrys
Crooklets Beach
MERIDOWN RD
KALE HOUSE RD
BELLE VUE
THE STRAND RD
SUMMERLEAZE CRES
STRATTON
Stratton Prim Sch
SKITCHES CNR
Bude Haven
Flexbury
CH
NEW RD
104
IRB Sta (summer only)
BUDE
Stratton
SMALLRIDGE LA
CROSS LANES
Compass Point
Tower
Mus Lib
Schs
BROADCLOSE HILL
PRIMROSE RD
ELIZABETH RD
Superstore
Diddies
DIDDIES RD
OLD DROVERS WAY
A3072
KILLERTON RD
VALLEY RD
Ctr
STRATTON RD
A3072
A39
BARNFIELD
PARK LA
A3072

6

For full street detail of the highlighted area see page 104.

7

D1
1 POUNDFIELD HILL
2 POUNDFIELD CL
3 BAY TREE COTTS
4 WARD CL
5 BENTLEY DR
6 UNION HILL
7 BRIDGE ST
8 WOODLEY CL
9 ST MICHAEL'S RD
10 GLADWELL GDNS
11 ST PETERS RD
12 ST ANDREW'S RD
13 ST OLAF'S RD
14 BOWDEN

E1
1 MAIDEN CL
2 COT HILL
3 MARKET ST
4 CHURCH SQ
5 CHURCH ST
6 GIBRALTER SQ
7 FORE ST
8 OLD POST OFFICE HILL
9 THE LEAT
10 HOWELL'S RD
11 SPICERS LA
12 SANCTUARY LA
13 BIDEFORD MEWS
14 TOWNSEND

15 HUNTFIELD GDNS

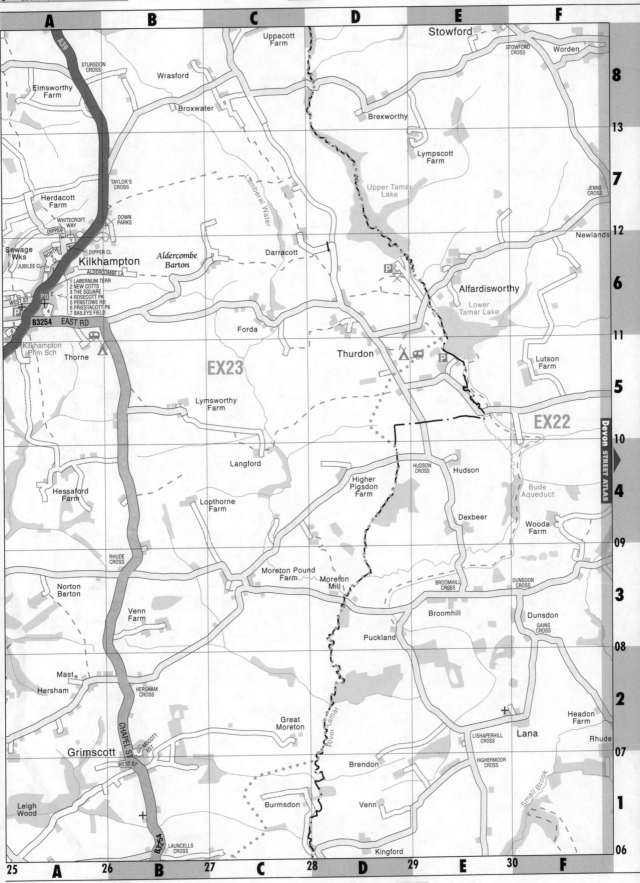

Scale: 1¾ inches to 1 mile

0   ¼   ½ mile
0   250m 500m 750m 1 km

A **B** **C** **D** **E** **F**

Stowford

STURSDON CROSS
Elmsworthy Farm
Wrasford
Uppacott Farm
STOWFORD CROSS
Worden
Broxwater
Brexworthy
Lympscott Farm
JENNS CROSS
TAYLOR'S CROSS
Lamberal Water
Upper Tamar Lake
Herdacott Farm
WHITECROFT WAY
DOWN PARKS
DIPPER
Newlands
NORTH RD
DIPPER CL
Aldercombe Barton
Darracott
Alfardisworthy
Sewage Wks
JUBILEE CL
Kilkhampton
Lower Tamar Lake
1 LABERNUM TERR
2 NEW COTTS
3 THE SQUARE
4 ROSECOTT PK
5 PENSTOWE RD
6 PRIESTACOTT PK
7 BAILEYS FIELD
ALDERCOMBE LA
WEST ST
B3254 EAST RD
Forda
Thurdon
Lutson Farm
Kilkhampton Prim Sch
Thorne
EX23
EX5
EX22
Lymsworthy Farm
Hudson Cross
Hudson
Langford
Higher Pigsdon Farm
Dexbeer
Bude Aqueduct
Hessaford Farm
Lopthorne Farm
Wooda Farm
Moreton Pound Farm
Moreton Mill
Broomhill Cross
Dunsdon Cross
Norton Barton
Venn Farm
Broomhill
Dunsdon
RHUDE CROSS
GAINS CROSS
Puckland
Mast
Hersham
HERSHAM CROSS
Lishaperhill Cross
Lana
Headon Farm
Rhude
Great Moreton
River Tamar
HIGHERMOOR CROSS
CHAPEL ST
GRIMSCOTT EST
Grimscott
WEST ST
Brendon
Venn
Small Brook
Leigh Wood
Burmsdon
Kingford
B3254
LAUNCELLS CROSS

8
13
7
12
6
11
5
10
4
09
3
08
2
07
1
06

25 **A** **26** **B** **27** **C** **28** **D** **29** **E** **30** **F**

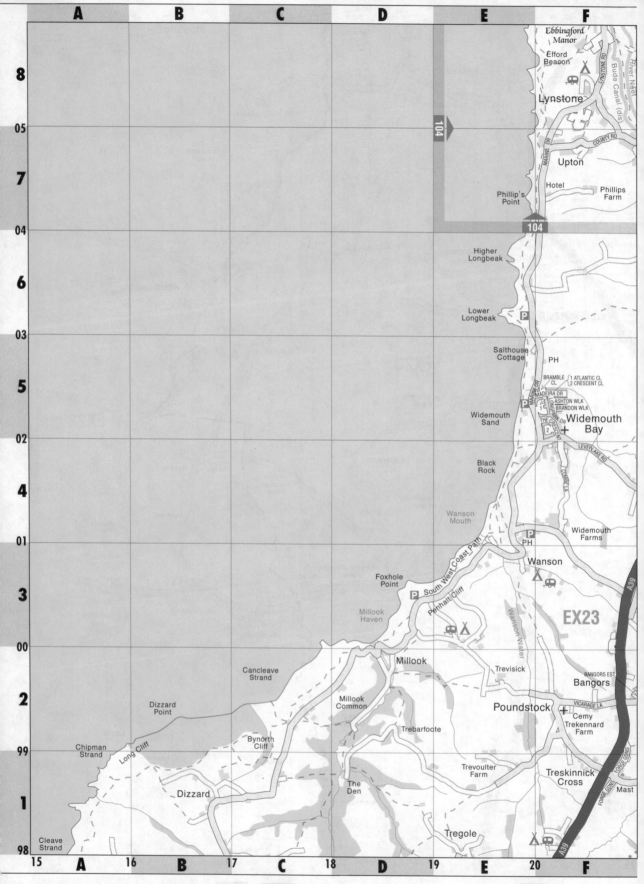

For full street detail of the highlighted area see page 104.

4

Scale: 1¾ inches to 1 mile

0   ¼   ½ mile

0   250m 500m 750m 1 km

Ebbingford Manor

Efford Beacon

Lynstone

Upton

Bude Canal (dis)

River Neet

LYNSTONE RD

COUNTY RD

MARINE DR

Hotel

Phillips Farm

Phillip's Point

104

Higher Longbeak

Lower Longbeak

P

Salthouse Cottage

PH

BRAMBLE CL

1 ATLANTIC CL
2 CRESCENT CL

MADEIRA DR

ASHTON WLK

BRANDON WLK

P

LONDSON DR

THE CRESCENT

Widemouth Sand

Widemouth Bay

Black Rock

LEVERLAKE RD

Wanson Mouth

COMBE LA

Widemouth Farms

P

PH

Wanson

South West Coast Path

Foxhole Point

P

Pennalt Cliff

Millook Haven

Wanson Water

EX23

A39

Millook

Trevisick

Cancleave Strand

Bangors

BANGORS EST

Millook Common

Dizzard Point

Trebarfoote

Poundstock

VICARAGE LA

Cemy Trekennard Farm

Chipman Strand

Long Cliff

Bynorth Cliff

Trevoulter Farm

Treskinnick Cross

FORGE GDNS

Mast

Dizzard

The Den

Cleave Strand

Tregole

A39

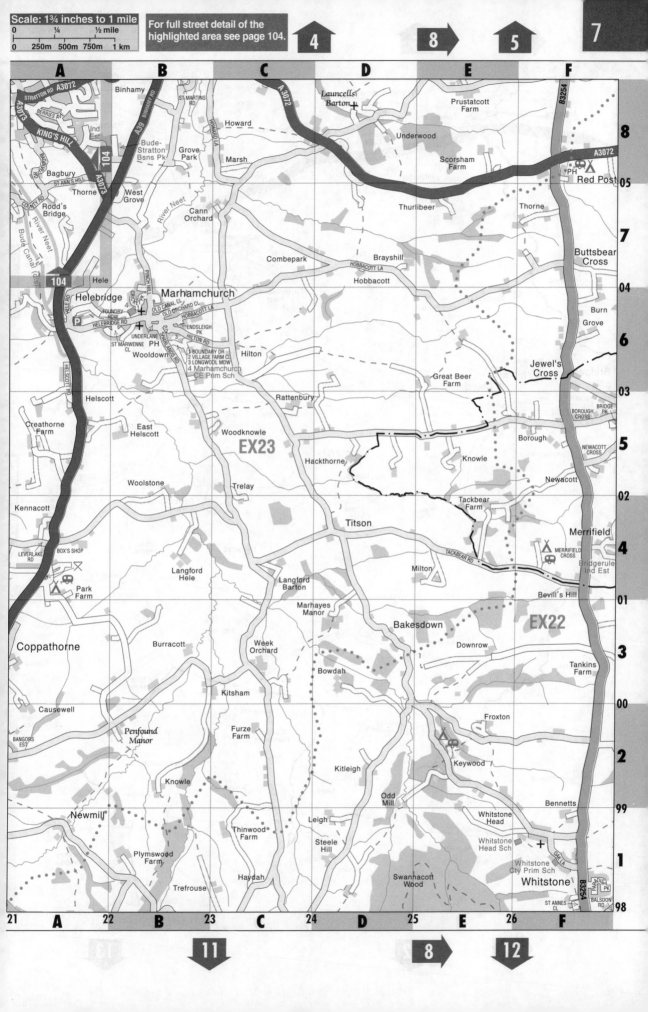

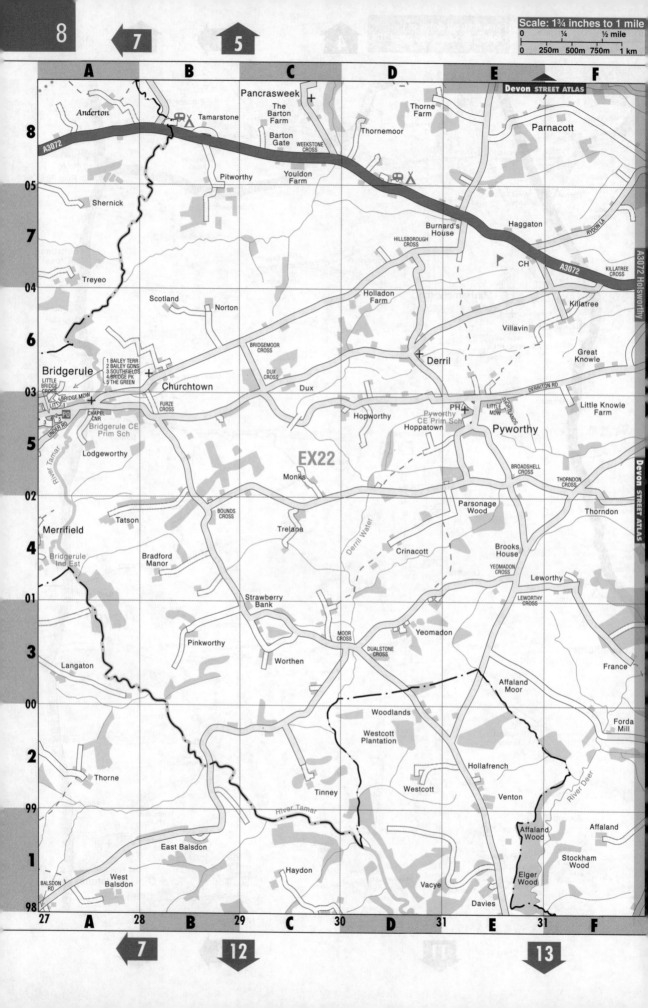

Scale: 1¾ inches to 1 mile

0   ¼   ½ mile
0 250m 500m 750m 1 km

Devon STREET ATLAS

A B C D E F

Anderton

A3072

Tamarstone

Pancrasweek

The Barton Farm

Barton Gate

WEEKSTONE CROSS

Thorne Farm

Thornemoor

Parnacott

8

05

Shernick

Pitworthy

Youldon Farm

Burnard's House

HILLSBOROUGH CROSS

Haggaton

RYDON LA

7

Treyeo

CH

A3072

Killatree CROSS

04

Scotland

Norton

Holladon Farm

Killatree

Villavin

6

Bridgemoor CROSS

DUX CROSS

Derril

Great Knowle

Bridgerule

1 BAILEY TERR
2 BAILEY GDNS
3 SOUTHFIELDS
4 BRIDGE PK
5 THE GREEN

Churchtown

FURZE CROSS

Dux

Hopworthy

Pyworthy CE Prim Sch

Hoppatown

PH

LITTLE MDW

DERRITON RD

SCOTLANDS

Little Knowle Farm

03

LITTLE BRIDGE CROSS

BRIDGE MDW

CHAPEL CNR

Bridgerule CE Prim Sch

Pyworthy

PO

UNDER RD

Lodgeworthy

EX22

Monks

BROADSHELL CROSS

THORNDON CROSS

05

River Tamar

02

Tatson

BOUNDS CROSS

Trelana

Parsonage Wood

Thorndon

Merrifield

Bridgerule Ind Est

Bradford Manor

Crinacott

Brooks House

YEOMADON CROSS

Leworthy

4

Strawberry Bank

Derril Water

LEWORTHY CROSS

01

Pinkworthy

Worthen

MOOR CROSS

Yeomadon

France

3

Langaton

DUALSTONE CROSS

Affaland Moor

00

Woodlands

Forda Mill

Westcott Plantation

Thorne

Hollafrench

River Deer

2

Tinney

Westcott

Venton

99

River Tamar

Affaland Wood

Affaland

East Balsdon

Stockham Wood

1

Haydon

Vacye

Elger Wood

98

BALSDON RD

West Balsdon

Davies

27 A 28 B 29 C 30 D 31 E 31 F

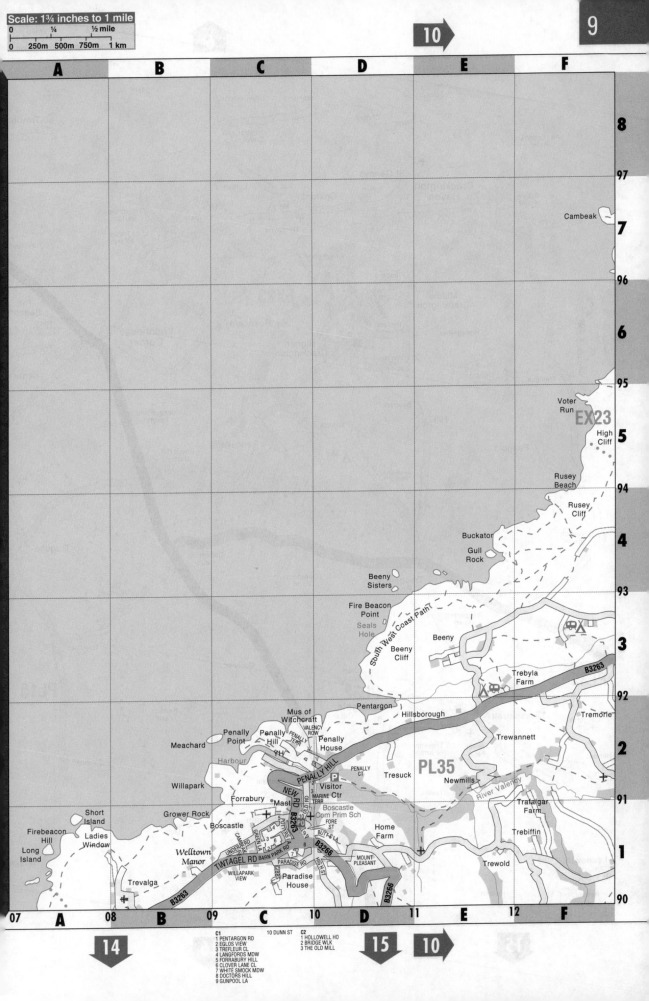

A   B   C   D   E   F

8

97

7

96

6

95

Cambeak

Voter Run

EX23

5

High Cliff

Rusey Beach

94

Rusey Cliff

4

Buckator

Gull Rock

Beeny Sisters

93

Fire Beacon Point

Seals Hole

Beeny

3

Beeny Cliff

South West Coast Path

Trebyla Farm

B3263

92

Pentargon

Hillsborough

Tremorle

Mus of Witchcraft

Trewannett

Penally Point

Penally Hill

Penally Terr

Valency Row

Penally House

2

Meachard

YH

PENALLY HILL

PENALLY CT

PL35

Newmills

Harbour

Tresuck

River Valency

Willapark

P

Visitor Ctr

Trafalgar Farm

91

Forrabury

Mast

MARINE TERR

Boscastle Com Prim Sch

Grower Rock

NEW RD

FORE ST

Home Farm

Trebiffin

Short Island

Firebeacon Hill

Ladies Window

Boscastle

B3263

BUTTS LA

Trewold

1

Long Island

Welltown Manor

TINTAGEL RD

BARN PARK RD

PARADISE RD

HIGH ST

B3266

MOUNT PLEASANT

WILLAPARK VIEW

GIBBS

Paradise House

B3266

Trevalga

90

C1
1 PENTARGON RD
2 EGLOS VIEW
3 TREFLEUR CL
4 LANGFORDS MDW
5 FORRABURY HILL
6 CLOVER LANE CL
7 WHITE SMOCK MDW
8 DOCTORS HILL
9 GUNPOOL LA

C2
1 HOLLOWELL HO
2 BRIDGE WLK
3 THE OLD MILL

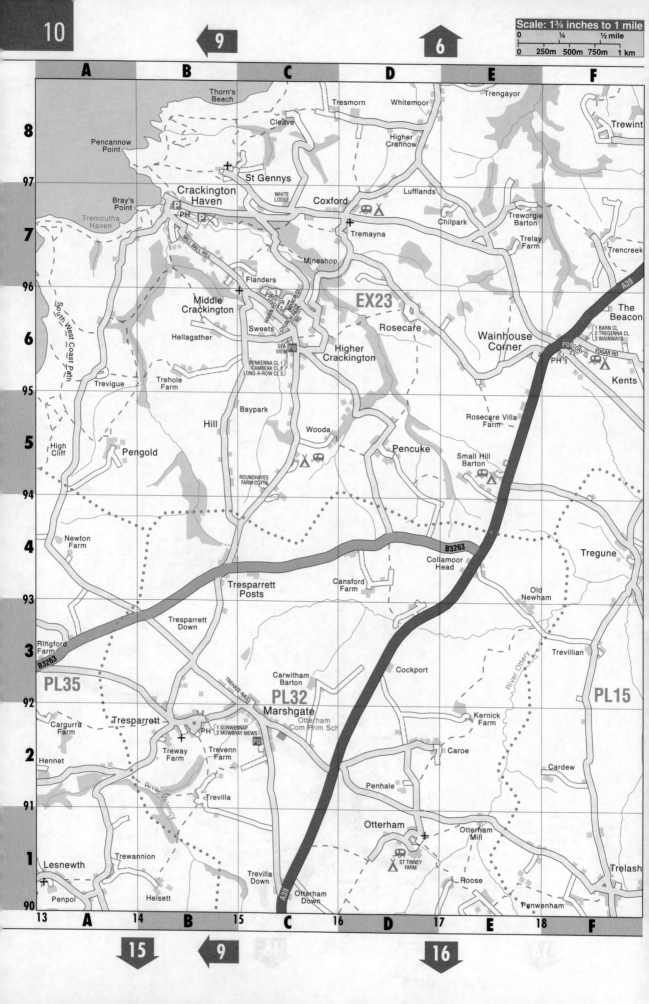

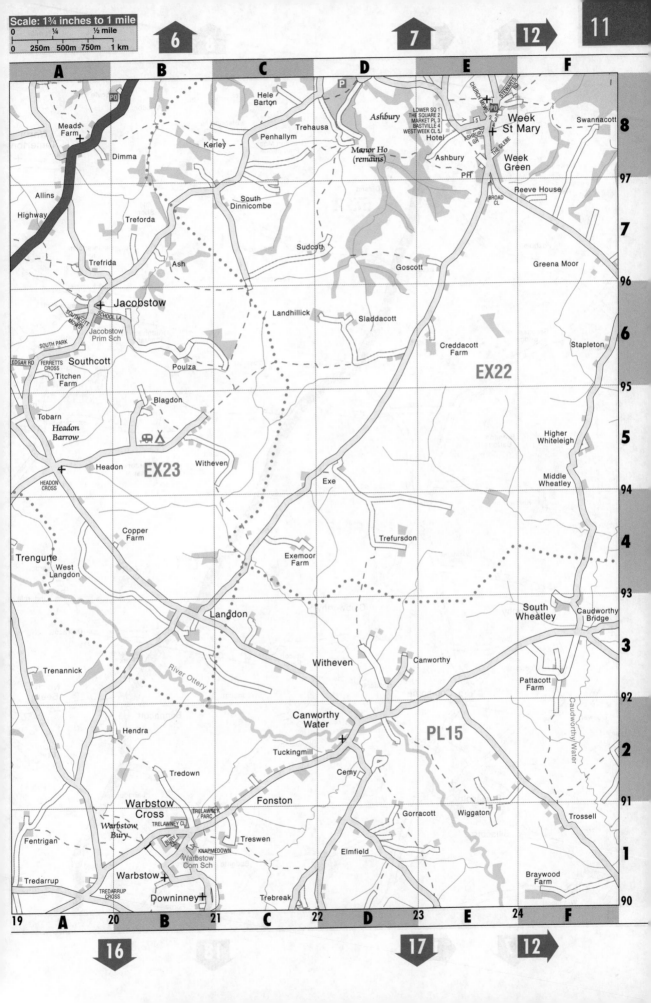

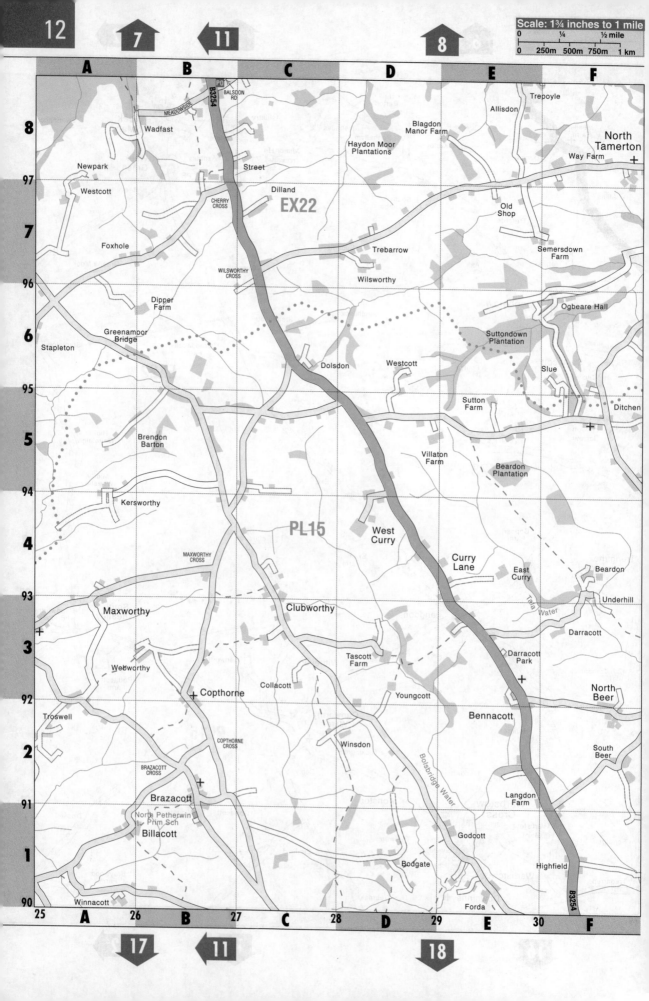

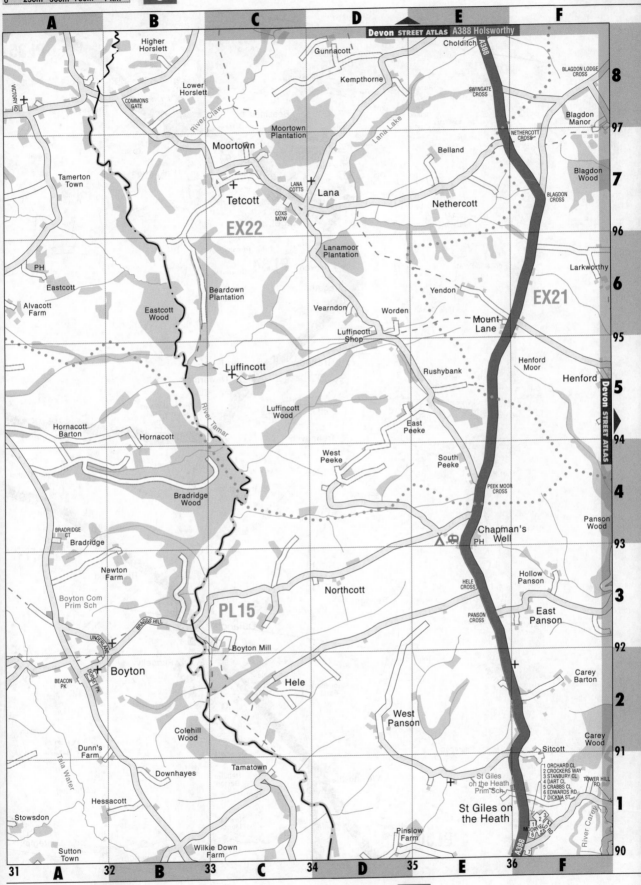

Scale: 1¾ inches to 1 mile

0   ¼   ½ mile
0   250m 500m 750m 1 km

Devon STREET ATLAS A388 Holsworthy

A B C D E F

Higher Horslett

Lower Horslett

COMMONS GATE

River Claw

Gunnacott

Kempthorne

Choldlitch

SWINGATE CROSS

NETHERCOTT CROSS

BLAGDON LODGE CROSS

Blagdon Manor

8

97

VICTORY RD

Moortown Plantation

Moortown

Tetcott

LANA COTTS

Lana

Belland

Nethercott

Blagdon Wood

BLAGDON CROSS

7

Tamerton Town

EX22

COXS MDW

Lana Lake

96

Larkworthy

EX21

6

PH

Eastcott

Alvacott Farm

Eastcott Wood

Beardown Plantation

Lanamoor Plantation

Vearndon

Worden

Luffincott Shop

Yendon

Mount Lane

Henford Moor

Henford

95

Devon STREET ATLAS

Luffincott

Rushybank

5

Hornacott Barton

Hornacott

River Tamar

Luffincott Wood

East Peeke

94

Bradridge Wood

West Peeke

South Peeke

PEEK MOOR CROSS

Panson Wood

4

BRADRIDGE CT

Bradridge

Newton Farm

BRIGGS HILL

Boyton Com Prim Sch

Northcott

Chapman's Well

PH

HELE CROSS

Hollow Panson

East Panson

93

PL15

PANSON CROSS

3

UNDERLANE

Boyton Mill

DORSET PK

Boyton

BEACON PK

Hele

West Panson

Carey Barton

Carey Wood

2

92

91

Dunn's Farm

Colehill Wood

Tamatown

Sitcott

1 ORCHARD CL
2 CROCKERS WAY
3 STANBURY CL
4 DART CL
5 CRABBS CL
6 EDWARDS RD
7 DICKNA ST

TOWER HILL RD

Tala Water

Downhayes

St Giles on the Heath Prim Sch

Stowsdon

Hessacott

St Giles on the Heath

MOOR...

River Carey

1

90

Sutton Town

Wilkie Down Farm

Pinslow Farm

A388

31 A 32 B 33 C 34 D 35 E 36 F

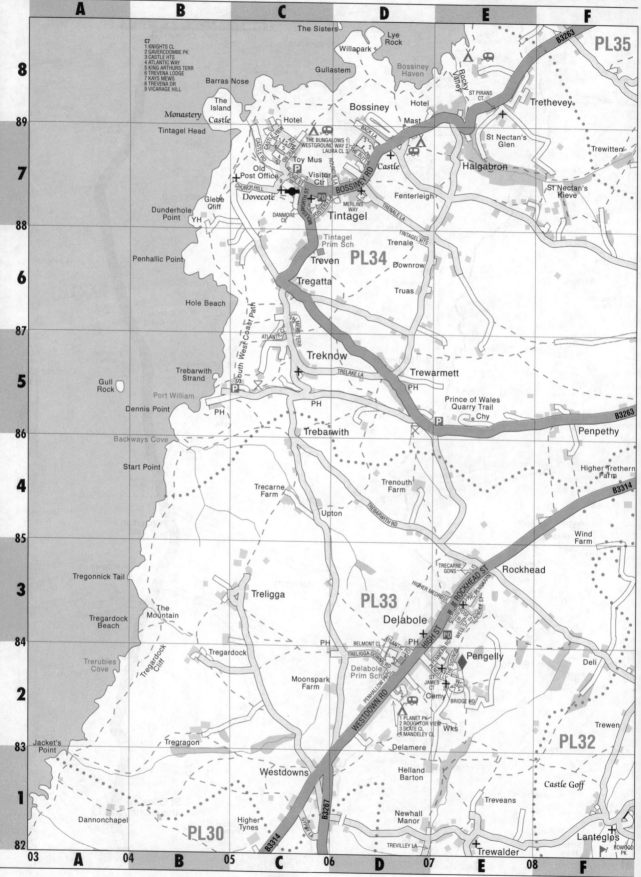

PL35

PL34

PL33

PL32

PL30

The Sisters
Willapark
Lye Rock
Gullastem
Bossiney Haven
Rocky Valley
St Pirans CT
Trethevey
Barras Nose
Bossiney
Hotel
Mast
St Nectan's Glen
Trewitten
The Island
Monastery
Castle
Hotel
Castle
Halgabron
St Nectan's Kieve
Tintagel Head
CASTLE VIEW
Toy Mus
Visitor Ctr
Fenterleigh
Old Post Office
CHURCH HILL
Dovecote
MERLINS WAY
TRENALE LA
Tintagel
Trenale
Glebe Cliff
DANMORE CL
TINTAGEL HTS
Dunderhole Point
YH
Tintagel Prim Sch
Trenale
Penhallic Point
Treven
Downrow
Tregatta
Truas
Hole Beach
Trebarwith Strand
ATLANTIC
PALMERS TERR
Treknow
Trewarmett
PH
Gull Rock
Port William
South West Coast Path
Trelake La
Prince of Wales Quarry Trail
Chy
Dennis Point
PH
PH
Trebarwith
Penpethy
Backways Cove
Higher Trethern Farm
Start Point
Trecarne Farm
Trenouth Farm
Wind Farm
Upton
TREBARWITH RD
Tregonnick Tail
Trecarne Gdns
ROCKHEAD ST
Rockhead
Treligga
The Mountain
PL33
Delabole
Tregardock Beach
Pengelly
Deli
Trerubies Cove
Tregardock Cliff
Tregardock
PH
HIGH ST
Delabole Prim Sch
PH
Cemy
BRIDGE HO
Wks
Trewen
Moonspark Farm
WESTDOWN RD
Planet Pk
Jacket's Point
Tregragon
Delamere
Helland Barton
Castle Goff
Westdowns
Treveans
Dannonchapel
Higher Tynes
B3314
B3267
GYPSY LA
Newhall Manor
TREVILLEY LA
Trewalder
Lanteglos
BOWOOD PK

C7
1 KNIGHTS CL
2 GAVERCOOMBE PK
3 CASTLE HTS
4 ATLANTIC WAY
5 KING ARTHURS TERR
6 TREVENA LODGE
7 KAYS MEWS
8 TREVENA DR
9 VICARAGE HILL

THE BUNGALOWS 1
WESTGROUND WAY 2
LAURA CL 3

1 PLANET PK
2 ROUGHTOR VIEW
3 SCATE CL
4 MANDELEY CL

B3263
B3263
B3314

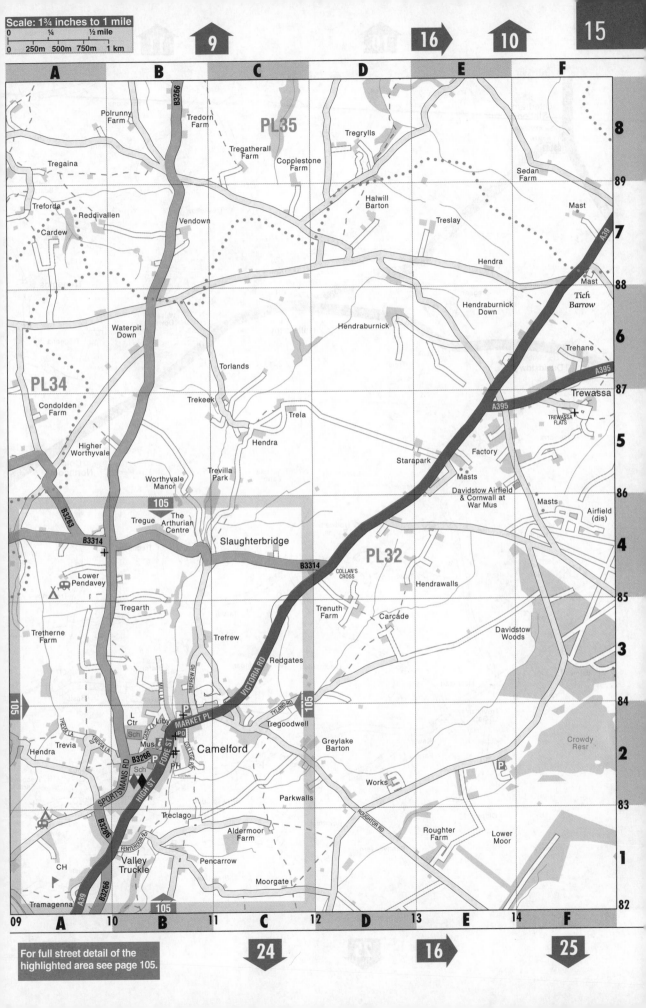

A   B   C   D   E   F

8

89

7

88

6

87

5

86

4

85

3

84

2

83

1

82

PL35

PL34

PL32

Polrunny Farm

Tredorn Farm

Tregaina

Tregatherall Farm

Tregrylls

Copplestone Farm

Sedan Farm

Treforda

Reddivallen

Vendown

Halwill Barton

Treslay

Mast

Cardew

Mast

Tich Barrow

Trehane

Hendra

Hendraburnick Down

Trewassa

Waterpit Down

Hendraburnick

A395

TREWASSA FLATS

Higher Worthyvale

Trekeek

Trela

Factory

Torlands

Starapark

Masts

Condolden Farm

Hendra

Davidstow Airfield & Cornwall at War Mus

Masts

Airfield (dis)

Trevilla Park

Worthyvale Manor

Tregue

The Arthurian Centre

Slaughterbridge

105

B3263

B3314

B3314

Collan's Cross

Hendrawalls

Lower Pendavey

Tregarth

Trefrew

Trenuth Farm

Carcade

Davidstow Woods

Tretherne Farm

Redgates

VICTORIA RD

TREFREW RD

TYLAND RD

105

Tregoodwell

Greylake Barton

Crowdy Resr

Hendra

Trevia

TREVIA LA

L Ctr

Sch

DARKIN LA

Liby

MARKET PL

PO

Mus

FORE ST

COLLEGE RD

Camelford

ROUGHTOR RD

SPORTSMANS RD

HIGH ST

B3266

Sch

PH

Works

105

Treclago

Parkwalls

Roughter Farm

Lower Moor

B3266

FENTEROUN RD

Valley Truckle

Aldermoor Farm

Pencarrow

CH

A39

B3266

Moorgate

Tramagenna

105

09   A   10   B   11   C   12   D   13   E   14   F

24

16

25

For full street detail of the highlighted area see page 105.

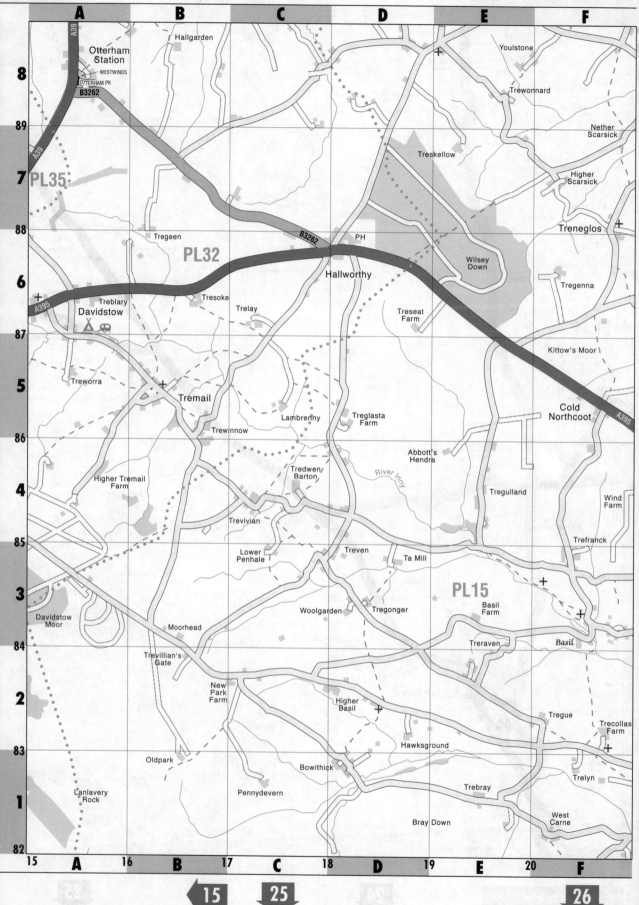

A   B   C   D   E   F

8

Otterham
Station
WESTWINDS
OTTERHAM PK
B3262

Hallgarden

Youlstone

Trewonnard

89

Nether
Scarsick

A39

7

PL35

Treskellow

Higher
Scarsick

88

Tregeen

B3262

PH

Treneglos

PL32

Hallworthy

Wilsey
Down

Tregenna

6

A395

Treblary
Davidstow

Tresoke

Trelay

Treseat
Farm

Kittow's Moor

87

5

Treworra

Tremail

Lambrenny

Treglasta
Farm

Cold
Northcoot

A395

Trewinnow

Abbott's
Hendra

River Inny

86

Higher Tremail
Farm

Tredwen
Barton

Tregulland

Wind
Farm

4

Trevivian

Trefranck

85

Lower
Penhale

Treven

Ta Mill

3

Davidstow
Moor

Moorhead

Woolgarden

Tregonger

PL15

Basil
Farm

Basil

84

Trevillian's
Gate

Treraven

Tregue

Trecollas
Farm

2

New
Park
Farm

Higher
Basil

Hawksground

83

Oldpark

Bowithick

Trebray

Trelyn

1

Lanlavery
Rock

Pennydevern

Bray Down

West
Carne

82

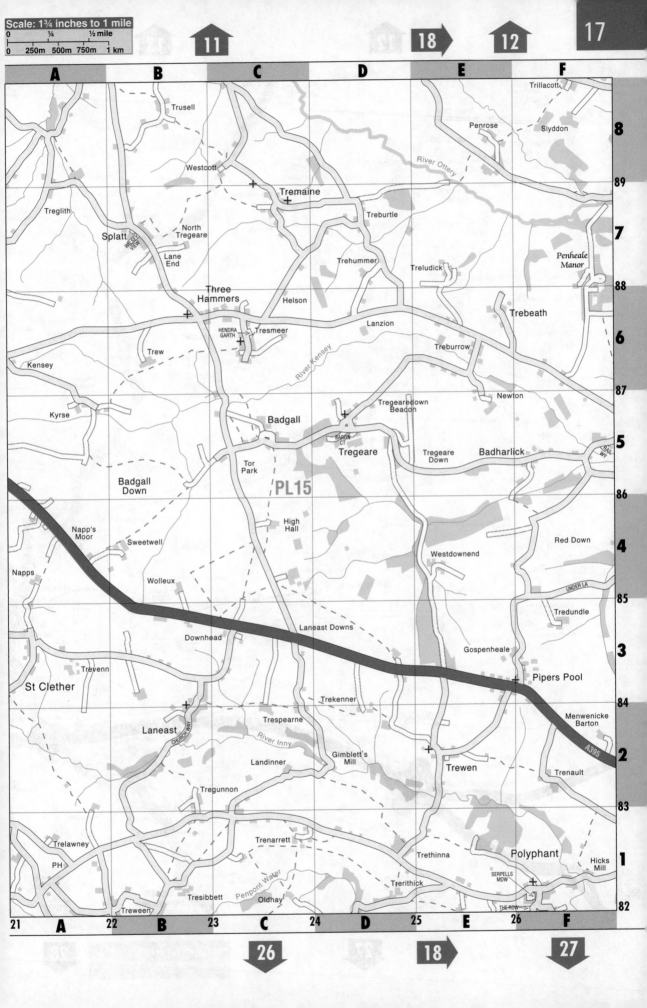

A   B   C   D   E   F

8

89

7

88

6

87

5

86

4

85

3

84

2

83

1

82

Trillacott

Penrose

Slyddon

River Ottery

Trusell

Westcott

Treglith

Tremaine

Treburtle

Penheale
Manor

Splatt

WEST VIEW

North
Tregeare

Lane
End

Trehummer

Treludick

Three
Hammers

Helson

Lanzion

Trebeath

HENDRA
GARTH

Tresmeer

River Kensey

Treburrow

Trew

Kensey

Newton

Tregearedown
Beacon

Kyrse

Badgall

BARON
CT

Tregeare

Tregeare
Down

Badharlick

RAIL
WAY

Tor
Park

PL15

Badgall
Down

Napp's
Moor

High
Hall

Red Down

Sweetwell

Westdownend

Napps

Wolleux

UNDER LA

Tredundle

Laneast Downs

Downhead

Gospenheale

3

Trevenn

Pipers Pool

St Clether

Menwenicke
Barton

Laneast

CHURCH WAY

Trespearne

Trekenner

Trewen

Trenault

River Inny

A395

Gimblett's
Mill

Landinner

Tregunnon

Trenarrett

Trethinna

Polyphant

Hicks
Mill

Trelawney

SERPELLS
MDW

PH

Trerithick

Tresibbett

Oldhay

Treween

Penpont Water

THE ROW

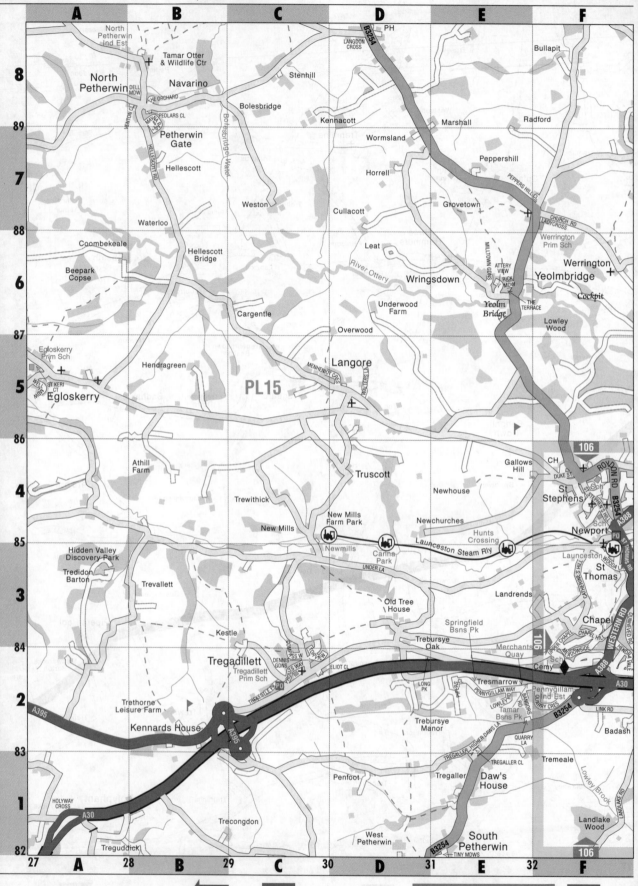

17 12
13

Scale: 1¾ inches to 1 mile
0   ¼   ½ mile
0   250m   500m   750m   1 km

A   B   C   D   E   F

8
89
7
88
6
87
5
86
4
85
3
84
2
83
1
82

North Petherwin Ind Est
Tamar Otter & Wildlife Ctr
North Petherwin
DELL MDW
Navarino
Stenhill
VENTON RD
THE ORCHARD
PEDLARS CL
Petherwin Gate
Bolesbridge
Kennacott
Wormsland
B3254
LANGDON CROSS
PH
Bullapit
Marshall
Radford
Peppershill
Hellescott
HELLESCOTT RD
Botesbridge Water
Weston
Cullacott
Grovetown
PEPPERS HILL CL
CHURCH RD
LADYCROSS
Werrington Prim Sch
Werrington
Waterloo
Horrell
Yeolmbridge
Hellescott Bridge
Leat
River Ottery
Wringsdown
MILLTOWN GDNS
ATTERY VIEW
RICK MDW
Cockpit
Coombekeale
Beepark Copse
Underwood Farm
Yeolm Bridge
THE TERRACE
Lowley Wood
Cargentle
Overwood
Hendragreen
Langore
MENHENIOT CRES
WALTER'S WAY
Egloskerry Prim Sch
WELL MDW
ST KERI CT
Egloskerry
PL15
106
CH
DUKE ST
ROYDON RD
B3254
St Stephens
A368
Athill Farm
Truscott
Newhouse
Gallows Hill
Newport
PO
Trewithick
New Mills
New Mills Farm Park
Newchurches
Hunts Crossing
Launceston Steam Rly
ST THOMAS RD
St Thomas
Hidden Valley Discovery Park
Newmills
Canna Park
UNDER LA
Landrends
Chapel
CHAPEL HILL
Tredidon Barton
Trevallett
Old Tree House
Springfield Bsns Pk
Merchants Quay
UPPER CHAPEL
MEADOWSIDE
WESTERN RD
HENDRA VALE
A388
Kestle
Trebursye Oak
106
Cemy
A30
Tregadillett
DENNIS GDNS
POWIS WAY
EXETER WAY
Tregadillett Prim Sch
THRESHERS LA
PO
ELIOT CL
LONG PK
Tresmarrow
PENNYGILLAM WAY
LOWLEY CL
Tamar Bsns Pk
BANGORS RD
QUARRY CRES
Pennygillam Ind Est
A30
LINK RD
Badash
A395
Trethorne Leisure Farm
Kennards House
A395
Trebursye Manor
Tregaller
QUARRY LA
TREGALLER HIGHER DAWS LA
TREGALLER CL
Daw's House
Tremeale
HOLYWAY CROSS
A30
Penfoot
Tregaller
Lowley Brook
LANDLAKE RD
Landlake Wood
Trecongodon
West Petherwin
B3254
South Petherwin
TINY MDWS
106
Treguddick

27   28   29   30   31   32

17 27
For full street detail of the highlighted area see page 106.
28

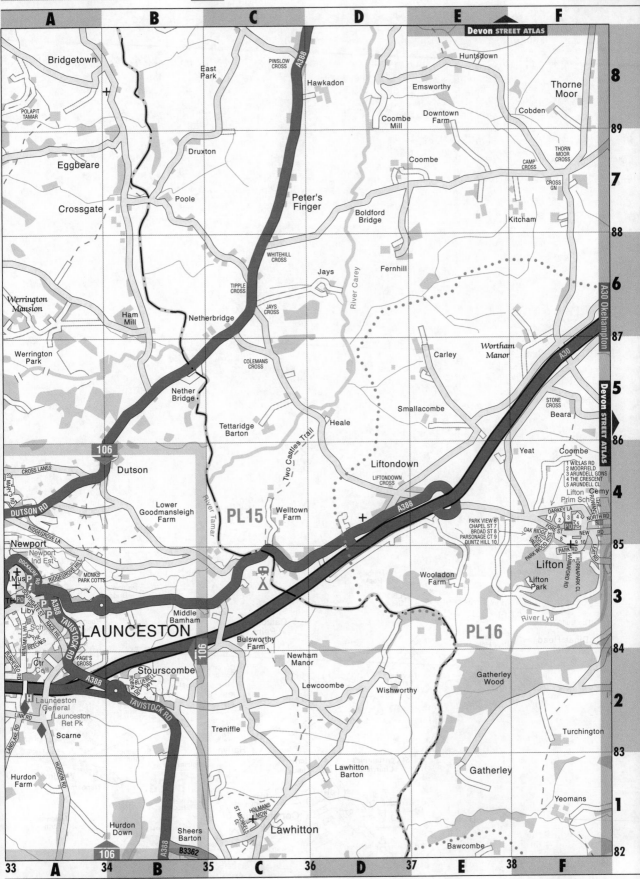

Scale: 1¾ inches to 1 mile

0   ¼   ½ mile
0 250m 500m 750m 1 km

Devon STREET ATLAS

A30 Okehampton

Devon STREET ATLAS

8
89
7
88
6
87
5
86
4
85
3
84
2
83
1
82

A   B   C   D   E   F

Bridgetown
The
POLAPIT TAMAR
Eggbeare
Crossgate
Werrington Mansion
Werrington Park
Newport
Newport Ind Est
Mus
LAUNCESTON
Liby
Sch
THE BEECHES
Ctr Call
Launceston General
Launceston Ret Pk
Scarne
Hurdon Farm
Hurdon Down

East Park
Druxton
Poole
Ham Mill
Netherbridge
Dutson
Lower Goodmansleigh Farm
Middle Bamham
Bulsworthy Farm
Stourscombe
Treniffle
Sheers Barton

CROSS LANES
RIDGEGROVE LA
DUTSON RD
DOCKACRE RD
RIDGEGROVE HILL
MONKS PARK COTTS
TAVISTOCK RD
RACE HILL
PAGE'S CROSS
BLUEBELL WY
ROBIN'S RD
LINK RD
LAND LAKE RD
HURDON RD
RIDGE RD
WINDMILL HILL
ST MARY'S RD

Pinslow Cross
Hawkadon
Peter's Finger
WHITEHILL CROSS
Jays
JAYS CROSS
TIPPLE CROSS
Nether Bridge
Tettaridge Barton
COLEMANS CROSS
Heale
Two Castles Trail
Welltown Farm
Newham Manor
Lewcoombe
Lawhitton Barton
Lawhitton
HOLMANS MDW
ST MICHAELS CL

PL15
River Tamar

Huntsdown
Emsworthy
Downtown Farm
Coombe Mill
Coombe
Boldford Bridge
Fernhill
River Carey
Liftondown
LIFTONDOWN CROSS
Wooladon Farm
Wishworthy
Bawcombe

Thorne Moor
Cobden
THORN MOOR CROSS
CAMP CROSS
CROSS GN
Kitcham
Wortham Manor
Carley
Smallacombe
STONE CROSS
Beara
Yeat
Coombe
1 WILLAS RD
2 MOORFIELD
3 ARUNDELL GDNS
4 THE CRESCENT
5 ARUNDELL CL
Lifton Prim Sch
Cemy
DARKEY LA
Lifton
Lifton Park
PARK VIEW 6
CHAPEL ST 7
BROAD ST 8
PARSONAGE CT 9
DUNTZ HILL 10
OAK RIDGE
FORE ST
VALE RD
PARK WOOD RD
NORTH RD
NEW RD
HORNAPARK RD
HAMMATT RD
HANNAFORD RD
LEAT RD
River Lyd
River Lyd
PL16
Gatherley Wood
Gatherley
Turchington
Yeomans

A388
A30
106
B3362
TAVISTOCK RD
A388

33   A   34   B   35   C   36   D   37   E   38   F

For full street detail of the highlighted area see page 106.

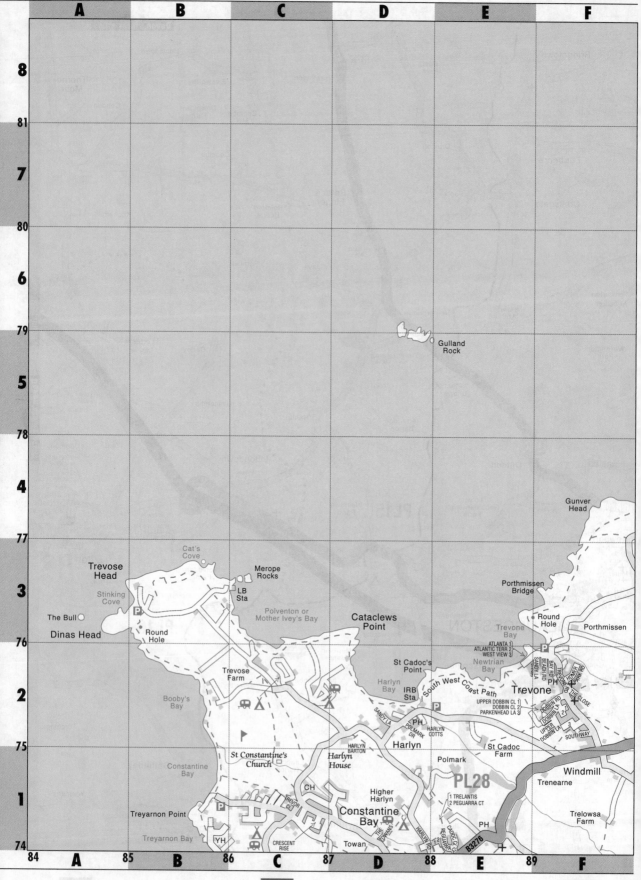

A   B   C   D   E   F

8
81
7
80
6
79

Gulland
Rock

5
78
4

77

Gunver
Head

Trevose
Head

Cat's
Cove

Merope
Rocks

Porthmissen
Bridge

3

Stinking
Cove

LB
Sta

Polventon or
Mother Ivey's Bay

Cataclews
Point

Round
Hole

Porthmissen

The Bull

P

Round
Hole

Dinas Head

Trevone
Bay

ATLANTA 1
ATLANTIC TERR 2
WEST VIEW 3

St Cadoc's
Point

76

Trevose
Farm

Harlyn
Bay

South West Coast Path

Newtrian
Bay

P

BAY RD
BEACH RD
SANDY LA
PH
TREVONE BAY RD
THE CLOSE
DOWNHILL PARK RD

Trevone

2

Booby's
Bay

IRB
Sta

UPPER DOBBIN CL 1
DOBBIN CL 2
PARKENHEAD LA 3

DOBBIN RD
DOBBIN LA
1 2

SANDY LA

POLMARK DR

PH

HARLYN
COTTS

P

UPPER
DOBBIN LA

SOUTHWAY

St Constantine's
Church

HARLYN
BARTON

Harlyn

St Cadoc
Farm

75

Constantine
Bay

Harlyn
House

Polmark

PL28

Windmill

Trenearne

CH

Higher
Harlyn

1 TRELANTIS
2 PEGUARRA CT

Trelowsa
Farm

1

P

TREVOR
RD

1

Treyarnon Point

YH

Constantine
Bay

THE TOWANS

HARLYN RD

CADOC CL
PEGUARRA CT
1
2

PH

B3276

74

Treyarnon Bay

CRESCENT
RISE

Towan

84   A   85   B   86   C   87   D   88   E   89   F

31   32

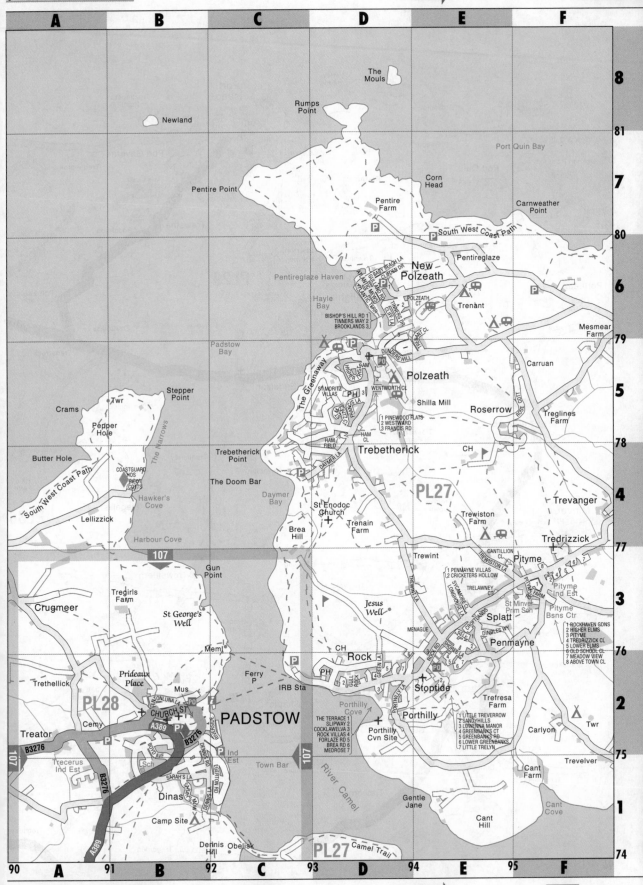

Scale: 1¾ inches to 1 mile

0   ¼   ½ mile
0 250m 500m 750m 1 km

A   B   C   D   E   F

8

The Mouls

Newland

Rumps
Point

81

Pentire Point

Port Quin Bay

7

Corn
Head

Pentire
Farm

Carnweather
Point

80

Pentireglaze Haven

Hayle
Bay

Pentire

South West Coast Path

New
Polzeath

Pentireglaze

6

POLZEATH
CT

Trenant

Mesmear
Farm

79

Padstow
Bay

BISHOP'S HILL RD 1
TINNERS WAY 2
BROOKLANDS 3

Carruan

The Greenaway

Crams

Twr

Stepper
Point

ST MORITZ
VILLAS

PH

Polzeath

Shilla Mill

Roserrow

Treglines
Farm

5

Pepper
Hole

WENTWORTH CL

1 PINEWOOD FLATS
2 WESTWARD
3 FRANCIS RD

HAM
CL

CH

78

Butter Hole

The Narrows

South West Coast Path

COASTGUARD
HOS
PILOT
COTTS

Trebetherick
Point

DAYMER LA

HAM
FIELD

Trebetherick

PL27

Trevanger

4

Lellizzick

The Doom Bar

Daymer
Bay

St Enodoc
Church

Trewiston
Farm

Tredrizzick

77

Hawker's
Cove

Harbour Cove

Brea
Hill

Trenain
Farm

Trewint

CANTILLION
CL

Pityme

107

Gun
Point

TREWISTON LA

PITYME LA

Pityme
Ind Est

Pityme
Bsns Ctr

Crugmeer

Tregirls
Farm

St George's
Well

Jesus
Well

1 PENMAYNE VILLAS
2 CRICKETERS HOLLOW

TRELAWNEY
CT

St Minver
Prim Sch

Splatt

1 ROCKHAVEN GDNS
2 HIGHER ELMS
3 PITYME
4 TREDRIZZICK CL
5 LOWER ELMS
6 OLD SCHOOL CL
7 MEADOW VIEW
8 ABOVE TOWN CL

3

MENAGUE

Penmayne

Trethellick

PL28

Mem

CH

Rock

GREEN LA

PO

76

PH

Prideaux
Place

Mus

Ferry
P

IRB Sta

GULL
ROCK

Stoptide

Trefresa
Farm

2

Treator

Cemy

ST ONLUNA LA

CHURCH ST

A389

PADSTOW

Porthilly
Cove

Porthilly

THE TERRACE 1
SLIPWAY 2
COCKLAWELVA 3
ROCK VILLAS 4
FORLAZE RD 5
BREA RD 6
MEDROSE 7

Porthilly
Cvn Site

1 LITTLE TREVERROW
2 SANDYHILLS
3 LOWENNA MANOR
4 GREENBANKS CT
5 GREENBANKS RD
6 LOWER GREENBANKS
7 LITTLE TRELYN

Carlyon

Twr

Trecerus
Ind Est

B3276

Sch

SARAH'S LA

Ind Est

Town Bar

107

River Camel

Cant
Farm

Trevelver

75

Dinas

Camp Site

Gentle
Jane

Cant
Hill

Cant
Cove

1

B3276

A389

Dennis
Hill

Obelisk

PL27

Camel Trail

74

90   A   91   B   92   C   93   D   94   E   95   F

For full street detail of the
highlighted area see page 107.

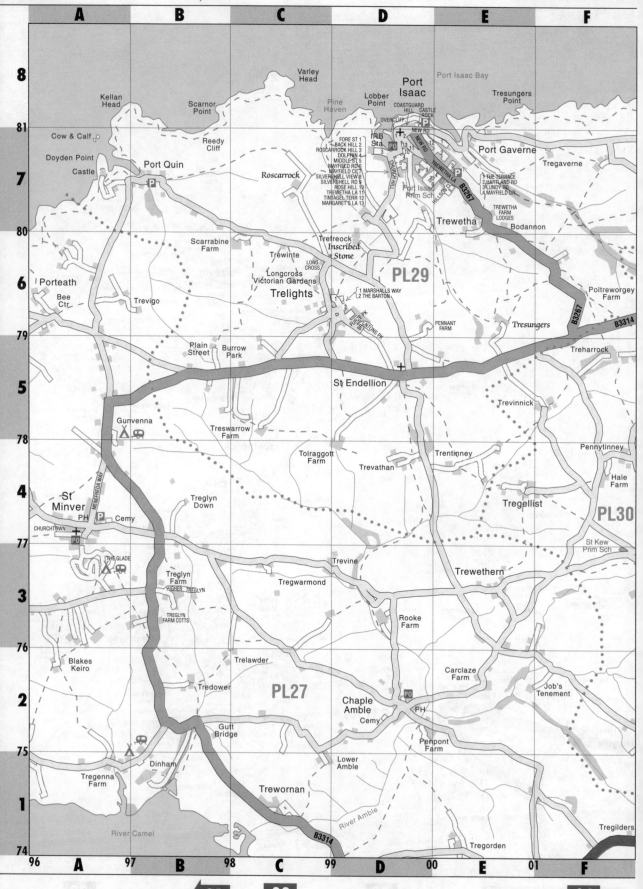

Scale: 1¾ inches to 1 mile

0   ¼   ½ mile
0   250m 500m 750m   1 km

Port Isaac Bay

Port Isaac

Tresungers Point

Kellan Head

Scarnor Point

Varley Head

Pine Haven

Lobber Point

COASTGUARD HILL CASTLE ROCK
OVERCLIFF
NEW RD

Tresungers Point

Cow & Calf

Reedy Cliff

Doyden Point
Castle

Port Quin

Roscarrock

FORE ST 1
BACK HILL 2
ROSCARROCK HILL 3
DOLPHIN 4
MIDDLE ST 5
MAYFIELD RD 6
MAYFIELD CLT 7
SILVERSHELL VIEW 8
SILVERSHELL RD 9
ROSE HILL 10
TREWETHA LA 11
TINTAGEL TERR 12
MARGARET'S LA 13

Port Gaverne

Tregaverne

IRB Sta

Port Isaac Prim Sch

CHURCH HILL

TREWETHA LA

B3267

1 THE TERRACE
2 HARTLAND RD
3 LUNDY RD
4 MAYFIELD DR

Trewetha

TREWETHA FARM LODGES

Bodannon

Scarrabine Farm

Trewinte

Tretreock Inscribed Stone

LONG CROSS

Longcross Victorian Gardens

Trelights

PL29

Porteath

Bee Ctr

Trevigo

1 MARSHALLS WAY
2 THE BARTON

PURZE PK

BENTONS PK

PENNANT FARM

Tresungers

Poltreworgey Farm

B3267

B3314

Treharrock

Plain Street

Burrow Park

St Endellion

Trevinnick

Pennytinney

Gunvenna

Treswarrow Farm

Tolraggott Farm

Trevathan

Trentinney

Tregellist

Hale Farm

PL30

St Minver

McNEFREDA WAY

PH

Cemy

CHURCHTOWN

THE GLADE

Treglyn Down

Treglyn Farm

HIGHER TREGLYN

TREGLYN FARM COTTS

Trevine

Tregwarmond

Trewethern

St Kew Prim Sch

Blakes Keiro

Trelawder

Tredower

PL27

Rooke Farm

Carclaze Farm

Job's Tenement

Gutt Bridge

Dinham

Chaple Amble

Cemy

PH

Penpont Farm

Tregenna Farm

Trewornan

Lower Amble

River Amble

B3314

Tregorden

Tregilders

River Camel

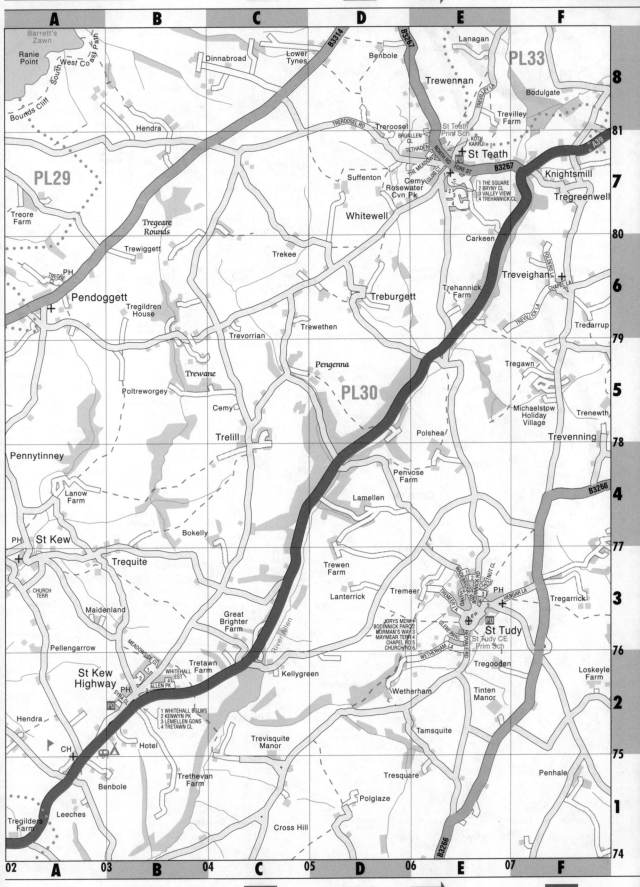

Scale: 1¾ inches to 1 mile

0   ¼   ½ mile
0 250m 500m 750m 1 km

PL33

PL29

PL30

Barrett's Zawn
Ranie Point
West Co ... Path
Bounds Cliff
South ...

Dinnabroad
Lower Tynes
B3314
B3267
Benbole
Lanagan
Trewennan
Bodulgate
Trevilley Farm

Hendra
Treroosel Rd
Treroosel
St Teath Prim Sch
KOTH KARRJI
A39
St Teath
FORE ST
B3267
Knightsmill
Tregreenwell

Treore Farm
PH
TREORE CL
Pendoggett
Tregildren House
Tregeare Rounds
Trewiggett
Suffenton
Cemy Rosewater Cvn Pk
Whitewell
THE MEADOWS
CLOSE CT
NORTH RD
1 THE SQUARE
2 BRYNY CL
3 VALLEY VIEW
4 TREHANNICK CL
Carkeen
Trehannick Farm
FOLDERS
Treveighans
CHAPEL LA
TREVILLICK LA
Tredarrup

Trekee
Treburgett
Trewethen
Trevorrian
Pengenna
Tregawn
Michaelstow Holiday Village
Trenewth
Trevenning

Trewane
Poltreworgey
Cemy
Trelill
Polshea
Penvose Farm
Lamellen
Bokelly

Pennytinney
Lanow Farm
B3266

St Kew
CHURCH TERR
Trequite
Great Brighter Farm
River Allen
Trewen Farm
Lanterrick
Tremeer
TREMEER LA
WADEBRIDGE RD
BODINNICK RD
CHESTNUT CL
PH
HENGAR LA
Tregarrick

Maidenland
Kellygreen
JORYS MDW 1
BODINNICK PARC 2
NORMAN'S WAY 3
MAYMEAR TERR 4
CHAPEL RD 5
CHURCH RD 6
GLEBE PARC
REVVAE RD
WETHERHAM LA
St Tudy CE Prim Sch
St Tudy
PO
Tregooden
Loskeyle Farm

Pellengarrow
MEADOWSIDE CL
WHITEHALL EST
ALLEN PK
St Kew Highway
PH
PO
SYRE CL
1 WHITEHALL BGLWS
2 KENWYN PK
3 LEMELLEN GDNS
4 TRETAWN CL
Tretawn Farm
Wetherham
Tinten Manor

Hendra
CH
Hotel
Trevisquite Manor
Tamsquite

Benbole
Trethevan Farm
Tresquare
Penhale

Tregilders Farm
Leeches
Cross Hill
Polglaze
B3266

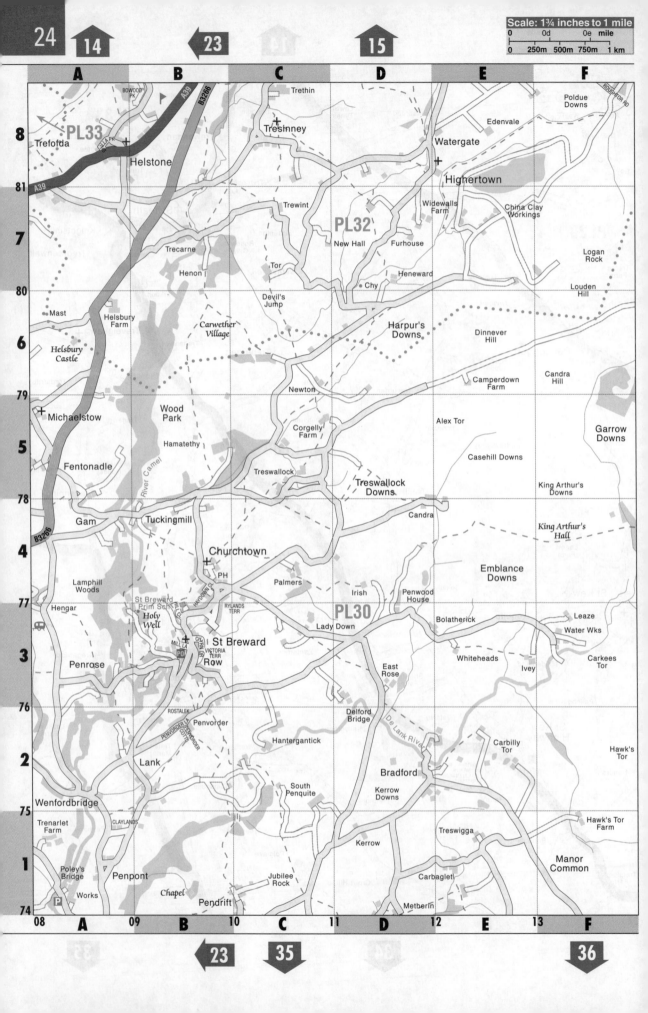

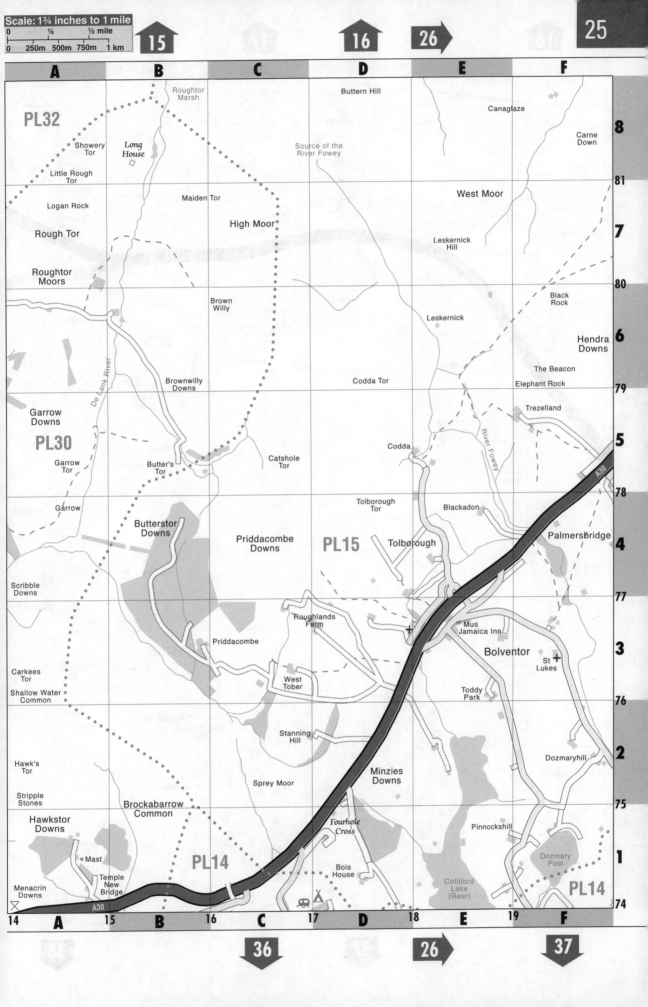

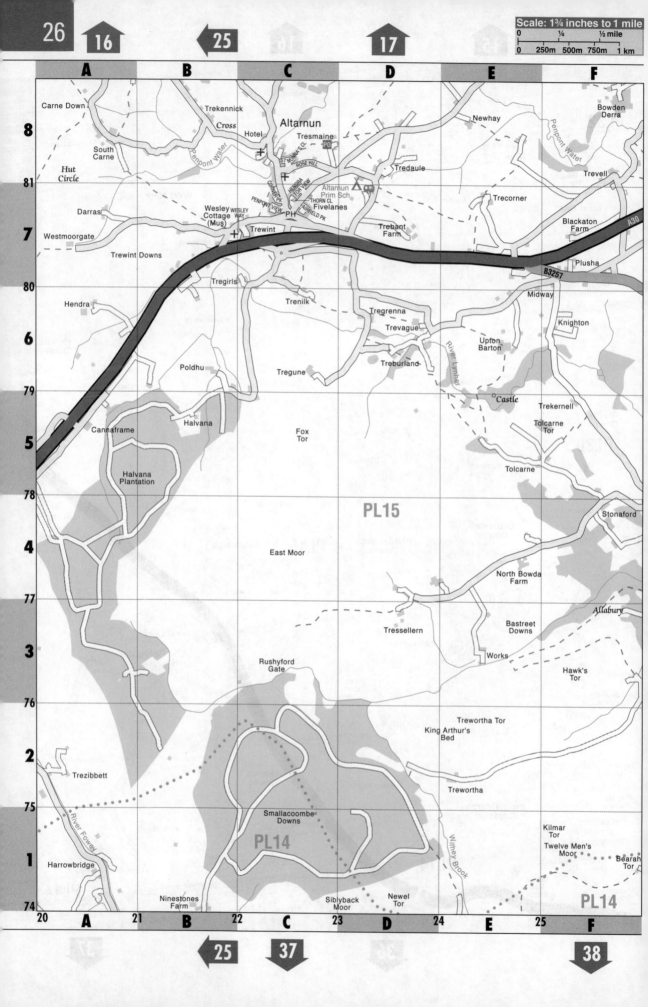

Scale: 1¾ inches to 1 mile

A30

B3257

Altarnun

PL15

PL14

Carne Down
Trekennick
Cross
Hotel
Tresmaine
Newhay
Bowden Derra
South Carne
Hut Circle
St Nonna Sch.
ROSE HILL
Tredaule
Trevell
Darras
CORNER PK.
HENDRA
TOR VIEW
Altarnun Prim Sch
Trecorner
Wesley Cottage (Mus)
WESLEY WAY
PENPONT VIEW
THORN CL
Fivelanes
Blackaton Farm
Westmoorgate
PH
FAIRFIELD PK
Trebant Farm
Plusha
Trewint
Trewint Downs
Tregirls
Midway
Hendra
Trenilk
Tregrenna
Knighton
Tregune
Trevague
Upton Barton
Poldhu
Treburland
Castle
Trekernell
Cannaframe
Halvana
Tolcarne Tor
Fox Tor
Tolcarne
Halvana Plantation
Stonaford
East Moor
North Bowda Farm
Allabury
Tressellern
Bastreet Downs
Hawk's Tor
Rushyford Gate
Works
Trewortha Tor
King Arthur's Bed
Trezibbett
Treworthus
Smallacoombe Downs
Kilmar Tor
Harrowbridge
River Fowey
PL14
Twelve Men's Moor
Bearah Tor
Ninestones Farm
Siblyback Moor
Newel Tor
Witney Brook
PL14

Penpont Water

River Lynher

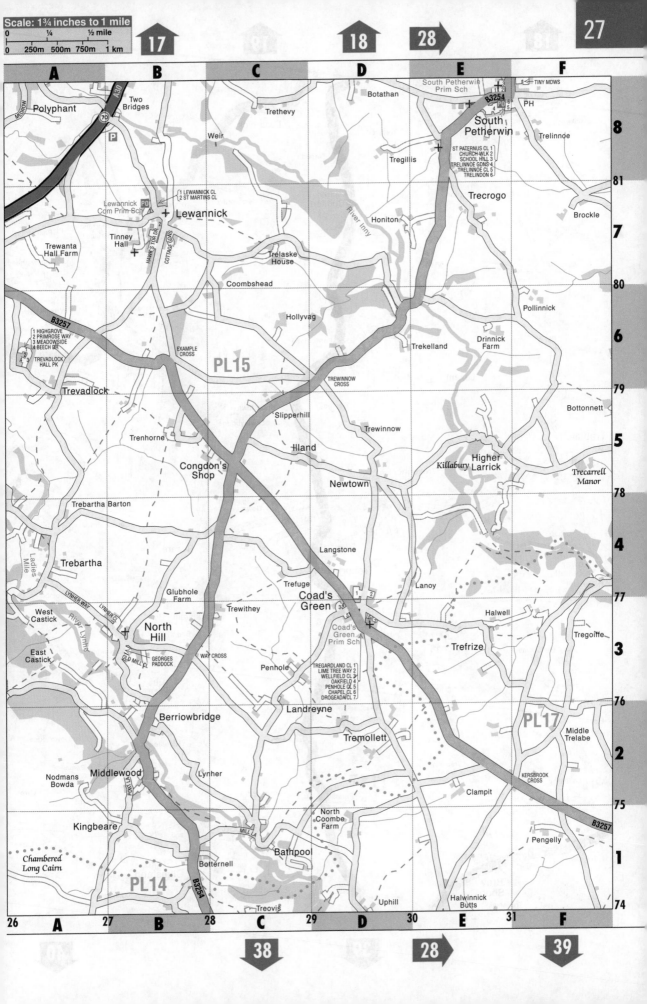

A B C D E F

17 **18** **28**

8
81
7
80
6
79
5
78
4
77
3
76
2
75
1
74

Polyphant
Two Bridges
A30
P
70

Trethevy
Botathan

South Petherwin Prim Sch
B3254
PO
PH
TINY MDWS

South Petherwin

Trelinnoe

1 LEWANNICK CL
2 ST MARTINS CL

Lewannick Com Prim Sch
PO
Lewannick

Weir

Tregillis

Tregillis

ST PATERNUS CL 1
CHURCH WLK 2
SCHOOL HILL 3
TRELINNOE GDNS 4
TRELINNOE CL 5
TRELINDON 6

Trecrogo

Brockle

Tinney Hall

Trewanta Hall Farm

Hawk's Tor Dr

Cottage Gdns

Trelaske House

Honiton

River Inny

Coombshead

Pollinnick

B3257

1 HIGHGROVE
2 PRIMROSE WAY
3 MEADOWSIDE
4 BEECH DR

TREVADLOCK HALL PK

Trevadlock

Hollyvag

Trekelland

Drinnick Farm

PL15

Example Cross

Trewinnow Cross

Bottonnett

Slipperhill

Trenhorne

Hland

Trewinnow

Higher Larrick

Killabury

Trecarrell Manor

Congdon's Shop

Newtown

Trebartha Barton

Langstone

Lanoy

Ladies Mile

Trebartha

Trefuge

Coad's Green

Trewithey

Halwell

Tregoiffe

Glubhole Farm

Lynher Way

Lynher Cl

River Lynher

West Castick

North Hill

Coad's Green Prim Sch

Trefrize

1
2

East Castick

Old Mill Cl

Georges Paddock

Way Cross

Penhole

TREGARDLAND CL 1
LIME TREE WAY 2
WELLFIELD CL 3
OAKFIELD 4
PENHOLE CL 5
CHAPEL CL 6
DROGEADA CL 7

PL17

Middle Trelabe

Berriowbridge

Landreyne

Tremollett

Kersbrook Cross

Nodmans Bowda

Middlewood

Lynher

Por La

Clampit

Kingbeare

Mill La

North Coombe Farm

B3257

Pengelly

Chambered Long Cairn

Bathpool

PL14

B3254

Botternell

Treovis

Uphill

Halwinnick Butts

26 A 27 B 28 C 29 D 30 E 31 F

38 **28** **39**

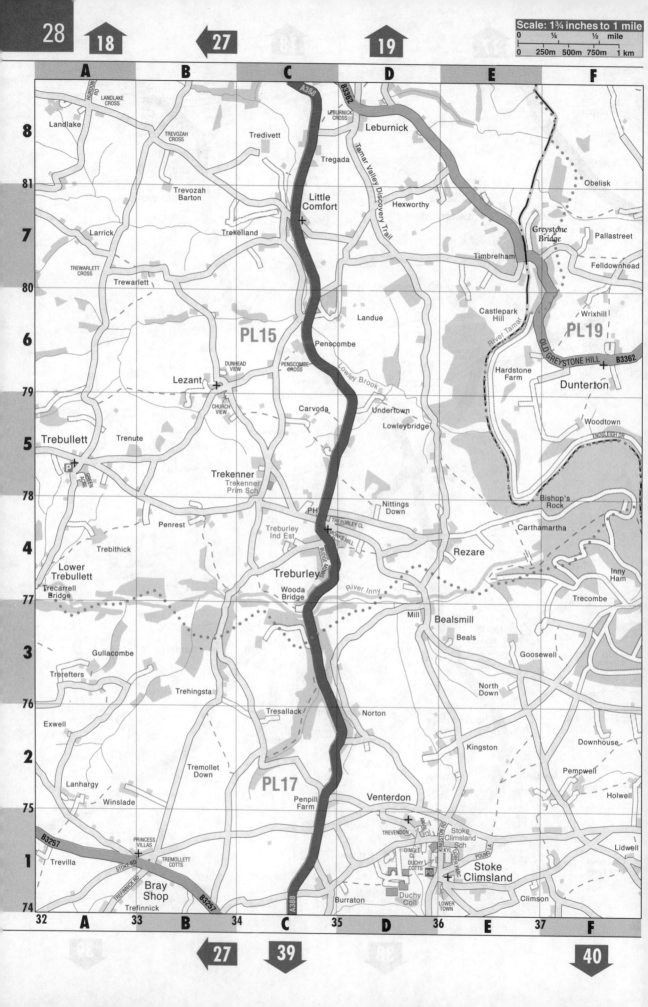

A · B · C · D · E · F

Devon STREET ATLAS

8
81
7
80
6
79
5
78
4
77
3
76
2
75
1
74

38 · A · 39 · B · 40 · C · 41 · D · 42 · E · 43 · F · 74

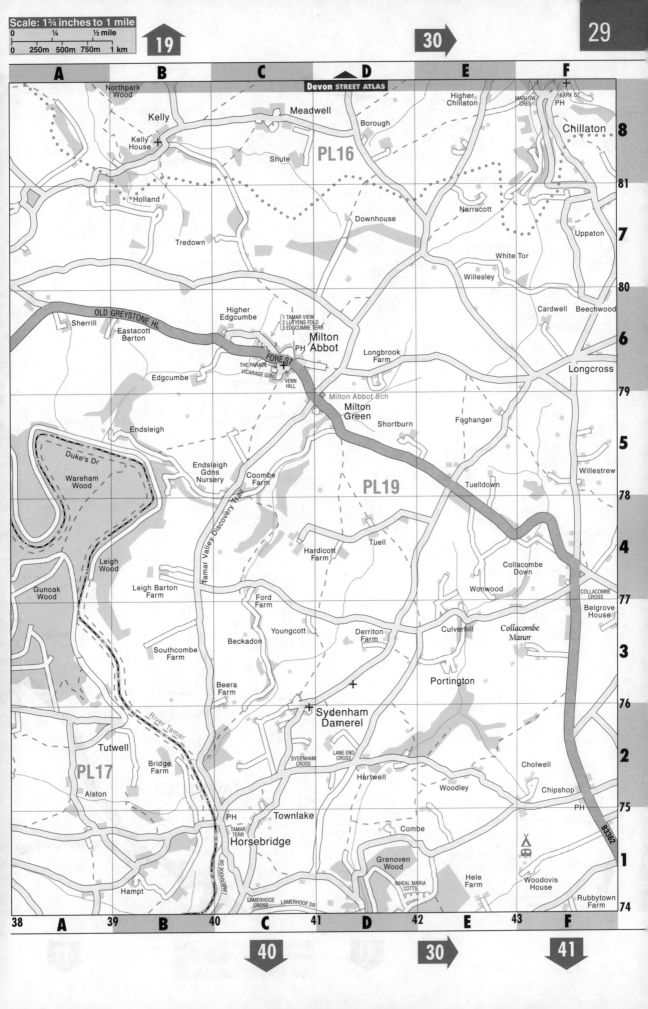

Northpark Wood
Kelly
Kelly House
Holland
Tredown
Meadwell
Borough
Shute
Downhouse
PL16
Higher Chillaton
MARLOW CRES
PARK OT PH
Chillaton
Narracott
Uppaton
White Tor
Willesley
OLD GREYSTONE HL
Sherrill
Eastacott Barton
Higher Edgcumbe
1 TAMAR VIEW
2 LUTYENS FOLD
3 EDGCUMBE TERR
Milton Abbot
PH
Longbrook Farm
Cardwell
Beechwood
Longcross
Edgcumbe
FORE ST
THE PARADE
VICARAGE GDNS
VENN HILL
Milton Abbot Sch
Milton Green
Shortburn
Foghanger
Endsleigh
Duke's Dr
Wareham Wood
Endsleigh Gdns Nursery
Coombe Farm
PL19
Tuelldown
Willestrew
Leigh Wood
Gunoak Wood
Leigh Barton Farm
Ford Farm
Hardicott Farm
Tuell
Collacombe Down
Wonwood
COLLACOMBE CROSS
Belgrove House
Southcombe Farm
Beckadon
Youngcott
Derriton Farm
Culverhill
Collacombe Manor
Beera Farm
Portington
Tutwell
Bridge Farm
Sydenham Damerel
Cholwell
PL17
Sydenham Cross
Lane End Cross
Hartwell
Woodley
Chipshop
Alston
River Tamar
PH
TAMAR TERR
Townlake
Combe
PH
B3362
Horsebridge
LAMERHOOE DR
Hampt
LAMERHOOE CROSS
LAMERHOOE DR
Grenoven Wood
WHEAL MARIA COTTS
Hele Farm
Woodovis House
Rubbytown Farm

Tamar Valley Discovery Trail

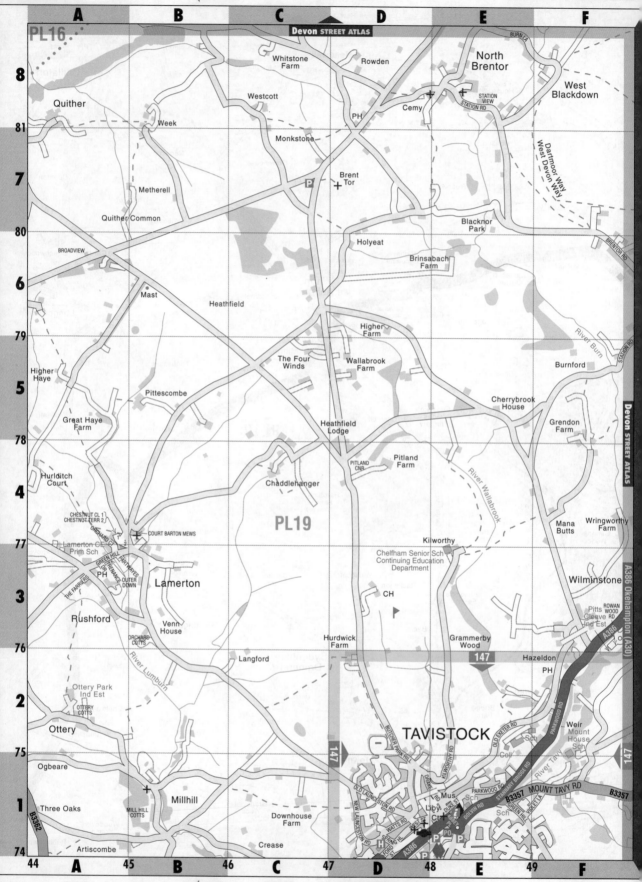

Scale: 1¾ inches to 1 mile
0   ¼   ½ mile
0   250m 500m 750m 1 km

PL16

Devon STREET ATLAS

Devon STREET ATLAS

8
Quither
North Brentor
West Blackdown
Whitstone Farm
Rowden
Westcott
Cemy
81
Week
Monkstone
PH
STATION VIEW
STATION RD
BURN LA

7
Metherell
Brent Tor
Dartmoor Way
West Devon Way
P

80
Quither Common
Holyeat
Blacknor Park
BROADVIEW
Brinsabach Farm
River Burn

6
Mast
Heathfield
Higher Farm
STATION RD
BRENTOR RD

79
The Four Winds
Wallabrook Farm
Burnford

5
Higher Haye
Pittescombe
Cherrybrook House
Grendon Farm

78
Great Haye Farm
Heathfield Lodge
Pitland Farm
Pitland CNR

4
Hurlditch Court
Chaddlehanger
PL19
Mana Butts
Wringworthy Farm
River Wallabrook
CHESTNUT CL 1
CHESTNUT TERR 2
ORCHARD CT
Kilworthy
ROWAN WOOD IND EST
Pitts Cleave
A386 Okehampton (A30)

77
Lamerton CE Prim Sch
Court Barton Mews
Chelfham Senior Sch Continuing Education Department
Wilminstone
PITTS CLEAVE RD
GREEN HILL
EARTHAYES
DRY HANGE

3
THE FARRIERS
PH
Lamerton
OUTER DOWN
CH
Grammerby Wood
Rushford
Venn House
Hazeldon
PH
ORCHARD COTTS
Hurdwick Farm
147
147

76
Langford
River Lumburn
TAVISTOCK
Weir Mount House Sch
147

2
Ottery Park Ind Est
OTTERY COTTS
BUTCHER PARK HILL
OLD EXETER RD
Sch
PARKWOOD RD

75
Ottery
Coll
River Tavy
Ogbeare
OLD LAUNCESTON RD
NEW LAUNCESTON RD
DRAKE RD
KILWORTHY RD
PARKWOOD RD
B3357 MOUNT TAVY RD
B3357

1
Three Oaks
Millhill
MILL HILL COTTS
Downhouse Farm
Crease
Mus
Liby Ctr
H
WATTS RD
SPRING HILL
FORD ST
PD
DOLVIN RD
GREEN HILL
PLYMOUTH RD
B3362
Artiscombe
A386

29

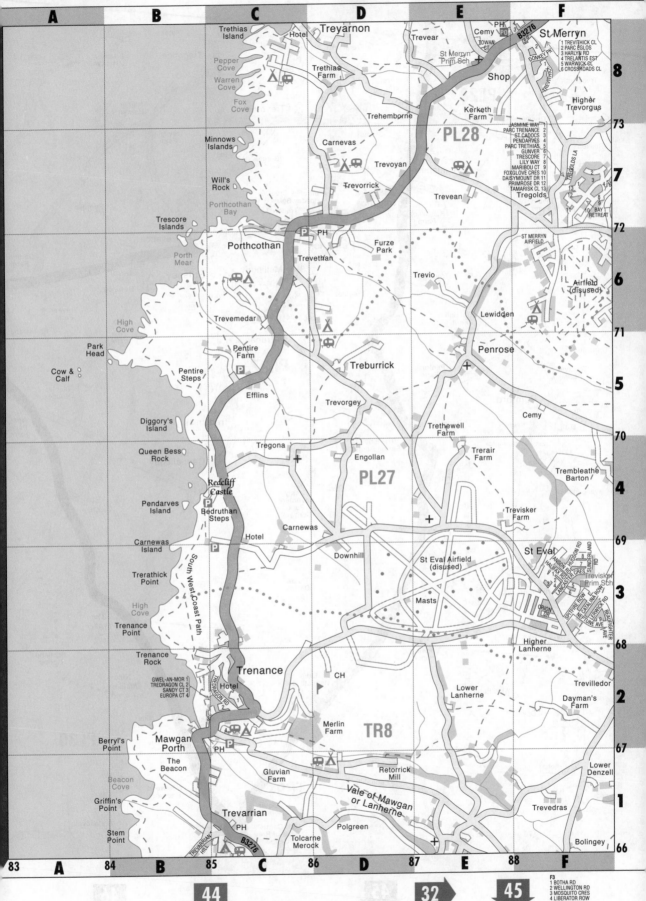

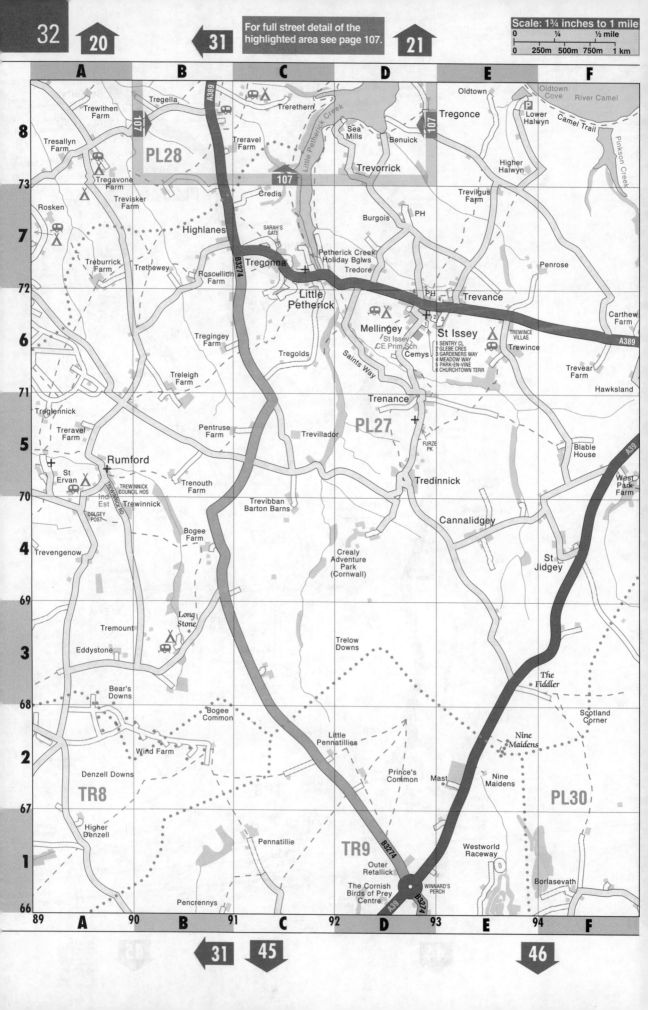

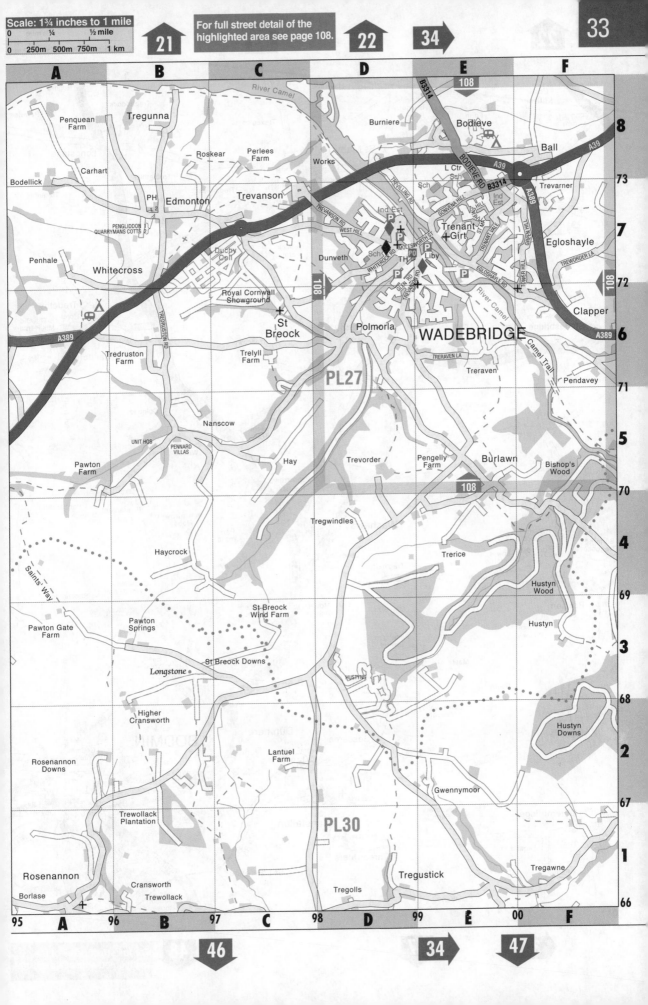

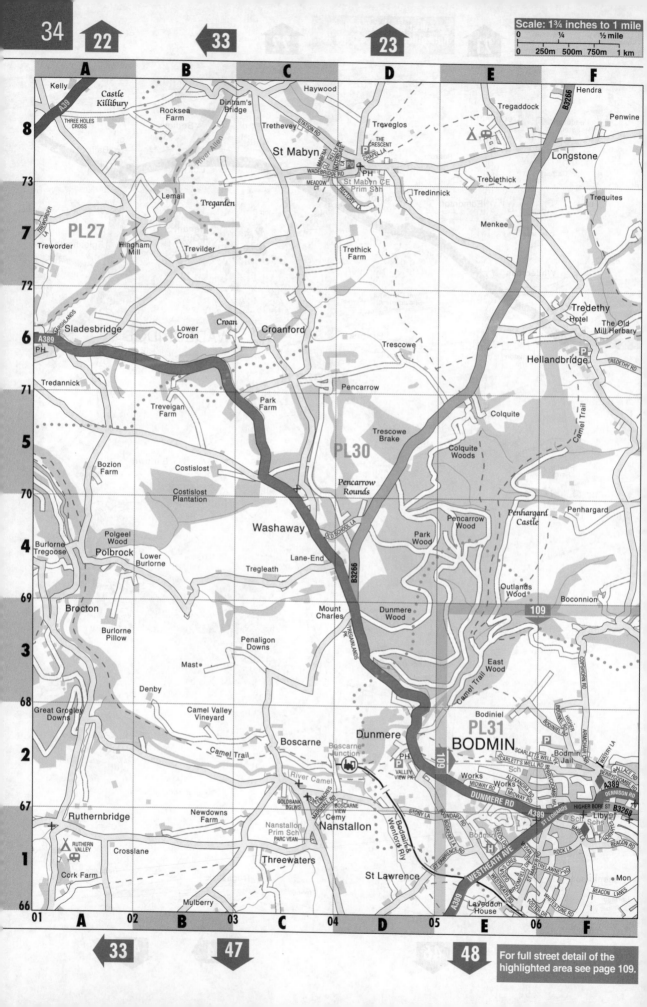

Scale: 1¾ inches to 1 mile

0 ¼ ½ mile
0 250m 500m 750m 1 km

A **B** **C** **D** **E** **F**

Kelly
Castle Killibury
THREE HOLES CROSS
A39
Rocksea Farm
Dinham's Bridge
Haywood
Trethevey
Trethevey
St Mabyn
STATION RD
THE CRESCENT
CHAPEL LA
Tregaddock
Hendra
Penwine
Longstone
B3266

8

River Allen
Lemail
Tregarden
PH
WADEBRIDGE RD
MEADOW CT
RECTORY LA
St Mabyn CE Prim Sch
Treveglos
Treblethick
Tredinnick
Trequites

73

PL27
Treworder
Hingham Mill
Trevilder
Trethick Farm
Menkee

7

72

Sladesbridge
A389
PH
Lower Croan
Croan
Croanford
Trescowe
Pencarrow
Tredethy
Hotel
The Old Mill Herbary
Hellandbridge
P
TREDETHY RD

6

Tredannick
Treveigan Farm
Park Farm
Colquite
Camel Trail

71

Costislost
PL30
Trescowe Brake
Colquite Woods

5

Bozion Farm
Costislost Plantation
Pencarrow Rounds
Penhargard Castle
Penhargard

70

Burlorne Tregoose
Polgeel Wood
Polbrock
Lower Burlorne
Washaway
OLD SCHOOL LA
Pencarrow Wood
Park Wood

4

Lane-End
Tregleath
B3266
Outlands Wood
Boconnion

69

Brocton
Burlorne Pillow
Penaligon Downs
Mount Charles
Dunmere Wood
109

Great Grogley Downs
Mast
Denby
Camel Valley Vineyard
TREGAINLANDS PK
East Wood
Bodiniel
PL31
BODMIN
Bodmin Jail
WATERY LA

3

68

Camel Trail
Camel Trail
Boscarne
Dunmere
PH
VALLEY VIEW PK
109
Works
Works
Sch
Scarlett's Well Rd
BERRYCOOMBE HILL
DENNISON RD
A389
B3266

2

67

Ruthernbridge
RUTHERN VALLEY
Newdowns Farm
GOLDBANK BGLWS
MARSHALL RD
Boscarne Junction
BOSCARNE VIEW
Cemy
Nanstallon
Nanstallon Prim Sch
PARC VEAN
River Camel
STONY LA
Bodmin & Wenford Rly
BOSCARTH LA
DUNMERE RD
A389
HIGHER BORE ST
ST LEONARDS
Liby Sch Schs

1

Cork Farm
Crosslane
Threewaters
Mulberry
St Lawrence
Laveddon House
ST LAWRENCE RD
A389
WESTHEATH AVE
WESTHEATH RD
WHITSTONE RD
Mon
BEACON LANES

66

01 **A** 02 **B** 03 **C** 04 **D** 05 **E** 06 **F**

For full street detail of the highlighted area see page 109.

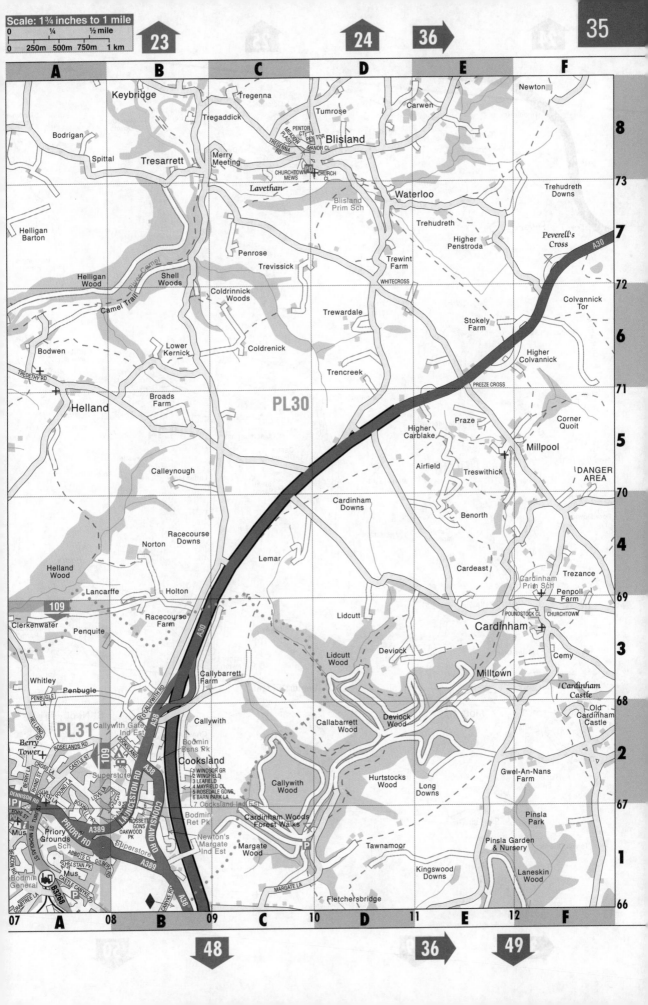

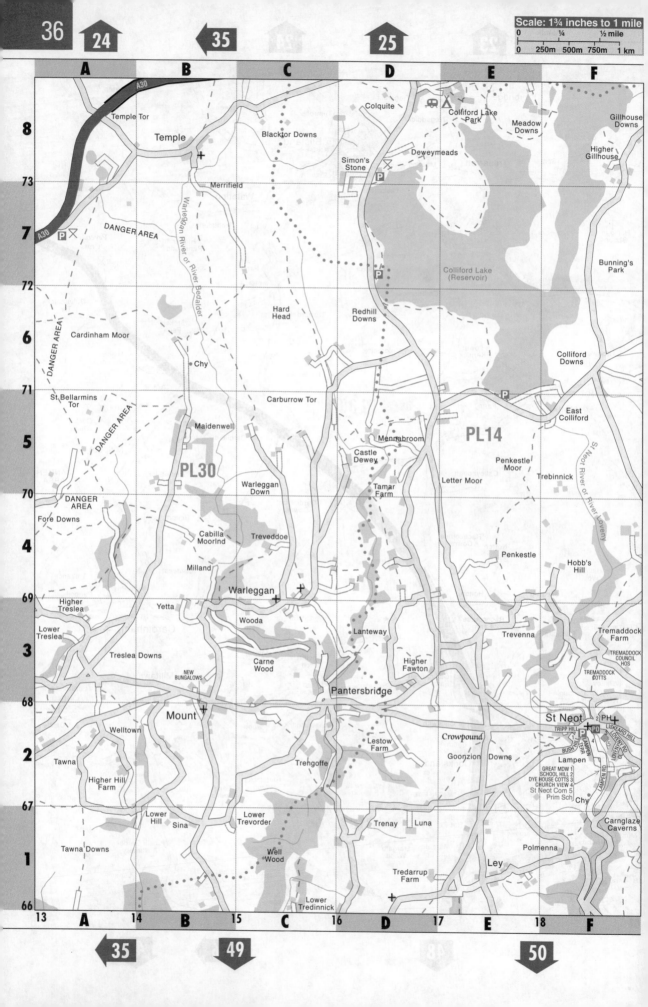

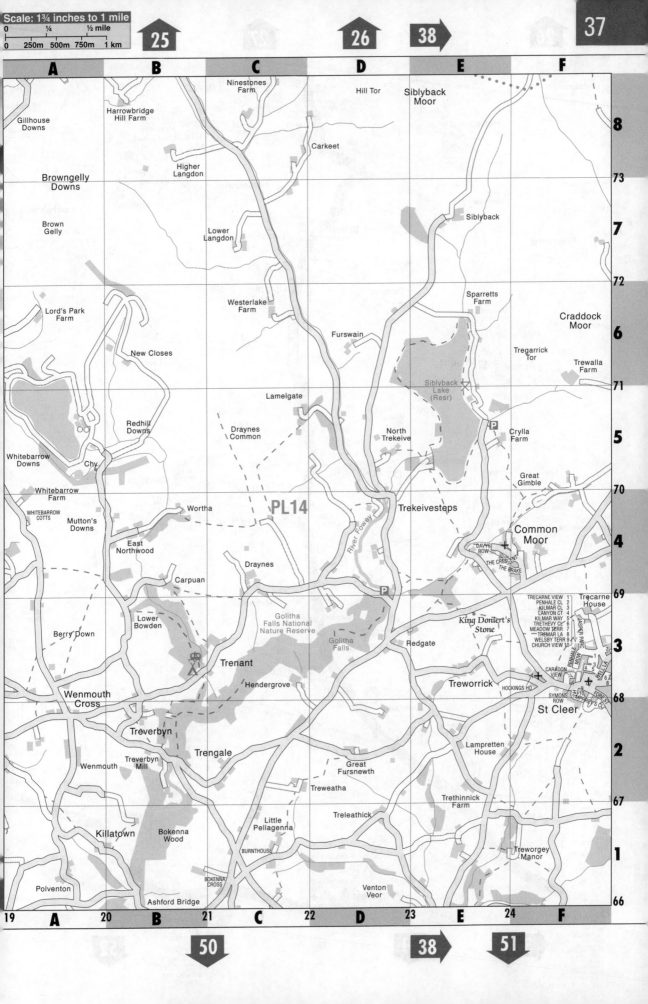

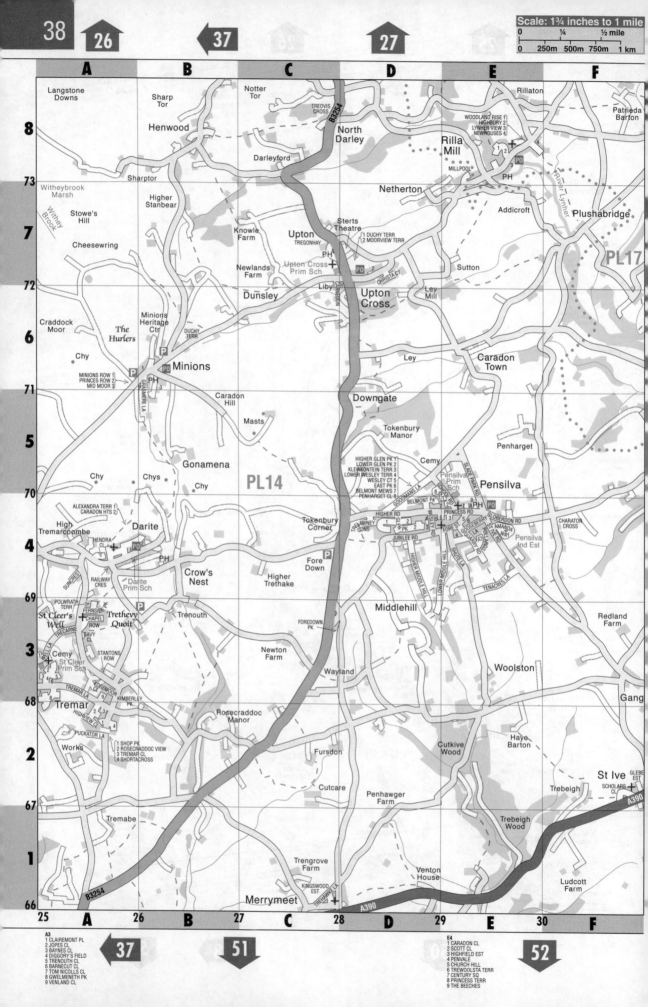

A   B   C   D   E   F

8

Langstone Downs
Sharp Tor
Henwood
Notter Tor
TREOVIS CROSS
B3254
North Darley
Rillaton
Patrieda Barton
WOODLAND RISE 1
HIGHBURY 2
LYNHER VIEW 3
NEWHOUSES 4
Rilla Mill
MILLPOOL
PH

73

Witheybrook Marsh
Sharptor
Darleyford
Netherton
Addicroft
Plushabridge

7

Withey Brook
Stowe's Hill
Higher Stanbear
Knowle Farm
Sterts Theatre
Upton
TREGONHAY
1 DUCHY TERR
2 MOORVIEW TERR
Sutton
PL17
Cheesewring
Newlands Farm
Upton Cross Prim Sch
PH
PO
CHRISTA CT
Upton Cross
Ley Mill

72

Craddock Moor
The Hurlers
Minions Heritage Ctr
DUCHY TERR
Dunsley
Liby
Ley
Caradon Town

6

Chy
P
P
PO
Minions
PH
Caradon Hill
Downgate
Penharget

71

MINIONS ROW 1
PRINCES ROW 2
MID MOOR 3
GRASMERE LA
Masts
Tokenbury Manor
Penharget

5

Chy
Chys
Gonamena
Chy
PL14
HIGHER GLEN PK 1
LOWER GLEN PK 2
KLEINFONTEIN TERR 3
LOWER WESLEY TERR 4
WESLEY CT 5
EAST PK 6
BELMONT MEWS 7
PENHARGET CL 8
Cemy
Pensilva Prim Sch
Pensilva

70

ALEXANDRA TERR 1
CARADON HTS 2
High Tremarcoombe
Darite
HENDRA CL
PO
Tokenbury Corner
GOODMAN LA
SLADE PARK RD
Belmont Pk
SCHOOL RD
Princess Rd
PH
PO
GLOBERDON RD
CHARATON CROSS

4

SUNCREST
RAILWAY CRES
Darite Prim Sch
PH
Crow's Nest
Higher Trethake
Fore Down
P
Higher Rd
TRELAWNEY GDNS
Jubilee Rd
HIGHER MIDDLE HILL
SHUTE LA
AMANDA WAY
Pensilva Ind Est
TENACRES LA

69

POLWRATH TERR
FERNSIDE
PK
Trethevy Quoit
Trenouth
Middlehill
Redland Farm

3

St Cleer's Well
CHAPEL ROW
DAVY CL
TRECARNE
Cemy
St Cleer Prim Sch
STANTONS ROW
Newton Farm
Wayland
Woolston
Gang

68

EDGEMOOR
TREMAR LA
KIMBERLEY PK
HIGHVIEW CL
Tremar
Rosecraddoc Manor
Cutkive Wood
Haye Barton

2

Works
PUCKATOR LA
1 SHOP PK
2 ROSECRADDOC VIEW
3 TREMAR CL
4 SHORTACROSS
Fursdon
Cutkive Wood
St Ive
GLEBE EST
SCHOLARS CL
A390

67

Tremabe
Cutcare
Penhawger Farm
Trebeigh
Trebeigh Wood
Ludcott Farm

1

Trengrove Farm
KINGSWOOD EST
TREAWKE LA
Venton House
Merrymeet

66

B3254
Merrymeet
A390

25   A   26   B   27   C   28   D   29   E   30   F

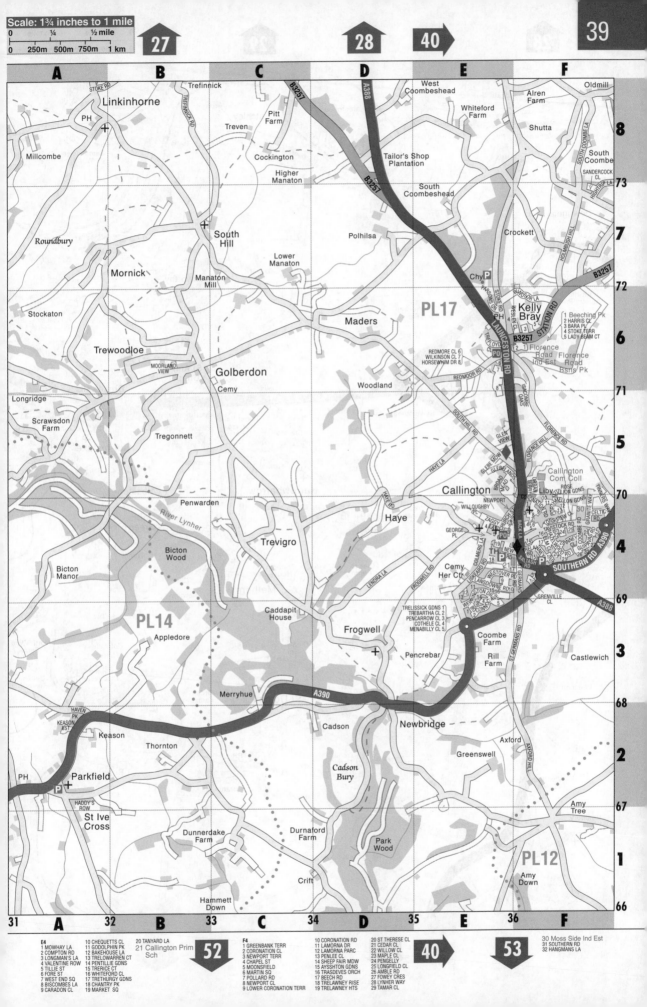

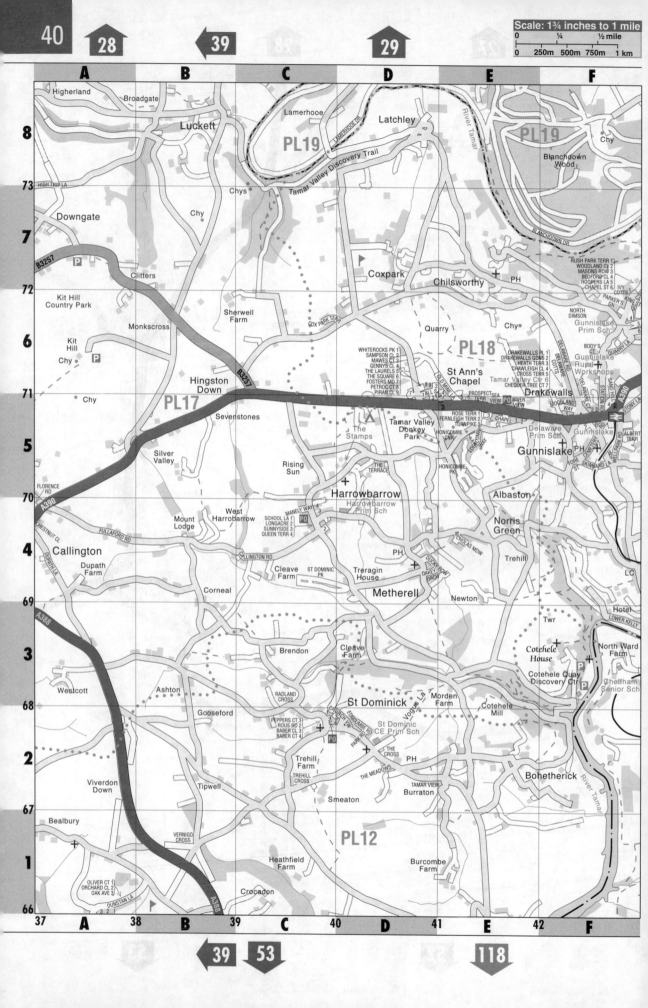

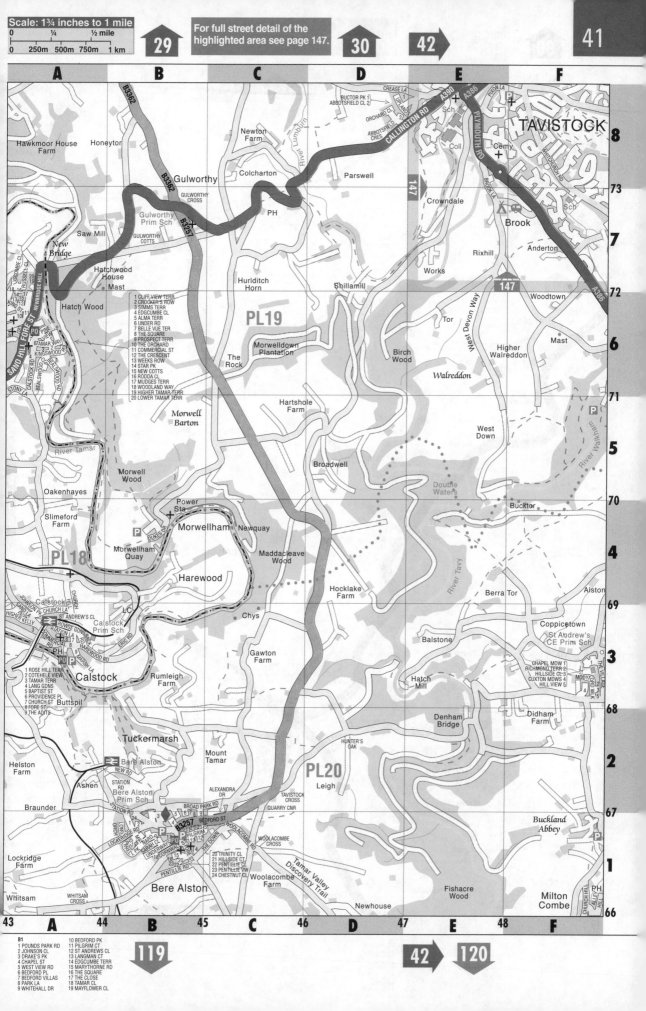

Scale: 1¾ inches to 1 mile

0   ¼   ½ mile

0   250m 500m 750m 1 km

29

For full street detail of the
highlighted area see page 147.

30   42

41

A   B   C   D   E   F

TAVISTOCK

8

73

7

72

6

71

5

70

4

69

3

68

2

67

1

66

PL19

PL18

PL20

B3362
B3362
B3257
A390
A386

CALLINGTON RD
PLYMOUTH RD
A386

147
147
147

Hawkmoor House Farm

Honeytor

Gulworthy

Gulworthy Cross

Saw Mill

Gulworthy Prim Sch

Gulworthy Cotts

New Bridge

Hatch Wood

Hatchwood House

Mast

SAND HILL FORE ST
NEWBRIDGE HILL

Newton Farm

Colcharton

Parswell

PH

Hurlditch Horn

Shillamill

The Rock

Morwelldown Plantation

Morwell Barton

River Tamar

Oakenhayes

Morwell Wood

Slimeford Farm

Power Sta

Morwellham

Newquay

Morwellham Quay

Harewood

Maddacleave Wood

Hartshole Farm

Broadwell

West Down

Double Waters

Bucktor

Chys

Hocklake Farm

Gawton Farm

Balstone

Berra Tor

Alston

Coppicetown

St Andrew's CE Prim Sch

Hatch Mill

River Tavy

West Devon Way

Higher Walreddon

Walreddon

Tor

Mast

Woodtown

Birch Wood

Crownvale

Brook

Rixhill

Works

Anderton

Didham Farm

Calstock

St Andrew's Cl

Calstock Prim Sch

Rowse Gdns

Eric Rd

L C

Harewood Rd

Rumleigh Farm

Buttspil

PH

Tuckermarsh

Helston Farm

Ashen

Braunder

Mount Tamar

Bere Alston Prim Sch

New Rd

Station Rd

Bere Alston

Alexandra Dr

Tavistock Cross

Quarry Cnr

Leigh

Hunter's Oak

Denham Bridge

Tamar Valley Discovery Trail

Buckland Abbey

Fishacre Wood

Milton Combe

Lockridge Farm

Whitsam

Whitsam Cross

Newhouse

Woolacombe Farm

Woolacombe Cross

B3257

Broad Park Rd

Bedford St

Woolacombe Rd

1 CLIFF VIEW TERR
2 CROCKER'S ROW
3 SIMMS TERR
4 EDGCUMBE CL
5 ALMA TERR
6 UNDER RD
7 BELLE VUE TER
8 THE SQUARE
9 PROSPECT TERR
10 THE ORCHARD
11 COMMERCIAL ST
12 THE CRESCENT
13 WEEKS ROW
14 STAR PK
15 NEW COTTS
16 RODDA CL
17 MUDGES TERR
18 WOODLAND WAY
19 HIGHER TAMAR TERR
20 LOWER TAMAR TERR

1 ROSE HILL TERR
2 COTEHELE VIEW
3 TAMAR TERR
4 LANG GDNS
5 BAPTIST ST
6 PROVIDENCE PL
7 CHURCH ST
8 FORE ST
9 THE ADITS

20 TRINITY CL
21 HILLSIDE CT
22 PENTILLIE CL
23 PENTILLIE VW
24 CHESTNUT CL

CHAPEL MDW 1
RICHMOND TERR 2
HILLSIDE CT 3
CUXTON MDWS 4
HILL VIEW 5

43   A   44   B   45   C   46   D   47   E   48   F

119   42   120

B1
1 POUNDS PARK RD
2 JOHNSON CL
3 DRAKE'S PK
4 CHAPEL ST
5 WEST VIEW RD
6 BEDFORD PL
7 BEDFORD VILLAS
8 PARK LA
9 WHITEHALL DR
10 BEDFORD PK
11 PILGRIM CT
12 ST ANDREWS CL
13 LANGMAN CT
14 EDGCUMBE TERR
15 MARYTHORNE RD
16 THE SQUARE
17 THE CLOSE
18 TAMAR CL
19 MAYFLOWER CL

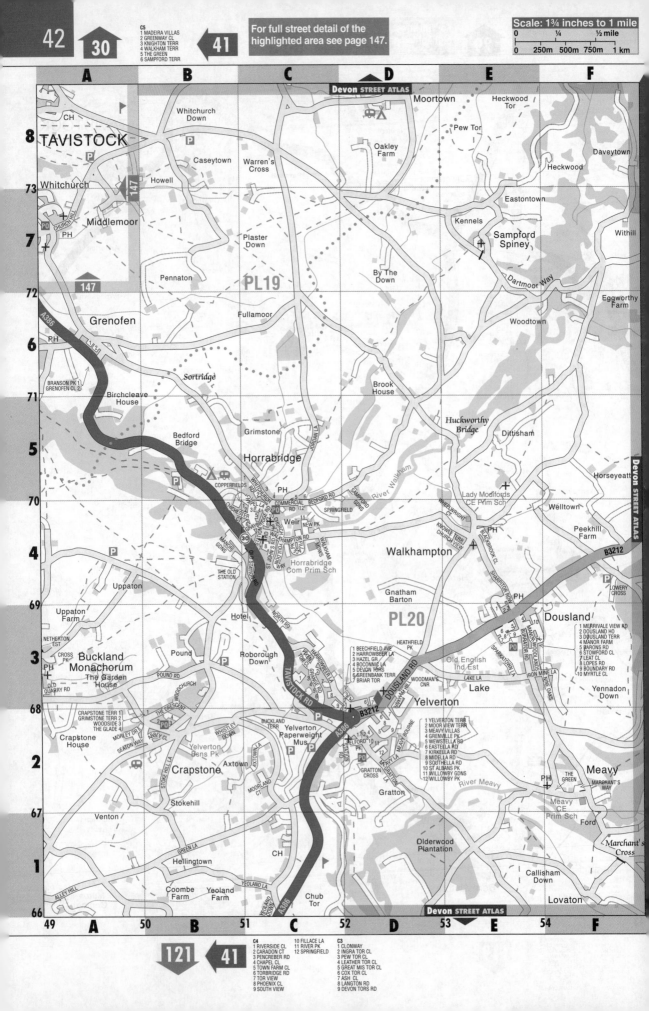

For full street detail of the highlighted area see page 147.

Devon STREET ATLAS

TAVISTOCK
Whitchurch
Middlemoor
Howell
Caseytown
Whitchurch Down
Warren's Cross
Moortown
Heckwood Tor
Daveytown
Heckwood
Oakley Farm
Pew Tor
Pennaton
Plaster Down
PL19
By The Down
Eastontown
Kennels
Sampford Spiney
Withill
Dartmoor Way
Eggworthy Farm
Grenofen
Fullamoor
Woodtown
BRANSON PK 1 / GRENOFEN CL 2
Sortridge
Birchcleave House
Brook House
Huckworthy Bridge
Dittisham
Horseyeatt
Bedford Bridge
Grimstone
Horrabridge
River Walkham
Lady Modifords CE Prim Sch
Welltown
COPPERFIELDS
COMMERCIAL RD
BEDFORD RD
SPRINGFIELD
Wheelwright
Peekhill Farm
Weir
NEW PK
Walkhampton
B3212
Horrabridge Com Prim Sch
THE OLD STATION
Gnatham Barton
PL20
Dousland
LOWERY CROSS
Uppaton
Hotel
NORTH RD
1 MERRIVALE VIEW RD / 2 DOUSLAND HO / 3 DOUSLAND TERR / 4 MANOR FARM / 5 BARONS RD / 6 STOWFORD CL / 7 LEAT CL / 8 LOPES RD / 9 BOUNDARY RD / 10 MYRTLE CL
Uppaton Farm
Buckland Monachorum
CROSS PK
The Garden House
Pound
Roborough Down
1 BEECHFIELD AVE / 2 HARROWBEER LA / 3 HAZEL GR / 4 BOCONNIC LA / 5 DEVON TORS / 6 GREENBANK TERR / 7 BRIAR TOR
HEATHFIELD PK
Old English Ind Est
Lake
Yennadon Down
QUARRY RD
TAVISTOCK RD
WOODMAN'S CNR
Yelverton
LAKE LA
IRON MINE LA
Hellingtown
Coombe Farm
Yeoland Farm
YEOLAND LA
A386
Chub Tor
CROSS
CRAPSTONE TERR 1 / GRIMSTONE TERR 2 / WOODSIDE 3 / THE GLADE 4
Crapstone House
MORLEY DRI
SEATON WAY
Yelverton Bsns Pk
Axtown
Crapstone
Stokehill
Venton
Buckland Terr
Yelverton Paperweight Mus
WHISTLEY DOWN
MOORLAND CT
GRATTON CROSS
B3212
ELFORD
Gratton
1 YELVERTON TERR / 2 MOOR VIEW TERR / 3 MEAVY VILLAS / 4 GRENVILLE RD / 5 WEWSTELLA RD / 6 EASTELLA RD / 7 KIRKELLA RD / 8 MIDELLA RD / 9 SOUTHELLA RD / 9 ST ALBANS PK / 10 WILLOWBY GDNS / 11 WILLOWBY PK / 12 WILLOWBY PK
River Meavy
THE GREEN
MARCHANT'S WAY
Meavy
Meavy CE Prim Sch
Ford
Olderwood Plantation
Callisham Down
Lovaton
Marchant's Cross

Devon STREET ATLAS

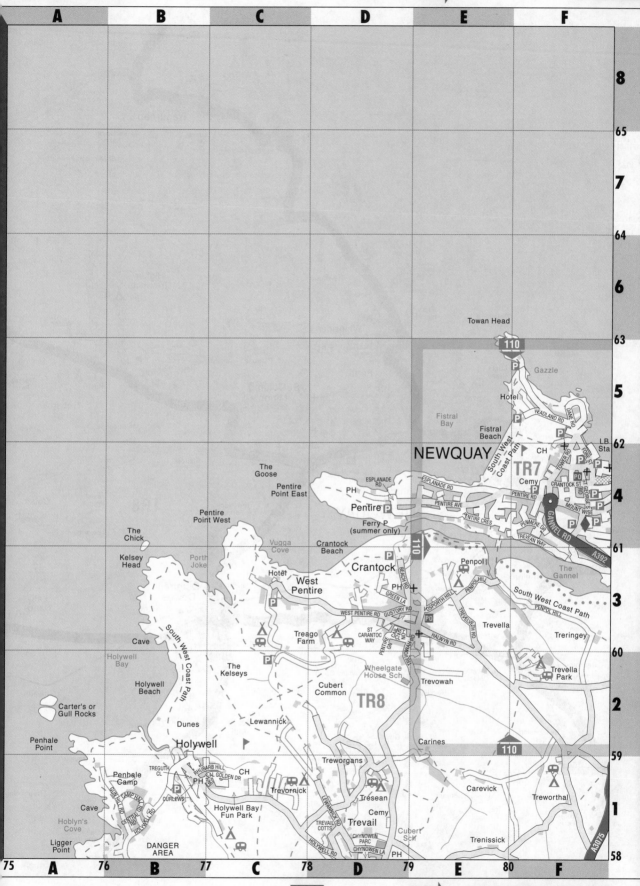

Scale: 1¾ inches to 1 mile

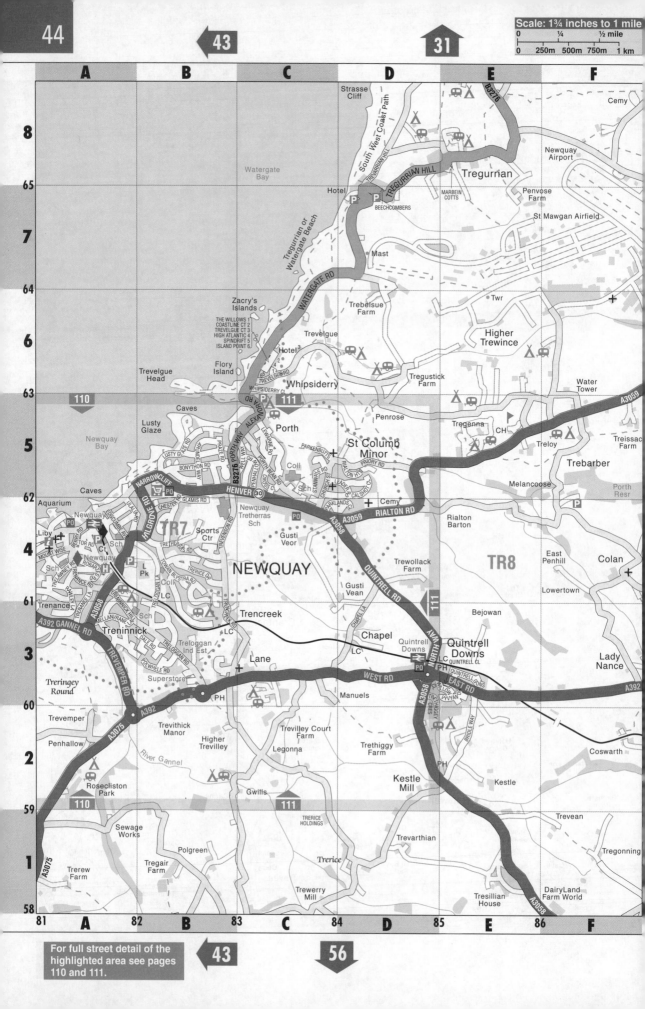

Scale: 1¾ inches to 1 mile

0 ¼ ½ mile

0 250m 500m 750m 1 km

31 32 46

D6
1 DINAS RD
2 BOSPOLVANS RD
3 BOSWORGEY CL
4 BEECH DR
5 MAPLE CL
6 CARLOGGAS GR
7 HAWTHORN CL
8 ELM DR
9 HAWKENS WAY
10 CARLOGGAS WAY
11 WREFORD CL
12 HIGH CROSS
13 HIGHFIELD AVE
14 BROWNING CL

E6
1 EAST ST
2 ROSEWIN ROW
3 ROSEWIN MEWS
4 STONEWOOD CT
5 HALVEOR CL
6 GLEBE CL
7 BROAD ST
8 GORDON PL
9 HIGHER EAST ST
10 TRETHEWEY CL
11 TREVENTON RISE
12 MEADOW RISE
13 WEST PK
14 HILLCREST CL
15 SPRINGFIELD PL
16 SOUTH PK
17 RACHEL'S WAY
18 BARN LA

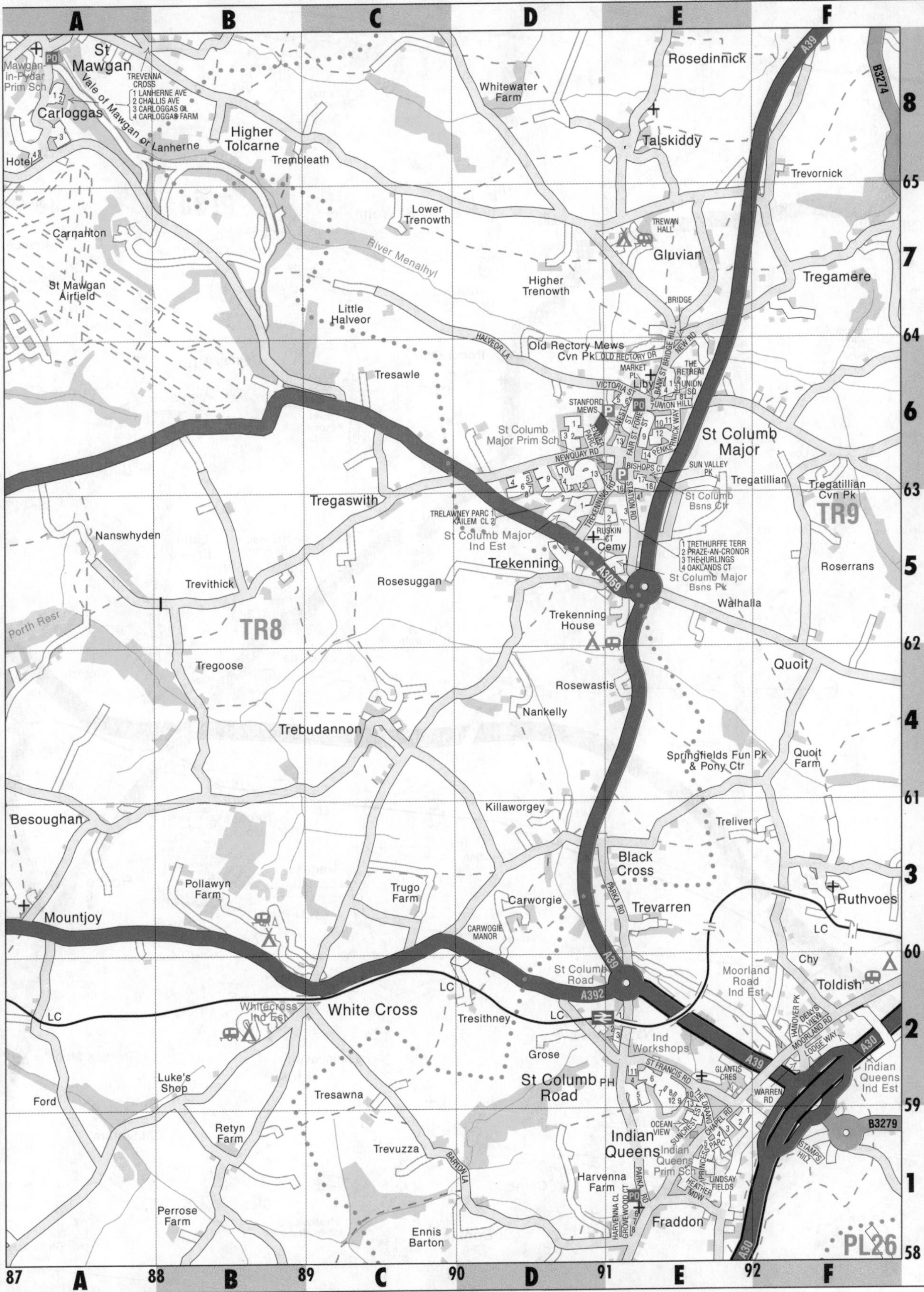

A B C D E F
St Mawgan
Mawgan-in-Pydar Prim Sch
TREVENNA CROSS
1 LANHERNE AVE
2 CHALLIS AVE
3 CARLOGGAS CL
4 CARLOGGAS FARM
Carloggas
Vale of Mawgan or Lanherne
Hotel
Higher Tolcarne
Trembleath
Whitewater Farm
Rosedinnick
Talskiddy
Trevornick
B3274
A39
Lower Trenowth
River Menalhyl
Carnanton
St Mawgan Airfield
TREWAN HALL
Gluvian
Higher Trenowth
Tregamere
Little Halveor
BRIDGE
HALVEOR LA
Old Rectory Mews Cvn Pk
OLD RECTORY DR
MARKET PL
THE RETREAT
Tresawle
VICTORIA ST
Liby
UNION SQ
UNION HILL
STANFORD MEWS
St Columb Major Prim Sch
St Columb Major
NEWQUAY RD
BISHOPS CT
SUN VALLEY PK
Tregatillian
Tregatillian Cvn Pk
Tregaswith
St Columb Bsns Ctr
TR9
TRELAWNEY PARC 1
KAILEM CL 2
St Columb Major Ind Est
RUSKIN CT
Nanswhyden
Cemy
Trekenning
1 TRETHURFFE TERR
2 PRAZE-AN-CRONOR
3 THE HURLINGS
4 OAKLANDS CT
Trevithick
Rosesuggan
A3059
St Columb Major Bsns Pk
Roserrans
Walhalla
Porth Resr
TR8
Trekenning House
Quoit
Tregoose
Rosewastis
Nankelly
Trebudannon
Springfields Fun Pk & Pony Ctr
Quoit Farm
Killaworgey
Besoughan
Treliver
Black Cross
Pollawyn Farm
Trugo Farm
Carworgie
PARKA RD
Trevarren
Ruthvoes
Mountjoy
CARWOGIE MANOR
LC
Chy
St Columb Road
Moorland Road Ind Est
Toldish
A392
Whitecross Ind Est
White Cross
Tresithney
HANOVER PK
DENYS VIEW
MOORLAND RD
LODGE WAY
Ind Workshops
Grose
A30
Indian Queens Ind Est
ST FRANCIS RD
GLANTIS CRES
Luke's Shop
St Columb Road
PH
WARREN RD
Ford
Tresawna
OCEAN VIEW
SUNCREST EST
THE DRANG
CHAPEL RD
B3279
Retyn Farm
Trevuzza
BARTON LA
Indian Queens
Indian Queens Prim Sch
PRINCESS PARC
STAMPS HILL
Harvenna Farm
HEATHER MDW
LINDSAY FIELDS
Perrose Farm
Ennis Barton
HARVENNA CL
GROVEWOOD CT
Fraddon
PL26
8 65 7 64 6 63 5 62 4 61 3 60 2 59 1 58
87 88 89 90 91 92

E1
1 HIGHGATE HILL
2 KEAST CL
3 BARNFIELD TERR
4 POCOHONTAS CRES
5 QUEENS CL
6 MELROSE TERR
7 OAKDENE VILLAS
8 MANDALAY VILLAS

57 46

E2
1 STATION RD
2 VICTORIA GDNS
3 STATION APP
4 WOODLAND TERR
5 FAIRVIEW PK
6 TREMEAR GN
7 CARWORGIE WAY
8 PARKA RD
9 HALLOON AVE
10 CARWORGIE CT
11 CLODAN MEWS
12 PARKA CL
13 THE MOWIE

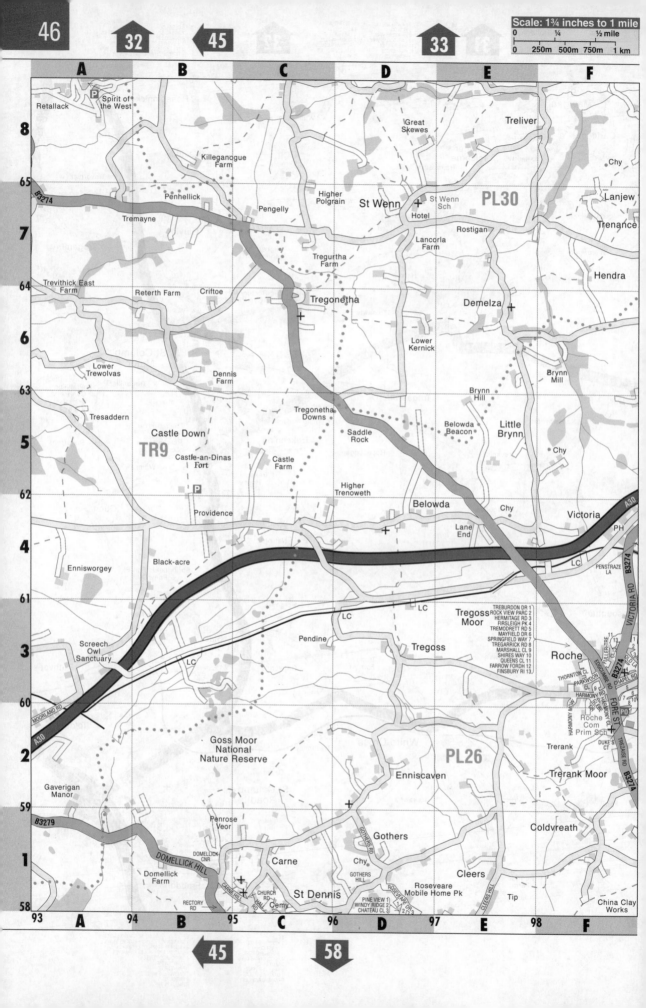

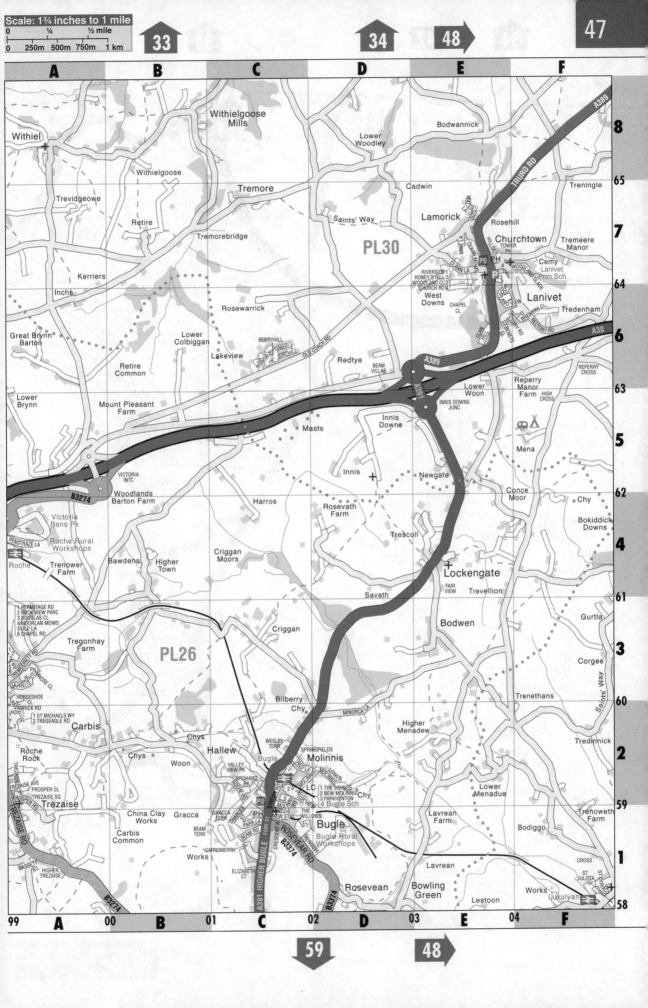

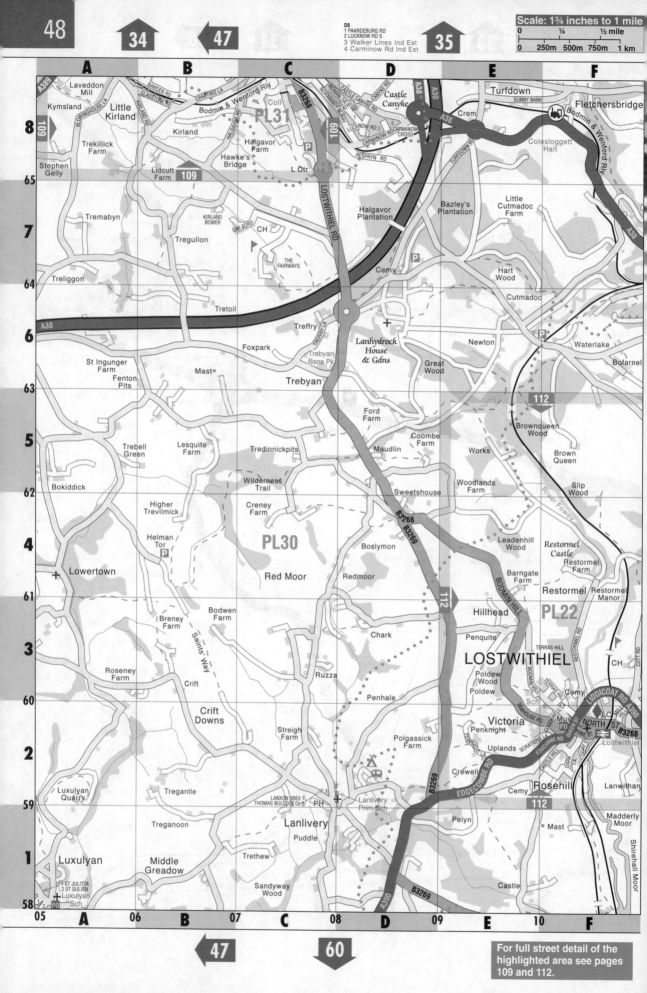

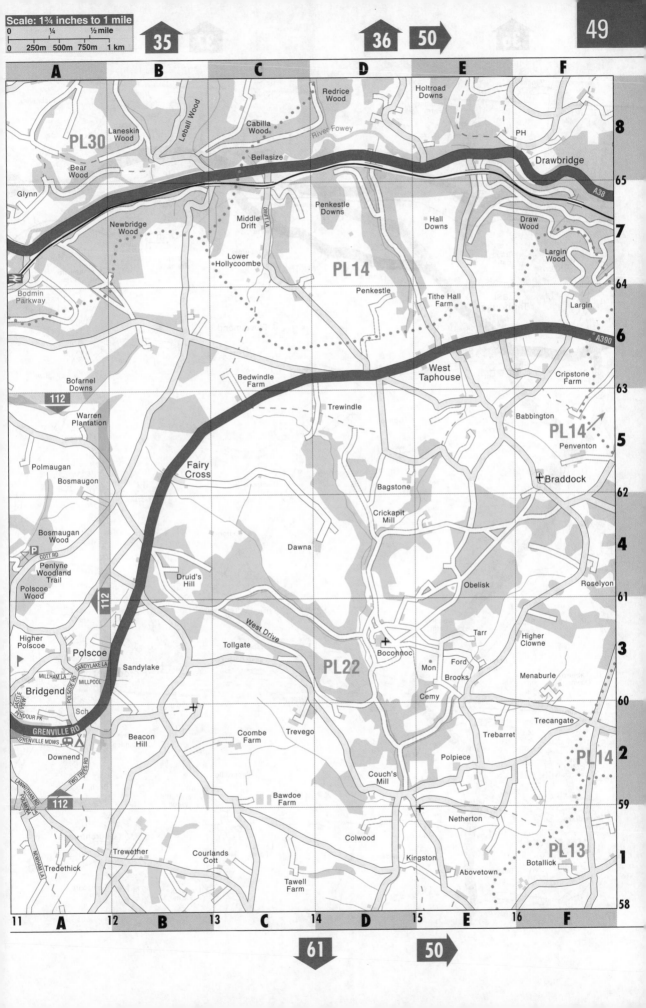

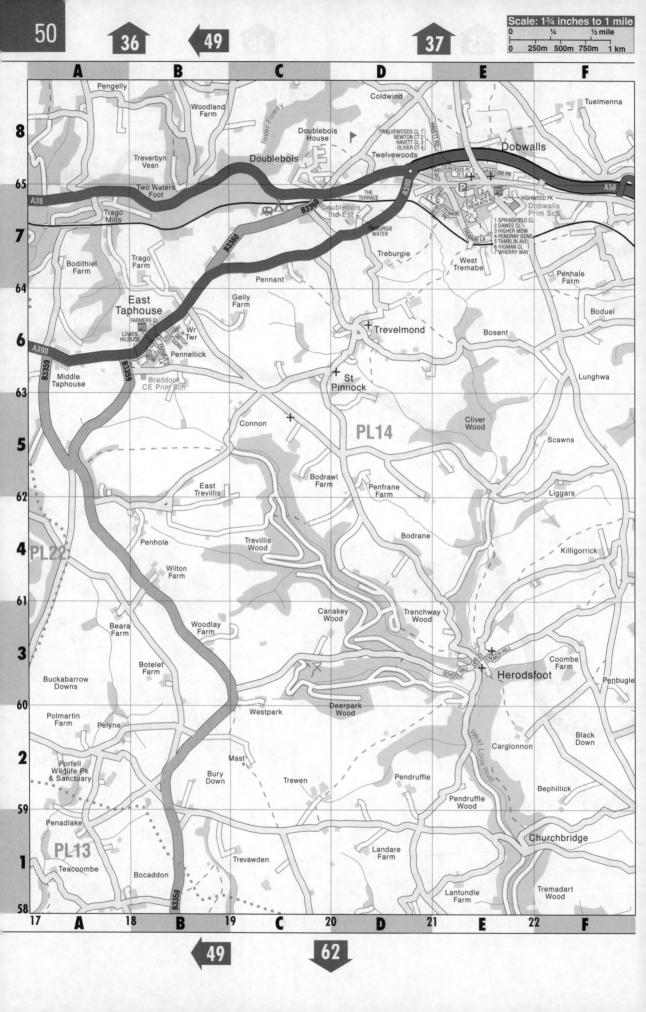

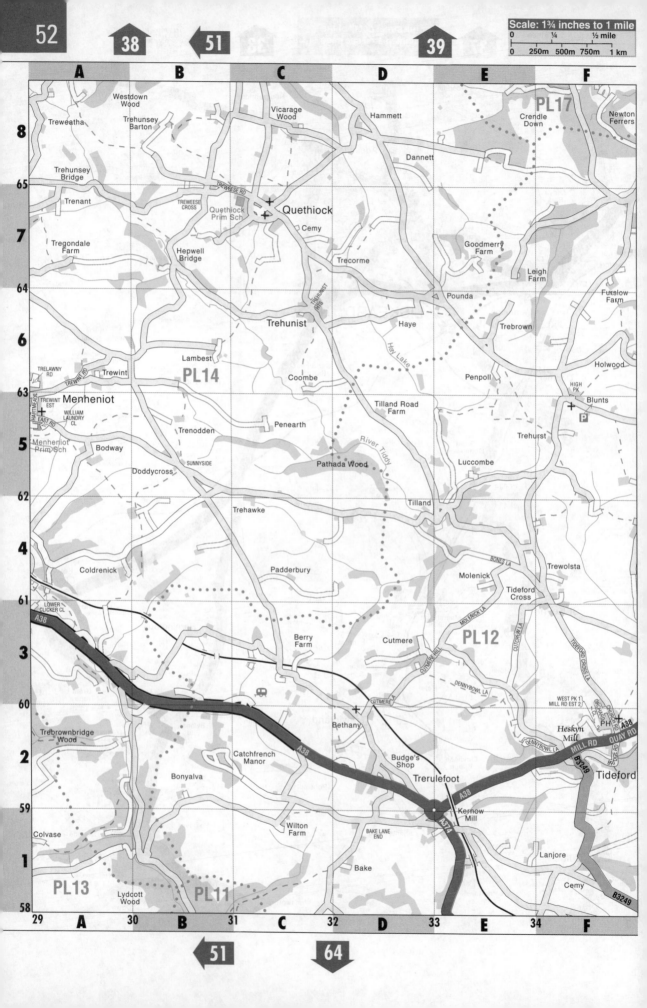

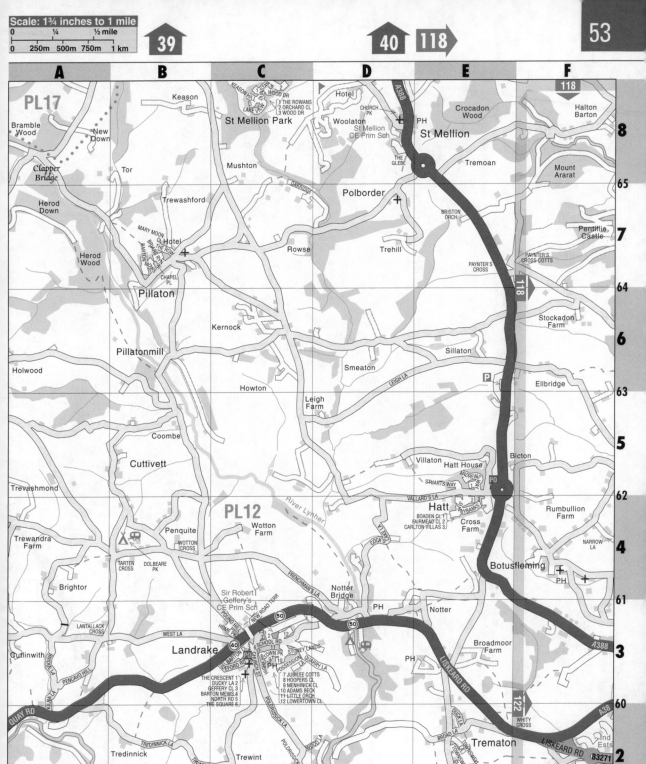

A   **B**   **C**   **D**   **E**   **F**

PL17

Bramble Wood

New Down

Clapper Bridge

Tor

Herod Down

Herod Wood

Holwood

Pillaton

MARY MOON CL
THE ROW
BRIAR RD
BARTON MEWS
CHAPEL PL

Pillatonmill

Trevashmond

Trewandra Farm

Brightor

Cutlinwith

8

65

7

64

6

63

5

62

4

61

3

60

2

59

1

58

Keason

St Mellion Park

KEASON HILL
AUSTIN
WOOD DR
LAKE VIEW
1 THE ROWANS
2 ORCHARD CL
3 WOOD DR

Mushton

Trewashford

Rowse

Kernock

Howton

Leigh Farm

Coombe

Cuttivett

PL12

Penquite

WOTTON CROSS

Wotton Farm

DOLBEARE PK

TARTEN CROSS

Sir Robert Geffery's CE Prim Sch
POUND HILL
NEW ROAD TERR
HOME PK

50

Landrake

40

WEST LA

LANTALLACK CROSS

PENCAVIO HILL

BRIDE LA

KILN LA

QUAY RD

Tredinnick

TREDINNICK LA

Trewint

TREWINT LA

River Tiddy

St Erney

Penimble

Lithiack

GALLERY LA

TREERO RD

Markwell

MARKWELL LA

Berry Hill

Poldrissick

Treluggan Manor

POLDRISSICK HILL
POLDRISSICK LA

WOOD LA

QUAY LA

Hotel

Woolaton

St Mellion CE Prim Sch

CHURCH PK

THE GLEBE

Polborder

Trehill

Leigh Farm

LEIGH LA

Smeaton

Notter Bridge

FRENCHMAN'S LA

Notter Bridge

PH

SCHOOL RD
OWN PK
POSSESSION
QUARRY LA
STONEY LANDS

THE CRESCENT 1
DUCKY LA 2
GEFFERY CL 3
BARTON MEWS 4
NORTH RD 5
THE SQUARE 6

7 JUBILEE COTTS
8 HOOPERS CL
9 MENHINICK CL
10 ADAMS BECK
11 LITTLE ORCH
12 LOWERTOWN CL

COCK'S LA

Notter

PH

LISKEARD RD

Trevollard

CUMBLE TOR LA

REVOLLARD LA

A388

PH

St Mellion

PH

Crocadon Wood

Halton Barton

Tremoan

Mount Ararat

Briston Orch

Pentillie Castle

PAYNTER'S CROSS

PAYNTER'S CROSS COTTS

118

Stockadon Farm

Sillaton

Ellbridge

Villaton

Hatt House

Bicton

ANDREW'S WAY

STUARTS WAY

P

PO

VALLARD'S LA

Hatt

RYBAM'S

Rumbullion Farm

BOADEN CL 1
FAIRMEAD CL 2
CARLTON VILLAS 3

Cross Farm

NARROW LA

Botusfleming

PH

Broadmoor Farm

122

DUCK LA

BROAD LA

WHITY CROSS

Trematon

CROSSWELL
TOWNSWELL
THORNWELL LA

VOSS RD

Burell House

Trevollard

LISKEARD RD

Ind Ests

Latchbrook

FELLDOWTOR RD

LONGLANDS LA

Longlands

Trehan

B3271

A38

For full street detail of the highlighted area see pages 118 and 122.

A   B   C   D   E   F

8
57
7
56
6
55
5
54
4
53
3
52
2
51
1
50

69   A   70   B   71   C   72   D   73   E   74   F

Shag Rock
Shafts (dis)
Cligga Head
Cligga Workshops 1
ST GEORGE'S TERR 2
Shafts (dis)
B3285
Hotel
TR6
Anchor
Hanover Cove
South West Coast Path
Airfield
Green Island
Trevellas Porth
Cross Coombe
Trevellas
Chy
Trevaunance Cove
Blue Hills
Trevellas Coombe
Blowinghouse
Newdowns Head
Heritage Trail
Shafts (dis)
PH
Perran View Holiday Pk
Crams
New Downs
Chy
Wheal Kitty Workshops
TR5
St Agnes Head
Chy
Trevaunance CL
Wheal Kitty
GOONLAZE TERR
Mithian Prim Sch
Carn Gowla
Higher Bal
Chy
Peterville
Barkla Shop
Tubby's Head
Chy
St Agnes Beacon
St Agnes Prim Sch
TOWN HILL
B3285
Chy
Mithian
PH
Liby
P
BEACON FARM
GREEN AVE
Mus
Cemy
B3277
St Agnes
Goonown
WATER LA

Bawden Rocks

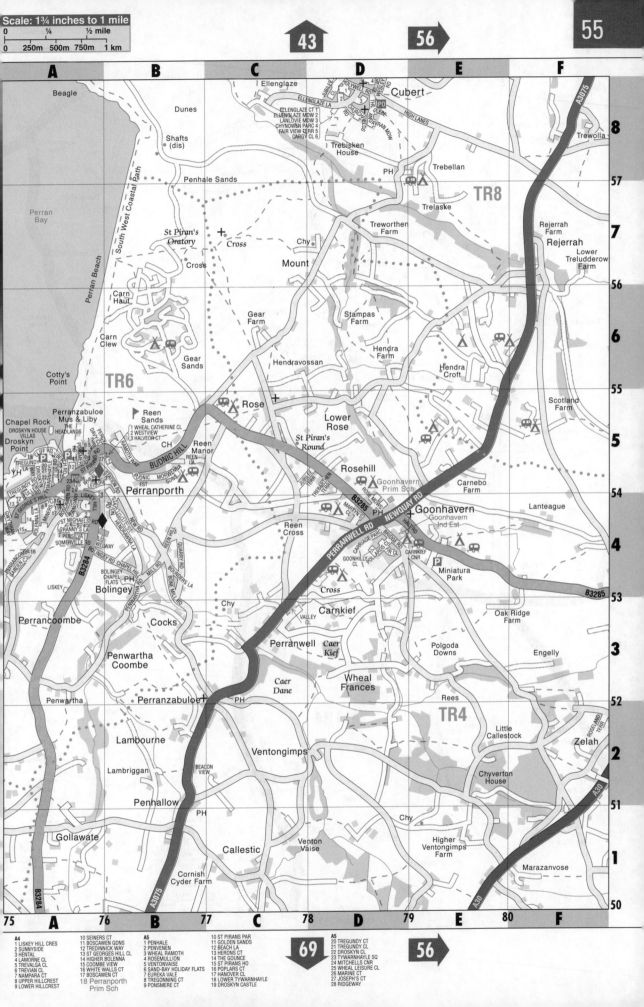

Scale: 1¾ inches to 1 mile
0   ¼   ½ mile
0   250m 500m 750m 1 km

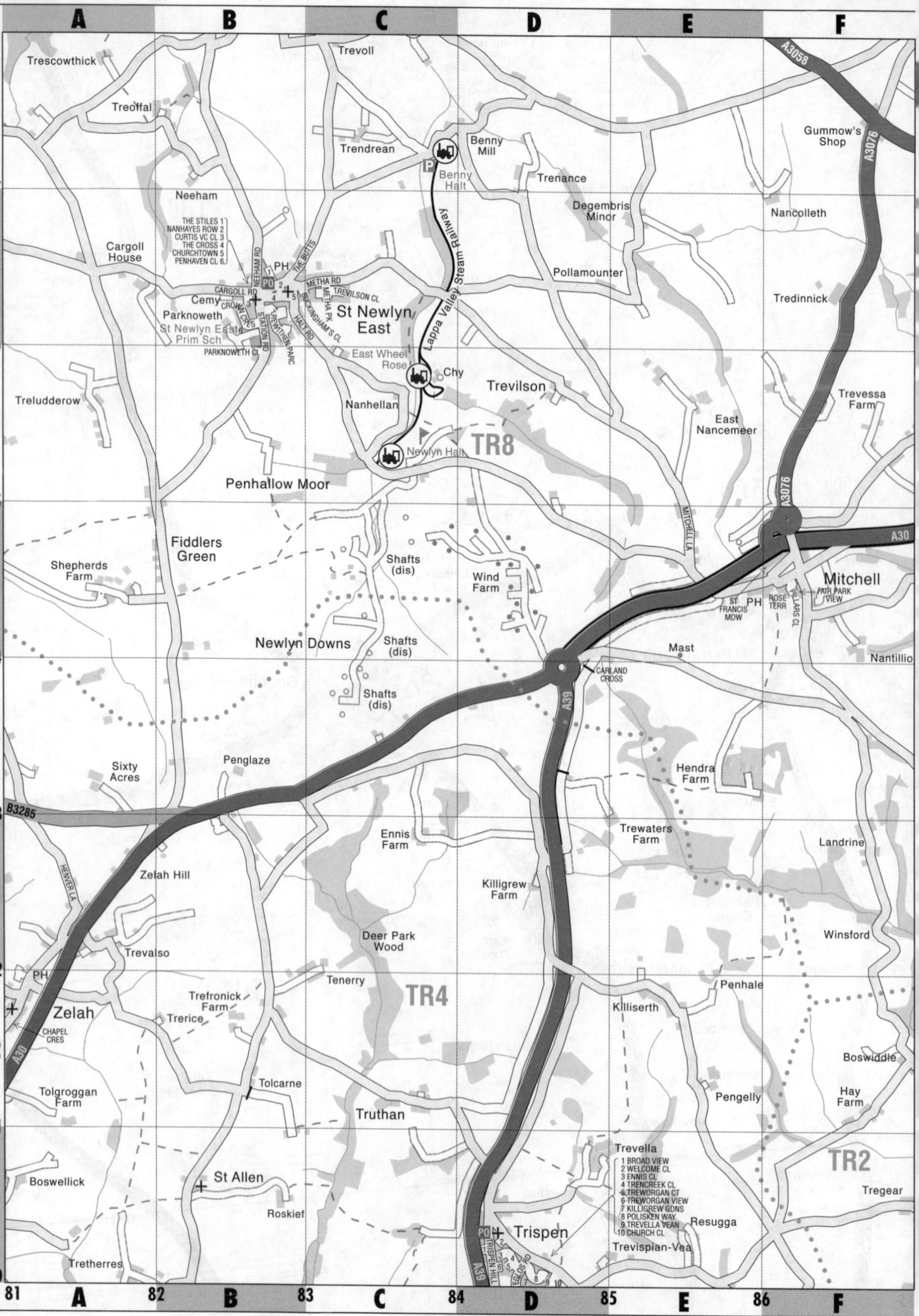

A   B   C   D   E   F

8
57
7
56
6
55
5
54
4
53
3
52
2
51
1
50

Trescowthick
Treoffal
Treffal
Trevoll
Trendrean
Benny Mill
Benny Halt
Gummow's Shop
A3058
A3076
Neeham
Trenance
Degembris Minor
Nancolleth
THE STILES 1
NANHAYES ROW 2
CURTIS VC CL 3
THE CROSS 4
CHURCHTOWN 5
PENHAVEN CL 6
Cargoll House
Pollamounter
Tredinnick
PH
Cemy
Cargoll Rd
CROWCLES
THE BUTTS
METHA RD
TREVILSON CL
St Newlyn East
Parknoweth
St Newlyn East Prim Sch
PARKNOWETH CL
STATION RD
BUCKINGHAM'S CL
HALE RD
TREVATHAN PARC
Lappa Valley Steam Railway
East Wheel Rose
Chy
Trevilson
Trevessa Farm
Treludderow
Nanhellan
East Nancemeer
TR8
Newlyn Halt
Penhallow Moor
Fiddlers Green
MITCHELL LA
A3076
A30
Mitchell
FAIR PARK VIEW
Shepherds Farm
Shafts (dis)
Wind Farm
ST FRANCIS MDW
PH
ROSE TERR
PILLARS CL
Newlyn Downs
Shafts (dis)
Mast
Nantillio
Shafts (dis)
CARLAND CROSS
A39
Sixty Acres
Penglaze
Hendra Farm
B3285
Ennis Farm
Trewaters Farm
Landrine
Zelah Hill
Killigrew Farm
HENVER LA
Winsford
Deer Park Wood
PH
Trevalso
Tenerry
Penhale
TR4
Killiserth
Boswiddle
Zelah
CHAPEL CRES
Trefronick Farm
Trerice
Pengelly
Hay Farm
A30
Tolcarne
Truthan
TR2
Tolgroggan Farm
Trevella
1 BROAD VIEW
2 WELCOME CL
3 ENNIS CL
4 TRENCREEK CL
5 TREWORGAN CT
6 TREWORGAN VIEW
7 KILLIGREW GDNS
8 POLISKEN WAY
9 TREVELLA YEAN
10 CHURCH CL
Tregear
Boswellick
St Allen
Roskief
PO
Trispen
TRISPEN HILL
A39
Resugga
Trevispian-Vea
Tretherres

81   82   83   84   85   86

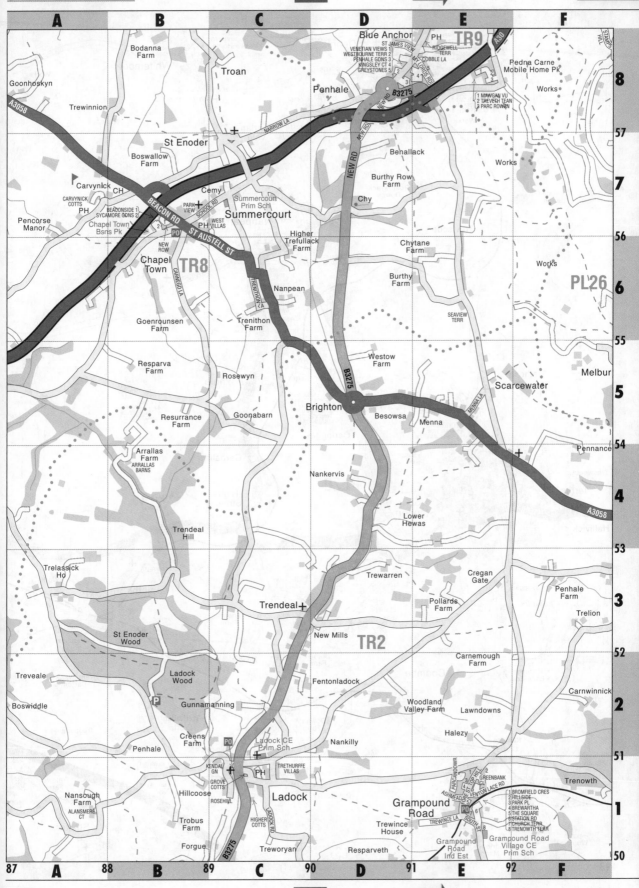

A B C D E F

8

57

7

56

6

55

5

54

4

53

3

52

2

51

1

50

Trerice Terr

Carsella Farm

Boscawen Pk

St Dennis Ind Est

MAPLE CL

B3279

Lby

P

PO

PH

St Dennis Com Prim Sch

St Dennis

Chateau Cl

Roseveare Mobile Home Pk

Crown Terr

North Terr

THE FIRS

GWENDRA LA

ALLENDALE

Whitemoor

Works

Trerice Manor Farm

GROSE MDWS 1
WHITEGATE MDWS 2
WHITEGATE 3
RECTORY RD 4
TREVALVOUR PRAZEY 5

HENDRA RD

PRAZEY

Works

Hendra

HENDRA HEIGHTS

Trelavour Downs

TRELAVOUR RD

BREWERS HILL

1 BOSCAWEN RD
2 ARUNDLE RD
3 HALIMOTE CL
4 CARNE CT
5 TRELAVOUR SQ
6 WELLINGTON RD
7 KENT CL
8 ROBARTES RD
9 TYNANCE CT

Currian Vale

Whitemoor Com Prim Sch

CROWN RD

PARK RD

CURRIAN HILL

Workings

Bodella

Chy

Chy

Rostowrack Downs

Treviscoe Barton

CENTRAL TREVISCOE

BARTON RD

Treviscoe

Works

Chy

CURRIAN RD

CURRIAN RD

POST OFFICE ROW

PO

HALLEW RD

Nanpean

GRENVILLE MDWS

VICTORIA TERR

Nanpean Prim Sch

ST GEORGES RD

OLD POUND

Goonamarth Farm

FERNLEIGH TERR

Chy

WHEALBRAKE LODGE

P

DRINNICK TERR

Works

GOVERSETH HILL

BRADDOCK RD

FORESCUE

MEADOW RISE

THE HEATHERS

GREYSTONE AVE

PL25

Trethosa

Stepaside

1 LITTLE STARK CL
2 WHEAL VIEW
3 HOMER WATER PK

GOONABARN COTTS

Goonabarn

GOONAVEAN PK

BEACON RD

WHEAL BULL

Foxhole Prim Sch

GOVERSETH TERR

GOVERSETH CVN PK

BEACON

CHEGWYN RD

POLGOOTH

CHAPEL RD

CREAZ-AN-BRE

PO

Foxhole

1 GUILDFORD CL
2 DUNSTABLE CL
3 FOLKSTONE CL
4 SOUTHBOURNE CL
5 KENILWORTH WAY
6 TODDINGTON LEA
7 FIR CRES
8 KINGS PIPPIN
9 LARKFIELD CL
10 CHICHESTER CL

CHEGWYNS 1
ROWES TERR 2
LOWER ROWES TERR 3
BEACON TERR 4
POND VIEW TERR 5
HENSBARROW MS 6

Carloggas

PL26

CARPALLA RD

CARPALLA TERR

Carpalla

B3279

CLEAVN DR

High Street

PETERS HILL

Hornick

Hornick Hill

St Stephen Church Town Prim Sch

CREAKAVOSE PK

TREVOSA CL

DOWNS CL

TREGARGUS VIEW

Tregargus Farm

P

Cemy

CHURCH RD

LAVINGTON RD

ADAMS CL

Tresweeta

Terras

A3058

TERRAS RD

Hallivick

FRIELD HO 4
GILBERT CL 5
MEADOW CL 6
CENTRAL CL 7
FORE ST 8

RECTORY GDNS

THE SQUARE

RESUGGA CL

CARNELS CL

St Stephen

P

PH

GWINDRA RD

Gwindra

LONG LA

High Street Ind Est

SCHOOL HILL

LC

GLENDALE TERR

BROOKFIELD CL

PH

PYRAMID CL

CARNE HILL

A3058

Works

River Fal

Resugga

Tolgarrick

The Brannel Sch

Gwindra Ind Est

Court Farm

Hay Farm

High Street Ind Est

COOMBE RD

Langerth Farm

Lanjeth

Hendra

Burngullow

TR2

Resugga Lane-End

Coombe

WOODLAND VIEW

Branell Farm

Chy

Tretbullan Castle

Nanphysick Barton

Tregandanel

Resugga Castle

COOMBE HILL

Dowgas Farm

Chy

Polclose

Ninnis Farm

A390

Terhowth House

Chapel

Treway Farm

Downderry

Chy

SOUTHDOWN CL 1
COTSWOLD CL 2
ASHDOWN CL 3
MARLBOROUGH WAY 4
MODUS LA 5

Trelower Farm

LITTLE TRELOWER PARK

TRE-POL

Trevan Wood

Garlenick Manor

Ventonwyn Farm

Chy

ST STEPHENS RD

THE PADDOCK

GLENLEIGH PK

LINDEN FIELD AVE

A390

PH

FORE ST

P

Sticker

ROSE HILL

CHURCH HILL

HAZEL HILL

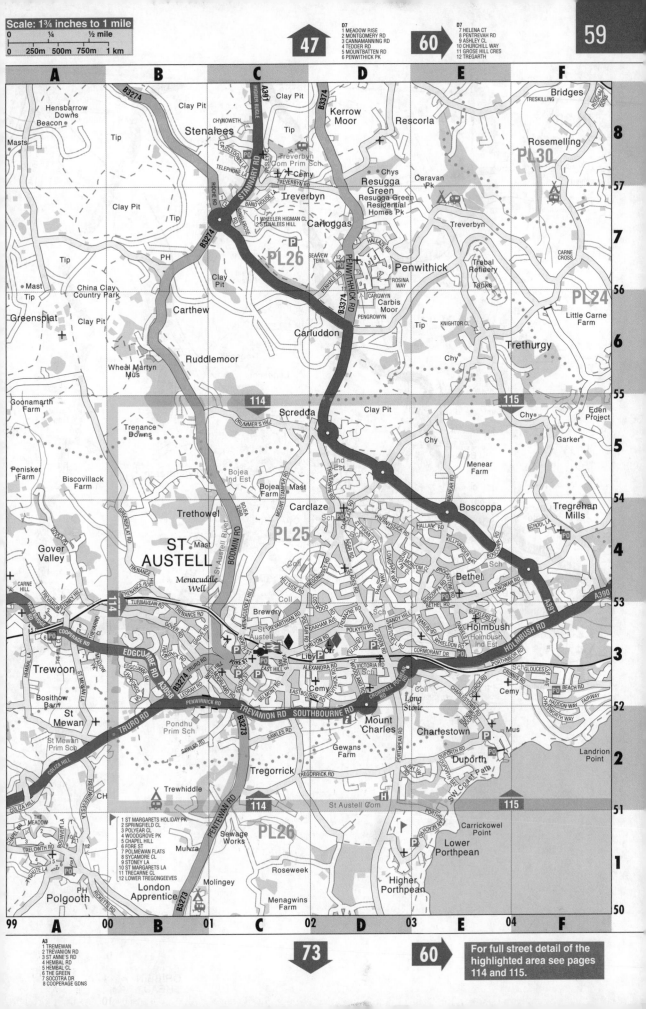

Scale: 1¾ inches to 1 mile
0   ¼   ½ mile
0 250m 500m 750m 1 km

47

60

59

D7
1 MEADOW RISE
2 MONTGOMERY RD
3 CANNAMANNING RD
4 TEDDER RD
5 MOUNTBATTEN RD
6 PENWITHICK PK

D7
7 HELENA CT
8 PENTREVAH RD
9 ASHLEY CL
10 CHURCHILL WAY
11 GROSE HILL CRES
12 TREGARTH

73

60

For full street detail of the
highlighted area see pages
114 and 115.

A3
1 TREMEWAN
2 TREVANION RD
3 ST ANNE'S RD
4 HEMBAL RD
5 HEMBAL CL
6 THE GREEN
7 SOCOTRA DR
8 COOPERAGE GDNS

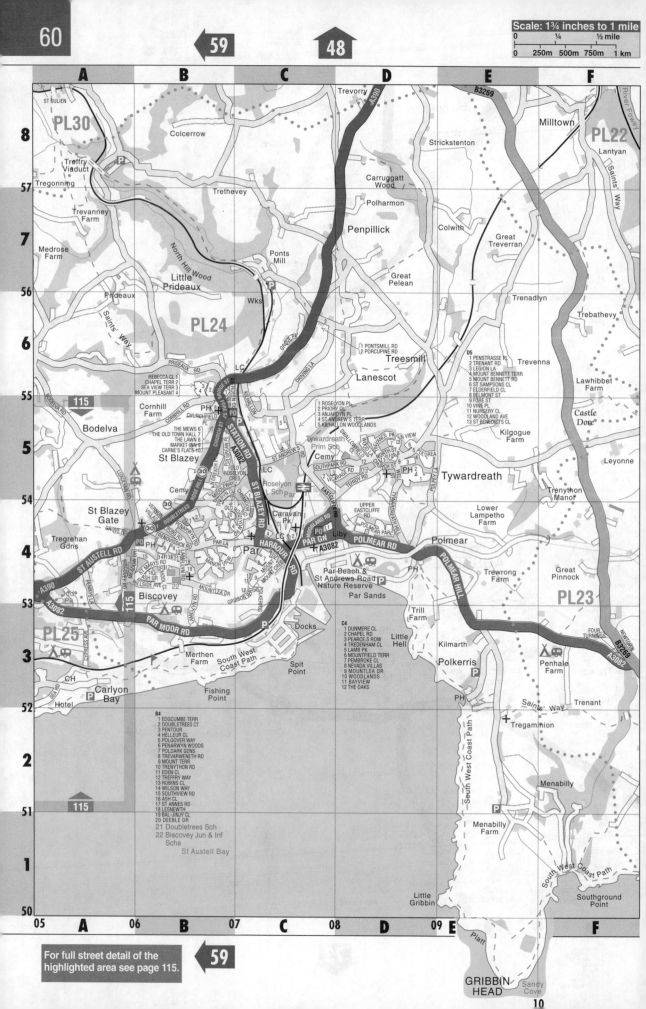

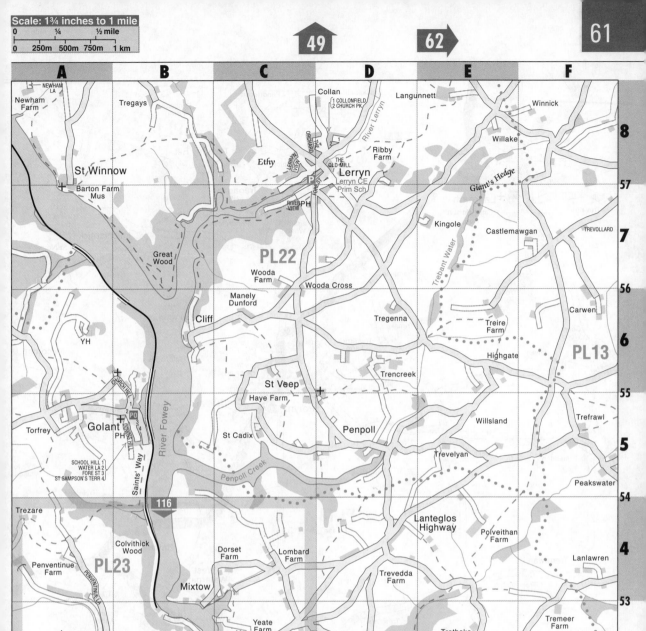

Scale: 1¾ inches to 1 mile

0 ¼ ½ mile

0 250m 500m 750m 1 km

A **B** **C** **D** **E** **F**

Newham LA

Newham Farm

St Winnow

Barton Farm Mus

Tregays

Ethy

Collan

1 COLLONFIELD
2 CHURCH PK

THE OLD MILL

Lerryn

Lerryn CE Prim Sch

Langunnett

Winnick

Willake

River Lerryn

THE ORCHARD

LERRYN VIEW

GREAT FORE ST

P

RIVER VIEW PH

Ribby Farm

Giant's Hedge

Kingole

Castlemawgan

TREVOLLARD

Great Wood

PL22

Wooda Farm

Wooda Cross

Trebant Water

Treire Farm

Carwen

YH

CHURCH HILL

Cliff

Manely Dunford

Tregenna

Highgate

PL13

St Veep

Haye Farm

Trencreek

Torfrey

Golant

PO

PH

TOWNS HILL

Saints' Way

River Fowey

St Cadix

Penpoll

Willsland

Trefrawl

SCHOOL HILL 1
WATER LA 2
FORE ST 3
ST SAMPSON'S TERR 4

Penpoll Creek

Trevelyan

Peakswater

Trezare

116

Lanteglos Highway

Polveithan Farm

Penventinue Farm

PL23

Colvithick Wood

PENGRATINUE LA

Dorset Farm

Lombard Farm

Trevedda Farm

Lanlawren

Mixtow

Lescrow

Yeate Farm

Trethake

Tremeer Farm

B3269

PASSAGE LA

Tristan Stone

B3415

116

Liby

P

P

PH

Lamellyon Hall Farm

Bodinnick

Pont

Tredudwell Manor

Carneggan Farm

Trevarder

TAVERN BAR

POLVILLION RD

CEMY

GREEN

PARK RD

PO

NEW ROAD HILL

LB Sta

116

Pendower House

P

Frogmore Farm

LANKELLY LA

RASHLEIGH LA

L Ctr

Coll

Sch

P

HANSON DR

ESPLANADE

Ferry (P)

TH

Mus

Mon

Pont Pill

Triggabrowne

P

West Coombe

FOWEY

P

TOWER PK

Readymoney

PO

WEST ST

ST SAVIOUR'S HILL

FORE ST

Essa

Churchtown Farm

St Catherine's Castle (remains of)

SWCP

Coombe Haven

Ferry (P) Summer only

P

Sch

TOWNSEND

Polruan

South West Coast Path

Lantivet Bay

Washing Rocks

Blackbottle Rock

Lantic Bay

Pencarrow Head

116

8
57
7
56
6
55
5
54
4
53
3
52
2
51
1
50

11 **A** 12 **B** 13 **C** 14 **D** 15 **E** 16 **F**

62

For full street detail of the highlighted area see page116.

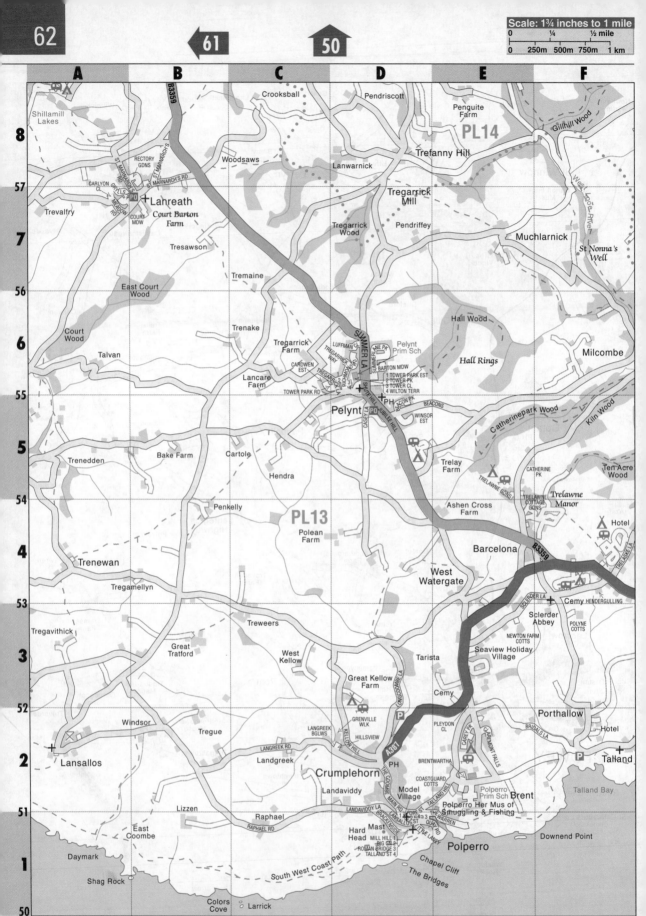

Scale: 1¾ inches to 1 mile
0   ¼   ½ mile
0   250m 500m 750m 1 km

8
Shillamill Lakes
Crooksball
Pendriscott
Penguite Farm
Gillhill Wood
PL14
Trefanny Hill
West Looe River

57
St MICHAELS
CARLYON CL
ST MARNARCH'S CL
RECTORY GDNS
MEADOW RD
ST MARNARCH'S RD
COURT MDW
PO
+Lanreath
Tregarrick Mill
Muchlarnick
Trevalfry
Court Barton Farm
Pendriffey
St Nonna's Well

7
Tresawson
Tremaine
Tregarrick Wood
Pendriffey

56
East Court Wood

6
Court Wood
Trenake
Tregarrick Farm
SUMMER LA
ONE PK
Luffman
Pelynt Prim Sch
Hall Wood
Milcombe
Talvan
Cardwen EST
TREGARRICK LA
RIDGMOUTH
Hall Rings
Lancare Farm
BARTON MDW
1 TOWER PARK EST
2 TOWER PK
3 TOWER CL
4 WILTON TERR
Hall Rings

55
TOWER PARK RD
CASEY LA
SHUTE HILL
PO
PH
BEACON PK
WINSOR EST
BEACONS
JUBILEE HILL
Catherinepark Wood
Kiln Wood
Pelynt

5
Trenedden
Bake Farm
Cartole
Hendra
Trelay Farm
CATHERINE PK
TRELAWNE GDNS
Ten Acre Wood
Trelawne Cottage
Trelawne Manor
TRELAWNE GDNS

54
Penkelly
Ashen Cross Farm

4
PL13
Polean Farm
West Watergate
Barcelona
B3359
Hotel
TRELASKE LA
Trenewan
Tregamellyn
Treweers

53
Tregavithick
SCLERDER LA
Cemy Hendergulling
Sclerder Abbey
NEWTON FARM COTTS
POLYNE COTTS

3
Great Tratford
West Kellow
Tarista
Seaview Holiday Village
CLAREMONT FALLS
CLAREMONT CL
Porthallow

52
Windsor
Tregue
Great Kellow Farm
GRENVILLE WLK
HILLSVIEW
Cemy
PLEYDON CL
Brentwartha
CARE PK
BRIDALS LA
Hotel
LONGCOOMBE LA
KELLOW HILL
P
LANGREEK BGLWS
P
Talland

2
Lansallos
Landgreek
LANGREEK RD
Landaviddy
THE COOMBE
A387
PH
COASTGUARD COTTS
Model Village
Polperro Prim Sch
Brent
Talland Bay
Windsor
RAPHAEL RD
RAPHAEL RD
MAIN RD
CORE ST
CARE ST
TALLAND HILL
Polperro Her Mus of Smuggling & Fishing
THE WARREN
Lizzen
Raphael
LANDAVIDDY LA
BRACKESIDE
CANSALLOS ST
E4 3
QUAY RD
THE LANEY
Downend Point

1
Daymark
East Coombe
Hard Head
Mast
MILL HILL 1
BIG GN 2
ROMAN BRIDGE 3
TALLAND ST 4
Chapel Cliff
Polperro
Shag Rock
South West Coast Path
The Bridges

50
Colors Cove
Larrick

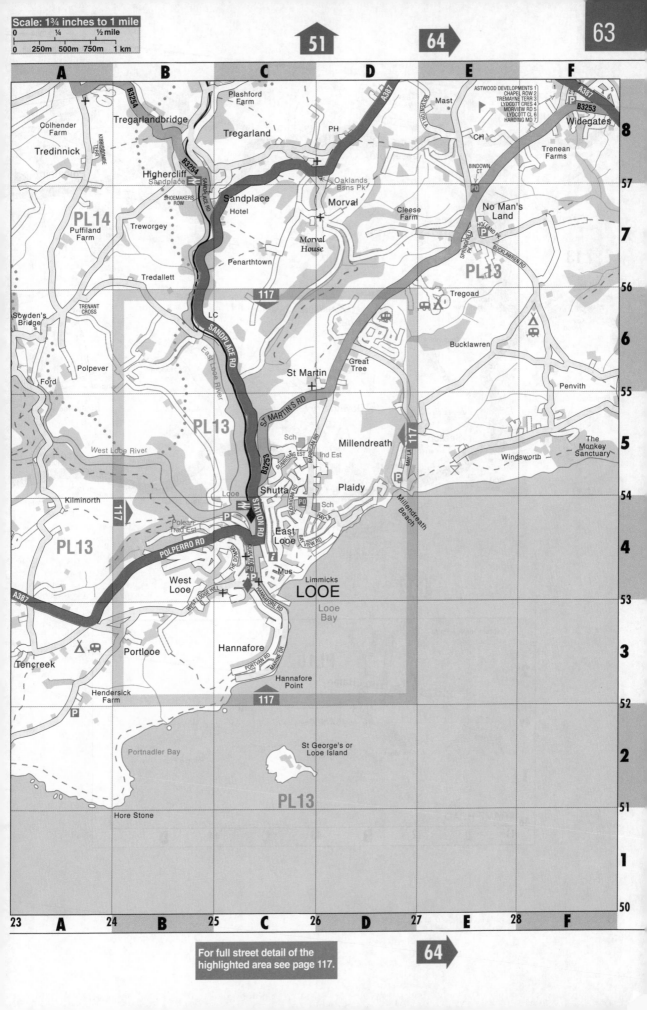

Scale: 1¾ inches to 1 mile

0   ¼   ½ mile
0   250m 500m 750m 1 km

51

64

A **B** **C** **D** **E** **F**

ASTWOOD DEVELOPMENTS 1
CHAPEL ROW 2
TREMAYNE TERR 3
LYDCOTT CRES 4
MORVIEW RD 5
LYDCOTT CL 6
HARDING MD 7

Widegates

B3253

A387

Mast

CH

Trenean
Farms

8

Colhender
Farm

Tredinnick

B3254

Tregarlandbridge

Plashford
Farm

Tregarland

PH

BINDOWN
CT

PO

No Man's
Land

57

PL14

Puffiland
Farm

Highercliff
Sandplace

B3254

SANDPLACE RD

SHOEMAKERS
ROW

Sandplace

Hotel

Oaklands
Bsns Pk

Morval

Cleese
Farm

SPRINGFIELD

HOLLAND PK

P

PL13

7

Treworgey

Tredallett

East Looe River

Penarthtown

Morval
House

BUCKLAWREN RD

Tregoad

56

Sowden's
Bridge

TRENANT
CROSS

Polpever

Ford

SANDPLACE RD

LC

117

Bucklawren

Penvith

6

West Looe River

St Martin

Great
Tree

The
Monkey
Sanctuary

55

PL13

ST MARTIN'S RD

Millendreath

Windsworth

5

Kilminorth

117

B3253

Sch

SUNRISING EST

BARBICAN RD

Ind Est

Plaidy

117

MAY LA

P

Millendreath
Beach

54

PL13

Looe

STATION RD

P

Shutta

BODRIGAN RD

PO

Sch

Millendreath
Beach

POLPERRO RD

Polean
Trad Est

THE DOWNS

East
Looe

BAY VIEW RD

HAYS

4

A387

West
Looe

PO

P

Mus

Limmicks
Rd

LOOE

WEST LOOE HILL

HANNAFORE RD

Looe
Bay

53

Tencreek

Portlooe

Hannafore

PORTVAN RD

MARINE DR

3

Hendersick
Farm

P

Hannafore
Point

117

52

Portnadler Bay

St George's or
Looe Island

2

PL13

51

Hore Stone

50

A 23 **B** 24 **C** 25 **D** 26 **E** 27 **F** 28

For full street detail of the
highlighted area see page 117.

64

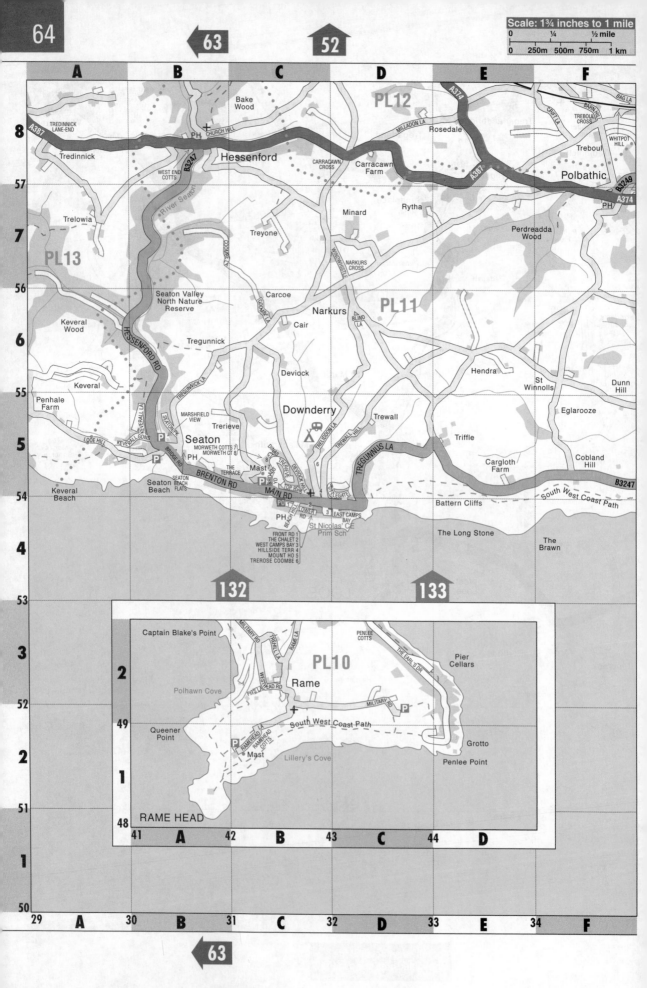

63
52

Scale: 1¾ inches to 1 mile

0   ¼   ½ mile

0   250m   500m   750m   1 km

A   B   C   D   E   F

PL 12

A374

BAG LA

CRIFT LA

BARN HILL

TREBOUL CROSS

WHITPOT HILL

Trebouil

8

A387

TREDINNICK LANE-END

PH

Tredinnick

CHURCH HILL

Bake Wood

Hessenford

CARRACAWN CROSS

Carracawn Farm

MILLADON LA

Rosedale

A387

Polbathic

B3249

A374

PH

57

WEST END COTTS

B3247

River Seaton

Minard

Rytha

Trelowia

Treyone

WINDMILL LA

NARKURS CROSS

Perdreadda Wood

7

PL13

COOMBE LA

56

Seaton Valley North Nature Reserve

COOMBE LA

Carcoe

Narkurs

Cair

BLIND LA

PL11

Keveral Wood

St Winnolls

Dunn Hill

6

Tregunnick

Deviock

Hendra

Eglarooze

Keveral

HESSENFORD RD

TREGUNNICK LA

Downderry

Trewall

Triffle

55

Penhale Farm

KEVERAL LA

SEATON LA

MARSHFIELD VIEW

Trerieve

TREWALL HILL

TREGUNNIS LA

Cobland Hill

Keveral

KEVERAL GDNS

LOOE HILL

P

Seaton

MORWETH COTTS 7

MORWETH CT 8

8

DINAS CRES

Cargloth Farm

B3247

5

BRIDGE RD

P

PH

THE TERRACE

Mast

TREGY RD

DEVIOCK HILL

TREGLADOM LA

6

WELLGATE

South West Coast Path

Keveral Beach

BRENTON RD

SEATON BEACH FLATS

P

TOP RD

BATTERY RD

Battern Cliffs

54

Seaton Beach

MAIN RD

PO

2

East Camps Bay

The Long Stone

The Brawn

PH

BEACH RD

LOWER RD

St Nicolas' CE Prim Sch

3

FRONT RD 1
THE CHALET 2
WEST CAMPS BAY 3
HILLSIDE TERR 4
MOUNT HO 5
TREROSE COOMBE 6

4

132
133

53

Captain Blake's Point

MILITARY RD

TREHILL LA

RAME LA

PENLEE COTTS

THE EARL'S DR

Pier Cellars

3

2

PL10

Rame

Polhawn Cove

PITTS LA

WEST HEAD RD

MILITARY RD

P

52

49

Queener Point

RAMEHEAD LA

RAMEHEAD COTTS

South West Coast Path

Grotto

2

P

Mast

Lillery's Cove

Penlee Point

1

51

48

RAME HEAD

41   A   42   B   43   C   44   D

50

29   A   30   B   31   C   32   D   33   E   34   F

63

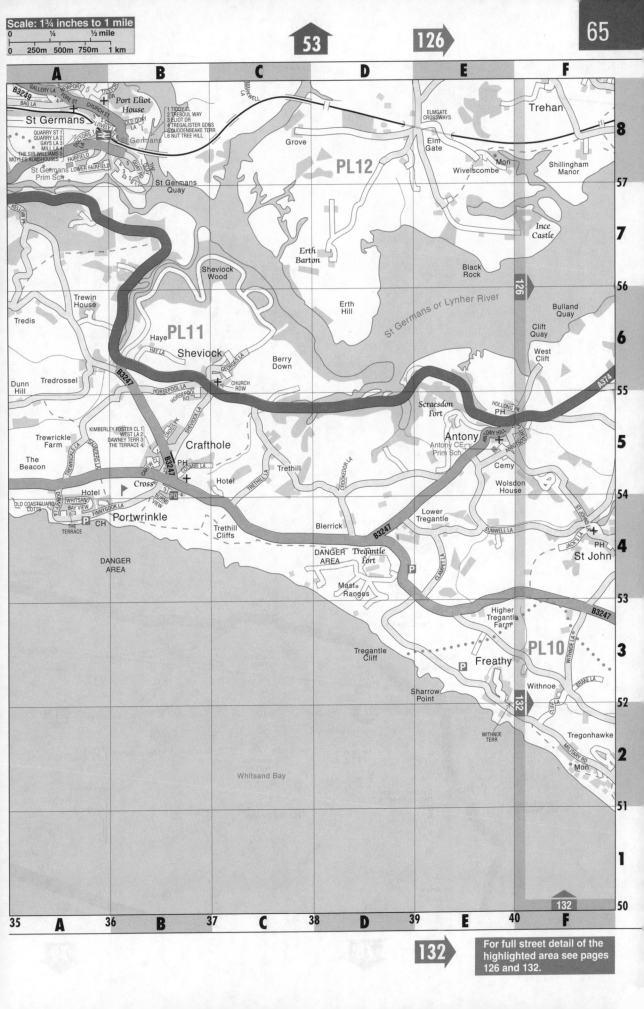

Scale: 1¾ inches to 1 mile

0   ¼   ½ mile
0   250m   500m   750m   1 km

A | **B** | **C** | **D** | **E** | **F**

B3249
Newport
Gore St
Tideford Rd
Church St
BAG LA
GALLERY LA
Port Eliot House
St Germans
LOVELY LA
OLD QUAY LA
QUAY RD
THE
1 TIDDY CL
2 TREBOUL WAY
3 ELIOT DR
4 TREGALISTER GDNS
5 DUDDENBEAKE TERR
6 NUT TREE HILL
MARKWELL

QUARRY ST 1
QUARRY LA 2
GAYS LA 3
MILL LA 4
THE SIR WILLIAMS 5
MOYLES ALMSHOUSES
St Germans Prim Sch
FAIRFIELD
LOWER FAIRFIELD
St Germans Quay

Grove

ELMGATE CROSSWAYS
Elm Gate
Trehan
Mon
Wivelscombe
Shillingham Manor

PL12

8

57

KELLOW PK
Trewin House
Tredis
Sheviock Wood
Erth Barton

Ince Castle

Black Rock

St Germans or Lynher River

126

Bulland Quay
Clift Quay
West Cliff

7

56

6

PL11
Haye
HAY LA
Sheviock
B3247
HORSEPOOL LA
HORSEPOOL RD
GEORGES LA
CHURCH ROW
Berry Down

Dunn Hill
Tredrossel

SHEVIOCK LA
CROSS PK
Trewrickle Farm
KIMBERLEY FOSTER CL 1
WEST LA 2
DAWNEY TERR 3
THE TERRACE 4
Crafthole
B3247
PH
COMBE LA
TREWRICKLE LA
SAUNDERS LA
The Beacon
DONKEY LA
WHITSAND BAY VIEW
CAREW CL
BURNS VIEW
Cross
PO
Hotel
TRETHILL LA
Trethill
CROOKEDOR LA
Screaesdon Fort
Antony
Antony CE Prim Sch
ANTONY HILL
ABBOTSCROFT
HOLLONG PK
PH
A374
Cemy
Wolsdon House
Scraesdon Fort

5

55

OLD COASTGUARD COTTS
THE TERRACE
P
CH
FINNYGOOK LA
Portwrinkle
Trethill Cliffs
Blerrick
B3247
Lower Tregantle
SUNWELL LA
CLAMPIT LA
ST JOHN'S RD
JACK'S LA
PH
St John

4

54

53

DANGER AREA
Tregantle Fort
P
DANGER AREA
Mast Ranges
Higher Tregantle Farm
WITHNOE LA
B3247
BRAKE LA
PL10
Withnoe

Tregantle Cliff
Sharrow Point
Freathy
P
132
CLIFF
Tregonhawke
MILITARY RD
WITHNOE TERR
Mon

3

52

2

Whitsand Bay

51

1

132

50

A | **B** | **C** | **D** | **E** | **F**
35   36   37   38   39   40

For full street detail of the highlighted area see pages 126 and 132.

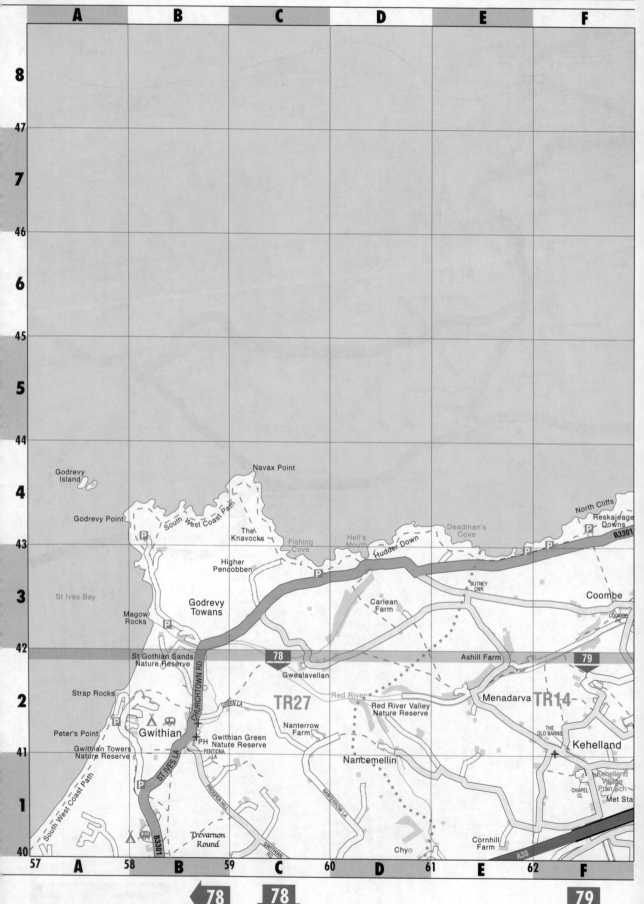

Scale: 1¾ inches to 1 mile

0   ¼   ½ mile

0   250m   500m   750m   1 km

A   B   C   D   E   F

8
47
7
46
6
45
5
44
4
3
42
2
1
40

Godrevy Island

Navax Point

North Cliffs

Reskajeage Downs

B3301

Godrevy Point

South West Coast Path

The Knavocks

Fishing Cove

Hell's Mouth

Hudder Down

Deadman's Cove

Coombe

St Ives Bay

Higher Pencobben

BUTNEY CNR

COOMBE PK

Godrevy Towans

Carlean Farm

Magow Rocks

St Gothian Sands Nature Reserve

Ashill Farm

78

79

Gwealavellan

Strap Rocks

CHURCHTOWN RD

GREEN LA

TR27

Red River

Menadarva

TR14

Red River Valley Nature Reserve

Peter's Point

Gwithian

Nanterrow Farm

THE OLD BARNS

Kehelland

PH

Gwithian Green Nature Reserve

PENTIDNA LA

Gwithian Towers Nature Reserve

ST IVES LA

Nancemellin

NANTERROW LA

CHAPEL CL

Kehelland Village Prim Sch

Met Sta

South West Coast Path

PROSSER HILL

B3301

Trevarnon Round

GWITHIAN RD

Chyo

Cornhill Farm

A30

57   A   58   B   59   C   60   D   61   E   62   F

78   78   79

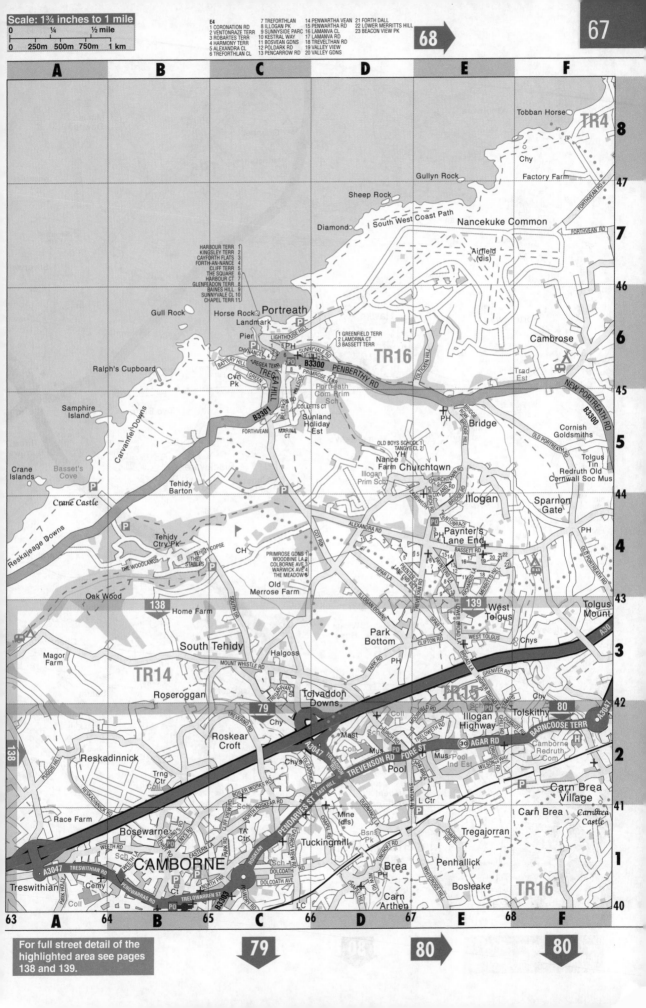

A   B   C   D   E   F

8

BEACON DR

Chapel Porth

Goonvrea

B3277

ALBANY GOONOWN RD

CHIVERTON GREENACRES

KERENSA GDNS

ALMA CL

1 BUTSON PK
2 HEAD LA

Mithian Downs

Goonbell

Shaft (dis)

Chy

49

Mingoose

HURLINGBARROW IND EST

TR5

Whitestreet

South West Coast Path

1 EASTCLIFF AVE NO 1
2 EASTCLIFF AVENUE NO 2
3 EASTCLIFF AVE NO
4 LOWER EASTCLIFF
5 GOYNE'S FIELD
6 SEASPRAY LEISURE FLATS
7 KINGSLEY COVE
8 OCEAN CT
9 SANDY COVE TRAVEL LODGE

Towan Cross

7

Silverwell Farm

TOWAN RD

PH

Silverwell

Porth Towan

Banns

Gover Farm

1 HENLEY CRES
2 HENLEY DR
3 HENLEY CL
4 SHORT CROSS MEWS
5 ALEXANDRA TERR
6 PENHALLOW CL
7 TRENITHICK MDW
8 GOVER CL
9 HIGH FIELD RD
10 MARSHALLEN RD
11 CHURCH RD
12 CHARLOTTE CL
13 ELLEN CL

48

Sandy Cove

SANDY RD

COAST RD

BARNS RD

PENHALL

ROPE WLK

RODDAS RD

Porthtowan

Trevissick Farm

Mount Hawke

PH

Chys

GLENDALE CRES

Works

Chy

1 BEACHSIDE CT
2 BEACHVIEW FLATS
3 TYWARHALE WAY
4 SOUTH VIEW PARC

Mount Hawke Com Prim Sch

SHORT CROSS RD

FORE ST

Chy

Penhallow Farm

TR4

6

Cemy

Goosewartha Farm

Two Burrows

B3277

PH

CHIVERTON CROSS

A3075

A30

47

Wheal Bassett Farm

Menagissey

1 HIGHVIEW CRES
2 HIGHVIEW
3 SOUTH VIEW TERR
4 SYMONDS CL
5 CORONATION TERR
6 PASSMORE CL

THE OLD CHAPEL

Three Burrows

A390

Manor Parsley

Blackwater

5

Skinners Bottom

Blackwater Prim Sch

PH

Laity Moor

Mawla

Stencoose

Carnhot

46

Chapel Hill

Forge

Wheal Plenty

1 LANSDOWNE PK
2 GWEL GWARTHE
3 PARK LEDER
4 TREVEN NOWETH
5 PRAS COTH

Chy

STATION RD

Boscawen Farm

4

Sinns Barton

GREEN LA

Chy

Wheal Busy

BROOKSIDE 1
BUCKINGHAM NIP 2
SERGEANTS HILL 3

45

B3300

Parc Erissey

Parc Erissey Ind Est

TR16

WHITE CROSS

Wheal Rose

Chys

SWANLS LA

Hallenbeagle

1 SCORIA CL
2 ADAMS ROW
3 RADNOR RD

Chacewater

WHEAL BUSY LA

THE TERRACE 1
2 3

HIGH ST

North Downs

PH

Motel

Scorrier

Chys

Salem

3

44

NEW PORTREATH RD

North Country

RADNOR RD

140

A3047

B3298

Scorrier House

Killifreth Farm

Cox Hill

CHURCH HILL

BASSETT RD

Treleigh

LC

SCORRIER HOUSE WORKSHOPS

Tregullow

1 TELEGRAPH HILL
2 NORTHFIELD CL
3 MILLS ST
4 SCORRIER ST
5 CHURCH ST
6 CAREW CL
7 BOSAWNA CL
8 MILLS GDNS

Creegbrawse

2

140

A3047

Highway

Treskerby

140

Todpool

A300

CARDREW WAY

SANDY LA

TREGANNON RD

REDRUTH HIGHWAY

HIGHWAY LA

Mount Ambrose

WHEAL GORLAND RD 1
CHYROSE RD 2
FORTH-AN-PRAZE 3
BALCOATH 4
TRENANT 5
CHAPEL ST 6
VOGUE TERR 7
BUCKINGHAM ST 8
TELEGRAPH ST 9
MARKET SQ 10
FORE ST 11
WEST END 12
CREW RD 13
FORTH-AN-GLOS 14
BURNWITHIAN TERR 15

Tolgullow

POLDICE TERR

Chy

KNIGHTS WAY

ROSELAND GDNS

EAST END

Vogue

SPRINGFIELD WAY

PINK MOORS

St Day

TREWELM LA

CHAPEL TERR

POLDICE LA

Goon Gumpas

1

TR15

MUROOCH CL

STRAWBERRY LA

DRUMP RD

A393

PH

Trefula

ST DAY DR

VOGUE HILL

VOLCAREW RD

BARRACK'S

VICARAGE HILL

HIGHER GOONGUMPAS LA

LOWER GOONGUMPAS LA

CLOSE HILL

TRELEIGH AVE

FORTH ST

REDRUTH

Ninnis

Crofthandy

WHEAL JEWEL

CHURCH HILL

B3298

Chys

42

A30/A17

TOLGUS HILL

B3300

FORDS ROW

Cemy

Redruth

Colle

BRICKWORKS HILL

St Day & Carharrack Com Sch

69   A   70   B   71   C   72   D   73   E   74   F

67   80   81

For full street detail of the highlighted area see page 140.

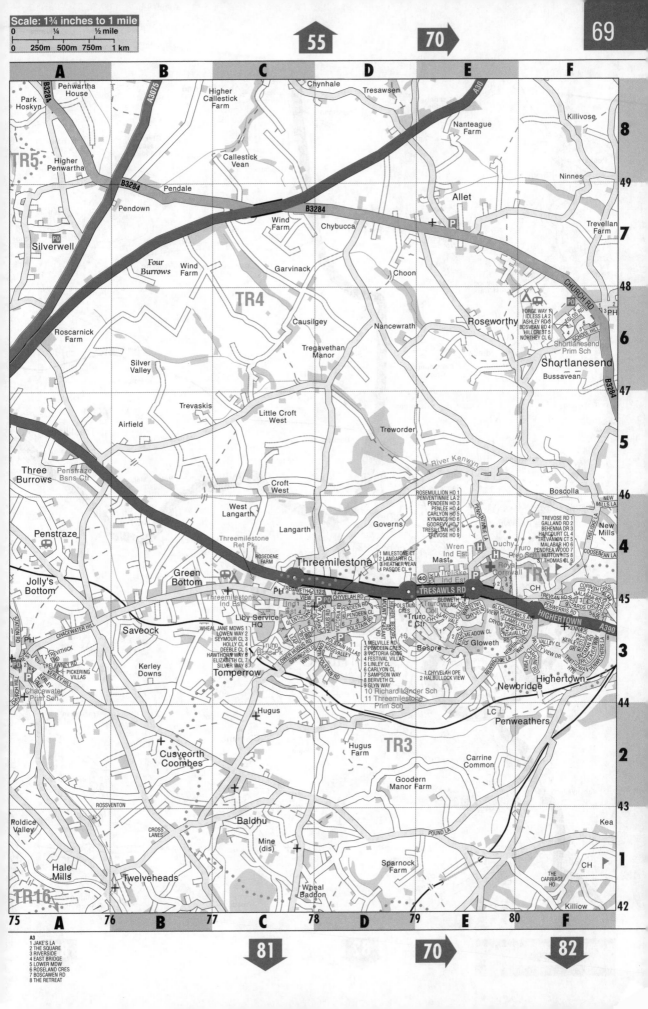

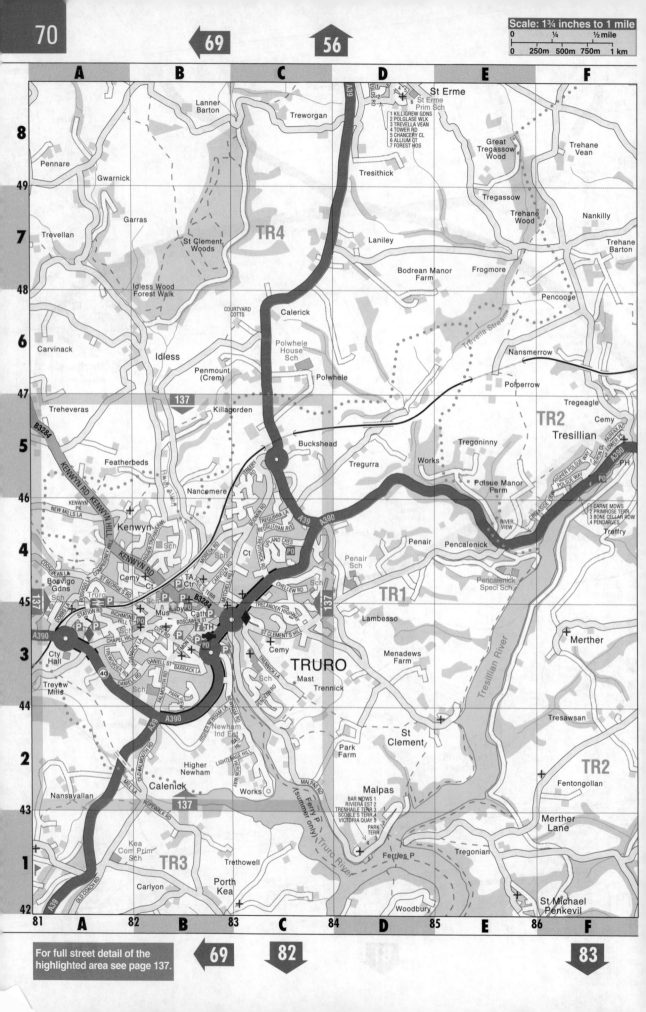

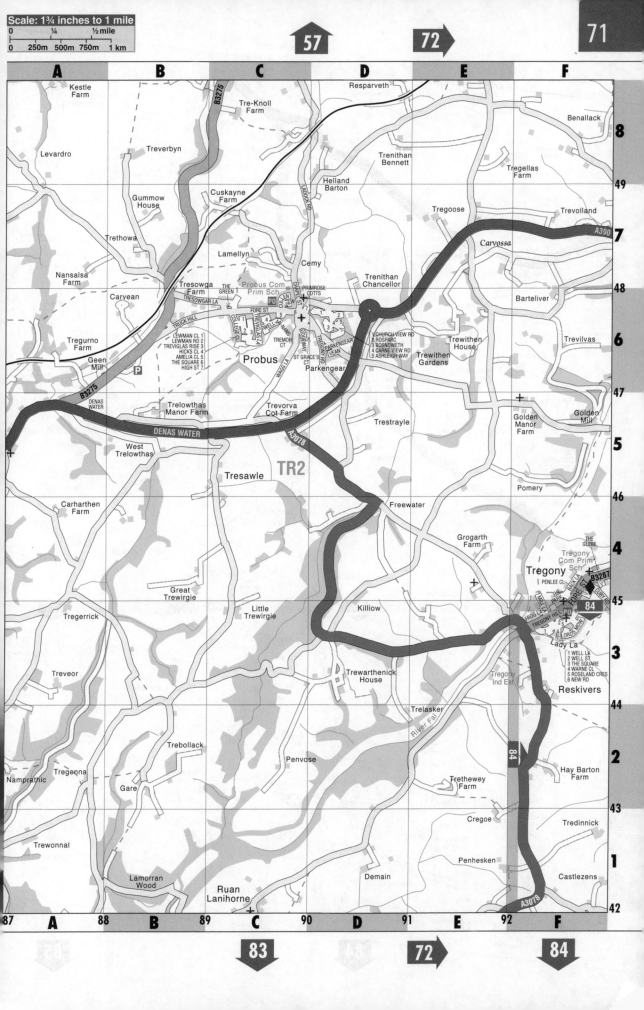

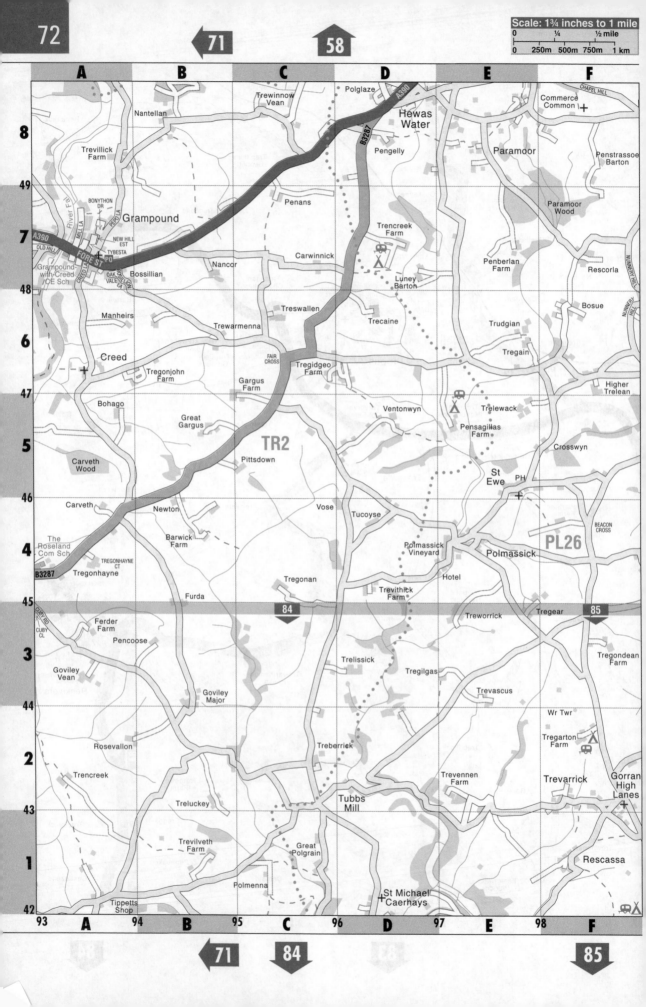

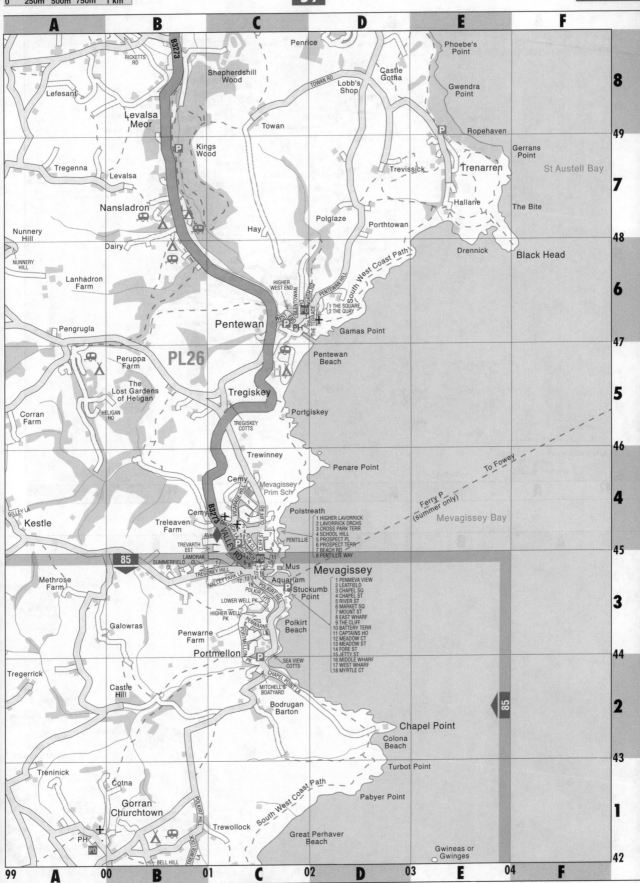

A   B   C   D   E   F

8

Penrice

RICKETTS RD

B3273

Shepherdshill Wood

Castle Gotha

Phoebe's Point

Lefesant

Levalsa Meor

Kings Wood

TOWAN RD

Lobb's Shop

Gwendra Point

49

Tregenna

Levalsa

Towan

Trevissick

Trenarren

Ropehaven

Gerrans Point

St Austell Bay

7

Nansladron

Hay

Polglaze

Hallane

The Bite

Nunnery Hill

Dairy

Porthtowan

48

NUNNERY HILL

South West Coast Path

Drennick

Black Head

6

Lanhadron Farm

HIGHER WEST END

PENTEWAN HILL

GLENTOWAN

THE TERRACE

WEST END

PO

1 THE SQUARE
2 THE QUAY

Pengrugla

PL26

Peruppa Farm

Pentewan

PH

Gamas Point

47

The Lost Gardens of Heligan

HELIGAN HO

Tregiskey

Pentewan Beach

5

Corran Farm

Portgiskey

46

Kestle

GILLEY LA

TREGISKEY COTTS

Trewinney

Penare Point

To Fowey

Ferry P (summer only)

Mevagissey Bay

Cemy

WICKARISE HILL

Mevagissey Prim Sch

Cemy

Treleaven Farm

B3273

CHURCH LA

CLIFF RD

Trewinney

Polstreath

1 HIGHER LAVORRICK
2 LAVORRICK ORCHS
3 CROSS PARK TERR
4 SCHOOL PL
5 PROSPECT PL
6 PROSPECT TERR
7 BEACH RD
8 PENTILLIE WAY

4

TREVARTH EST

LAMORAK

VALLEY RD

CLIFF ST

PENTILLIE

45

SUMMERFIELD CL

TREGONEY HILL

VALLEY PARK LA

PO

Mus

Mevagissey

1 PENMEVA VIEW
2 LEATFIELD
3 CHAPEL SQ
4 CHAPEL ST
5 RIVER ST
6 MARKET SQ
7 MOUNT ST
8 EAST WHARF
9 THE CLIFF
10 BATTERY TERR
11 CAPTAINS HO
12 MEADOW CT
13 MEADOW ST
14 FORE ST
15 JETTY ST
16 MIDDLE WHARF
17 WEST WHARF
18 MYRTLE CT

85

Methrose Farm

Galowras

POLKIRT HTS

Aquarium

Stuckumb Point

LOWER WELL PK

HIGHER WELL PK

PENWARNE LA

Polkirt Beach

3

Penwarne Farm

PORTMELLON PK

Portmellon

SEA VIEW COTTS

85

Tregerrick

Castle Hill

CHAPEL POINT LA

MITCHELL'S BOATYARD

44

Bodrugan Barton

Chapel Point

2

Colona Beach

Turbot Point

43

Treninick

Cotna

South West Coast Path

Pabyer Point

1

Gorran Churchtown

POLKIRT HILL

TREWOLLOCK LA

Trewollock

Great Perhaver Beach

Gwineas or Gwinges

PH

PO

BELL HILL

42

99   A   00   B   01   C   02   D   03   E   04   F

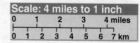

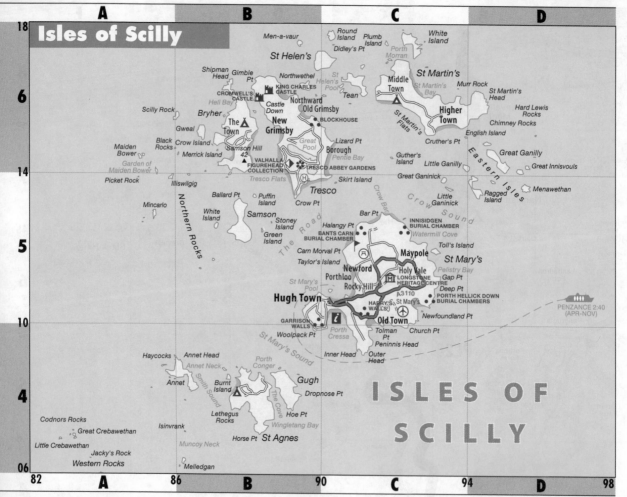

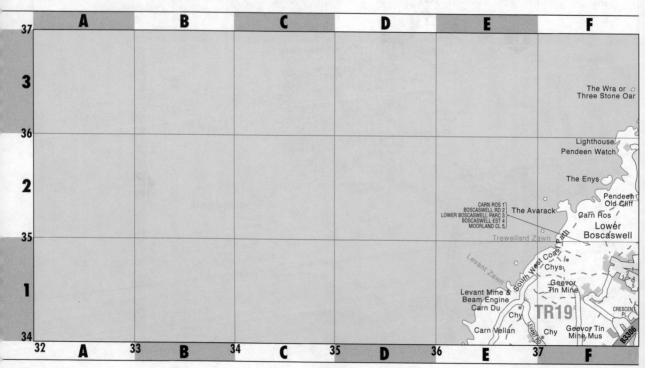

Scale: 1¾ inches to 1 mile

0   ¼   ½ mile
0   250m   500m   750m   1 km

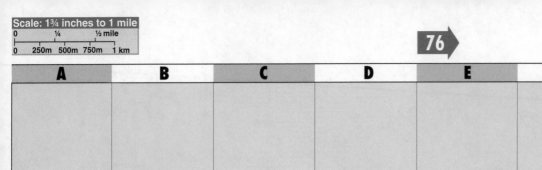

A   B   C   D   E   F

8
41
7
40
6
39
5
38
4
37
3
36
2
35
1
34

Porthglaze Cove

Gurnard's Head

TR26

Porthmeor Point

Porthmeor Cove

TREEN COTTS

Treen

PH

B3306

Great Zawn

Halldrine Cove

Bosigran Farm

Porthmeor

Porthmoina Cove

Bosigran Castle

Bosporthennis

Whirl Pool

Rosemergy

P

Carn Galver

Hannibal's Carn

Greeb Point

Long Carn

Little Galver

South West Coast Path

Chair Carn Lth

White Downs

Porthteras Cove

Carn Clough

Lower Chypraze

Watch Croft

TR20

Morvah

Trevean

Pendeen House

Trevowhan

Nine Maidens

Portheras Farm

TR19

ROSE VALLEY

ENYS COTTS

1 PETERS ROW
2 PARK-AN-PYTH
3 TREASE
4 BOSCASWELL TERR
6 CALARTHA TERR
6 CRESCENT PL
7 THE SQUARE
8 ST JOHN'S TERR
9 GWEL-MOR

ST IVES RD

Keigwin

The Carn

Bosullow Common

PONDS HILL

PORTHERAS CROSS

HIGHER BOJEWYAN

Tor Noon

Chun

Carn Downs

Bosullow Vean

Lanyon Farm

Pendeen

PH

PO

10 PORTHERAS VILLAS
11 PORTHERAS TERR
12 BOJEWYAN STENNACK

12

B3306

P

Little Bosullow

Bosiliack

BOSCASWELL DOWNS

B3318

Pendeen Prim Sch

Higher Boscaswell

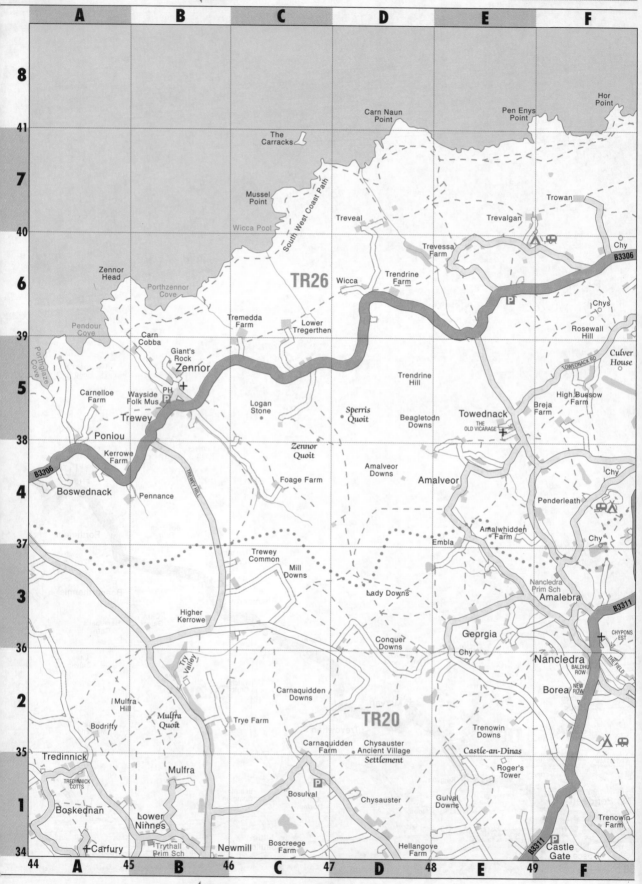

Scale: 1¾ inches to 1 mile

0   ¼   ½ mile

0   250m 500m 750m 1 km

A   B   C   D   E   F

8

41

The Carracks

Carn Naun Point

Pen Enys Point

Hor Point

7

Mussel Point

Wicca Pool

South West Coast Path

Treveal

Trowan

Trevalgan

40

Trevessa Farm

TR26

Zennor Head

Porthzennor Cove

Wicca

Trendrine Farm

B3306

Chy

6

Pendour Cove

Tremedda Farm

Lower Tregerthen

Chys

P

39

Porthglaze Cove

Carn Cobba

Giant's Rock

Rosewall Hill

TOWEDNACK RD

Culver House

Zennor

Trendrine Hill

5

Carnelloe Farm

Wayside Folk Mus.

PH
P

Logan Stone

Sperris Quoit

Beagletodn Downs

Towednack

THE OLD VICARAGE

High Bussow Farm

Breja Farm

Trewey

Poniou

38

Zennor Quoit

Chy

B3306

Kerrowe Farm

Amalveor Downs

Amalveor

4

Boswednack

Pennance

TREWEY HILL

Foage Farm

Penderleath

Chy

37

Embla

Amalwhidden Farm

Trewey Common

Mill Downs

Lady Downs

Nancledra Prim Sch

3

Higher Kerrowe

Conquer Downs

Georgia

Amalebra

B3311

CHYPONS EST

36

Try Valley

Chy

Nancledra

BALDHU ROW

THE FIELD

Carnaquidden Downs

Borea

NEW ROW

2

Mulfra Hill

Mulfra Quoit

Trye Farm

TR20

Trenowin Downs

Bodriffy

Castle-an-Dinas

Tredinnick

Mulfra

Carnaquidden Farm

Chysauster Ancient Village

Settlement

Roger's Tower

1

TREDINNICK COTTS

P

Boskednan

Lower Ninnes

Bosulval

Chysauster

Gulval Downs

Trenowin Farm

B3311

P

Castle Gate

34

Carfury

Trythall Prim Sch

Newmill

Boscreege Farm

Hellangove Farm

44   A   45   B   46   C   47   D   48   E   49   F

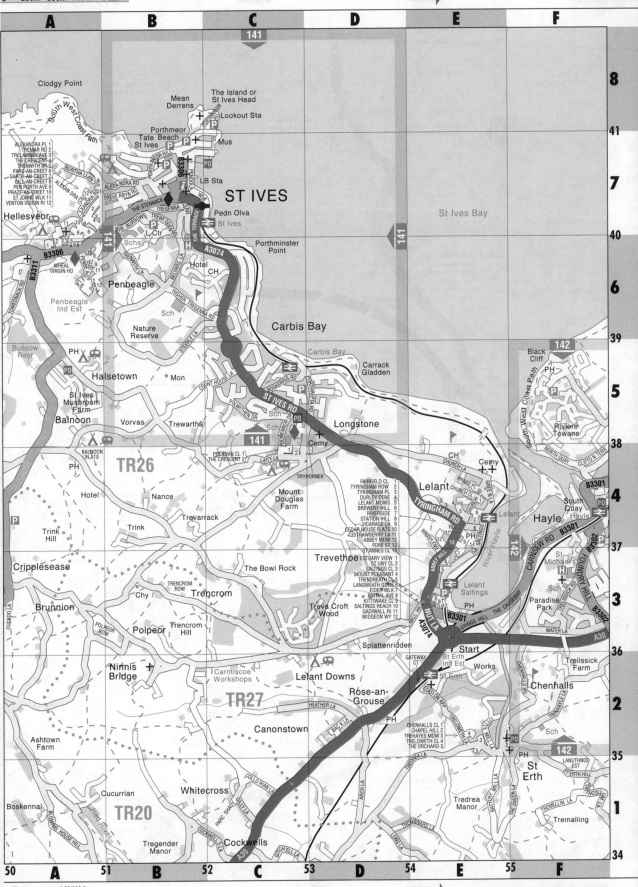

Scale: 1¾ inches to 1 mile

0   ¼   ½ mile

0   250m   500m   750m   1 km

78

ST IVES

St Ives Bay

Clodgy Point

South West Coast Path

Mean Derrens

The Island or St Ives Head

Lookout Sta

Porthmeor Beach

Tate St Ives

Mus

ALEXANDRA PL 1
TREMAR RD 2
TRELAWNEY AVE 3
THE CRESCENT 4
TRENWITH DR 5
PARC-AN-CREET 6
GARTH-AN-CREET 7
GILL-AN-CREET 8
PEN PORTH AVE 9
PRAZE-AN-CREET 10
ST JOHNS WLK 11
VENTON VISION RI 12

LB Sta

Pedn Olva
St Ives

Hellesveor

BURTHA LLAN LA

ALEXAN DRA RD

THE STENNACK

TREGENNA

TREVE RBYN RD

TREWI DDEN RD

THE BURROWS

Schs

L Ctr

Penbeagle

B3306

WHEAL VIRGIN HO

B3311

TOWEDNACK RD

B3306

Penbeagle Ind Est

HIGHER TREGENNA RD

Hotel

CH

A3074

Porthminster Point

Carbis Bay

Nature Reserve

Sch

Bussow Resr

PH

PO

Halsetown

Mon

St Ives Mushroom Farm

Balnoon

Vorvas

Trewartha

STEER E LA

COUNT HOUSE LA

POLWITHEN DR

Carbis Bay

ROSKERRIS RD

PORTHREPTA RD

ST IVES RD

Sch

PO

Sch

141

Cemy

Longstone

Carrack Gladden

142

Black Cliff

PH

Riviere Towans

South West Coast Path

NORTH QUAY

CLIFTON TERR

TR26

BALNOON FLATS

PH

Hotel

Nance

Trevarrack

Trink Hill

Trink

POLBREAN CL 1
THE CRESCENT 2

LATTY LA

TRYHORNEK

Mount Douglas Farm

FAIRFIELD CL 1
TYRINGHAM ROW 2
TYRINGHAM PL 3
DURLEY DENE 4
LELANT MDWS 5
BREWERY HILL 6
RIVERSIDE 7
STATION HILL 8
VICARAGE LA 9
CEDAR HOUSE FLATS 10
STRAWBERRY LA 11
ABBEY MDW 12
FORE ST 13
STANNES CL 14

Lelant

CHURCH LA

PRAED PL

GREEN LA

CHURCH CL

Cemy

CH

TYRINGHAM RD

BRUST CREE

Lelant

PH

Hayle

B3301

South Quay
Hayle

PO

B3301

St Michael's

Sch

H

Paradise Park

B3302

B3301

TRELISSICK RD

FOUNDRY HILL

B3302

Cripplesease

Brunnion

Chy

TRENCROM ROW

Trencrom

The Bowl Rock

ESTUARY VIEW 1
ST UNY CL 2
SALTINGS CL 3
MOUNT PLEASANT 4
TRENDREATH CL 5
LANGWEATH GDNS 6
EIDER WLK 7
PINTAIL AVE 8
KITTIWAKE CL 9
SALTINGS REACH 10
GADIWALL RI 11
WIDGEON WY 12

Trevethoe

ABBEY HILL

River Hayle

Lelant Saltings

142

CARNSEW RD

WATER LA

A30

PH

Polpeor

Trencrom Hill

Treva Croft Wood

MILL HILL

NUT LA

A3074

B3301

GRIGGS HILL

THE CAUSEWAY

Paradise Park

Chenhalls

CHENHALLS RD

TRELISSICK RD

Trelissick Farm

CUCKOO LA

POLROAR ROW

Nimnis Bridge

Carntiscoe Workshops

Lelant Downs

Splattenridden

GATEWAY CT

St Erth Ind Est

Start

St Erth

Works

TR27

HEATHER LA

BACK K LA

Rose-an-Grouse

STATION AP

TRENEERE MILL LA

Ashtown Farm

Canonstown

PH

CHENHALLS CL 1
CHAPEL HILL 2
TREHAYES MDW 3
TRELOWETH CL 4
THE ORCHARD 5

Sch

142

St Erth

ST ERTH HILL

LANUTHNOE EST

Boskennal

RED RIVER

Cucurrian

Whitecross

PARC SHADY

GULLY LA

COCKWELL'S LA

COLLO RIAN LA

ARCH LA

TREVINNARD LA

LONG LA

TREDREA LA

BATTERY MILL LA

Tredrea Manor

THE GREEN LA

TREMELLIN LA

Tremalling

BLOWING HOUSE HILL

TR20

Tregender Manor

Cockwells

A30

GILCH ELL LA

PH

PO

A6
1 CHYANDOUR CL
2 HELLESVEAN
3 HELLESVEAN CL
4 PARC-AN-STAMPS
5 CROWS-AN-EGLOS
6 PARC-AN-FORTH
7 PENBEAGLE TERR
8 PENBEAGLE CRES
9 CORVA RD
10 PRIORS CL
11 CORVA CL
12 PORTHIA RD
13 CARNSTABBA RD
14 ALAN HARVEY CL
15 JUBILEE CT
16 TINNERS WAY
17 PENBEAGLE CL

89

78

For full street detail of the highlighted area see pages 141 and 142.

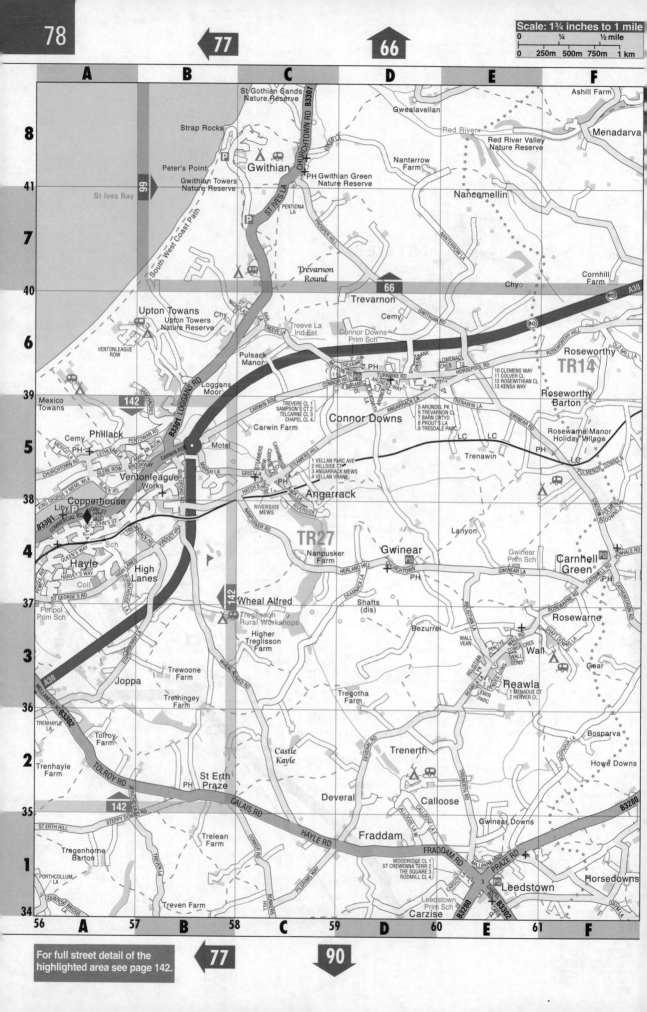

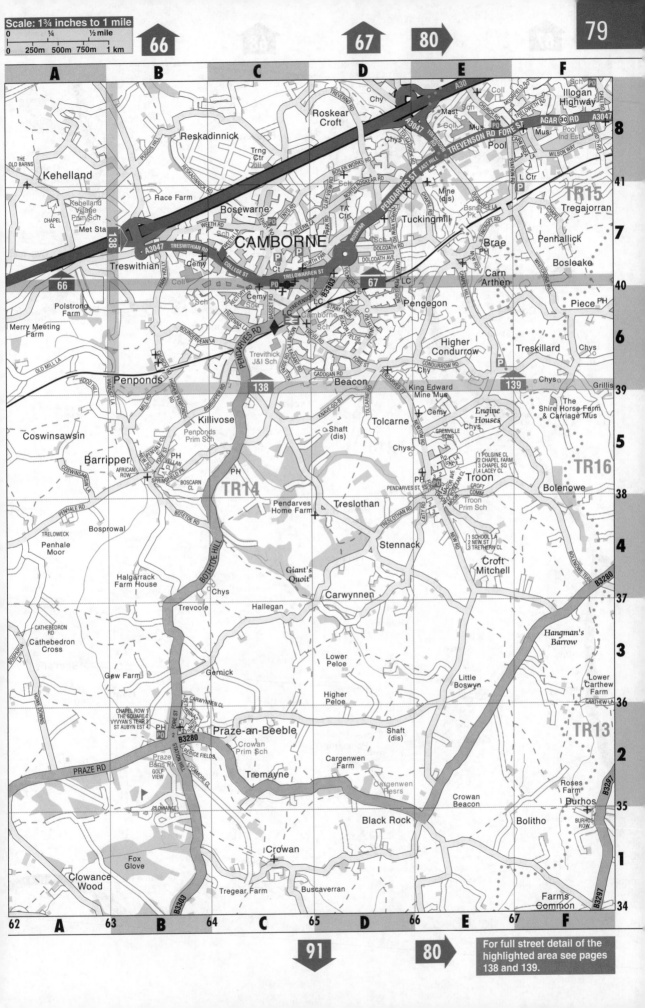

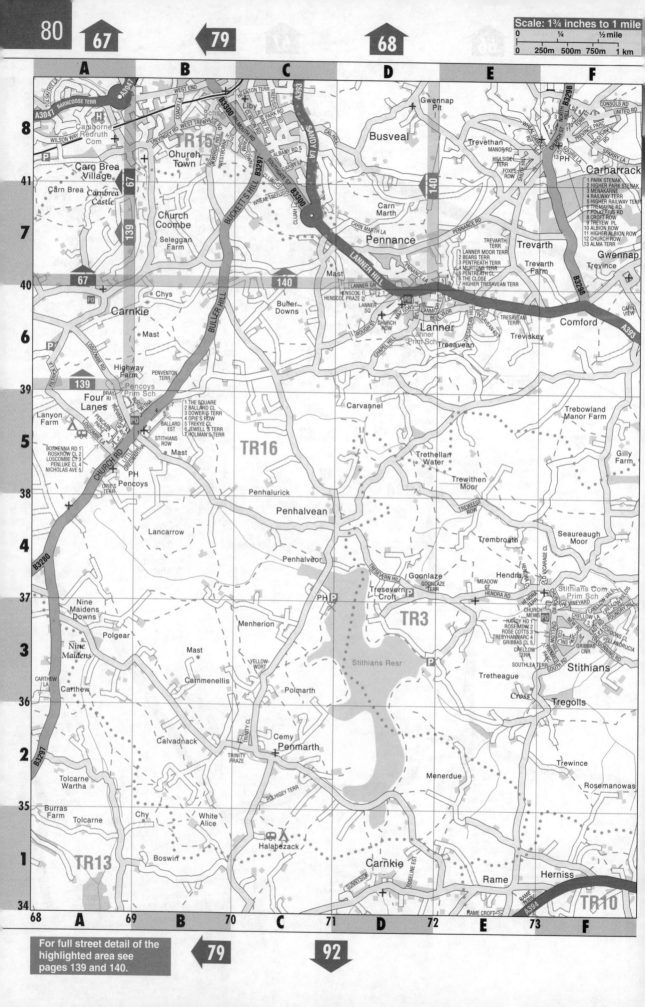

Scale: 1¾ inches to 1 mile

0 ¼ ½ mile

0 250m 500m 750m 1 km

A B C D E F

8

41

7

40

6

39

5

38

4

37

3

36

2

35

1

34

68 A 69 B 70 C 71 D 72 E 73 F

For full street detail of the highlighted area see pages 139 and 140.

CONSOLS RD
UNITED RD
B3298
Gwennap Pit
Carharrack
1 PARK STENAK
2 HIGHER PARK STENAK
3 MENAKARNE
4 RAILWAY TERR
5 HIGHER RAILWAY TERR
6 TREMAYNE RD
7 POLKERRIS RD
8 CROFT ROW
9 TREVEW PL
10 ALBION ROW
11 HIGHER ALBION ROW
12 CHURCH ROW
13 ALMA TERR

Busveal
Trevethan
MANOR RD
HILLSIDE TERR
FOXES ROW

Carn Marth
Trevarth
Trevince
Gwennap
Trevarth Farm

CARN MARTH LA
Pennance
PENNANCE RD
PENNANCE LA
B3298
Comford
A393
CARN VIEW

A3047
TOLSKITHY
BARNCOOSE TERR
WEST END
HEANTON TERR
Liby
B3300
SANDY LA
A393
Camborne Redruth Com
WILSON WAY
Carn Brea Village
Carn Brea
Cambrea Castle
TR15
Church Town
Church Coombe
Seleggan Farm

Mast
140
Mast
Carn Marth
Butter Downs
HENSCOL
HENSCOL PRAZE
LANNER SQ
Lanner
Lanner Prim Sch
Tresavean
Treviskey

Chys
Carnkie
Mast
BULLER HILL
LOSCOMBE RD
Highway Farm
PENVENTON TERR
139
Four Lanes
Lanyon Farm
Pencoys Prim Sch
1 BOSNENNA RD
2 ROSKROW CL
3 LOSCOMBE CT
4 PENLUKE CL
5 NICHOLAS AVE
STITHIANS ROW
1 THE SQUARE
2 BALLARD CL
3 DOWER'S TERR
4 OPIE'S ROW
5 TREKYE CL
6 JEWELL'S TERR
7 HOLMAN'S TERR
BALLARD EST
PH Pencoys
OPIE'S TERR
Mast
TR16

Trethellan Water
Trewithen Moor
Carvannel
Trebowland Manor Farm
Gilly Farm

Penhalurick
Penhalvean
TREVEEGE ROW
Trembroath
Seaureaugh Moor

Lancarrow
Penhalveor
TRESEVERN HILL
Goonlaze
GOONLAZE TERR
Tresevern Croft
Hendra
HENDRA RD
MEADOW CT
Stithians Com Prim Sch
OLD VICARAGE CL

B3280
Nine Maidens Downs
Polgear
Menherion
PH
TR3
CHURCH MEWS
HARDY HO
ROSE MDW
ROSE COTTS
TREBYHANNARC
GRIBBAS CL
CRELLOW TERR
SOUTHLEA TERR
Stithians

Nine Maidens
CARTHEW LA
Carthew
Mast
YELLOW-WORT
Carnmenellis
Polmarth
Stithians Resr
Tretheague
Cross
Tregolls

Burras Farm
Tolcarne Wartha
Tolcarne
Chy
White Alice
TRINITY CL
Cemy Penmarth
TRINITY PRAZE
POLHIGEY TERR
Menerdue
Trewince
Rosemanowas

B3297
TR13
Boswin
Halabezack
SUNNYSIDE
BOSELINE EST
Carnkie
Rame
RAME CROFT
A394
Herniss
TR10

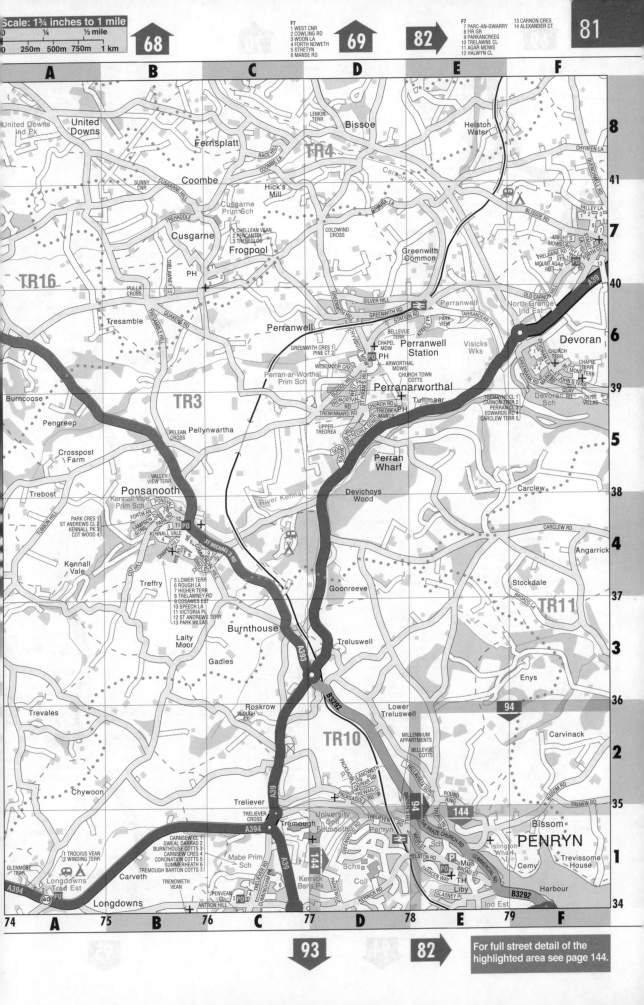

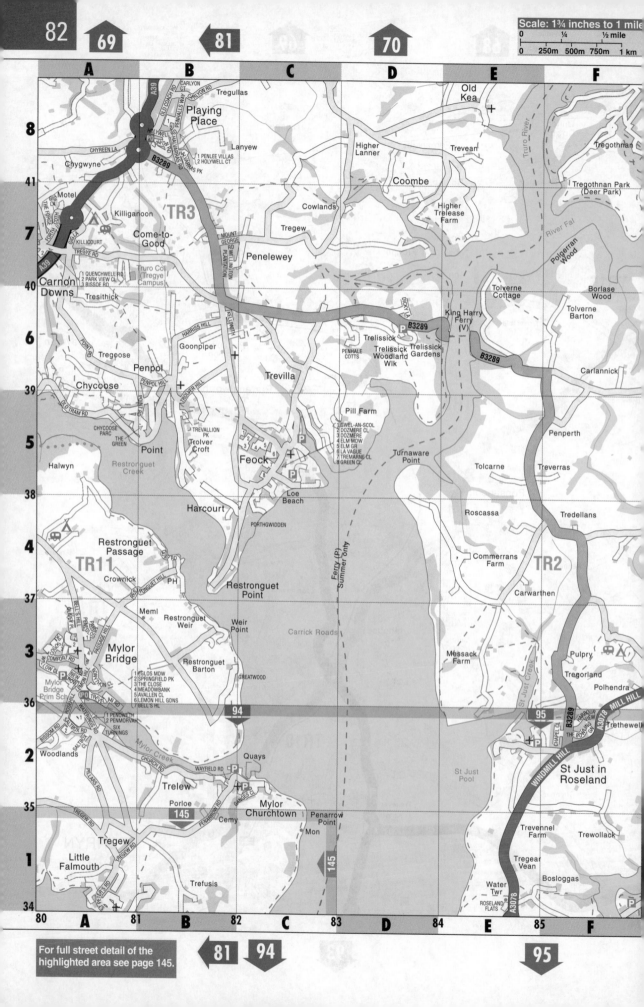

Scale: 1¾ inches to 1 mile
0   ¼   ½ mile
0 250m 500m 750m 1 km

A B C D E F

Old Kea

Tregullas

Playing Place

CARLYON CT
CARLYON RD

Lanyew

1 PENLEE VILLAS
2 HOLYWELL CT

Tregothnan

8

41

Chygwyne

Higher Lanner

Trevean

Tregothnan Park
(Deer Park)

Coombe

River Fal

Motel

TR3

Cowlands

Killiganoon

Come-to-Good

Tregew

Higher Trelease Farm

Polgerran Wood

7

KILLICOURT

Penelewey

MOUNT GEORGE RD
BELLINGTON PLANTATION

40

Carnon Downs

1 QUENCHWELL RD
2 PARK VIEW CL
3 BISSOE RD

Truro Coll
Tregye Campus

Tolverne Cottage

Borlase Wood

Tresithick

B3289

King Harry Ferry (V)

Tolverne Barton

6

HARRISS HILL

Goonpiper

Trelissick

DICK'S LA

B3289

Carlannick

Penpol

TROLVER HILL

Trevilla

Trelissick Woodland Wlk

Trelissick Gardens

PENHALE COTTS

39

PENPOL HILL

Chycoose

POINT RD

Pill Farm

1 GWEL-AN-SCOL
2 DOZMERE CL
3 DOZMERE
4 ELM MDW
5 ELM GR
6 LA VAGUE
7 TREMARNE CL
8 GREEN CL

Penperth

OLD TRAM RD

CHYCOOSE PARC

THE GREEN

Point

TREVALLION PK

Trolver Croft

Turnaware Point

Tolcarne

Treverras

5

Halwyn

Restronguet Creek

Feock

P

P

Loe Beach

Roscassa

38

Harcourt

PORTHGWIDDEN

Tredellans

4

Restronguet Passage

TR11

Crownick

PH

Restronguet Point

Commerrans Farm

TR2

37

Meml

Restronguet Weir

Weir Point

Carwarthen

3

Mylor Bridge

Restronguet Barton

GREATWOOD

Messack Farm

Pulpry

St Just Creek

Tregorland

Polhendra

Mylor Bridge Prim Sch

1 EGLOS MDW
2 SPRINGFIELD PK
3 THE CLOSE
4 MEADOWBANK
5 AVALLEN CL
6 LEMON HILL GDNS
BELL'S HL

Carrick Roads

94

95

B3289

A3078 MILL HILL

Trethewell

36

1 PENDWETH
2 PENMORVAH
SIX TURNINGS

HARBOUR VIEW

THE BOXING GA

+P

2

Woodlands

Mylor Creek

WAYFIELD RD

Quays

St Just Pool

WINDMILL HILL

St Just in Roseland

35

Trelew

Porloe

145

PENARROW RD

GANGES CL

Cemy

Mylor Churchtown

Penarrow Point

Mon

Trevennel Farm

Trewollack

1

Tregew

TREGEW RD

145

Little Falmouth

Tregear Vean

Bosloggas

Trefusis

Water Twr

A3078

ROSELAND FLATS

P

34

80 A 81 B 82 C 83 D 84 E 85 F

For full street detail of the highlighted area see page 145.

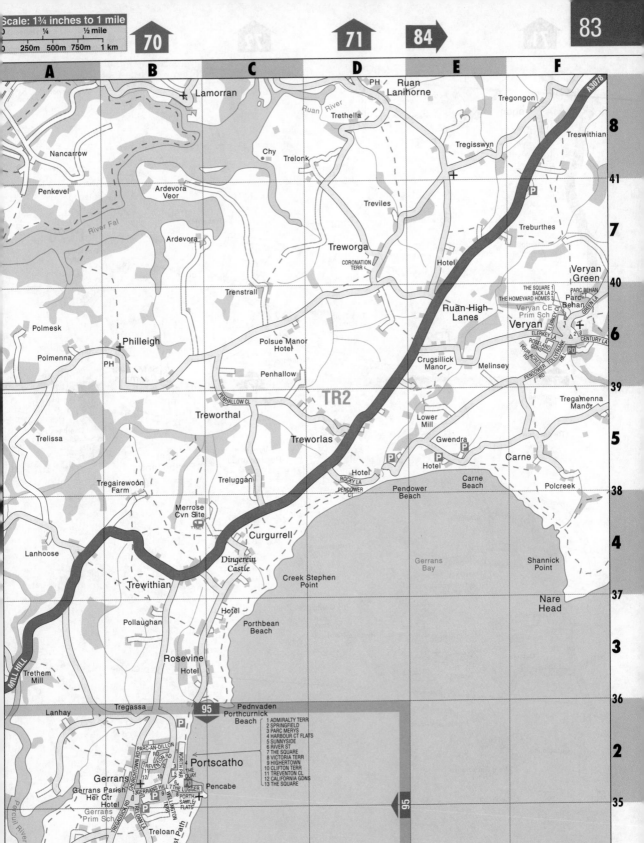

A B C D E F

8
41
7
40
6
39
5
38
4
37
3
36
2
35
1
34

Lamorran

Nancarrow

Penkevel

Polmesk

Polmenna

Philleigh
PH

Trelissa

Tregairewoon
Farm

Lanhoose

Trewithian

Pollaughan

Rosevine
Hotel

Lanhay

Tregassa

Gerrans
Gerrans Parish
Her Ctr
Hotel
Gerrans
Prim Sch

Tregassick

Percuil

River Fal

Ardevora
Veor

Ardevora

Trenstrall

Treworthal

Merrose
Cvn Site

Dingerein
Castle

Curgurrell

Creek Stephen
Point

Porthbean
Beach

Pednvaden
Porthcurnick
Beach

Portscatho

Pencabe

Trethella

Trelonk
Chy

Treworga

CORONATION
TERR

Polsue Manor
Hotel

Penhallow

PENHALLOW CL

Treworlas

Treluggan

Ruan River

PH Ruan
Lanihorne

Tregisswyn

Hotel

Ruan High
Lanes

Crugsillick
Manor

Lower
Mill

Hotel

ROCKY LA
PENDOWER
CL

Pendower
Beach

Tregongon

Treswithian

Treburthes

Veryan
Green

THE SQUARE 1
BACK LA 2
THE HOMEYARD HOMES 3

PARC BEHAN
Parc
Behan

Veryan CE
Prim Sch

Veryan

Melinsey

Gwendra

Hotel

Carne
Beach

Carne

Polcreek

Tregamenna
Manor

Shannick
Point

Nare
Head

Gerrans
Bay

TR2

1 ADMIRALTY TERR
2 SPRINGFIELD
3 PARC MERYS
4 HARBOUR CT FLATS
5 SUNNYSIDE
6 RIVER ST
7 THE SQUARE
8 VICTORIA TERR
9 HIGHERTOWN
10 CLIFTON TERR
11 TREVENTON CL
12 CALIFORNIA GDNS
13 THE SQUARE

South West Coast Path

Trethem
Mill
MILL HILL

Percuil River

86 87 88 89 90 91
A B C D E F

95

A3078

PO
PENDOWER RD TOLLYBANK
FOUR ACRES
ELERKEY LA
ROSELAND GDNS
CENTURY LA
GREEN LA

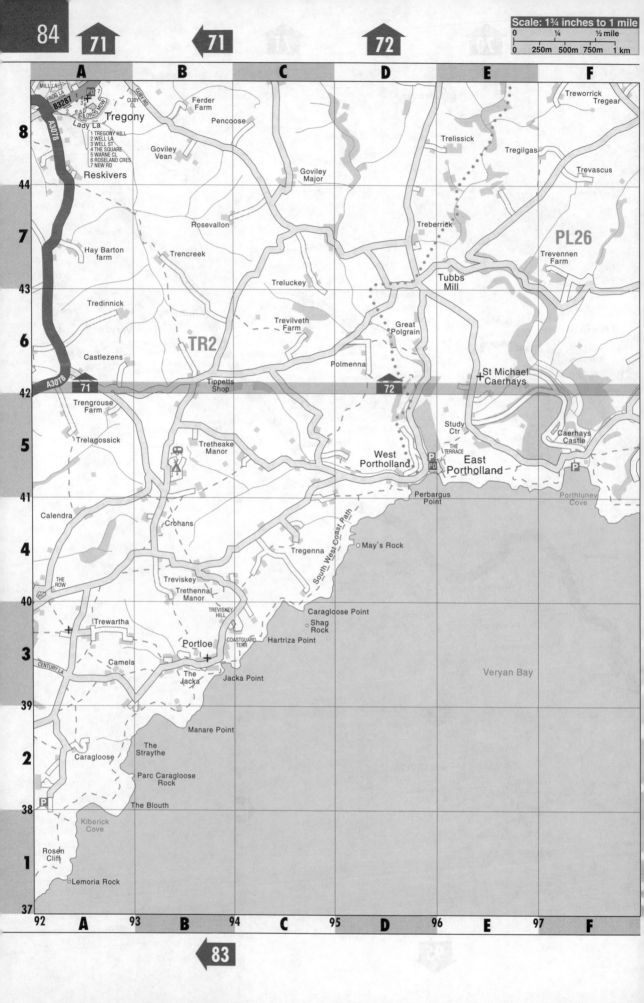

A   B   C   D   E   F

8

44

7

PL26

43

6

TR2

42

71   72

5

41

4

40

3

Veryan Bay

39

2

38

1

37

92   A   93   B   94   C   95   D   96   E   97   F

Place names and labels:

MILL LA
FROG LA
PO
B3287
LORDS MDW
CUBY RD
Tregony
CL
Lady La
1 TREGONY HILL
2 WELL LA
3 WELL ST
4 THE SQUARE
5 WARNE CL
6 ROSELAND CRES
7 NEW RD
Reskivers
A3078

Ferder Farm
Pencoose
Goviley Vean
Goviley Major
Rosevallon

Trelissick
Tregilgas
Trevascus
Treworrick
Tregear
Trevennen Farm

Hay Barton farm
Trencreek
Treluckey
Treberrick
Tubbs Mill

Tredinnick
Trevilveth Farm
Great Polgrain

Castlezens
Polmenna
St Michael Caerhays

A3078
Trengrouse Farm
Tippetts Shop
Study Ctr
Caerhays Castle

Trelagossick
Tretheake Manor
West Portholland
THE TERRACE
East Portholland
PO
PO
Porthluney Cove

Calendra
Crohans
Perbargus Point

THE ROW
Tregenna
May's Rock
South West Coast Path

Treviskey
Trethennal Manor
Caragloose Point
Shag Rock

Trewartha
TREVISKEY HILL
COASTGUARD TERR
Hartriza Point

Camels
Portloe

CENTURY LA
The Jacka
Jacka Point

Manare Point

Caragloose
The Straythe
Parc Caragloose Rock

P
The Blouth

Kiberick Cove

Rosen Cliff
Lemoria Rock

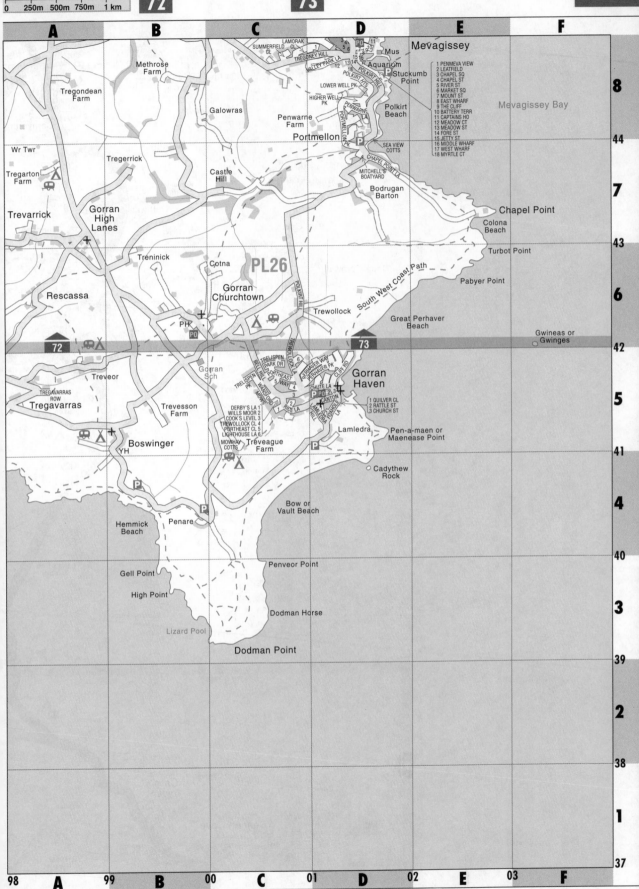

A   B   C   D   E   F

8
44
7
43
6
42
5
41
4
40
3
39
2
38
1
37

Mevagissey

1 PENMEVA VIEW
2 LEATFIELD
3 CHAPEL SQ
4 CHAPEL ST
5 RIVER ST
6 MARKET SQ
7 MOUNT ST
8 EAST WHARF
9 THE CLIFF
10 BATTERY TERR
11 CAPTAINS HO
12 MEADOW CT
13 MEADOW ST
14 FORE ST
15 JETTY ST
16 MIDDLE WHARF
17 WEST WHARF
18 MYRTLE CT

Mevagissey Bay

SUMMERFIELD
CL
LAMORAK
CL
TREGONEY HILL
VALLEY PARK LA
POLKIRT HILL
LOWER WELL PK
HIGHER WELL
PK
PENWARNE
LA
PENWARNE PK
PORTMELLON PK
Mus
Aquarium
Stuckumb
Point
Polkirt
Beach
SEA VIEW
COTTS

Methrose
Farm

Tregondean
Farm

Galowras

Penwarne
Farm

Portmellon

CHAPEL POINT LA
MITCHELL'S
BOATYARD

Chapel Point

Colona
Beach

Turbot Point

Pabyer Point

Bodrugan
Barton

Wr Twr

Tregarton
Farm

Tregerrick

Trevarrick

Gorran
High
Lanes

Castle
Hill

Treninick

Cotna

PL26

Gorran
Churchtown

Trewollock

South West Coast Path

Great Perhaver
Beach

Rescassa

PH
PO

Gwineas or
Gwinges

72

73

TRELISPEN
PARK DR
PERHAVER WAY
PERHAVER PK
CLIFF RD
Gorran
Sch
TRELISPEN
PK
BELL HILL
WATER LA
PORTHEAST
WAY
RICE LA
CHUTE LA
PO
CANTON
FOXHOLE LA
LAMLEDRA HILL
CHURCH HILL

Gorran
Haven

1 QUILVER CL
2 RATTLE ST
3 CHURCH ST

Treveor

Trevesson
Farm

TREGAVARRAS
ROW

Tregavarras

DERBY'S LA 1
WILLS MOOR 2
COOK'S LEVEL 3
TREWOLLOCK CL 4
PORTHEAST CL 5
LIGHTHOUSE LA 6

MOWHAY
COTTS

Treveague
Farm

Lamledra

Pen-a-maen or
Maenease Point

Boswinger
YH

Cadythew
Rock

P

Hemmick
Beach

Penare

Bow or
Vault Beach

Gell Point

Penveor Point

High Point

Dodman Horse

Lizard Pool

Dodman Point

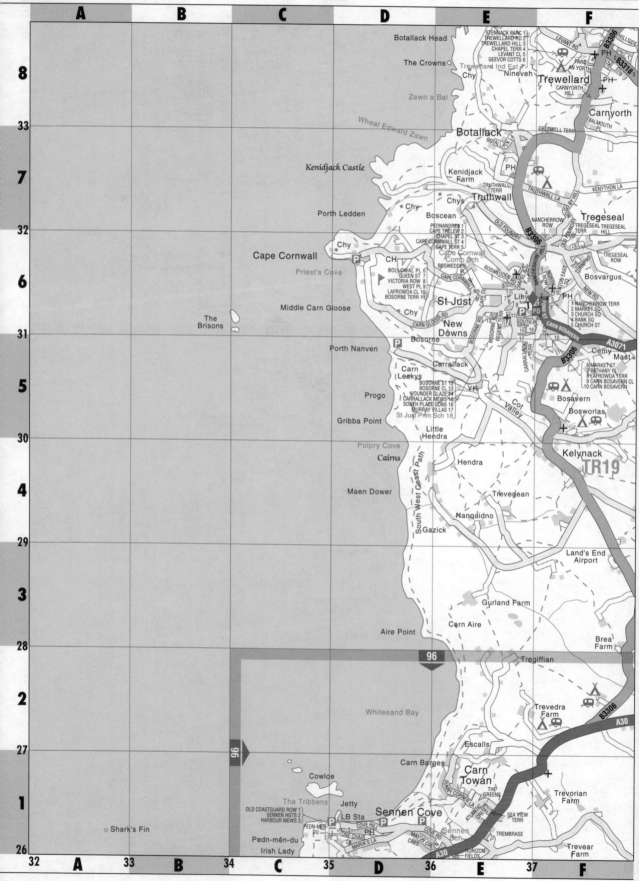

Scale: 1¾ inches to 1 mile

0   ¼   ½ mile
0   250m 500m 750m 1 km

A   B   C   D   E   F

8

33

7

32

6

31

5

30

4

29

3

28

2

27

1

26

Botallack Head
The Crowns
STENNACK PARC 1
TREWELLARD RD 2
TREWELLARD HILL 3
CHAPEL TERR 4
LEVANT CL 5
GEEVOR COTTS 6
Trewellard Ind Est
Chy
Nineveh
LEVANT RD
B3306
HILLSIDE
PARC
AN YORTH
Trewellard
PH
CARNYORTH
HILL
PH
B3318

Zawn a Bal
Carnyorth
FALMOUTH
PL

Wheal Edward Zawn
Botallack
BOTALLACK
CRESWELL TERR

Kenidjack Castle
Kenidjack
Farm
PH
TRUTHWALL
TERR
Truthwall
TRUTHWALL LA
KENYTHON LA

Chys
Chy
Chys
Boscean
Porth Ledden
Cape Cornwall
Comb Sch
NANCHERROW
ROW
OLD FOUNDRY
B3306
Tregeseal
Tregeseal TREGESEAL
HILL
TERR
TREGESEAL
ROW
BOSVARGUS

Chy
Cape Cornwall
CH
Priest's Cove
PEDNANDREA 1
CAPE TRELEW 2
CHAPEL ST 3
CAPE CORNWALL ST 4
CAPE TERR 5
BOLLOWAL PL 6
QUEEN ST 7
VICTORIA ROW 8
WEST PL 9
LAFROWDA CL 10
BOSORNE TERR 11
Cape Cornwall
BOSWEDDEN
PL
NANCHERROW
HILL
1 NANCHERROW TERR
2 MARKET SQ
3 CHURCH SQ
4 BANK SQ
5 CHURCH ST

Middle Carn Gloose
Carn Gloose
CAPE CORNWALL
RD
Chy
St Just
New
Downs
Lib
P
PH
VENTON EAST
SQ
THE TURNPIKE
NEW RD

The Brisons
Porth Nanven
P
Bosorne
Carrallack
CARN BOSAVERN
A3071
Cemy
Mast
6 MARKET ST
7 BETHANY PL
8 LAFROWDA TERR
9 CARN BOSAVERN CL
10 CARN BOSAVERN

Carn
Leskys
BOSORNE ST 12
BOSORNE CL 13
VOUNDER GLAZE 14
CARRALLACK MEWS 15
SOUTH PLACE GDNS 16
MURRAY VILLAS 17
St Just Prim Sch 18
YH
Cot
Valley
Bosavern
Boswarlas

Progo
Gribba Point
Little
Hendra
B3306
Kelynack
TR19

Polpry Cove
Cairns
South West Coast Path
Hendra
Maen Dower
Trevegean
Gazick
Nanquidno
Land's End
Airport

Carn Aire
Gurland Farm
Aire Point
Brea
Farm

Tregiffian

Whitesand Bay
Trevedra
Farm
B3306
A30

Escalls
Cowloe
Carn Barges
Carn
Towan
Trevorian
Farm

The Tribbens
Jetty
THE
GREENS
SEA VIEW
TERR
Shark's Fin
OLD COASTGUARD ROW 1
SENNEN HGTS 2
HARBOUR MEWS 3
LB Sta
P
PH
P
Sennen Cove
Sennen
Sch
TREMBRASE
Trevear
Farm
Pedn-mên-du
STONE CHAIR
PH
COVE RD
ATLANTIC
CRES
Pedn-mên-du
MARIA'S LA
MAYON
CRES
HORIZON
FIELDS
A30
Irish Lady

32   A   33   B   34   C   35   D   36   E   37   F

Scale: 1¾ inches to 1 mile

0   ¼   ½ mile

0   250m   500m   750m   1 km

A B C D E F

B3311   B3309   CASTLE RD   B3309

TREASSOWE RIDING   Treassowe Manor

Trythall Farm

Crankan

Noongallas

GARRIS COTTS

8

Boswarthen

Trezelah

BADGER'S CROSS

33

Chapel (rems of)

Bosoljack

TR20

Gear Farm

Rosemorran Farm

Kenegie Manor

7

Madron Well Cross

Kennels

Trevaylor

Bone

Tremearne

1 TRENEGLOS TERR
2 TREVARRACK ROW
3 BARNFIELD GDNS
4 VELLANOGGAN MEWS
5 MILLFIELD
6 BRANWELL LA
7 FOXES FIELD
8 EASTERN GREEN PK
9 FRESHBROOK CL
10 GWEL LEWERN
11 MOUNT'S BAY HOL FLTS
12 THE CHALETS

Tolver

Pleming

Tregarthen

32

MOUNT VIEW   PARC CABRAC   ALDREATH RD

FORE ST   PO

1 ALDREATH CL
2 TREGODDICK CL
3 VINGOE'S LA
4 HILLSIDE PARC
5 TRAFALAR FIELDS

143

Madron

Gulval

SCHOOL LA   Gulval Prim Sch

Trevarrack

Longrock

A30

6

Trengwainton House

Poltair

Sch

H

Heamoor

Trythogga

TR18

B3311

Heliport

EASTERN GN

PONIOU ROCK HILL   LC

Trengwainton Gdns

BOSCATHNOE LA   BOSCATHNOE WAY   B3312   MADRON RD   ROSCADHILL RD

Heamoor Prim Sch

Cemy

Coll

COOMBE RD

Schs

CHYANDOUR LA

CHYANDOUR CLIFF

2 PONIOU WAY

P   LC

31

Tremethick Cross

Boscathnoe Resr

ST CLARE   Schs

L Ctr   West Cornwall

CALVERNE

PO   H

P

Penzance

Chyandour

Superstore

CHY-AN-MOR   1
Penwith Bsns Ctr   2
Long Rock Bsns Pk   3
Long Rock Ind Est   4
CUXHAVEN WAY   5
PONIOU WAY   6
BAY VILLAS   7
EASTERN GREEN TERR   8
GLADSTONE TERR   9
CASTLE VIEW   9
TOLVERTH TERR   10
TRESCOE RD   11
DARLINGTON RD   12

Long Rock

A3071

Bosehill

Ct

Liby

THE QUAY

P

PENZANCE

Cressars

Western Cressar

Ryeman

5

LESINGEY LA

Castle Horneck

YH   Lesingey Round

Sch

ALVERTON RD   MARKET JEW ST   WHARF RD

Gall & Mus

Piers

Tremethick Farm

STRINGERS HILL

143

B3315

A3071

Tregavarah

Treife

PO

LOVE LA   ALEXANDRA RD

Wherry Town

WESTERN PROMENADE RD

St Mary's CE Prim Sch

The Gear

30

Trewidden

Trewidden Gdn

Ind Est

Tolcarne

CREEPING LA   NEW RD

Sch

4

Buryas Bridge

THE COOMBE

Newlyn Art Gall

29

The Pilchard Wks

P   PO

Tredavoe

STRAND

LB Sta

NEWLYN

Pier

Tidal Observatory

Gwavas Lake

Ferry (P) Isles of Scilly

3

A30

GURNICK RD   FORBES RD   CHYWOONE HILL   GWAVAS RD   FORE ST

PO

Chyenhal

Hotel

143

28

Tresvennack

97

Tresvennack Pillar

TREWARVENETH FARM COTTS

CHYWOONE GROVE

GWAVAS

ROSKILLY COTTS

CLIFF RD

Skilly

2

TR19

Kerris

Paul

1 ST POL DE LEON VIEW
2 TRUNGLE TERR
3 TRUNGLEMOOR COTTS
4 TRUNGLE PARC
5 BOSLANDEW HILL

Roskilly

27

Rosevale Farm Penaluna

QUARRY LA   LONG ROW

97

Cemy

PH

PARC AN GATE   MOUSEHOLE LA

Meml

Penlee Point

Sheffield

FOUR LANES END

LOWER SHEFFIELD

Trevithal

Mousehole Prim Sch

CLIFF LA   LOW LEE RD   THE PARADE

PH

KEIGWIN PL

1 PARADE HILL
2 CARN TODDEN

1

Redhouse

Halwyn Farm

B3315

MOUNT PLEASANT TERR

PO

Mousehole

St Clements Isle

26

A 44 B 45 C 46 D 47 E 48 F 49

C1
1 LYNWOOD COTTS
2 PREVENNA RD
3 GWELENYS RD
4 PARKRYN RD
5 FOXES LA
6 MARCWHEAL
7 DUMBARTON TERR
8 SOUTHVIEW TERR
9 DUCK ST

10 COMMERCIAL RD
11 QUAY ST
12 NORTH CLIFF
13 FORE ST
14 NORTH ST
15 CHERRY GDN ST
16 VIRGIN PL
17 BROOK ST
18 SOUTH CLIFF
19 GRENFELL ST

20 MILL LA
21 CHAPEL ST
22 THE WHARF
23 PORTLAND PL
24 GURNICK ST
25 RAGINNIS HILL
26 ST CLEMENTS TERR
27 SALTPONDS

For full street detail of the highlighted area see page 143.

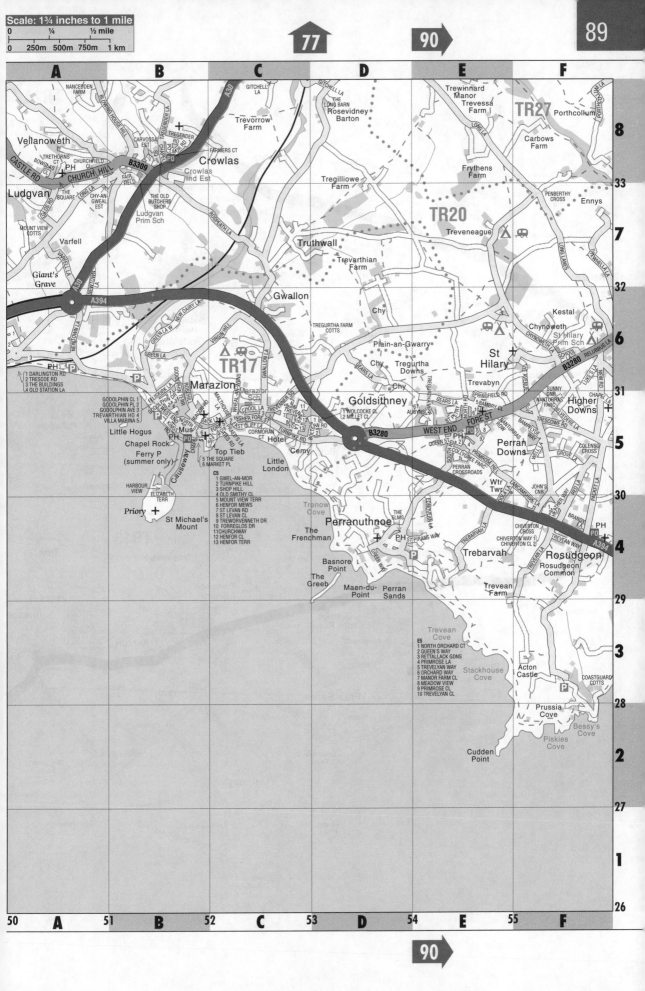

Scale: 1¾ inches to 1 mile

0 ¼ ½ mile
0 250m 500m 750m 1 km

77
90

A B C D E F

8 33 7 32 6 31 5 30 4 29 3 28 2 27 1 26

Nancedden Farm
Vellanoweth
Trethorns CT
Bowglas CL
PH
CHURCH HILL
CASTLE RD
Ludgvan
THE SQUARE
Long La
CROSS RD
Mount View Cotts
Varfell
Giant's Grave
A30
A394
NEWTOWN LA
BLOWINGHOUSE HILL
TREGENDER LA
TREGENDER RD
CARVOSSA EST
CHURCHFIELD
FAIR FIELD
B3309
PO
Crowlas Ind Est
Chy-an-Gweal Est
THE OLD BUTCHERS SHOP
Ludgvan Prim Sch
ROSPEATH LA
GITCHELL LA
Trevorrow Farm
Crowlas
GITCHELL LA
THE LONG BARN
Rosevidney Barton
Tregilliowe Farm
Truthwall
Trevarthian Farm
Gwallon
Chy
Tregurtha Farm Cotts
Plain-an-Gwarry
Chy
Tregurtha Downs
Chy
GEARS LA
Goldsithney
1 WOLCOCKE CL
2 MILLET CL
St Aubyns
GEARS LA
TREGURTHA LA
TREGENDER RD

Trewinnard Manor
Trevessa Farm
Porthcollum
TR27
Carbows Farm
Frythens Farm
TR20
Treveneague
PENBERTHY CROSS
Ennys
Kestal
Chynoweth
St Hilary Prim Sch
St Hilary
Trevabyn
CHYNOWETH LA
LUKE'S LA
NEW RD
RELUBBUS LA
TREMELLA LA
LONG LANES
LONG LA
B3280
SPRINGFIELD LA
SUNNY CNR
NANTORRAS PARC
Higher Downs
COLENSO CROSS
Perran Downs
THE AVENUE
SCHOOL LA
5 AMBRY LA
TRESCOWE RD
BAMPFYLDE WAY
NANTURRAS ROW
PRIMROSE HILL
GROVE LA
JOHN'S CNR
Brandy La
PO
PH
A394
Rosudgeon
Rosudgeon Common
Trevean Farm
TREVEAN WAY
CHIVERTON CROSS
1 CHIVERTON WAY
2 CHIVERTON CL
Trebarvah
TREBARVAH LA

TR17
Marazion
Marazion Sch
SCHOOL LA
WHEAL REETH
HIGHER FORE ST
TREVENNER SQ
TREVENNER LA
BACK LA
GWALLON LA
VIRGIN HILL
GREEN LA
GREEN LA W
NEW DAIRY LA
NEWTOWN LA
GODOLPHIN TER
FORE ST
THE SQUARE
TURNPIKE RD
CORMORAN Hotel
CEMY
Little London
WEST END
FORE ST
B3280
PERRAN CROSSROADS
COLLYGREE PARC
QUEEN'S WAY
SOUTH RD
EDENVEAN
Wtr Twr
LANCASHIRE HILL
DOCK LA
PACKET LA
RED LA
KEN WAY
PH

1 DARLINGTON RD
2 TRESCOE RD
3 THE BUILDINGS
4 OLD STATION LA
P
PH
GODOLPHIN CL 1
GODOLPHIN PL 2
GODOLPHIN AVE 3
TREVARTHIAN HO 4
VILLA MARINA 5
Little Hogus
Chapel Rock
Top Tieb
Ferry P
(summer only)
Causeway
HARBOUR VIEW
ELIZABETH TERR
Priory
St Michael's Mount
5 THE SQUARE
6 MARKET PL
C5
1 GWEL-AN-MOR
2 TURNPIKE HILL
3 SHOP HILL
4 OLD SMITHY CL
5 MOUNT VIEW TERR
6 HENFOR MEWS
7 ST LEVAN RD
8 ST LEVAN CL
9 TREWORVENNETH DR
10 FORREGLOS DR
11 CHURCHWAY
12 HENFOR CL
13 HENFOR TERR

Trenow Cove
Perranuthnoe
The Frenchman
ST PIRANS WAY
THE ELMS
GREEB WAY
Basnore Point
The Greeb
Maen-du-Point
Perran Sands

Trevean Cove
E5
1 NORTH ORCHARD CT
2 QUEEN'S WAY
3 RETTALLACK GDNS
4 PRIMROSE LA
5 TREVELYAN WAY
6 ORCHARD WAY
7 MANOR FARM CL
8 MEADOW VIEW
9 PRIMROSE CL
10 TREVELYAN CL
Stackhouse Cove
Acton Castle
COASTGUARD COTTS
Prussia Cove
Bessy's Cove
Piskies Cove
Cudden Point
P

50 A 51 B 52 C 53 D 54 E 55 F

90

Scale: 1¾ inches to 1 mile
0   ¼   ½ mile
0   250m 500m 750m 1 km

A B C D E F

Binners
Down
TR14

Keskeys

8

Paul's
Green
Binnerton
Manor

33

Trannack

Kerthen
Wood

TR27

Noonvares

Trenwheal

Townshend

Gwedna

Pengelly
Cross

7

Gurlyn

BOSENCE RD

River Hayle

32

Relubbus

Pengelly
Barton

Chy
Tregembo

Chy

Godolphin
House

Godolphin Prim Sch

Godolphin
CRES

6

1 TREWHELLA LA
2 TREWHELLA TERR

Chy

Chy

Godolphin
Hill

Godolphin
Cross

PH

31

Halamanning

Retallack

Chy

Trescowe

TREWITHEN
TERR

Chy

Broadlane

Polladras

TR20

SPARNON
CROSS

TREGONNING TERR 1
CHYTODDEN TERR 2

5

Millpool

Boscreege

Castle
Pencaire

Carleen

30

Colenso

Balwest

Meml

Tregonning
Hill

TR13

4

A394

Kenneggy
Downs

Newtown

Germoe

Cemy

Germoe
Cty
Prim Sch

Tresowes Hill

Trew

PH

Evans Way

Chys

Tresowes
Green

Trevena

29

Kenneggy

CH

THE LINKS

Chy

Germoe
Cross Roads

Chys

Motel

PROSPECT PL 1
TREGONNING CL 2
PROSPECT ROW 3
PRIORS ROW 4
HIGHER ROW 5

FOWLFIELD ROW 1
REPPERSFIELD ROW 2
BAKERS ROW 3
PELLOR FIELDS 4
COACHES CNR 5
COULTHARD DR 6
SETHNOE WAY 7
ST BREACA CL 8

Breage

Pengersick
Castle

Pengersick

PARC

Ashton

MIDDLE ROW

PH

TREVENA
CROSS

3

Pentreath

PO

CASTLE DR

TREVURVAS LA

HENDRA CV

MOUNTS BAY
TERR

VICARAGE
ROW

PH

PH

Praa Sands

PO

Breage
CE Sch

PENTREATH LA

28

Kenneggy
Sands

SANDY COVE BGLWS 1
PARC MORREP 2
PENWERRIS RISE 3

Hotel

Hendra

Rinsey
Croft

Penhale
Jakes

Colvorry

SCHOOL RD

Hoe
Point

Praa Sands

Lesceave
Farm

HENDRA LA

RINSEY LA

Trewithick

Tregunno
Farm

2

Rinsey

Trevena

Tranno

27

Rinsey
Head

Chy

Trewavas

Trequean

Tremearne

South West Coast Path

1

Chys

Trewavas
Head

26

56 A 57 B 58 C 59 D 60 E 61 F

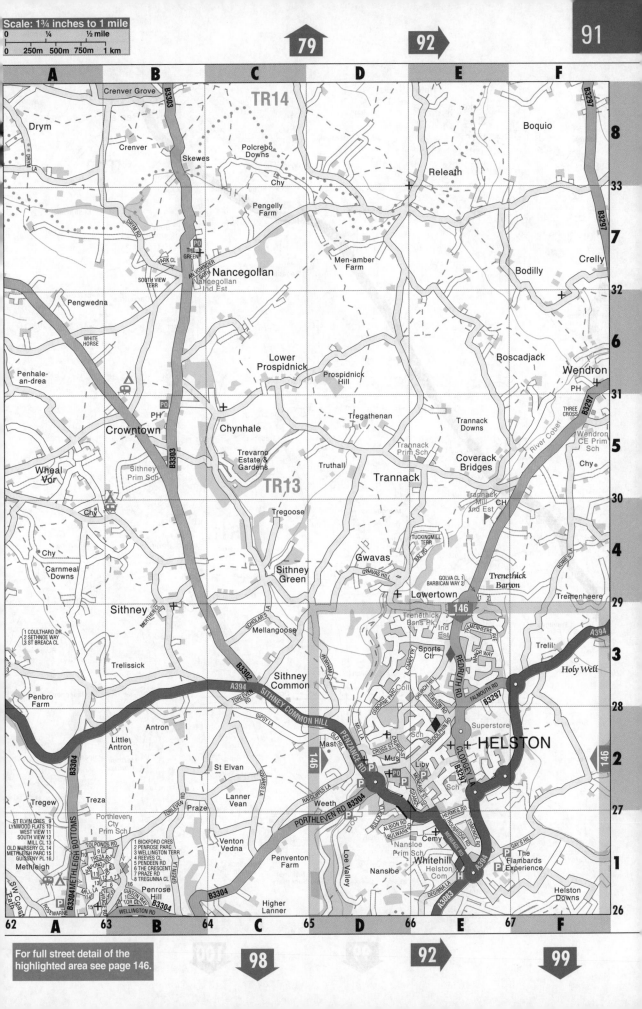

Scale: 1¾ inches to 1 mile

0   ¼   ½ mile
0   250m 500m 750m 1 km

A   B   C   D   E   F

8
33
7
32
6
31
5
30
4
29
3
28
2
27
1
26

TR14

Drym

Crenver Grove

Crenver

Skewes

Polcrebo Downs

Chy

Releath

Boquio

Pengelly Farm

Men-amber Farm

Crelly

THE GREEN
PO
PARK CL
SOUTH VIEW TERR
Nancegollan
Nancegollan Ind Est

Bodilly

Pengwedna

Lower Prospidnick

Boscadjack

Wendron
PH

WHITE HORSE

Prospidnick Hill

Penhale-an-drea

Tregathenan

Trannack Downs

THREE CROSS

Wendron CE Prim Sch

PO
PH
Crowntown

Chynhale

Trevarno Estate & Gardens

Trannack Prim Sch

Coverack Bridges

River Cober

B3297

Chy

Wheal Vor

Sithney Prim Sch

TR13

Truthall

Trannack

Trelissick

Tregoose

Trannack Mill Ind Est
CH

Chy

Chy
Carnmeal Downs

Sithney Green

Gwavas

TUCKINGMILL TERR
BEL RD

GOLVA CL 1
BARBICAN WAY 2

Trenethick Barton

Tremenheere

GWAVAS HILL

Lowertown

Sithney

MERTHER CL

Mellangoose

SCHOLAR'S

1 COULTHARD DR.
2 SETHNOE WAY
3 ST BREACA CL

Trenethick Bsns Pk
Ind Est

146

A394

Trelill

Holy Well

Sithney Common

NEWHAM LA

Sports Ctr

CAREPK

Superstore

HELSTON

B3302
TORLEVEN RD
GIPSY LA

A394

SITHNEY COMMON HILL

OLD HILL
PENZANGE RD
MILL LA
CROSS ST
CHURCH ST
Sch
Mus
Liby
Sch
CLODGEY LA
B3297

Antron

Little Antron

Mast

146

Weeth

P
P
P
P

Penbro Farm

B3304

St Elvan

SQUIRES LA

RATCLIFFES LA

PORTHLEVEN RD B3304

P

ALBION RD
BULWARK

HERMES RD
TROSBRIDGE RD

Tregew

Treza

Praze

Lanner Vean

Nansloe Prim Sch

Whitehill
Helston Com
H

The Flambards Experience
P

ST ELVIN CRES 9
LYNWOOD FLATS 10
WEST VIEW 11
SOUTH VIEW 12
MILL CL 13
OLD NURSERY CL 14
METHLEIGH PARC 15
GUISSENY PL 16

Porthleven Cty Prim Sch

1 BICKFORD CRES
2 PENROSE PARC
3 WELLINGTON TERR
4 REEVES CL
5 PENDEEN RD
6 THE CRESCENT
7 PRAZE RD
8 TREGUNNA CL

Venton Vedna

Penventon Farm

Loe Valley

Nansloe

Cemy

Gay's Hill

Helston Downs

Methleigh

METHLEIGH BOTTOMS
TOLPONDS RD
TREZA RD
GIBSON WAY
TOR CL
WELLINGTON RD

Penrose Hill

B3304

Higher Lanner

DEGIBNA LA
A3083
A394

SW COAST PATH

62   63   64   65   66   67

A   B   C   D   E   F

For full street detail of the highlighted area see page 146.

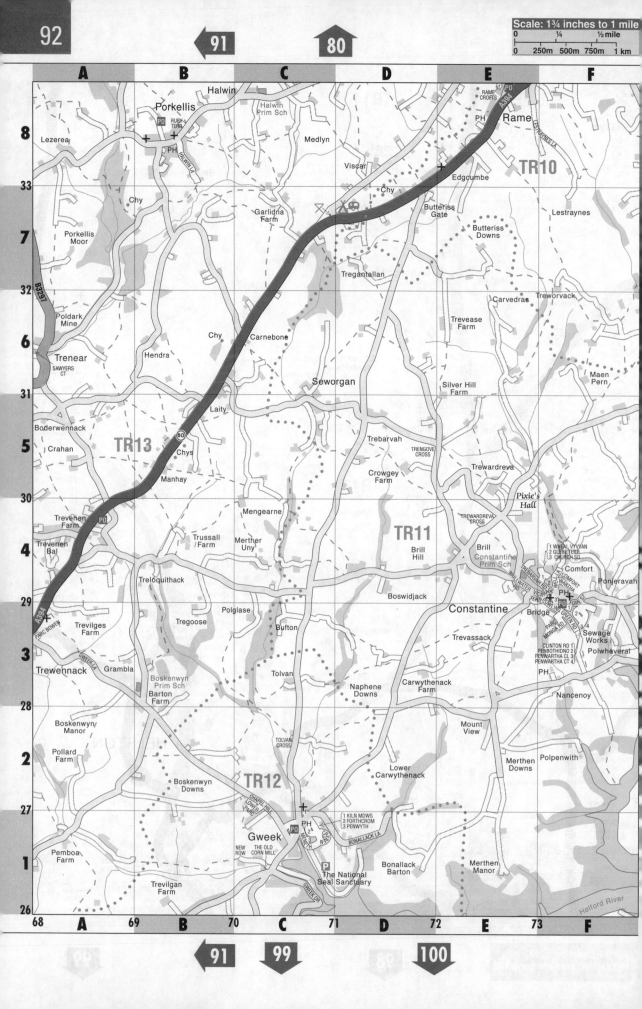

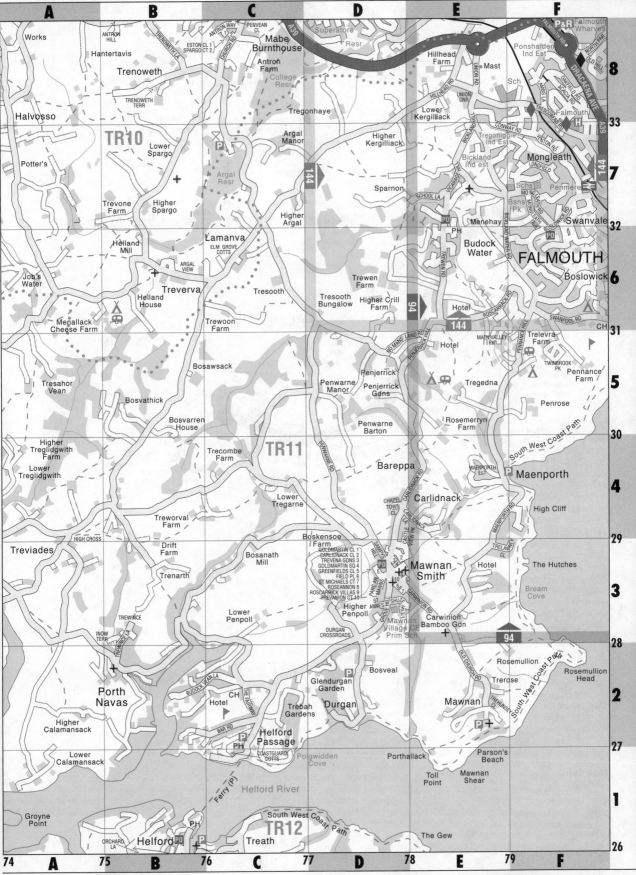

A   B   C   D   E   F

Works

Halvosso

TR10

Job's
Water

Treviades

Porth
Navas

Higher
Calamansack

Lower
Calamansack

Groyne
Point

Hantertavis

Antron
Hill

Trenoweth
Trenoweth Terr

Lower
Spargo

Trevone
Farm

Higher
Spargo

Potter's

Helland
Mill

Treverva

Helland
House

Menallack
Cheese Farm

Tresahor
Vean

Bosvathick

Bosvarren
House

Higher
Treglidgwith
Farm

Lower
Treglidgwith

Trecombe
Farm

TR11

High Cross

Drift
Farm

Trenarth

Bosanath
Mill

Lower
Penpoll

Trewince

Trewince La

Inow Terr

Buddock Vean La

The Fairway

Bar Rd

Hotel

CH

Helford
Passage

Trebah
Gardens

Coastguard
Cotts

Helford River

Orchard La

Helford

Treath

TR12

Eston Cl 1
Spargo Ct 2

Antron Way

Churchtown

Penvean
Cl

Mabe
Burnthouse

Antron
Farm

College
Resr

Argal
Manor

Lamanva

Elm Grove
Cotts

Argal
View

Argal
Resr

Higher
Argal

Tresooth

Trewoon
Farm

Bosawsack

Penwarne
Manor

Penjerrick

Lower
Tregarne

Treworval
Farm

Boskensoe
Farm

Goldmartin Cl 1
Carlidnack Cl 2
Trevena Gdns 3
Goldmartin Sq 4
Greenfields Cl 5
Field Pl 6
St Michaels Ct 7
Roseannon 8
Roscarrick Villas 9
Trevanion Ct 10

Higher
Penpoll

Durgan
Crossroads

Glendurgan
Garden

Durgan

Bosveal

Polgwidden Cove

Superstore
Resr

A39

144

Tregonhaye

Higher
Argal

Higher
Kergilliack

Sparnon

Trewen
Farm

Tresooth
Bungalow

Higher Crill
Farm

94

144

Penjerrick
Gdns

Penwarne
Barton

Bareppa

Chapel
Town
Cl

Carlidnack

Mawnan
Smith

Mawnan
Village CE
Prim Sch

Carwinion
Bamboo Gdn

Porthallack

South West Coast Path

Hillhead
Farm

Lower
Kergilliack

Union
Rd

Mast

Sch

Union
Cnr

School La

Bickland
Ind est

Bickland
Ind Est

PO

PH

Menehay

Budock
Water

Hotel

Roscarrack Rd

Hotel

Rosemerryn
Farm

Maenporth
Est

Maenporth

Carlidnack Rd

Castle
View Pk

Maenporth Rd

Hotel

The Hutches

Bream
Cove

High Cliff

Trelary
Cl

Old Church Rd

Rosemullion

Trerose

Mawnan

94

Rosemullion
Head

Parson's
Beach

Mawnan
Shear

The Gew

Toll
Point

P&R

Falmouth
Wharves

Ponsharden
Ind Est

Dracaena Ave

North Par

Old Hill

Falmouth A39

144

Mongleath

Penmere

Swanvale

FALMOUTH

Boslowick

Swanpool Rd

CH

Trelevra
Farm

Twinbrook
Pk

Pennance
Farm

Penrose

Tregedna

Hillhead Rd

Higher
Kergilliack

Tregoniggie
Ind Est

Longfield

Bsns
Pk

Schs

Conway Rd

Vauton Rd

Trescobeas Rd

Acacia Rd

Oakfield Rd

Lakes La

Bickland Water Rd

Mongleath Rd

Boslowick Rd

Pennance Hill

Maen Valley Pk

H

8

33

7

32

6

31

5

30

4

29

3

28

2

27

1

26

74   A   75   B   76   C   77   D   78   E   79   F

100

101

For full street detail of the
highlighted area see page 144.

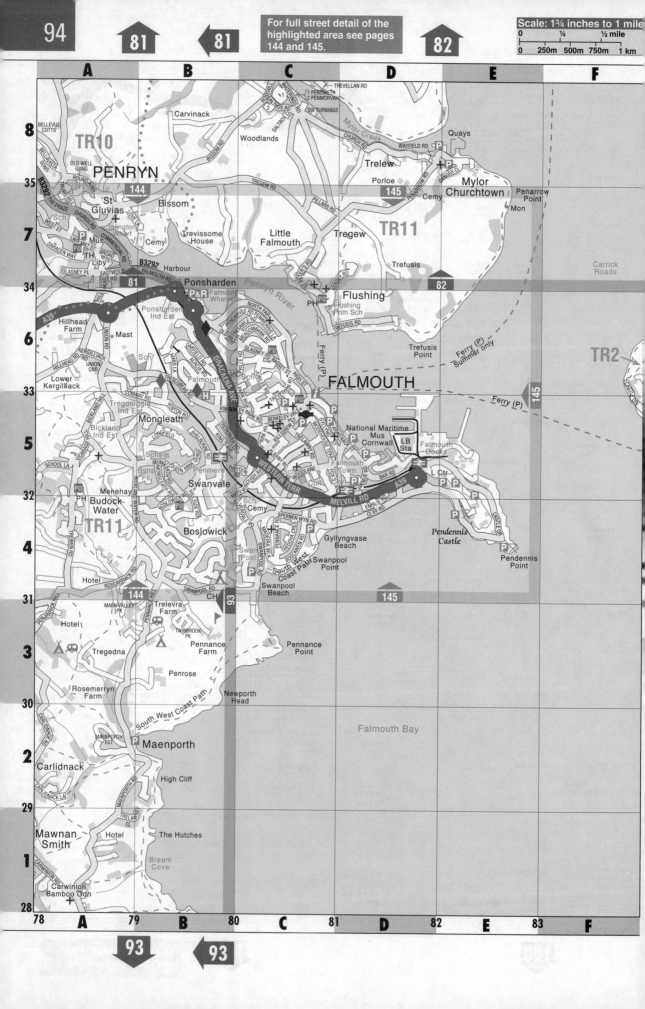

81 ← 81   82

For full street detail of the
highlighted area see pages
144 and 145.

Scale: 1¾ inches to 1 mile

0   ¼   ½ mile
0 250m 500m 750m 1 km

A   B   C   D   E   F

BELLEVUE
COTTS

TR10

PENRYN

Carvinack

Woodlands

TREVELLAN RD
PENDEWETH
PENMORVAH
SIX TURNINGS
SALTBOX RD
WATERINGS RD
ROSEHILL

MYLOR CREEK

Quays

Trelew

WAYFIELD RD

GANGES CL

CHURCH RD

Mylor
Churchtown

Porloe

Penarrow
Point

Mon

144

145

St
Gluvias

Bissom

ROUND RING

Cemy

Trevissome
House

Little
Falmouth

Tregew

Cemy

TR11

Trefusis

Carrick
Roads

THE PRAZE
WEST ST
SARACEN WAY
GLASNEY PL
Mus
Liby
TH
PO
EASTWOOD
LW
BROAD ST
COMMERCIAL RD
CHURCH HILL
RD/PO HILL
BELLAIR RD
B3292
B3292

Harbour
FALMOUTH RD

B3292

81

Islington
Wharf

PILLARS RD
TREGEW RD
PETER'S RD
CHURCH RD

Penryn River

Ponsharden

82

Flushing

Flushing
Prim Sch

PH
PO

A39

Hillhead
Farm

Mast

Ponsharden
Ind Est

P&R

Falmouth
Wharves

NORTH PAR
PENDARVES RD
OLD HILL
PENWERRIS LA
MEADOWBANK RD
GLASNEY VILLE
BASSET ST
HIGH ST
GREVILLE RD
JUBILEE RD
PO

TREFUSIS RD

Trefusis
Point

Ferry (P)
Summer only

TR2

Lower
Kergilliack

KERGILLIACK
UNION
CNR
HILLHEAD RD
UNION RD
JAMES ST
ACACIA RD
OAKFIELD RD
TRESCOBEAS RD
DRACAENA AVE
Falmouth

Sch

H

FALMOUTH

Ferry (P)

145

CONWAY RD
Tregoniggie
Ind Est
VEYTON RD
KIMBERLEY PARK RD
PARK RD
KINGS AVE
BERKELEY VALE
GROVE PL
TREVETHAN RD

i
PO

P

PO

P

National Maritime
Mus Cornwall

LB
Sta

Falmouth
Docks

Bickland Hill
Bickland
Ind Est
LONGFIELD
SHELBOURNE RD
MONGLEATH RD
TREGENVER RD
ALBANY RD
TRELAWNEY RD
WOODHOUSE TERR
FOX'S
KILLIGREW ST
MARLBOROUGH RD

Mongleath

Schs
Bsns
Pk
QUEEN ANNE
Penmere
BOSLOWICK RD
HILLSIDE RD

Swanvale

THEYDON RD

WESTERN TERR

Falmouth
Town

Sch

Coll

P

P

Falmouth
Docks

L Ctr

SCHOOL LA

PH
Budock
Water

TR11

Menehay

PH

PO

Boslowick

Sch Cemy

SPERNEN WYN RD
TRURONIA CRES
BOSCAWEN RD
DRACAENA AVE

Cemy

MELVILL RD

EMSLIE RD
BAR RD
CLIFF RD
CASTLE DR

A39

P

P

P

P

Pendennis
Castle

P

144

Hotel

ROSCARRACK RD

SWANPOOL RD

CH

93

Swan
Pool

MAGFIRA WLK
SWANPOOL RD

Gyllyngvase
Beach

South West
Coast Path
Swanpool
Point

Pendennis
Point

PENWERRIS HILL
PENNANCE HILL

MAEN VALLEY
PK

Trelevra
Farm

TWINBROOK
PK

Swanpool
Beach

Hotel

Tregedna

Penrose

Pennance
Farm

Pennance
Point

Rosemerryn
Farm

South West Coast Path

Newport
Head

Falmouth Bay

CARLIDNACK RD

MAENPORTH
EST

P

Maenporth

Carlidnack

High Cliff

MAENPORTH RD
TRELAWNE
CL

CARLIDNACK LA

**Mawnan
Smith**

Hotel

The Hutches

Bream
Cove

CARWINION RD

Carwinion
Bamboo Gdn

78   A   79   B   80   C   81   D   82   E   83   F

8
35
7
34
6
33
5
32
4
31
3
30
2
29
1
28

Scale: 1¾ inches to 1 mile

0   ¼   ½ mile
0 250m 500m 750m 1 km

82

83

A B C D E F

Messack Point

St Just Pool

Trethewell

Lanhay

Tregassa

Porthcurnick Beach

Pednvadan

1 ADMIRALTY TERR
2 SPRINGFIELD
3 PARC MERYS
4 HARBOUR CT FLATS
5 SUNNYSIDE
6 RIVER ST
7 THE SQUARE
8 VICTORIA TERR
9 HIGHERTOWN
10 CLIFTON TERR
11 TREVENTON CL
12 CALIFORNIA GDNS
13 THE SQUARE

WINDMILL HILL

CHAPEL CL

B3289

HARBOUR VIEW
BOWLING GN

A3078

St Just in Roseland

PARC-AN-DILLON RD

TREVENTON RD

NORTH PAR

Portscatho

THE QUAY

Gerrans

THE LUGGER

Gerrans Parish Hall Ctr Hotel

Pencabe

PORTH SAWLE FLATS

Trevennel Farm

Trewollack

Gerrans Prim Sch

8

35

Tregear Vean

Bosloggas

Tregassick

CHURCH HILL

Treloan

TRELOAN LA

TREGASSICK RD

GERRANS HILL

WELLINGTON TERR

Treloan

7

Water Twr

ROSELAND FLATS

82

TR2

Percuil

South West Coast Path

34

St Mawes

UPPER CASTLE RD

POLVARTH RD

WATERLOO

NEWTON RD

1 PORTH VIEW
2 PERCUIL VIEW
3 PEN BREA CL

POLVARTH EST

FENWHAM LA

Trewince

TREWINCE MANOR

Rosteague

Greeb Point

83

6

St Mawes Prim Sch

A3078

TREBARTHA

PROWSE

GRVE

CARRICK WAY

FRESHWATER LA

PEN-MORVAH

HILLSIDE

Quay

Froe

33

St Mawes Castle

RIVIERA

LOWER CASTLE RD

MARINE PAR

THE QUAY

TREDENHAM RD

PO

Ferry P (summer only)

St Mawes Harbour

Porth Farm

Towan Beach

5

Castle Point

Carricknath Point

St Anthony

Bohortha

Killigerran Head

32

A6
1 MANOR CT
2 ST AUSTELL ROW
3 THE SQUARE
4 KINGS RD
5 COMMERCIAL RD
6 GIBRALTAR TERR
7 CHURCH HILL
8 PEN-EGLOS
9 THE ROPE WLK
10 CHAPEL TERR
11 SEA VIEW CRES
12 SEA VIEW RD
13 NEWTON PK
14 HANCOCK LA
15 PLACE VIEW RD
16 KENNERLEY TERR
17 BROOKLYN TERR
18 BROOKLYN FLATS
19 BEECH HALL FLATS
20 BOHELLA RD

Place House

Porthbeer Beach

Porthmellin Head

4

St Anthony Head

Place Barton

MILITARY RD

31

Zone Point

3

30

2

29

1

28

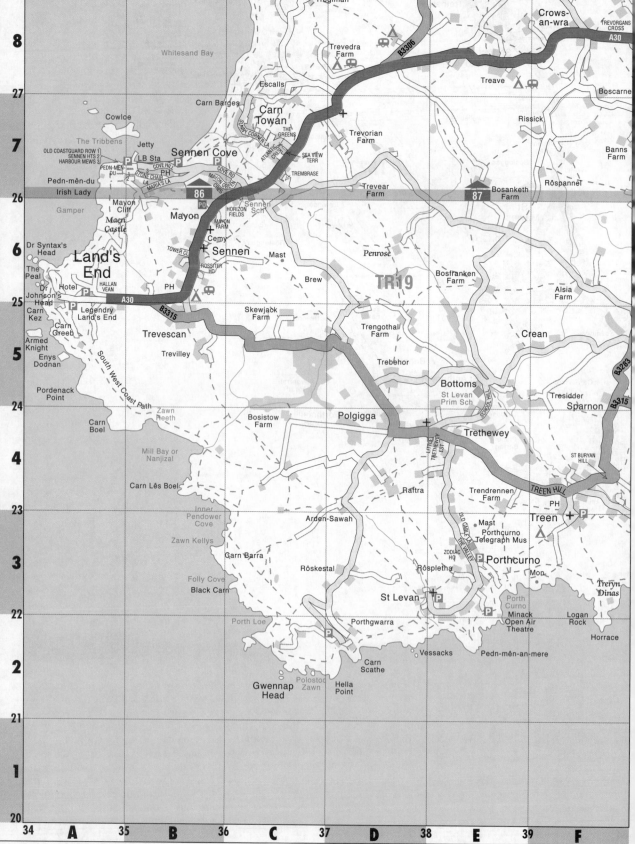

Scale: 1¾ inches to 1 mile

0   ¼   ½ mile

0   250m 500m 750m 1 km

A   B   C   D   E   F

8

27

7

26

6

25

5

24

4

23

3

22

2

21

1

20

Tregiffian

Crows-an-wra

TREVORGANS CROSS

A30

Whitesand Bay

Trevedra Farm

B3306

Treave

Boscarne

Escalls

Carn Barges

Carn Towan

THE GREENS

Trevorian Farm

Rissick

Banns Farm

Cowlce

The Tribbens

Jetty

Sennen Cove

OLD COASTGUARD ROW 1
SENNEN HTS 2
HARBOUR MEWS 3

LB Sta

PEDN-MEN-DU

PH

ATLANTIC CREST

SLAPY CORNER LA

SEA VIEW TERR

Trevear Farm

Bosanketh Farm

Rôspannel

COVE HILL

ZONE CHAIR LA

COVE RD

MAYON GREEN

MARIA'S LA

MAYON CRES

TREMBRASE

Pedn-mên-du

86

P.O.

87

Irish Lady

Gamper

Mayon Cliff

Mayon

HORIZON FIELDS

Sennen Sch

Maen Castle

MAYON FARM

Dr Syntax's Head

Land's End

TOWER CL

Cemy

Sennen

Mast

Penrose

Bosfranken Farm

The Peal

Dr Johnson's Head

Carn Kez

Hotel

HALLAN VEAN

ROSSITER HD

PH

Brew

TR19

Alsia Farm

Carn Greeb

Legendry Land's End

A30

B3315

Skewjack Farm

Trengothal Farm

Trebehor

Crean

Armed Knight

Trevescan

Trevilley

Trebehor

B3283

Enys Dodnan

South West Coast Path

Zawn Reeth

Bosistow Farm

Polgigga

Bottoms

St Levan Prim Sch

Tresidder

Sparnon

B3315

Pordenack Point

Carn Boel

Trethewey

SCHOOL HILL

ST BURYAN HILL

Carn Lês Boel

Mill Bay or Nanjizal

LITTLE TRETHEWEY EST

Trendrennen Farm

TREEN HILL

PH

Inner Pendower Cove

Raftra

Arden-Sawah

Mast

Treen

Zawn Kellys

Carn Barra

Rôskestal

Rôspletha

Porthcurno Telegraph Mus

Treryn Dinas

Folly Cove

Black Carn

ZODIAC HQ

THE VALLEY

OLD CABLE LA

Porthcurno

Mon

St Levan

Porth Curno

Logan Rock

Porth Loe

Porthgwarra

Minack Open Air Theatre

Horrace

Gwennap Head

Polostoc Zawn

Hella Point

Carn Scathe

Vessacks

Pedn-mên-an-mere

34   A   35   B   36   C   37   D   38   E   39   F

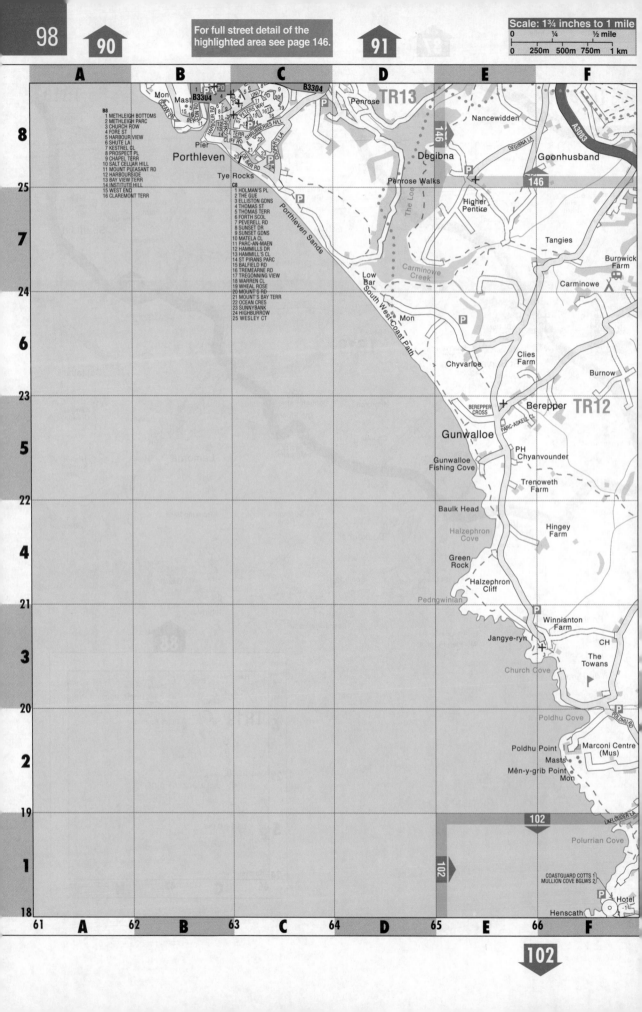

A   B   C   D   E   F

B8
1 METHLEIGH BOTTOMS
2 METHLEIGH PARC
3 CHURCH ROW
4 FORE ST
5 HARBOUR VIEW
6 SHUTE LA
7 KESTREL CL
8 PROSPECT PL
9 CHAPEL TERR
10 SALT CELLAR HILL
11 MOUNT PLEASANT RD
12 HARBOURSIDE
13 BAY VIEW TERR
14 INSTITUTE HILL
15 WEST END
16 CLAREMONT TERR

C8
1 HOLMAN'S PL
2 THE GUE
3 ELLISTON GDNS
4 THOMAS ST
5 THOMAS TERR
6 FORTH SCOL
7 PEVERELL RD
8 SUNSET DR
9 SUNSET GDNS
10 MATELA CL
11 PARC-AN-MAEN
12 HAMMILLS DR
13 HAMMILL'S CL
14 ST PIRANS PARC
15 BALFIELD RD
16 TREMEARNE RD
17 TREGONNING VIEW
18 WARREN CL
19 WHEAL ROSE
20 MOUNT'S RD
21 MOUNT'S BAY TERR
22 OCEAN CRES
23 SUNNYBANK
24 HIGHBURROW
25 WESLEY CT

Mon   Mast   B3304   PO   UNITY RD   B3304   Penrose   TR13
ST PETERS WAY   Nancewidden
Pier   Porthleven   Degibna   Goonhusband
Tye Rocks   Penrose Walks
Porthleven Sands   Higher Pentire   DEGIBNA LA   146   A3083
The Loe   Tangies
Carminowe Creek   Burnwick Farm
Low Bar   Carminowe
South West Coast Path   Mon   Clies Farm   Burnow
Chyvarloe   Berepper Cross   Berepper   TR12
Gunwalloe   PARC-ASKELL CL   PH   Chyanvounder
Gunwalloe Fishing Cove   Trenoweth Farm
Baulk Head   Hingey Farm
Halzephron Cove
Green Rock   Halzephron Cliff
Pedngwinian   Winnianton Farm
Jangye-ryn   CH   The Towans
Church Cove
Poldhu Cove
Poldhu Point   Marconi Centre (Mus)
Masts
Mên-y-grib Point   Mon
102   Polurrian Cove
102   LAFLOUDER LA
COASTGUARD COTTS 1
MULLION COVE BGLWS 2
Henscath   Hotel

61   A   62   B   63   C   64   D   65   E   66   F

102

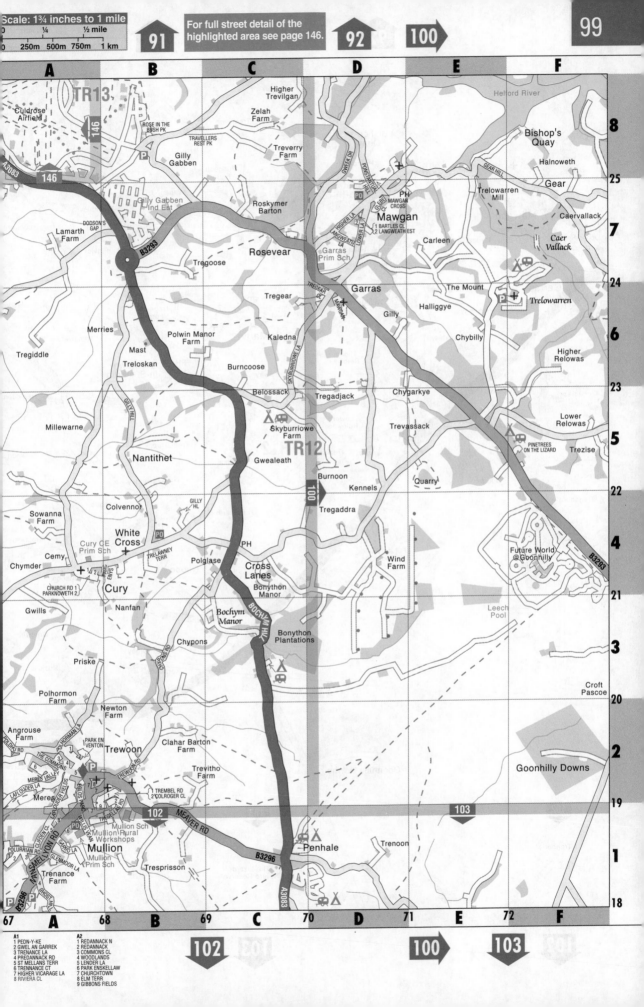

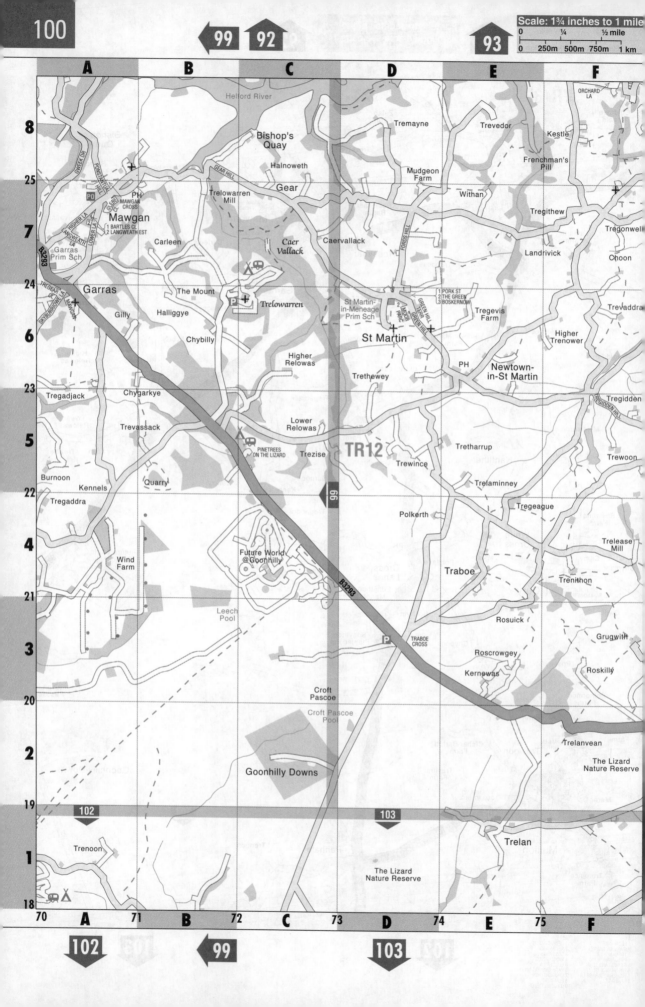

Scale: 1¾ inches to 1 mile
0   ¼   ½ mile
0 250m 500m 750m 1 km

A   B   C   D   E   F

8

ORCHARD LA

Helford River

Bishop's Quay

Tremayne

Trevedor

Kestle

Frenchman's Pill

25

Halnoweth

Gear Hill

Gear

Mudgeon Farm

Withan

Tregithew

PO

Trelowarren Mill

PH

MAWGAN CROSS

Mawgan

1 BARTLES CL
2 LANGWEATH EST

Landrivick

Tregonwell

7

Carleen

Caer Vallack

Caervallack

FORDS HILL

Choon

Garras Prim Sch

B3293

24

Garras

The Mount

Gilly

Halliggye

P

Trelowarren

St Martin-in-Meneage Prim Sch

1 PORK ST
2 THE GREEN
3 BOSKERNOW

Tregevis Farm

Trevaddra

GREEN HILL

Higher Trenower

6

Chybilly

St Martin

PH

Newtown-in-St Martin

Higher Relowas

Trethewey

23

Tregadjack

Chygarkye

Lower Relowas

Tretharrup

TREGIDDEN HILL

Tregidden

5

Trevassack

Trezise

TR12

Trewince

Trelaminney

Trewoon

Burnoon

Kennels

Quarry

PINETREES ON THE LIZARD

Trezise

99

Tregeague

Trelease Mill

22

Tregaddra

Polkerth

4

Wind Farm

Future World @Goonhilly

B3293

Traboe

Trenithon

21

Leech Pool

Rosuick

Grugwith

3

P

TRABOE CROSS

Roscrowgey

Roskilly

Kernewas

Croft Pascoe

20

Croft Pascoe Pool

Trelanvean

The Lizard Nature Reserve

2

Goonhilly Downs

19

102
103

Trelan

1

Trenoon

The Lizard Nature Reserve

18

70   A   71   B   72   C   73   D   74   E   75   F

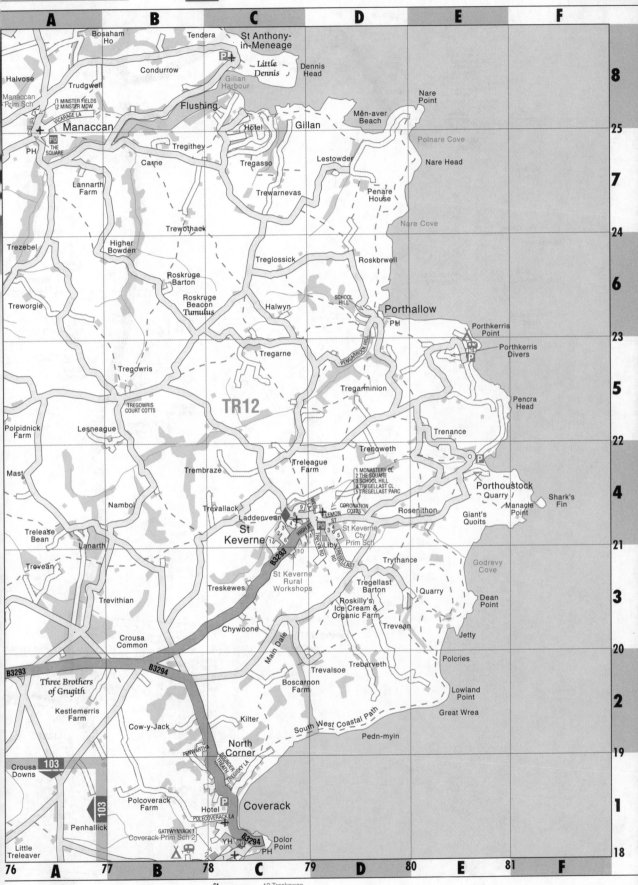

A   B   C   D   E   F

Halvose
Bosaham Ho
Tendera
St Anthony-in-Meneage
Trudgwell
Condurrow
Little Dennis
Dennis Head
8
Manaccan Prim Sch
1 MINSTER FIELDS
2 MINSTER MDW
VICARAGE LA
Flushing
Gillan Harbour
Gillan
Mên-aver Beach
Nare Point
Manaccan
PO THE SQUARE
PH
Tregithey
Hotel
25
Carne
Tregasso
Lestowder
Polnare Cove
Lannarth Farm
Trewarnevas
Penare House
Nare Head
7
Trewothack
Nare Cove
Trezebel
Higher Bowden
Treglossick
Roskorwell
24
Roskruge Barton
Halwyn
SCHOOL HILL
Porthallow
6
Treworgie
Roskruge Beacon Tumulus
PH
Porthkerris Point
Tregowris
Tregarne
PENGARROCK HILL
Porthkerris Divers
23
Polpidnick Farm
Lesneague
TR12
Tregarminion
Pencra Head
5
TREGOWRIS COURT COTTS
Trenance
Mast
Trembraze
Treleague Farm
Trenoweth
22
Nambol
1 MONASTERY CL
2 THE SQUARE
3 SCHOOL HILL
4 TREGELLAST CL
5 TREGELLAST PARC
Porthoustock
Quarry
Shark's Fin
4
Trevallack
CORONATION COTTS
Rosenithon
Giant's Quoits
Manacle Point
Trelease Bean
Laddenvean
St Keverne
HIGH ST
St Keverne Cty Prim Sch
21
Lanarth
PO
B3293
Godrevy Cove
Trevean
St Keverne Rural Workshops
Trythance
Dean Point
3
Trevithian
Treskewes
Tregellast Barton
Quarry
Chywoone
Roskilly's Ice Cream & Organic Farm
Trevean
Jetty
Crousa Common
Main Dale
20
B3293
B3294
Trevalsoe
Trebarveth
Polcries
Three Brothers of Grugith
Boscarnon Farm
Lowland Point
2
Kestlemerris Farm
Cow-y-Jack
Kilter
South West Coastal Path
Pedn-myin
Great Wrea
19
Crousa Downs
103
North Corner
PENWARTHA
BEMMICK TREATH
TREGISKY LA
1
103
Polcoverack Farm
Hotel
Coverack
Penhallick
GATEWYNNYACK 1
Coverack Prim Sch 2
POLCOVERACK LA
YH PO
B3294
Dolor Point
PH
Little Treleaver
18

76   A   77   B   78   C   79   D   80   E   81   F

C4
1 TRESKEWES EST
2 TREVALLACK VIEW
3 TREVALLACK PARC
4 LANHEVERNE PARC
5 DOCTORS HILL
6 POLVENTON PARC
7 PENMENNER EST
8 COMMERCIAL RD
9 TREGONNING PARC

10 Treskewes Ind Est

Scale: 1¾ inches to 1 mile

0 ¼ ½ mile
0 250m 500m 750m 1 km

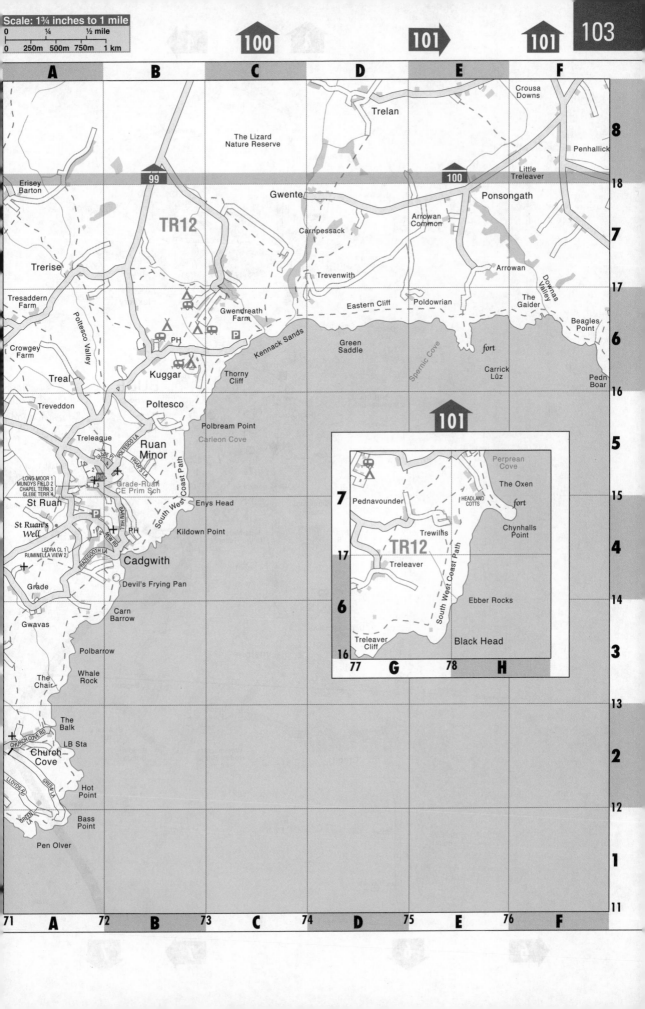

A B C D E F

8

Crousa Downs

The Lizard Nature Reserve

Trelan

Penhallick

99 100

Little Treleaver

18

Erisey Barton

Gwente

Ponsongath

7

TR12

Carnpessack

Arrowan Common

Trerise

Arrowan

17

Tresaddern Farm

Trevenwith

Eastern Cliff

Poldowrian

The Gaider

Downas Valley

Beagles Point

6

Crowgey Farm

Poltesco Valley

PH

Gwendreath Farm

P

Kennack Sands

Green Saddle

Spernic Cove

fort

Carrick Lûz

Pedn Boar

Treal

Kuggar

Thorny Cliff

16

Treveddon

Poltesco

Polbream Point

Treleague

Carleon Cove

5

POLTESCO LA

Ruan Minor

GLEBE PL
TRUAN LA

LONG MOOR 1
MUNDYS FIELD 2
CHAPEL TERR 3
GLEBE TERR 4

PO

Grade-Ruan CE Prim Sch

South West Coast Path

Enys Head

101

15

BARN HILL
KEW RD

P

St Ruan

PH

St Ruan's Well

LEDRA CL 1
RUMINELLA VIEW 2

PRAZEGOOTH LA

Cadgwith

Kildown Point

4

Grade

Devil's Frying Pan

14

Gwavas

Carn Barrow

13

Polbarrow

The Chair

Whale Rock

The Balk

13

Church Cove RD

LB Sta

2

GREEN LA

Church Cove

LLOYDS RD

Hot Point

Bass Point

12

Pen Olver

1

11

71 A 72 B 73 C 74 D 75 E 76 F

Inset map:

101

Perprean Cove

7

Pednavounder

HEADLAND COTTS

The Oxen

fort

17

TR12

Trewillis

15

Treleaver

Chynhalls Point

6

South West Coast Path

Ebber Rocks

14

16

Treleaver Cliff

Black Head

3

77 G 78 H

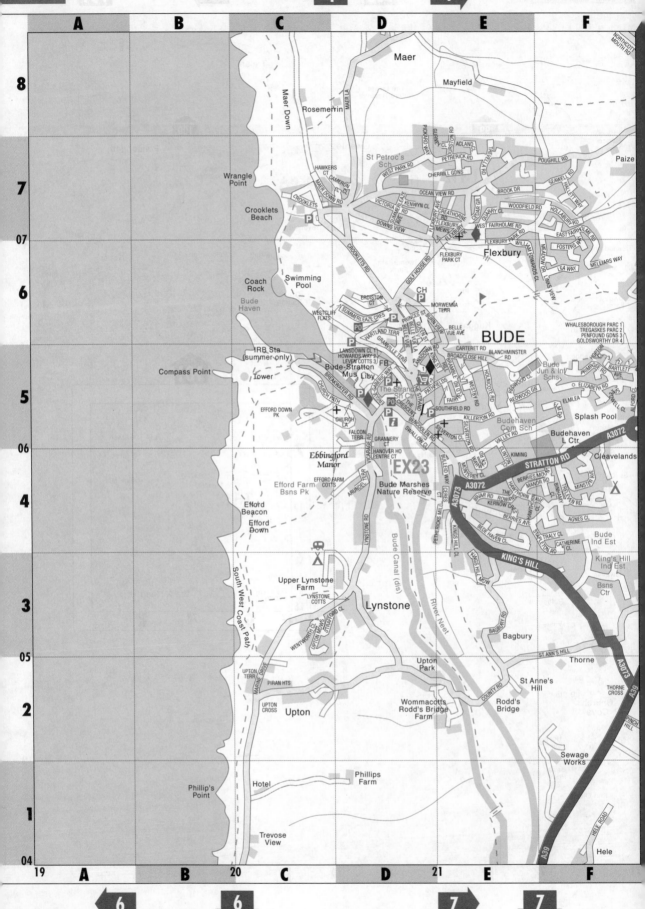

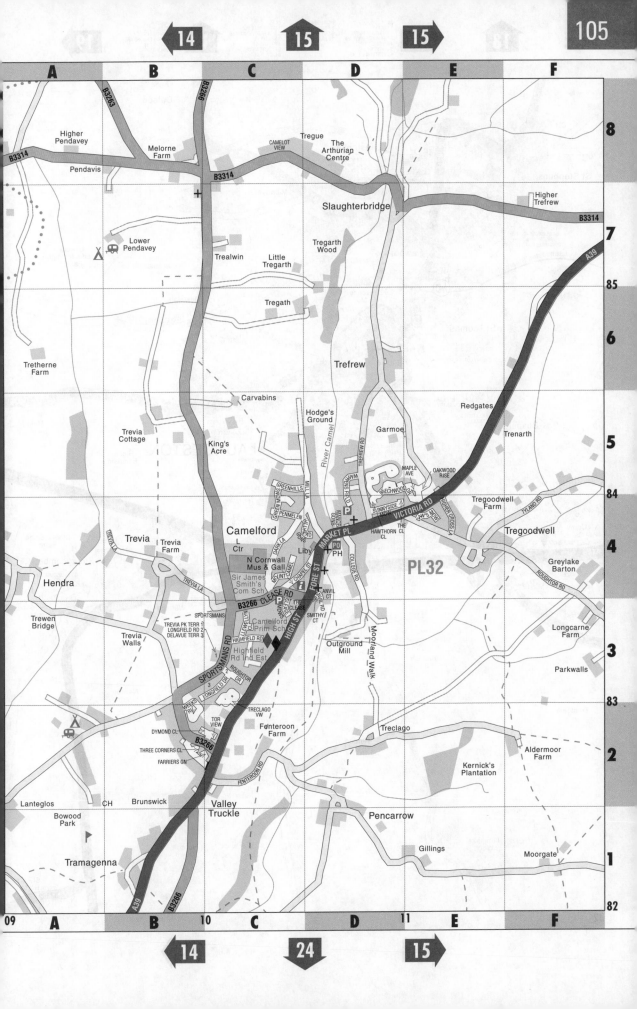

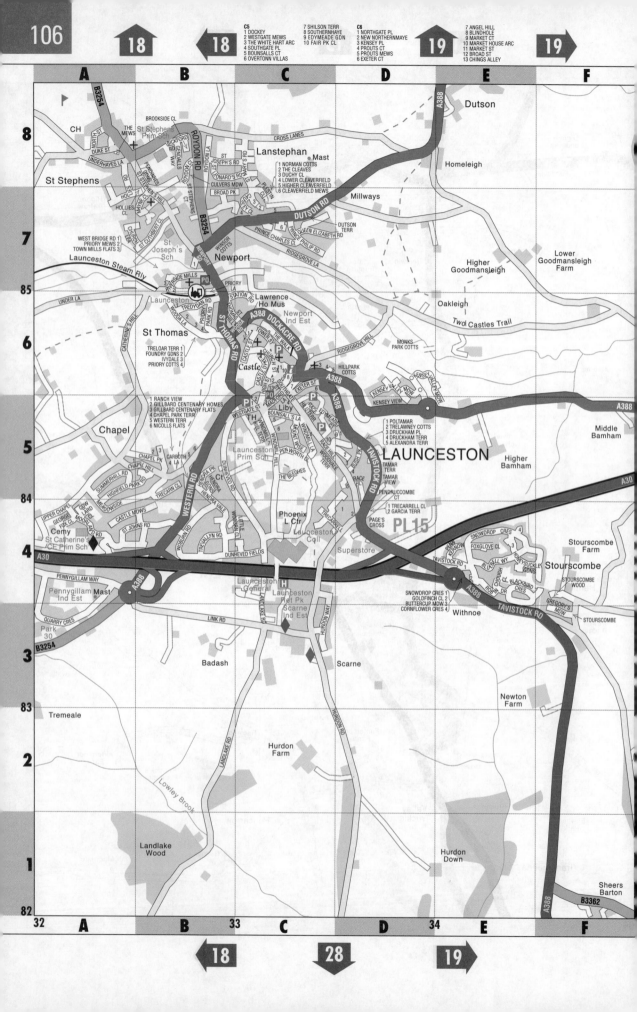

A   B   C   D   E   F

8

Gun Point

South West Coast Path

Crugmeer

St George's Well

Tregirls Farm

7

PL27

South West Coast Path

76

Meml

Ferry P (Low Water)

Trethillick

6

Ferry P (High Water)

IRB Sta

Prideaux Place

PL28

1 NORTH QUAY PAR
2 WATERS EDGE
3 THE OLD BOAT-YARD

National Lobster Hatchery

River Camel

FENTONLUNA LA

ST SAVIOUR'S LA

Cemy

HIGH ST

CHURCH ST

DUKE ST

1 OLD SCHOOL CT
2 ST EDMUNDS LA
3 COACHYARD MEWS
4 COMMERCIAL TERR
5 AVERY S ROW
6 STRAND ST
7 BROAD ST
8 CHAPEL CT
9 LANADWELL ST
10 MARKET PL
11 MARKET STRAND
12 MILL SQ
13 MIDDLE ST
14 ALMA PL
15 BARRY S LA
16 RUTHY S LA
17 CROSS ST

5

B3276

A389

CHURCH LA

Mus
Liby

Treator Cotts

ST PETROCS MDW

Treator

B3276

P

Trecerus Ind Est

HAWKINS RD

RALEIGH RD

DRAKE RD

SARAH'S CL

LODENEK AVE

DENNIS RD

ALAN RD

CAMEL CL

SCHOOL HILL

NEW ST

STATION RD

TREVORRYN RD

Padstow Harbour Ind Est

75

Padstow Workshop Units

B3276

GREWVILLE RD

PELLEW CL

Padstow Sch

SARAH'S LA

NETHER

TRELAWNEY RD

MOYLE RD

EGERTON RD

PORTHILLY VIEW

Town Bar

4

PADSTOW

Dinas

SARAH'S VIEW

ANNETHY LOWEN

DENNIS LA

MEADOW CT

SARAH'S MDW

LITTLE DINAS

Camel Trail

3

Dennis Hill

Obelisk

74

Tregella

Trerethern

Little Petherick Creek

2

Saints Way

Sea Mills

Tregonce

A389

Benuick

Treravel Farm

Trevorrick

PL27

1

73

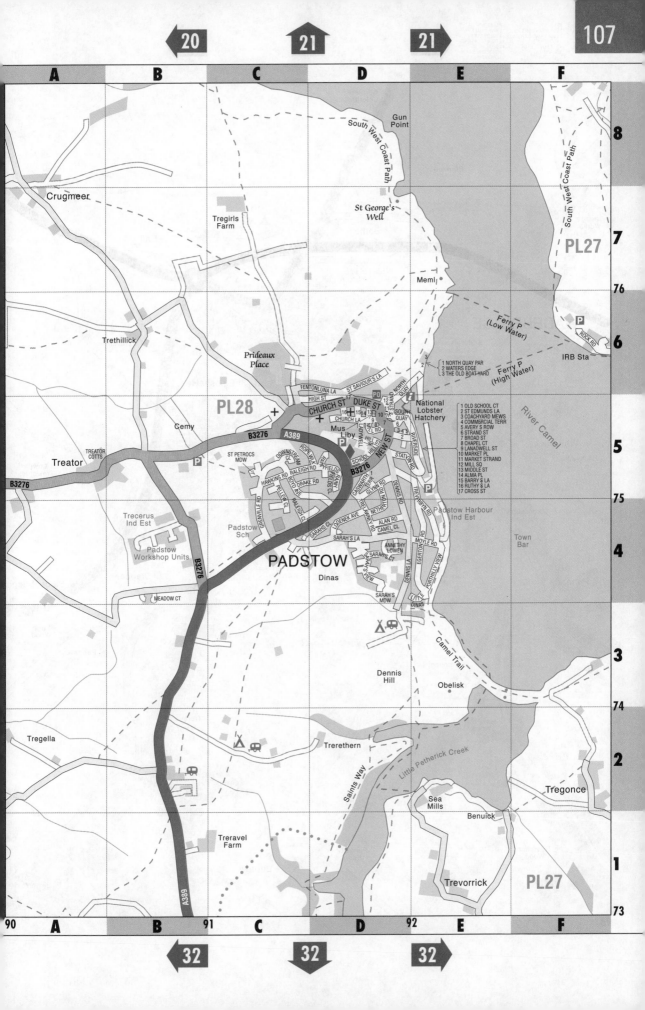

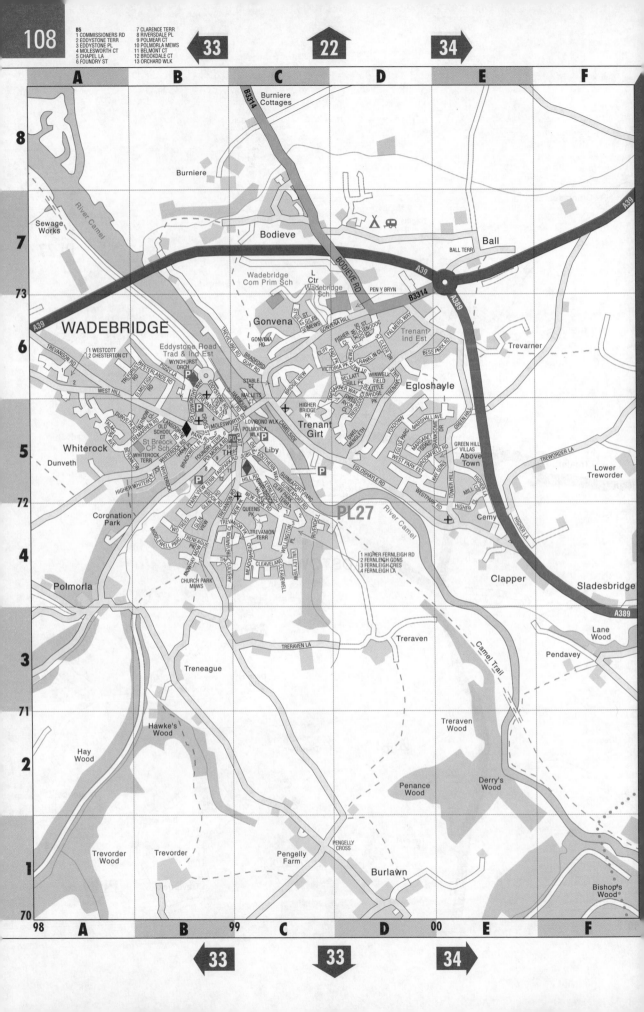

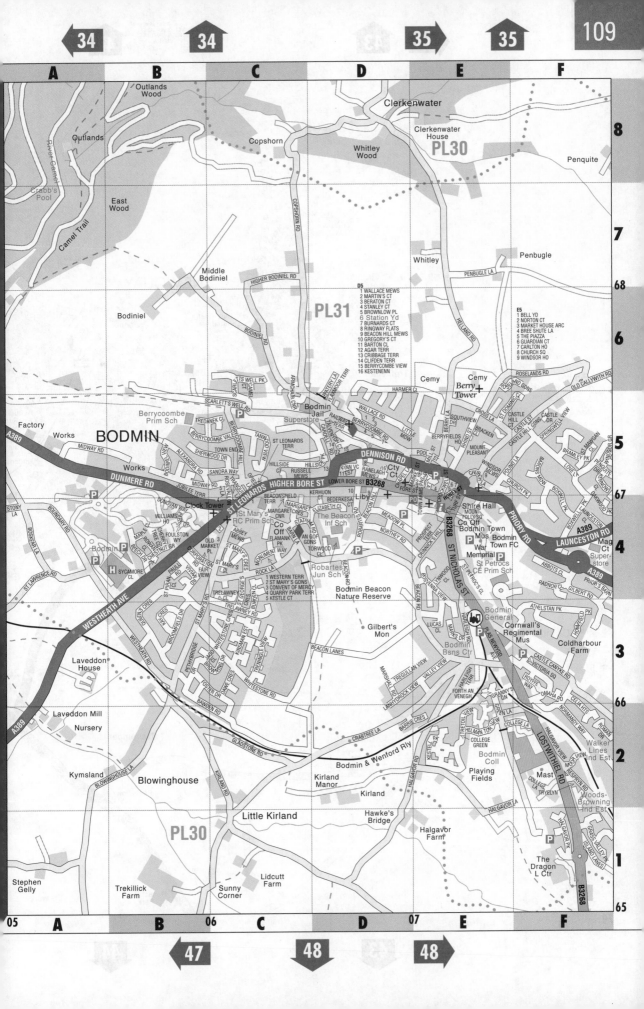

A   B   C   D   E   F

8

Clerkenwater

Outlands Wood

Copshorn   Whitley Wood   Clerkenwater House   PL30   Penquite

Outlands

Crabb's Pool

East Wood

Camel Trail

7

HIGHER BODINIEL RD

Whitley   Penbugle

PENBUGLE LA

68

Middle Bodiniel

PL31

6

Bodiniel

BODINIEL RD

COPSHORN RD

ARMCHAIR CNR

D5
1 WALLACE MEWS
2 MARTIN'S CT
3 BERATON CT
4 STANLEY CT
5 BROWNLOW PL
6 Station Yd
7 BURNARDS CT
8 RINGWAY FLATS
9 BEACON HILL MEWS
10 GREGORY'S CT
11 BARTON CL
12 AGAR TERR
13 CRIBBAGE TERR
14 CLIFDEN TERR
15 BERRYCOOMBE VIEW
16 KESTENENN

E5
1 BELL YD
2 NORTON CT
3 MARKET HOUSE ARC
4 BREE SHUTE LA
5 THE PIAZZA
6 GUARDIAN CT
7 CARLTON HO
8 CHURCH SQ
9 WINDSOR HO

Cemy   Cemy   Berry Tower

ROSELANDS RD
OLD CALLYWITH RD

Berrycoombe Prim Sch

SCARLETT'S WELL PK

Bodmin Jail Superstore   HARMER CL

WALLACE RD

5

BODMIN

Factory   Works

A389

Works

MIDWAY RD   DUNMERE RD

St Leonards Terr   ST LEONARDS   HIGHER BORE ST   DENNISON RD   B3268

67

Lower Bore St

Clock Tower   St Mary's RC Prim Sch   Liby

Cty Ct   PO   Shire Hall

4

Bodmin   H   SYCAMORE CL   Co Off

St Lawrence Rd   Old Market   The Beacon Inf Sch   Co Off   Bodmin Town Mus   Bodmin Town FC   Mag Ct

War Memorial   St Petrocs CE Prim Sch   Super-store

A389   LAUNCESTON RD   A389

PRIORY RD

Robartes Jun Sch   PRIOR'S BARN

Bodmin Beacon Nature Reserve

1 WESTERN TERR
2 ST MARY'S GDNS
3 CONVENT OF MERCY
4 QUARRY PARK TERR
5 KESTLE CT

Gilbert's Mon   RADNOR CL

ATHELSTAN PK

3

WESTHEATH AVE

Bodmin General   Cornwall's Regimental Mus   Coldharbour Farm

Laveddon House   Bodmin Bsns Ctr

VICTORIA SQ

Laveddon Mill Nursery   BEACON LANES

CRABTREE LA   Bodmin & Wenford Rly   College Green   Bodmin Coll   Playing Fields

HALGAVOR RD   LOSTWITHIEL RD

66

2

Kymsland   Blowinghouse   Kirland Manor   Kirland   Hawke's Bridge

BLOWINGHOUSE LA   KIRLAND RD   GLADSTONE RD

College La   Tryelyn   Woods-Browning Ind Est

Mast

PL30   Little Kirland   Halgavor Farm   The Dragon L Ctr

1

Stephen Gelly   Trekillick Farm   Sunny Corner   Lidcutt Farm

B3268

65

43 43 44

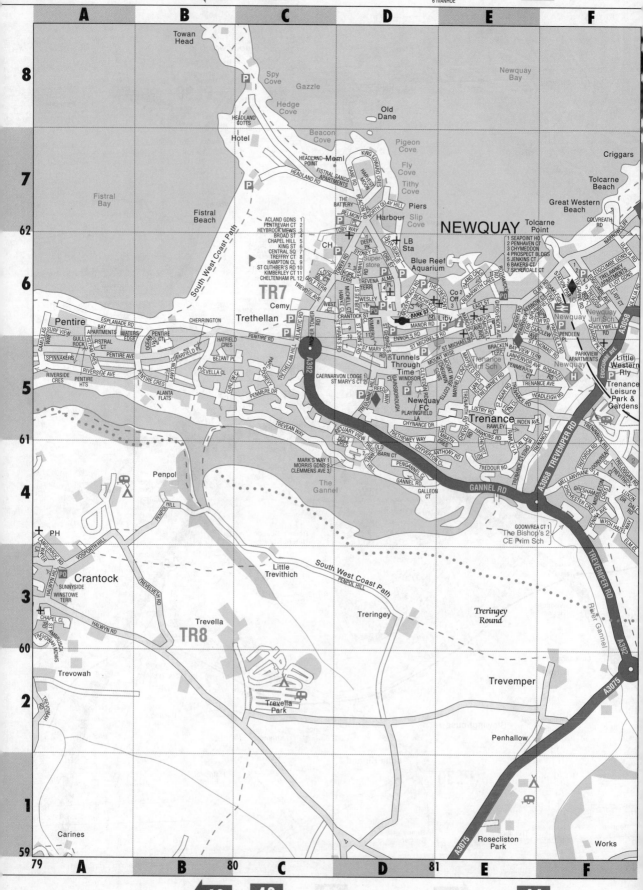

43 43 44

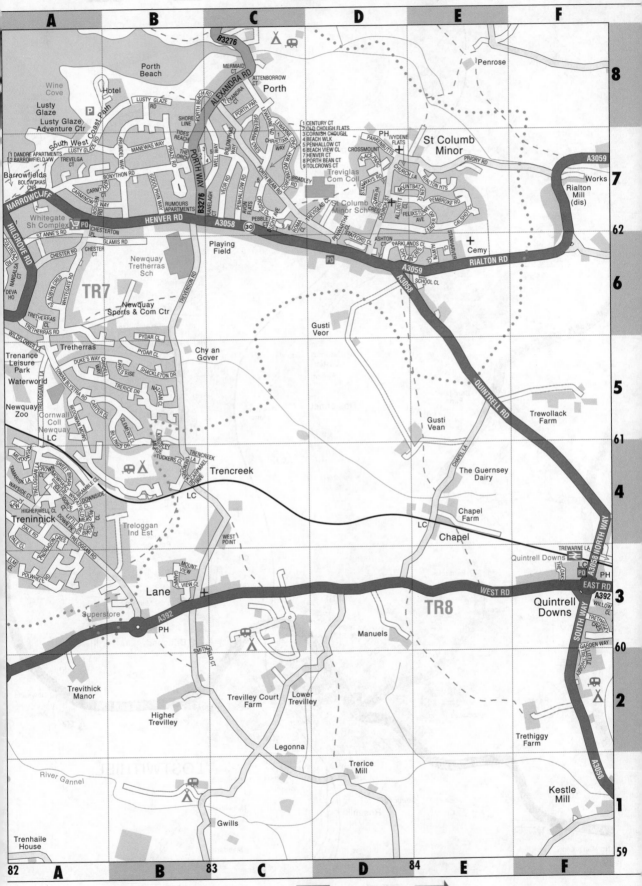

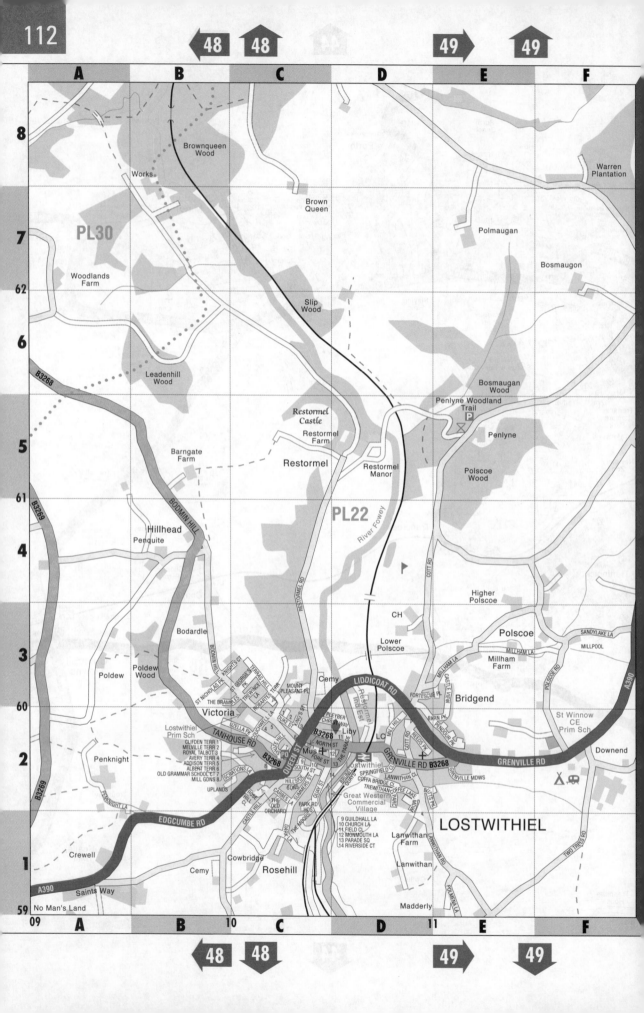

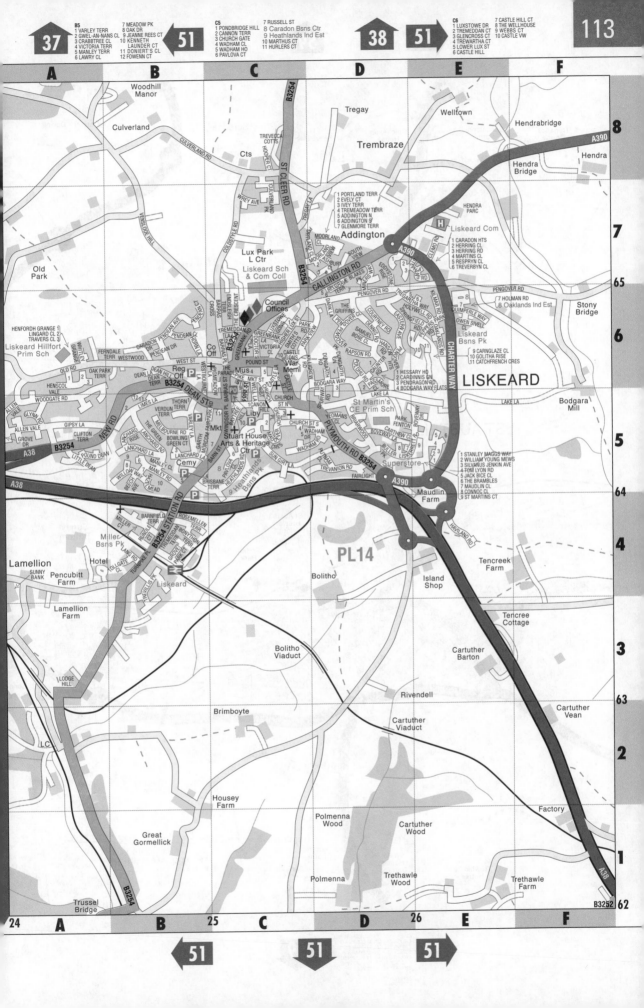

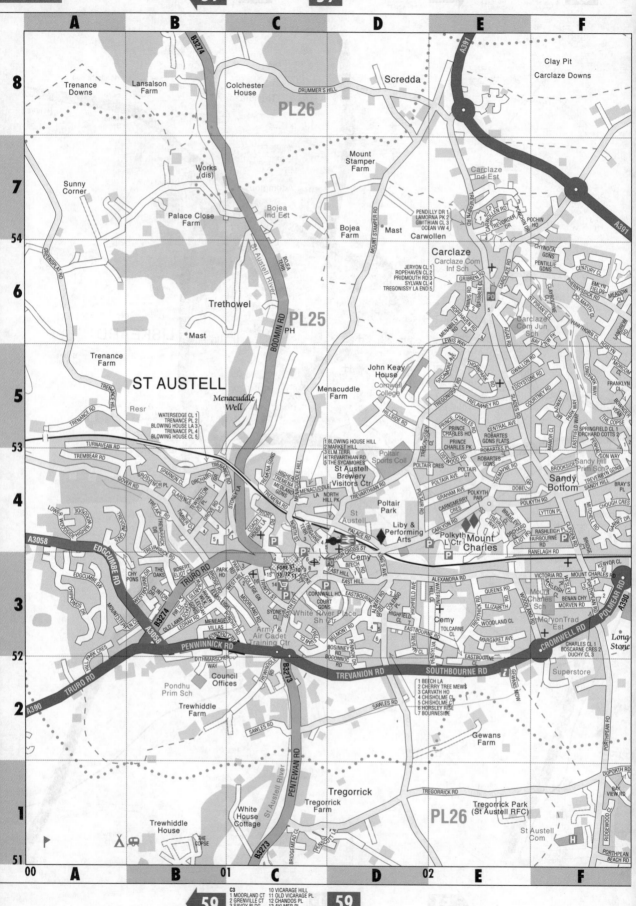

C3
1 MOORLAND CT
2 GRENVILLE CT
3 SAVOY BLDG
4 GRANT'S WLK
5 BIDDICK'S CT
6 MARKET ST
7 CROSS LA
8 CHURCH ST
9 VICTORIA PL
10 VICARAGE HILL
11 OLD VICARAGE PL
12 CHANDOS PL
13 AYLMER PL
14 AYLMER SQ
15 BURTON HO
16 WEST HILL CT

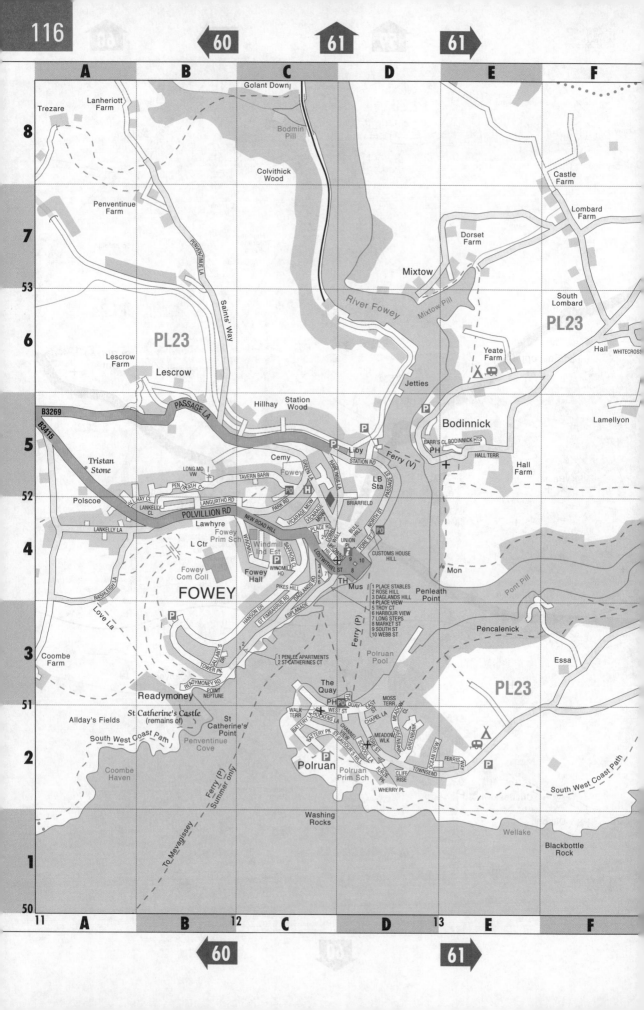

A B C D E F

8
7
53
6
5
52
4
3
51
2
1
50

Trezare
Lanheriott Farm
Golant Down
Bodmin Pill

Colvithick Wood

Penventinue Farm

PENVENTINUE LA

Saints' Way

PL23

River Fowey
Mixtow
Mixtow Pill

Castle Farm
Lombard Farm
Dorset Farm

South Lombard

PL23

Hall
WHITECROSS

Lescrow Farm
Lescrow

Yeate Farm

Lamellyon

Hillhay
Station Wood

Jetties

PASSAGE LA
B3269
B3415

Tristan Stone

Polscoe
PVL HAY CL
LANKELLY CL
LANKELLY LA

LONG MD VW
PEN HEATH CL
LANGURTHO RD

POLVILLION RD
Lawhyre
Fowey Prim Sch
NEW ROAD HILL

L Ctr

Cemy
Fowey
GREEN LA
RAWLINGS LA
Liby
STATION RD
Ferry (V)
LB Sta
PASSAGE

Bodinnick
BARR'S CL BODINNICK HTS
PH
HALL TERR
Hall Farm

Hall Terr

TAVERN BARN
PARK RD
VICARAGE MDW
H
VICARAGE MDW

Briarfield

Mon

WINDMILL
SAFFRON
PLACE RD
Windmill Ind Est
WINDMILL HO

Fowey Com Coll

Fowey Hall

FOWEY

RASKLEIGH LA

Love La

Coombe Farm

HANSON DR
ST FIMBARRUS RD
DAGLANDS RD
PIKES HILL
ESPLANADE

GALLANTS DR
TOWER PK
READYMONEY RD
POINT NEPTUNE
Readymoney

St Catherine's Castle (remains of)

Allday's Fields

South West Coast Path

Coombe Haven

Ferry (P) Summer only

To Mevagissey

St Catherine's Point

Penventinue Cove

CHURCH
BULL HILL
UNION
LOSTWITHIEL ST
NORTH ST
FORE ST
PO
TH
Mus

1 PLACE STABLES
2 ROSE HILL
3 DAGLANDS HILL
4 PLACE VIEW
5 TROY CT
6 HARBOUR VIEW
7 LONG STEPS
8 MARKET ST
9 SOUTH ST
10 WEBB ST

CUSTOMS HOUSE HILL
Penleath Point
Pont Pill

Pencalenick
Essa

1 PENLEE APARTMENTS
2 ST CATHERINES CT

Ferry (P)
Polruan Pool

PL23

The Quay
PH
PO
WEST ST
THE QUAY
EAST ST
MOSS TERR
CHAPEL ST
MEADOW CL
GREENBANK

WALK TERR
HOCKENS LA
ST SAVIOUR'S HILL
CHANNEL VIEW
SCHOOL LA
FORE ST
MEADOW WLK
GREENBANK
OCEAN VIEW
FERRIS WAY

BATTERY TERR
BATTERY PK
PRUTE PK
Polruan
Polruan Prim Sch
CLIFF RISE
WHERRY PL
TOWNSEND

Washing Rocks

Wellake

South West Coast Path

Blackbottle Rock

11 A B 12 C D 13 E F

A   B   C   D   E   F

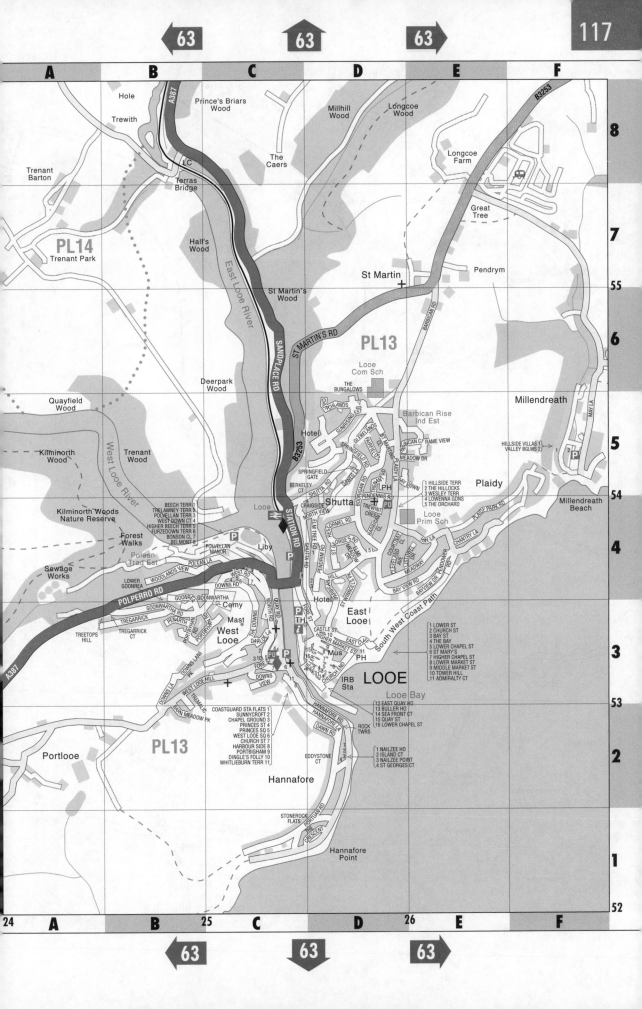

8

7

55

6

PL14
Trenant Park

Hole
Trewith

Trenant
Barton

Prince's Briars
Wood

Millhill
Wood

Longcoe
Wood

LC
Terras
Bridge

The Caers

Longcoe
Farm

Great
Tree

East Looe River

SANDPLACE RD

Hall's
Wood

St Martin's
Wood

St Martin

Pendrym

ST MARTIN'S RD

PL13

Deerpark
Wood

Looe
Com Sch

Millendreath

Quayfield
Wood

West Looe River

Trenant
Wood

B3253

THE BUNGALOWS

HIGHLANDS

Barbican Rise
Ind Est

HILLSIDE VILLAS 1
VALLEY BGLWS 2

Kilminorth
Wood

SUNRISINGS EST

GLEBELANDS

BARBICAN CT RAME VIEW

P

5

54

Kilminorth Woods
Nature Reserve

Forest
Walks

Sewage
Works

Hotel

FAIRFIELDS

SPRINGFIELD RD

ST MARTIN'S RD

TREWINT RD

PLAIDY LA

BAY DOWN

MEADOW DR

Plaidy

Millendreath
Beach

SPRINGFIELD
GATE
BERKELEY
CT

SHUTTA RD

CRAIGSIDE
NORTH VIEW

DANES LA

BARBICAN RD

PH
Shutta

PENDENNIS RD

PO

Looe
Prim Sch

PLAIDY PARK RD

1 HILLSIDE TERR
2 THE HILLOCKS
3 WESLEY TERR
4 LOWENNA GDNS
5 THE ORCHARD

CHANTRY LA

BEECH TERR 1
TRELAWNEY TERR 2
POLVELLAN TERR 3
WEST DOWN CT 4
HIGHER BEECH TERR 5
FURZEDOWN 6
BONSON CL 7
BELMONT 8

Looe
≠

STATION RD

CORMEL RD

COURTENAY
AVE

TRELAWNEY RD
KEYSTONE CL

HRY LA

54

POLVELLAN
MANOR

P

Liby

P

ELM TREE RD

ST GEORGE'S RD

FLAIR
MEADOW

MEADWAY

4

Polean
Trad Est

POLEAN LA

WOODLANDS VIEW

LOWER
GOONREA

POLPERRO RD

DOWNS RD

WEST RD

GOONREA

GOONWARTHA RD

GOONR
CL

GOONWARTHA

PENMARTH

PORTBYHAN

THE DOWNS

NORTH RD

QUAY RD

SHUTTA RD

RICHMOND
HILL

HANNAFORE RD

PRIMROSE
HILL

BAY VIEW RD

BAYVIEW DR PRIDOWER

South West Coast Path

1 LOWER ST
2 CHURCH ST
3 BAY ST
4 THE BAY
5 LOWER CHAPEL ST
6 ST MARY'S
7 HIGHER CHAPEL ST
8 LOWER MARKET ST
9 MIDDLE MARKET ST
10 TOWER HILL
11 ADMIRALTY CT

A387

TREETOPS
HILL

TREGARRICK

TREGARRICK
CT

Mast

West
Looe

Cemy

+

DARLOE LA

FORE ST

CASTLE ST

HIGHER MARKET ST

EAST CLIFF

EAST QUAY

Hotel

East
Looe

3

P

TH
i

Mus

PH

LOOE

53

DOWNS LANE

DOWNS
VIEW

WEST LOOE HILL

TREMAINE

+

FORE ST

CHURCH END

IRB
Sta

Looe Bay

12 EAST QUAY HO
13 BULLER HO
14 SEA FRONT CT
15 QUAY ST
16 LOWER CHAPEL ST

53

DOWNS LA

BARN MEADOW PK

COASTGUARD STA FLATS 1
SUNNYCROFT 2
CHAPEL GROUND 3
PRINCES ST 4
PRINCES SQ 5
WEST LOOE SQ 6
CHURCH ST 7
HARBOUR SIDE 8
PORTBIGHAM 9
DINGLE'S FOLLY 10
WHITLIEBURN TERR 11

HANNAFORE LA

DAWN RD

ROCK
TWRS

EDDYSTONE
CT

1 NAILZEE HO
2 ISLAND CT
3 NAILZEE POINT
4 ST GEORGES CT

2

PL13

Portlooe

Hannafore

STONEROCK
FLATS

PORTUAN RD

THE CRESCENT

Hannafore
Point

1

52

53
40

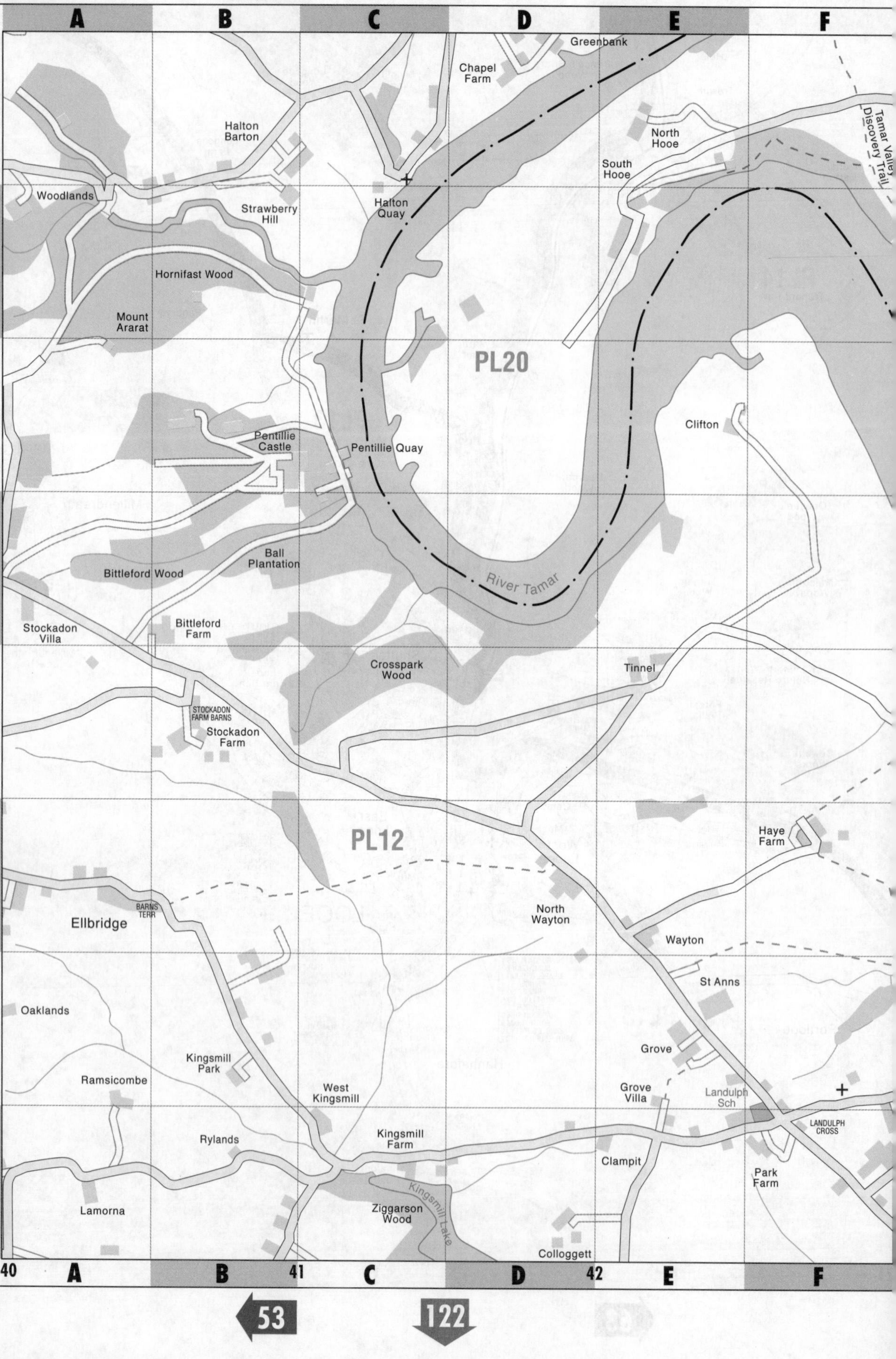
A
B
C
D
E
F
8
7
6
5
4
3
2
1
65
64
63
62
40
41
42
Greenbank
Chapel Farm
Halton Barton
North Hooe
South Hooe
Tamar Valley Discovery Trail
Woodlands
Strawberry Hill
Halton Quay
Hornifast Wood
Mount Ararat
PL20
Clifton
Pentillie Castle
Pentillie Quay
Ball Plantation
Bittleford Wood
River Tamar
Stockadon Villa
Bittleford Farm
Crosspark Wood
Tinnel
STOCKADON FARM BARNS
Stockadon Farm
PL12
Haye Farm
BARNS TERR
Ellbridge
North Wayton
Wayton
St Anns
Oaklands
Grove
Kingsmill Park
Ramsicombe
West Kingsmill
Grove Villa
Landulph Sch
LANDULPH CROSS
Rylands
Kingsmill Farm
Clampit
Park Farm
Kingsmill Lake
Lamorna
Ziggarson Wood
Colloggett

53
122

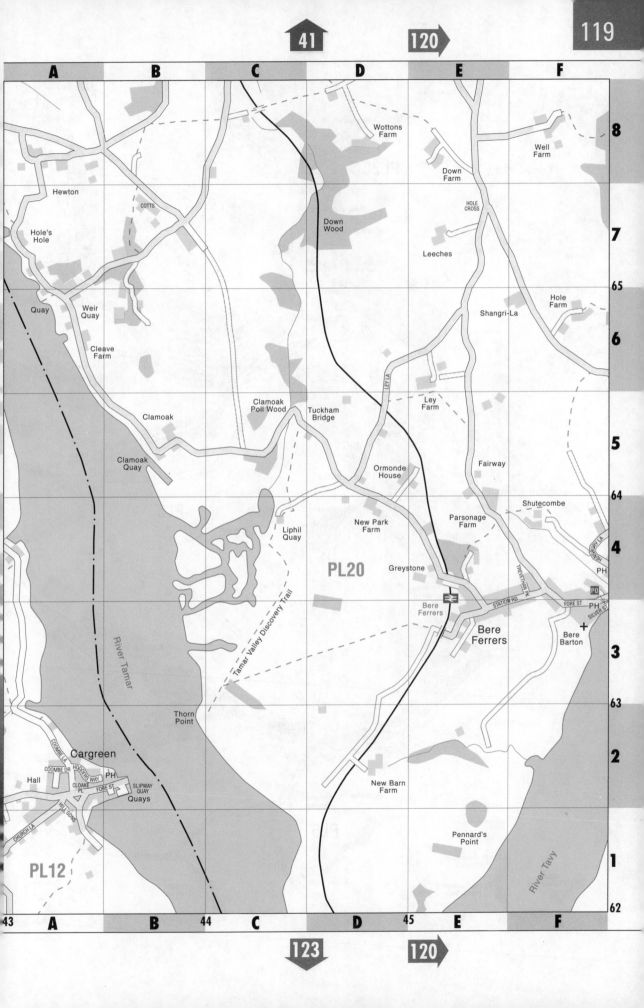

119 41

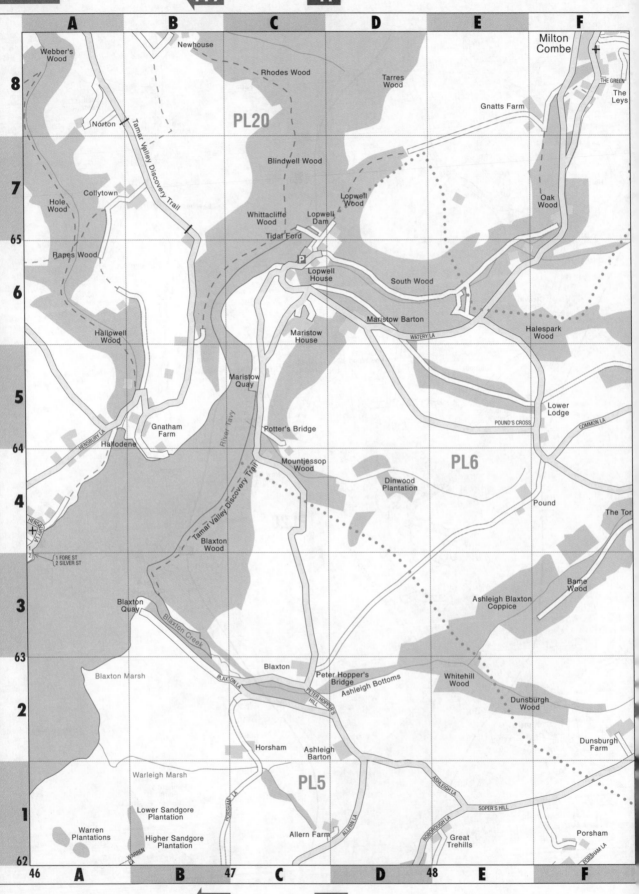

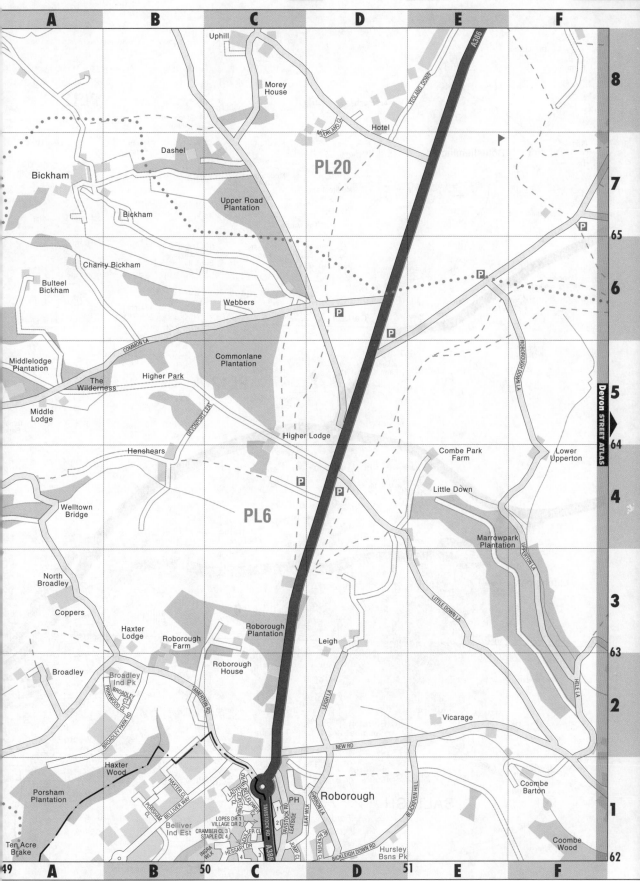

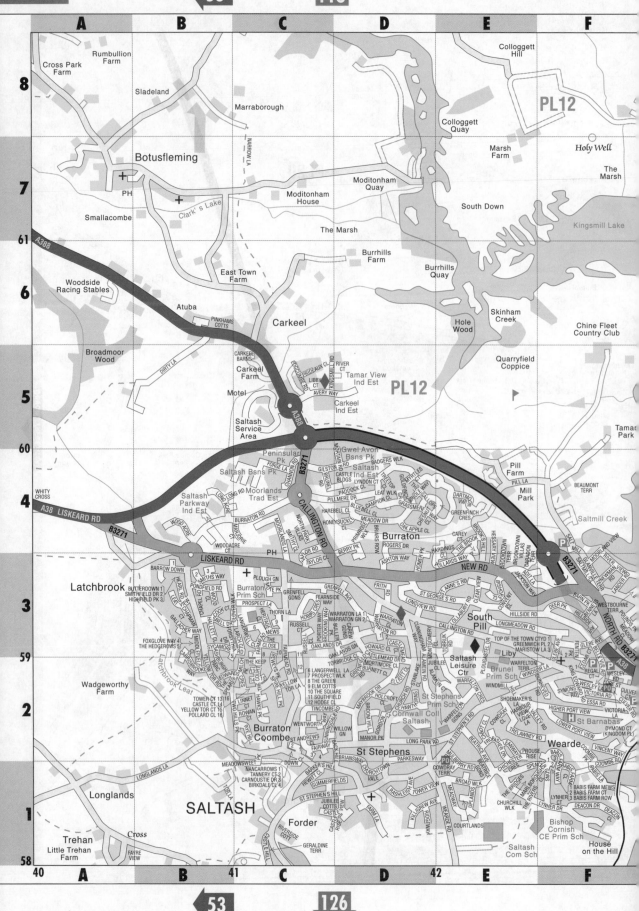

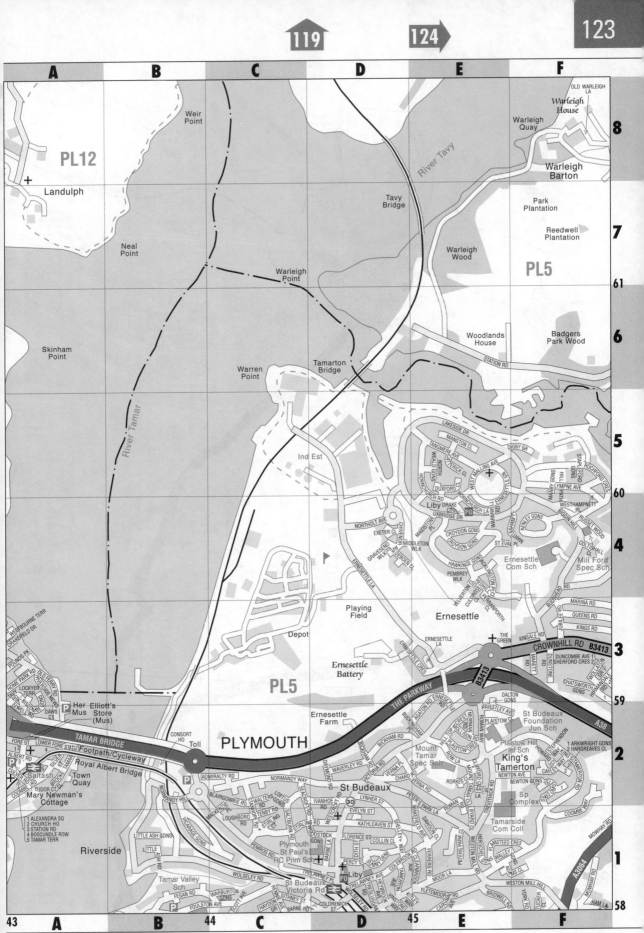

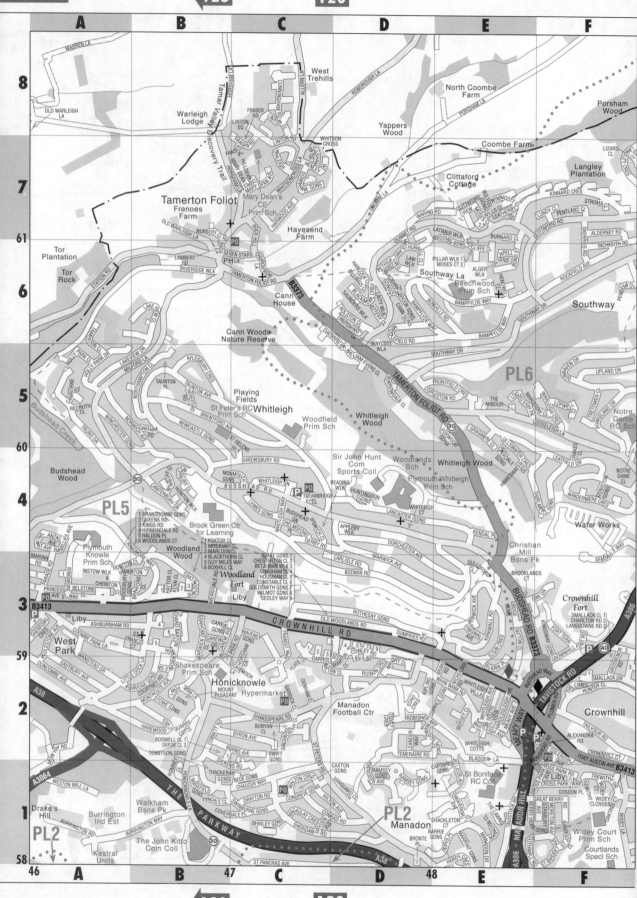

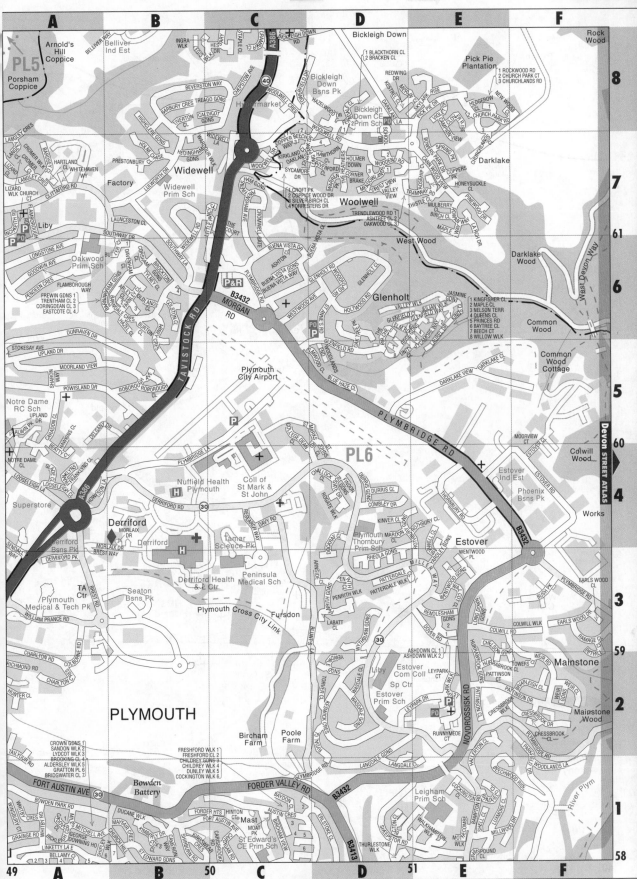

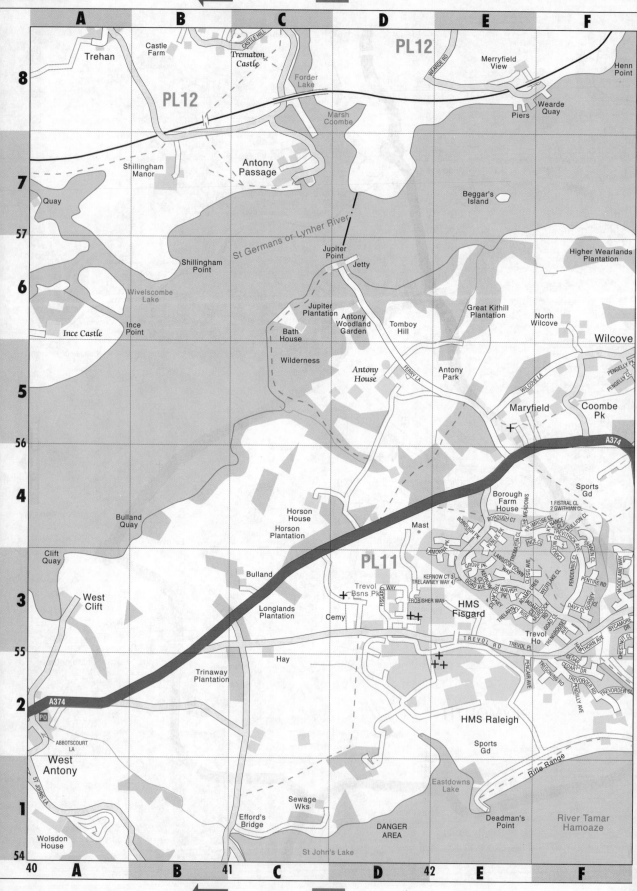

PL12

PL12

PL11

F5
1 NEPEAN ST
2 ADELAIDE ST
3 BRUNEL TERR
4 EPWORTH TERR
5 SUSSEX TERR
6 RAILWAY COTTS
7 YORK TERR
8 ST MAWES TERR

A　B　C　D　E　F

8
7
57
6
5
56
4
55
2
1
54

1 HARBOUR ST
2 ELLIOT SQ
3 ST JAMES CT
4 BELLEVUE SQ
5 ARTHUR TERR
6 HOOPER ST
7 WESLEY CT
8 CORNERSTONE CT
9 DEVONSHIRE CT

RIVERSIDE PL 1
CHAPMANS OPE 2
MORICE SQ 3
WASHBOURNE CL 4
GRANBY PL 5

1 PRINCES ST
2 LOFOTEN CL
3 VAAGSO CL
4 DIEPPE CL
5 ST NAZAIRE APP
6 ST THERESE'S CT

1 CUMBERLAND ST
2 MONUMENT ST
3 RAGLAN GDNS
4 RAGLAN CT
5 THEATRE OPE
6 GEORGE SQ
7 SUTTON CT
8 JAMES ST

F3
1 CLARENDON HO
2 GARFIELD TERR
3 TRAFALGAR PL
4 THE MEWS
5 NELSON GDNS
6 BEYROUT PL
7 ST MICHAEL'S CT
8 ST MICHAEL'S TERR
9 PORTLAND CT
10 MOLYNEAUX PL
11 CLARENDON LA
F4
1 ST GEORGES CT
2 HORNBY ST
3 PHILLIMORE ST
4 FREMANTLE GDNS
5 FAIRFAX TERR
6 HARGOOD TERR
7 HARRISON ST
8 KEPPEL TERR
9 HEALY CT
10 BRUNSWICK PL

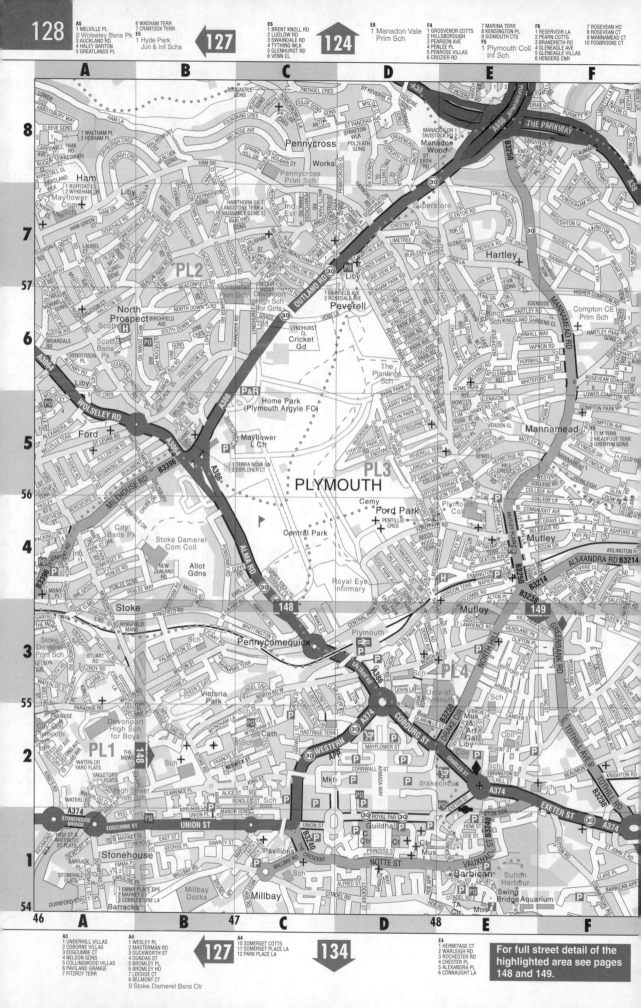

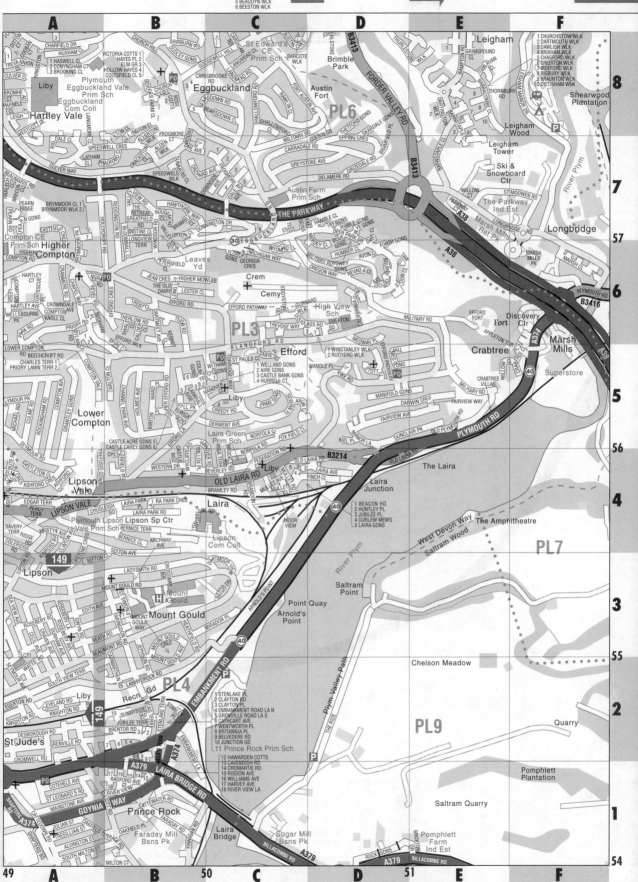

C7
1 BRAMBLE WLK
2 BOWHAYS WLK
3 BRISMAR WLK
4 MOORFIELD AVE
5 BEAUDYN WLK
6 BEESTON WLK

For full street detail of the highlighted area see page 149.

135   130

E7
1 PERSEVERANCE COTTS
2 BLANCHARD PL

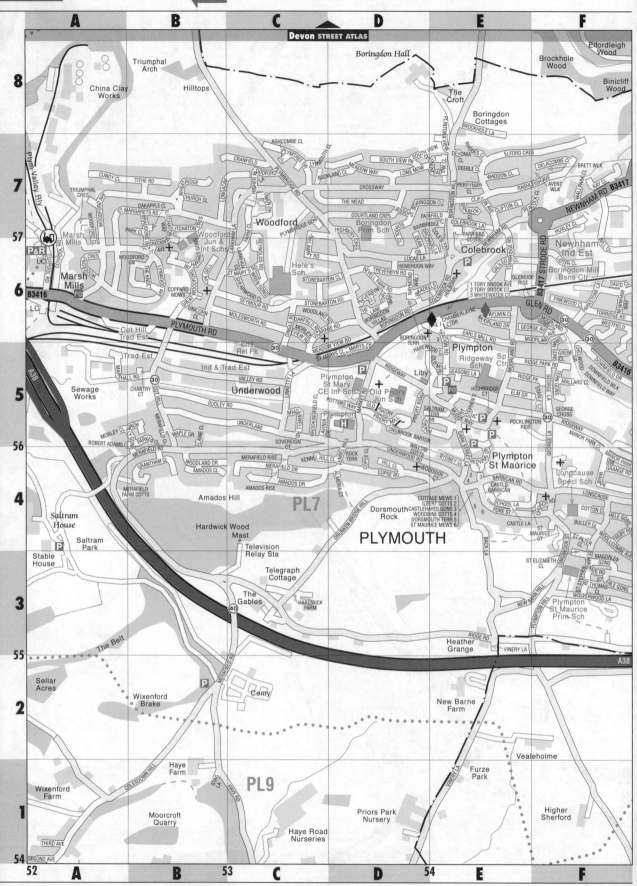

Devon STREET ATLAS

133
128

For full street detail of the highlighted area see pages 148 and 149.

A | B | C | D | E | F

8

ADMIRAL'S HARD
THE QUARTERDECK
TELEGRAPH WHARF
FREEMANS WHARF
THE MANSION HO
MOUNT STONE RD
ADMIRALTY COTTS
PL1
Tower
Firestone Bay
Western King Point

STRAND ST
CREMYL ST
POUND ST
DURNFORD ST
ADMIRALTY ST
ST PAUL'S ST
ROYAL WILLIAM RD
148

Ferryport
Ferryport
CAMBER RD
Millbay Docks

Eastern King Point

St George's CE (Prim Sch)

TA Ctr
WEST HOE RD
WALKER TERR
CLIFF RD
PIER ST
RADFORD RD
GREAT WESTERN RD
GRAND PAR
West Hoe
West Hoe Pier

The Hoe
Smeaton's Tower
HOE RD

The Citadel
MADEIRA RD
ARHAY HILL
P
P

Coxside
TEATS HILL RD

148

149

7

P
P
Spinnaker Quay
Mount Batten Breakwater
Mount Batten Point
Mount Batten Tower
LAWRENCE RD
SHAW WAY
Clovelly Bay

53

Mount Batten Ctr
LORD LOUIS CRES

6

Drake's or St Nicholas's Island
Mast
PL1
The Bridge

Ferry P (Summer Only)

Batten Bay
PL9

Dunstone Point

Rum Bay

5

52

Jennycliff Bay

4

The Sound

3

Ramscliff Point
Rams Cliff
South West Coast Path
Wall
PL9

51

Leekbed Bay

2

Bovisand Pier
Staddon Point
Bovisand Fort
BOVISAND CT
COASTGUARD COTTS

Breakwater Fort

1

Plymouth Breakwater

50

46 | A | | B | 47 | C | | D | 48 | E | | F

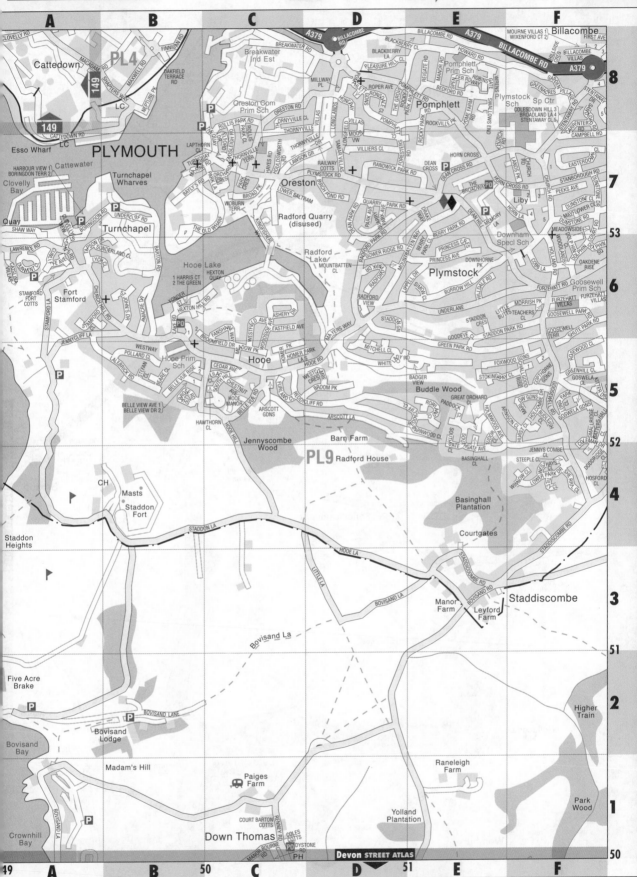

For full street detail of the highlighted area see page 149.

129

136

135

F5
1 CHALLGOOD CL
2 ORCHARDTON TERR

F7
1 THE DUKES RYDE
2 MAPLE CT
3 MAGNOLIA CT
4 HORN LANE FLATS
5 SELKIRK HO

A B C D E F

8

7

53

6

5

52

4

51

3

2

1

50

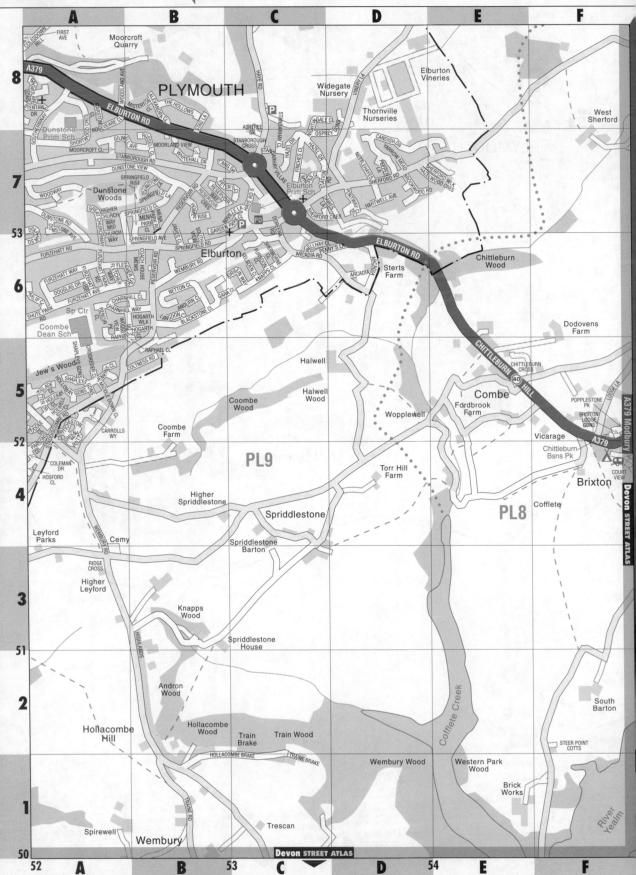

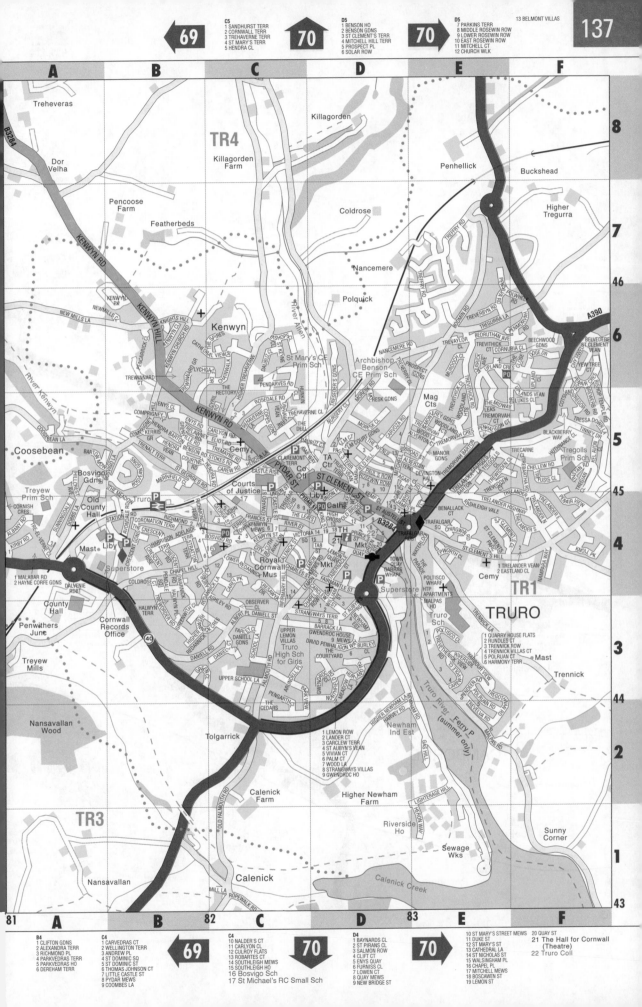

C5
1 SANDHURST TERR
2 CORNWALL TERR
3 TREHAVERNE TERR
4 ST MARY'S TERR
5 HENDRA CL

D5
1 BENSON HO
2 BENSON GDNS
3 ST CLEMENT'S TERR
4 MITCHELL HILL TERR
5 PROSPECT PL
6 SOLAR ROW

D5
7 PARKINS TERR
8 MIDDLE ROSEWIN ROW
9 LOWER ROSEWIN ROW
10 EAST ROSEWIN ROW
11 MITCHELL CT
12 CHURCH WLK

13 BELMONT VILLAS

137

◄ 69   ▲ 70   ► 70

B4
1 CLIFTON GDNS
2 ALEXANDRA TERR
3 RICHMOND PL
4 PARKVEDRAS TERR
5 PARKVEDRAS HO
6 DEREHAM TERR

C4
1 CARVEDRAS CT
2 WELLINGTON TERR
3 ANDREW PL
4 ST DOMINIC SQ
5 ST DOMINIC ST
6 THOMAS JOHNSON CT
7 LITTLE CASTLE ST
8 PYDAR MEWS
9 COOMBES LA

C4
10 NALDER'S CT
11 CARLYON CL
12 CULROY FLATS
13 ROBARTES CT
14 SOUTHLEIGH MEWS
15 SOUTHLEIGH HO
16 Bosvigo Sch
17 St Michael's RC Small Sch

D4
1 BAYNARDS CL
2 ST PIRANS CL
3 SALMON ROW
4 CLIFT CT
5 LEWIS'S QUAY
6 FURNISS CL
7 LOWEN CT
8 QUAY MEWS
9 NEW BRIDGE ST

10 ST MARY'S STREET MEWS
11 DUKE ST
12 ST MARY'S ST
13 CATHEDRAL LA
14 ST NICHOLAS ST
15 WALSINGHAM PL
16 CHAPEL PL
17 MITCHELL MEWS
18 BOSCAWEN ST
19 LEMON ST

20 QUAY ST
21 The Hall for Cornwall (Theatre)
22 Truro Coll

◄ 69   ▲ 70   ► 70

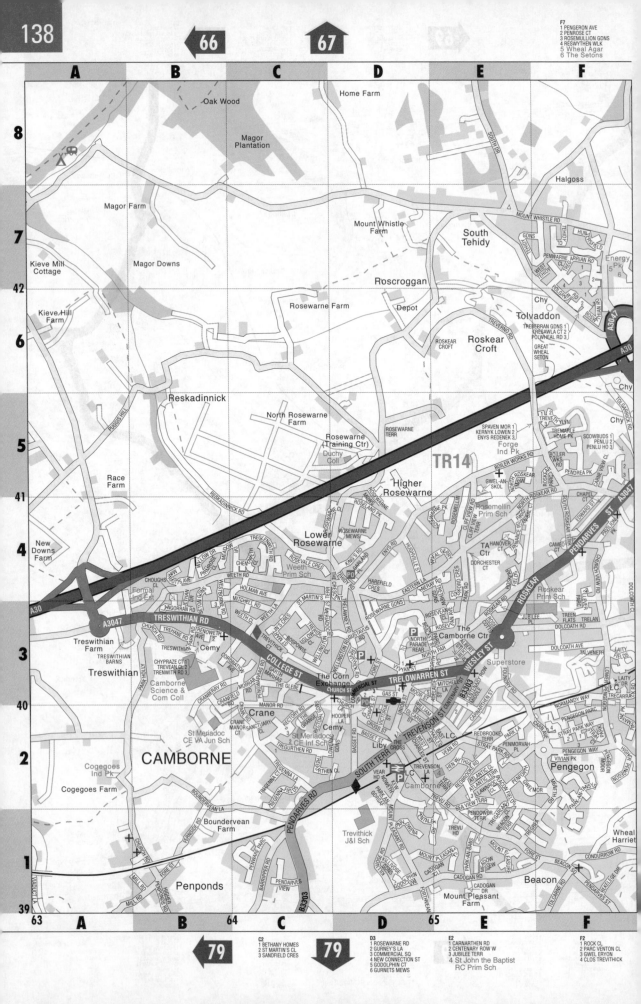

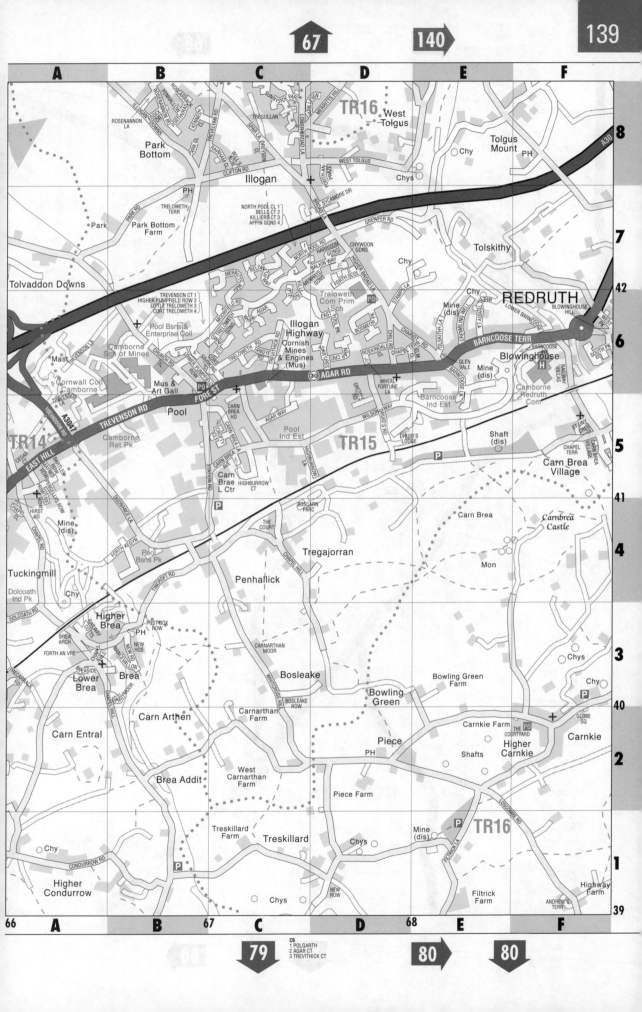

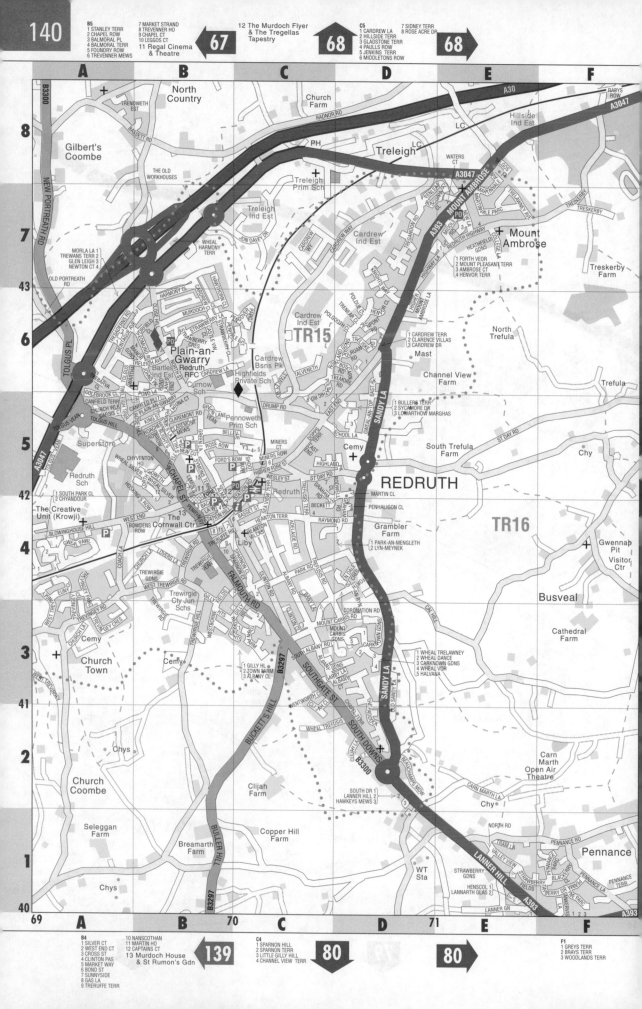

B5
1 STANLEY TERR
2 CHAPEL ROW
3 BALMORAL PL
4 BALMORAL TERR
5 FOUNDRY ROW
6 TREVENNER MEWS
7 MARKET STRAND
8 TREVENNER HO
9 CHAPEL CT
10 LEGGOS CT
11 REGAL CINEMA
& THEATRE

12 The Murdoch Flyer
& The Tregellas
Tapestry

C5
1 CARDREW LA
2 HILLSIDE TERR
3 GLADSTONE TERR
4 PAULLS ROW
5 JENKINS TERR
6 MIDDLETONS ROW
7 SIDNEY TERR
8 ROSE ACRE DR

← 67   68   68 →

North Country

Gilbert's Coombe

TRENOWETH EST

THE OLD WORKHOUSES

Treleigh

Church Farm

RADNOR RD

PH

Treleigh Prim Sch

Treleigh Ind Est

Hillside Ind Est

A30

A3047

BABYS ROW

LC

LC

WATERS CT

A3047

Mount Ambrose

Treskerby Farm

Trefula

MORLA LA 1
TREWANS TERR 2
GLEN LEIGH 3
NEWTON CT 4

OLD PORTREATH RD

WHEAL HARMONY TERR

JON DAVEY DR

Cardrew Ind Est

TR15

Cardrew Ind Est

Mast

North Trefula

Channel View Farm

1 FORTH VEOR
2 MOUNT PLEASANT TERR
3 AMBROSE CT
4 HENVOR TERR

1 CARDREW TERR
2 CLARENCE VILLAS
3 CARDREW DR

Plain-an-Gwarry

Redruth RFC

Cardrew Bsns Pk

Highfields Private Sch

Cardrew Prim Sch

1 BULLERS TERR
2 SYCAMORE DR
3 LOWARTHOW MARGHAS

South Trefula Farm

Superstore

Redruth Sch

Chyventon Ho

Cemy

REDRUTH

TR16

Busveal

1 SOUTH PARK CL
2 CHYANDOUR

The Creative Unit (Krowji)

The Bowdens Cornwall Ctr

BLOWINGHOUSE HILL

WEST END ROW

FORE ST

Redruth

Liby

MARTIN CL

PENHALIGON CL

Grambler Farm

1 PARK-AN-MENGLETH
2 LYN-MEYNEK

Cathedral Farm

Church Town

Cemy

Cemy

WEST TREWIRGIE RD

TREWIRGIE GDNS

WEST TREWIRGIE RD

Trewirgie Cty Jun Schs

FALMOUTH RD

1 GILLY HL
2 TOWN FARM
3 ALBANY CL

B3297

SOUTHGATE ST

SOUTH DOWNS

CORONATION RD

Mount Carbis Gdns

1 WHEAL TRELAWNEY
2 WHEAL DANCE
3 CARKNOWN GDNS
4 WHEAL VOR
5 HALVANA

Busveal

Church Coombe

Seleggan Farm

Clijah Farm

BUCKETT'S HILL

BULLER HILL

Copper Hill Farm

Breamarth Farm

B3297

B3300

Carn Marth Open Air Theatre

SOUTH DR 1
LANNER HILL 2
HAWKEYS MEWS 3

WT Sta

Chy

NORTH RD

TRAM LA

STRAWBERRY GDNS

Pennance

LANNER HILL

A393

HENSCOL
LANNARTH GLAS

1 GREYS TERR
2 BRAYS TERR
3 WOODLANDS TERR

B4
1 SILVER CT
2 WEST END CT
3 CROSS ST
4 CLINTON PAS
5 MARKET WAY
6 BOND ST
7 SUNNYSIDE
8 GAS LA
9 TRERUFFE TERR
10 NANSCOTHAN
11 MARTIN HO
12 CAPTAINS CT
13 MURDOCH HOUSE
& ST RUMON'S GDN

C4
1 SPARNON HILL
2 SPARNON TERR
3 LITTLE GILLY HILL
4 CHANNEL VIEW TERR

F1
1 GREYS TERR
2 BRAYS TERR
3 WOODLANDS TERR

← 139   80   80 →

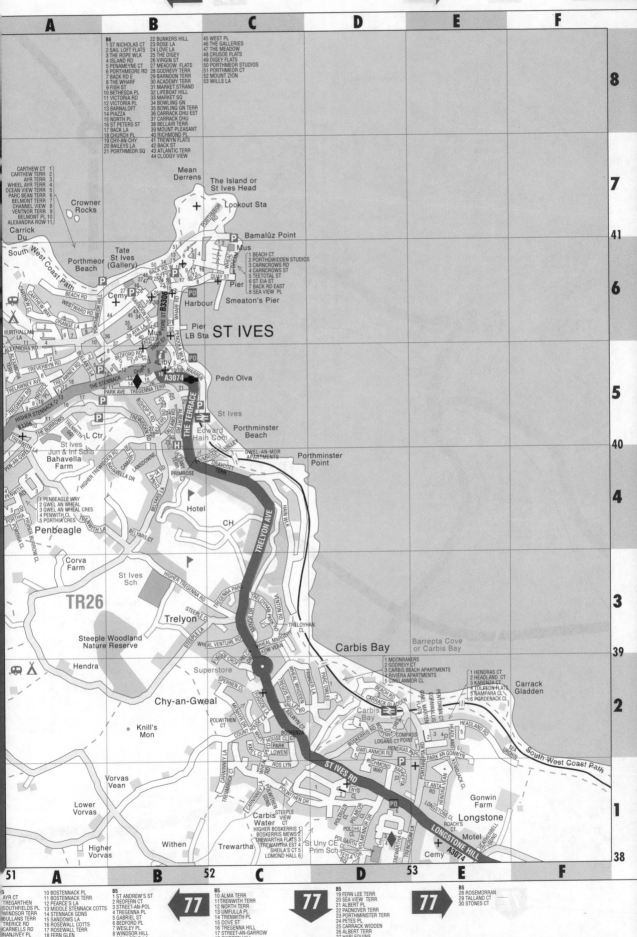

A   B   C   D   E   F

B6
1 ST NICHOLAS CT
2 SAIL LOFT FLATS
3 THE ROPE WLK
4 ISLAND RD
5 PENAMEYNE CT
6 PORTHMEOR RD
7 BACK RD E
8 THE WHARF
9 FISH ST
10 BETHESDA PL
11 VICTORIA RD
12 VICTORIA PL
13 BARNALOFT
14 PIAZZA
15 NORTH PL
16 ST PETERS ST
17 BACK LA
18 CHURCH PL
19 CHY-AN-CHY
20 BAILEYS LA
21 PORTHMEOR SQ

22 BUNKERS HILL
23 ROSE LA
24 LOVE LA
25 THE DIGEY
26 VIRGIN ST
27 MEADOW FLATS
28 GODREVY TERR
29 BARNOON TERR
30 ACADEMY TERR
31 MARKET STRAND
32 LIFEBOAT HILL
33 MARKET SQ
34 BOWLING GN
35 BOWLING GN TERR
36 CARRACK DHU EST
37 CARRACK DHU
38 BELLAIR TERR
39 MOUNT PLEASANT
40 RICHMOND PL
41 TREWYN FLATS
42 BACK ST
43 ATLANTIC TERR
44 CLODGY VIEW

45 WEST PL
46 THE GALLERIES
47 THE MEADOW
48 CRUSOE FLATS
49 DIGEY FLATS
50 PORTHMEOR STUDIOS
51 PORTHMEOR ST
52 MOUNT ZION
53 WILLS LA

CARTHEW CT 1
CARTHEW TERR 2
AYR TERR 3
WHEEL AYR TERR 4
OCEAN VIEW TERR 5
PARC BEAN TERR 6
BELMONT TERR 7
CHANNEL VIEW 8
VENTNOR TERR 9
BELMONT PL 10
ALEXANDRA ROW 11

1 PENBEAGLE WAY
2 GWEL AN WHEAL
3 GWEL AN WHEAL CRES
4 PENWITH CL
5 PORTHIA CRES

1 BEACH CT
2 PORTHGWIDDEN STUDIOS
3 CARNCROWS RD
4 CARNCROWS ST
5 TEETOTAL ST
6 ST EIA ST
7 BACK RD EAST
8 SEA VIEW PL

1 MOONRAKERS
2 GODREVY CT
3 CARBIS BEACH APARTMENTS
4 RIVIERA APARTMENTS
5 GWELANMOR CL

1 HENDRAS CT
2 HEADLAND CT
3 KARENZA CT
4 TOLPEDN FLATS
5 NAMPARA CT
6 PORDENACK CL

ST IVES

Carbis Bay

TR26

Penbeagle

Trelyon

Chy-an-Gweal

Carbis Water

Longstone

51   A   B   52   C   D   53   E   F

5
AYR CT
TREGARTHEN
SOUTHFIELDS PL
WINDSOR TERR
BULLANS TERR
TRERICE RD
CARNELLS RD
NANJIVEY PL
NANJIVEY TERR

10 BOSTENNACK PL
11 BOSTENNACK TERR
12 PEARCE'S LA
13 MIDDLE STENNACK COTTS
14 STENNACK GDNS
15 SANDOWS LA
16 ROSEWALL COTTS
17 ROSEWALL TERR
18 FERN GLEN
19 LITTLE-IN-SIGHT

B5
1 ST ANDREW'S ST
2 REDFERN CT
3 STREET-AN-POL
4 TREGENNA PL
5 GABRIEL ST
6 BEDFORD PL
7 WESLEY PL
8 WINDSOR HILL
9 DRILLFIELD LA

B5
10 ALMA TERR
11 TRENWITH TERR
12 NORTH TERR
13 UMFULLA PL
14 TRENWITH PL
15 DOVE ST
16 TREGENNA HILL
17 STREET-AN-GARROW
18 SKIDDEN HILL

B5
19 FERN LEE TERR
20 SEA VIEW TERR
21 ALBERT PL
22 PADNOVER TERR
23 PORTHMINSTER TERR
24 PETES PL
25 CARRACK WIDDEN
26 ALBERT ROW
27 HARLEQUINS

B5
28 ROSEMORRAN
29 TALLAND CT
30 STONES CT

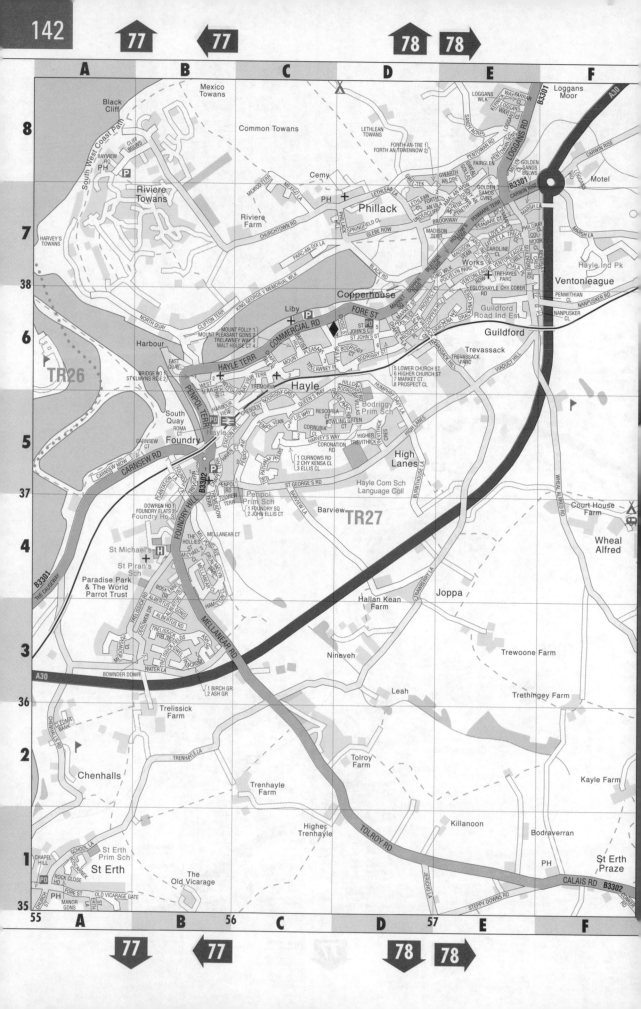

C7
1 ROSCADGHILL PARC
2 HEABROOK PARC
3 NICHOLAS PARC
4 MYTHYON CT
5 HEA COTTS
6 HAIG PL

7 POLTAIR TERR
8 BROOKWARD TERR
9 HOLLY TERR
10 CARMEN SQ
11 WESLEY ST
12 SYLVERTON PL
13 JAMAICA TERR

14 JAMAICA PL
15 PLEASANT PL
16 NEVADA PL
17 MELBOURNE TERR
D5
1 GREENBANK
2 HAWKINS CT

3 TREVEAN GDNS
4 ALVERTON TERR
5 STANFORD CL
6 WEETHES COTTS
7 ALVERNE BLDGS
8 CARMINOWE CRES

TR20

Madron

Trescrowan

TR20

Boskenwyn Manor

Polmennor Farm

Higher Trannack

Trythogga

B3372

St Madderns CE Sch

Poltair

Tretorvic

Chapel Rd

Ridged Mill 1
Helnoweth Cotts 2
Chyandaune Cl 3
Chyandaunce Terr 4
Gulval Almshouses 5
Gulval Cross 6
School La 7
The Mead Hos 8

Heamoor

Mount's Bay Sch

Treneere

Chyandour

Boscathnoe Resr

Heamoor Prim Sch

North Lodge

Nancealverne Spec Sch

Penzance CC Council Offices

Penwith Coll

Humphry Davy Sch

St Mary's RC Sch

Chycornick Terr 9
Chynoweth Gdns 10
Chy-an-hall 11
Trythogga Hill 12
Trevarrack Cl 13
Trevarrack Pl 14
Trevarrack 15
Trevarrack La 16
Pendrea Pl 18
Pendrea 17
Gwedhennek 19

Chyandour Terr 1
The Coach Ho 2
Chyandour Sq 3

Rosehill

Jack Stephens Est 1
Pendarves Flats 2
Chyanclare 3
St Clare Flats 4
Windsor Terr 5

Penzance L Ctr West Cornwall

PENZANCE

Lescudjack Terr 1
Mount Royal Cl 2
Coastguard Cres 3
Penrose Ct 4
Lannoweth Rd 5
Penrose Terr 6
Trafalgar Cl 7
Mabbots Ct 8
Leskinnick St 9
The Old Bakehouse Flats 10

Willowfield 1
Castle Horneck Cl 2
Alverton Ho 3
Cherrytree 4

The Bolitho Sch

Lesingey Round

Castle Horneck

YH

Lansdowne Ct

Penzance Sch of Art

Penlee House Gall & Mus

TR18

Penzance Art Gall

Harbour Pier

Dock Pier

Custom House Pier

Wherry Town

Penzance CE Prim Sch

Trenoweth Cres

A30

A3071

B3315

TR20

Trereife

Alverton

Jubilee Pool (Lido)

Under Chapel Yd 1
Coinagehall Pl 2
The Mission 3
Green St 4
Coinagehall St 5
Barbican La 6

E4
1 REDINNICK TERR
2 NORTH TERR
3 PENLEE VIEW TERR
4 REDINNICK GDNS
5 SOUTH PLACE FOLLY
6 QUEEN'S PL
7 MARINE TERR
8 COULSON'S TERR
9 COULSON S PL
10 COULSON'S BLDGS
11 CARNE'S BLDGS
12 SOUTH TERR

E5
1 TRENDEAL GDNS
2 CAMELOT CT
3 TARVEOR TERR
4 OLD BREWERY YD
5 ALMA PL
6 THE ARCADE
7 ST JOHNS CT
8 ST PIRANS CT
9 Wharfside Village
10 HANOVER CT
11 ST MICHAEL'S COTTS
12 PRINCESS CT
13 ST PIRANS CT
14 CHERRY GDNS
15 HARBOUR CT
16 CUSTOM HOUSE LA
17 KITTS CT
18 ST MICHAELS CT
19 ABBEY CT
20 VOUNDERVOUR LA
21 REGENT SQ
22 CHIRGWIN CT
23 CHANCERY LA
24 QUEEN'S SQ
25 MARKET PL
26 THE GREENMARKET
27 UNION ST
28 PARK CT
29 PARADE PASS
30 SIMPSONS CT
31 VICTORIA PL
32 BURITON ROW
33 SOUTH PAR
34 MORRAB PL
35 MORRAB TERR
36 REGENT BLDGS
37 The Exchange (Gall)
38 Acorn Arts Ctr

E6
1 BARWIS TERR
2 PENARE GDNS
3 THE MEWS
4 ST HENRY ST
5 ST FRANCIS ST
6 ST WARREN ST
7 ST PHILIP ST
8 ST DOMINIC ST
9 GWAVAS ST
10 PENLEE ST
11 PENWITH ST
12 TREWARTHA TERR
13 CROSS ST
14 LESKINNICK PL
15 VICTORIA CT
16 VICTORIA SQ
17 VICTORIA MEWS
18 ALBERT TERR
19 ALBERT BLDGS
20 BELLE VUE TERR
21 MEDROSE TERR
22 ROSE TERR
23 EMPRESS AVE
24 GARLIDNA
25 PROSPECT PL
26 FOUNTAIN CT
27 BULLOCK MARKET TERR
28 WINDSOR PL
29 CLARENCE PL
30 CLARENCE TERR

The Gear

Tolcarne

Newlyn Prim Sch

Stable Hobba Ind Est

The Coombe

The Pilchard Wks

Newlyn Art Gall

1 MOUNT PROSPECT TERR
2 WEST TERR
3 TRENEGLOS TERR
4 CHARLES ST
5 FLORENCE PL
6 TOLCARNE TERR
7 ART GALLERY TERR

NEWLYN

Pier

Pier

Gwavas Lake

Tredavoe

Gurnick Est

LB Sta

Pier

Tidal Observatory

Pier

BOSKERNICK CL 1
TREGLYN CL 2
GLOUCESTER CRES 3
PENKERNICK CL 4

1 HIGHER GREEN ST
2 LOWER GREEN ST
3 PRIMROSE TERR

TR 19

Hotel

B3315

C1
1 TREVENETH PL
2 TREWINCE TERR
3 HIGHER GWAVAS RD
4 GWAVAS BGLWS
5 BOWJEY TERR
6 SEA VIEW TERR
7 LYN TERR
8 MEADOW VILLAS
9 BOWJEY CT

10 NAVY INN CT
11 HARBOUR LIGHTS
12 EBENEZER PL
13 EDEN TERR
14 EDEN GDNS
15 CHURCH ST
16 FRANWILL TERR
17 PARC VILLAS
18 PARK RD
19 PARC TERR

20 JUBILEE BGLWS
21 BOUNDARY CL

C2
1 NORTH CNR
2 MALT HOUSE GDNS
3 THE MALT HOUSE
4 ANTOINE CL
5 WESLEY ST
6 STRICKLAND COTTS
7 GWAVAS QUAY
8 FARMERS MDW
9 CHAPEL ST

10 ORCHARD HO
11 ORCHARD RD
12 THE FRADGAN
13 THE BRIDGE HO
14 CLIFTON HILL
15 CLIFTON TERR
16 PENSWEL
17 BARLANDHU
18 BON VILLAS
19 HIGHFIELDS

20 ORCHARD TERR
21 LANE REDDIN TERR
22 HILLSIDE TERR
23 ANTOINE TERR
24 MOUNT VIEW TERR
25 ELMS CLOSE TERR
26 BAY VIEW TERR
27 GLOUCESTER PL

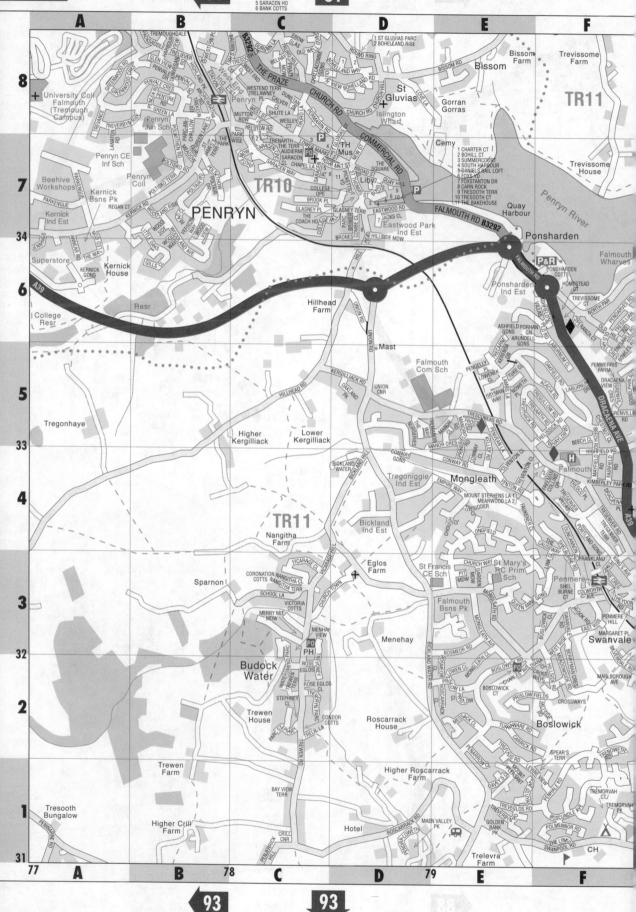

82   **82**

TR11

Cemy

Tregew

Little
Falmouth

ORCHARD
VALE

Trefusis

VINEFIELD
CT

1 POPLAR TERR
2 RIVER VIEW

KERSEY
CL

Penarrow
Point

Mon

Kilnquay
Wood

Falmouth
Wharves

Flushing

PH

Flushing
Prim Sch

Penryn River

Trefusis
Point

Ferry (P)
Summer only

B5

Inner
Harbour

Ferry (P)

Falmouth
Docks

Eastern
Breakwater

FALMOUTH

Poly Arts
& Science

TR11

National Maritime
Mus
Cornwall

LB Sta &
Coastguard
Ctr

Falmouth
Docks

Ships &
Castles
L Ctr

Middle
Point

Killigrew
Mon

Univ Coll
Falmouth

Falmouth
Town

King Charles
CE Prim Sch

MELVILL RD

Marlborough
Sch

Cemy

Pendragon HO
2 ROEBUCK VILLAS
3 TREGUNTER MEWS
4 RAILWAY COTTS
5 PENDENNIS RISE
6 BAY VIEW CRES
7 MANOR COTTS
8 PENDENNIS CT
9 IMPERIAL CT
10 CASTLE HILL

Pendennis
Castle

Pendennis Castle
Road Race
Commemoration Stone

Crab
Quay

Princess
Pavilion

GREYFRIARS
BOSCAWEN 2

Gyllyngvase
Beach

Pendennis
Point

Swan
Pool
Nature
Reserve

Swanpool
Point

Swanpool
Beach

South West Coast Path

Falmouth Bay

94   **94**

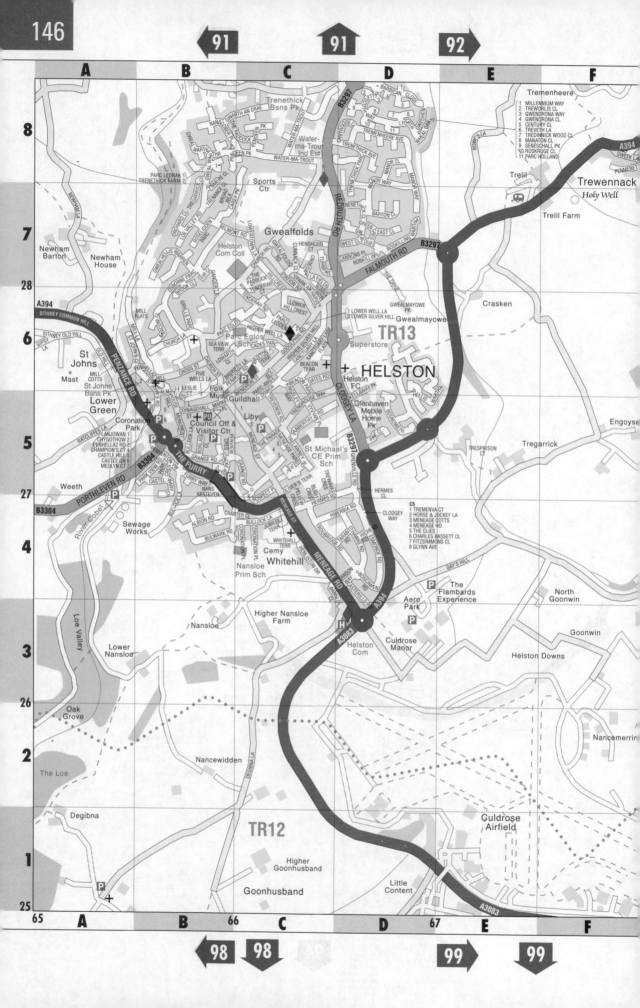

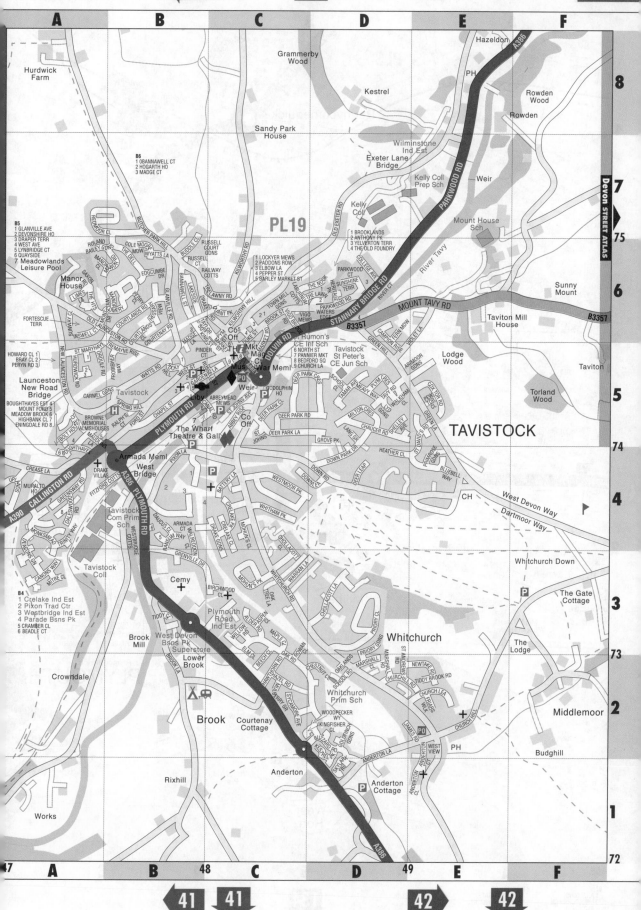

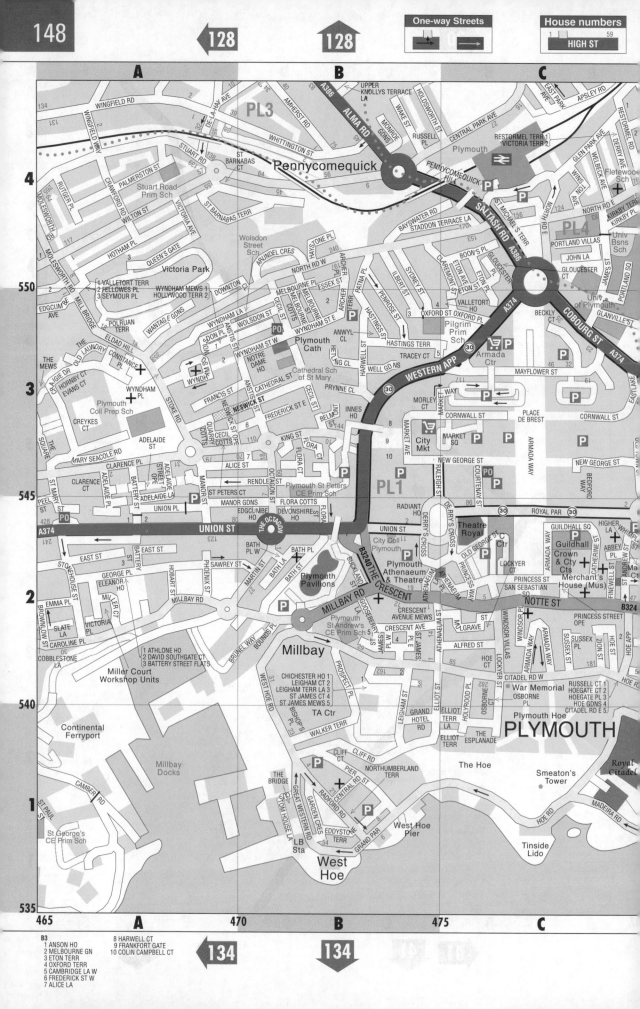

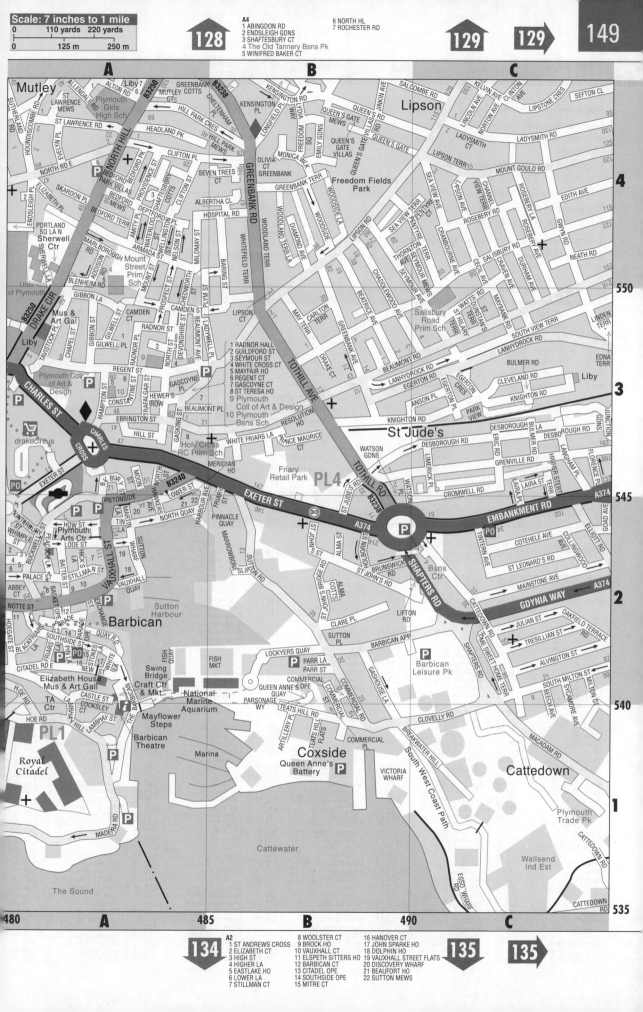

Index

Church Rd **6** Beckenham BR2.........**53** C6

Place name May be abbreviated on the map

Location number Present when a number indicates the place's position in a crowded area of mapping

Locality, town or village Shown when more than one place has the same name

Postcode district District for the indexed place

Page and grid square Page number and grid reference for the standard mapping

Cities, towns and villages are listed in CAPITAL LETTERS

Public and commercial buildings are highlighted in magenta   **Places of interest** are highlighted in blue with a star★

Abbreviations used in the index

Acad	Academy	Comm	Common	Gd	Ground	L	Leisure	Prom	Promenade
App	Approach	Cott	Cottage	Gdn	Garden	La	Lane	Rd	Road
Arc	Arcade	Cres	Crescent	Gn	Green	Liby	Library	Recn	Recreation
Ave	Avenue	Cswy	Causeway	Gr	Grove	Mdw	Meadow	Ret	Retail
Bglw	Bungalow	Ct	Court	H	Hall	Meml	Memorial	Sh	Shopping
Bldg	Building	Ctr	Centre	Ho	House	Mkt	Market	Sq	Square
Bsns, Bus	Business	Ctry	Country	Hospl	Hospital	Mus	Museum	St	Street
Bvd	Boulevard	Cty	County	HQ	Headquarters	Orch	Orchard	Sta	Station
Cath	Cathedral	Dr	Drive	Hts	Heights	Pal	Palace	Terr	Terrace
Cir	Circus	Dro	Drove	Ind	Industrial	Par	Parade	TH	Town Hall
Cl	Close	Ed	Education	Inst	Institute	Pas	Passage	Univ	University
Cnr	Corner	Emb	Embankment	Int	International	Pk	Park	Wk, Wlk	Walk
Coll	College	Est	Estate	Intc	Interchange	Pl	Place	Wr	Water
Com	Community	Ex	Exhibition	Junc	Junction	Prec	Precinct	Yd	Yard

Index of towns, villages, streets, hospitals, industrial estates, railway stations, schools, shopping centres, universities and places of interest

Abb–AND

A

Abbey Cl PL20 . . . . 42 B2
Abbey Ct
  19 Penzance TR18 . . . . . . 143 E5
  Plymouth PL1 . . . . 149 A2
Abbey Hill TR26 . . . . 77 E3
Abbey Mdw TR26 . . . . 77 E4
Abbeymead Mews PL19 . 147 C5
Abbey Mews PL31 . . . . . . 109 C4
Abbey Pl
  Plymouth PL1 . . . . 148 C2
  Tavistock PL19 . . . . 147 C5
Abbey Rise PL19 . . . . 147 C5
Abbey St TR18 . . . . 143 E5
Abbotsbury Way PL2 . . . . 127 F8
Abbots Cl PL31 . . . . 109 F4
Abbotscourt La PL11 . . . . 126 A2
Abbotsfield Cl PL19 . . . . . 41 D8
Abbotsfield Cres PL19 . . . . 41 D8
Abbotts Rd PL3 . . . . 128 E6
Aberdeen Ave PL5 . . . . . . 124 D1
Aberdeen Ct PL24 . . . . 60 B6
Aberfal Ho **1** PL11 . . . . . . 145 C3
Abingdon Rd **1** PL4 . . . . . 149 A4
Abney Cres PL6 . . . . 125 B6
Above Town Cl PL27 . . . . . 21 F3
Abscott La PL9 . . . . 135 C5
Acacia Rd TR11 . . . . 144 F5
Academy Terr **30** TR26 . . 141 B6
Acklington Pl PL5 . . . . 123 E4
Acland Cl EX23 . . . . 104 E7
Acland Gdns TR7 . . . . 110 D6
Acorn Arts Ctr★ **38** TR18 143 E5
Acorn Dr PL25 . . . . 115 A3
Acre Pl PL1 . . . . 127 F3
Acre Cotts PL1 . . . . 127 F3
Adams Cl
  Plymouth PL5 . . . . 123 F1
  Torpoint PL11 . . . . 126 F3
Adams Cres PL11 . . . . 126 E3
Adams Row TR16 . . . . 68 D3
ADDINGTON 113 D7
Addington N PL14 . . . . . . 113 D6
Addington S PL14 . . . . . . 113 D6
Addison Rd PL4 . . . . 149 A4
Addison Terr PL22 . . . . . . 112 C2
Adelaide La PL1 . . . . 148 A2

Adelaide Pl PL1 . . . . 148 A3
Adelaide Rd TR15 . . . . . . 140 C4
Adelaide St
  Camborne TR14 . . . . 138 E3
  Penzance TR18 . . . . 143 E6
  2 Plymouth, Ford PL2 . . 127 F5
  Plymouth PL1 . . . . 148 A3
Adelaide Street Ope PL1 148 A3
Adelaide Terr TR1 . . . . . . 137 B4
Adela Rd PL11 . . . . 127 A3
Adit La
  Newlyn TR18 . . . . 143 C1
  Saltash PL12 . . . . 122 E3
Adits The PL18 . . . . 41 A3
Admiral's Hard PL1 . . . . . 134 A8
Admirals Quay **4** TR11 . 145 B5
Admiralty Cotts PL1 . . . . . 134 A7
Admiralty Ct PL13 . . . . . . 117 D3
Admiralty Rd
  Plymouth, Millbay PL1 . . 134 A8
  Plymouth, St Budeaux PL5 123 C2
Admiralty St
  Plymouth, Keyham PL2 . . 127 E6
  Plymouth, Millbay PL1 . . 134 A8
Admiralty Terr TR2 . . . . . . 83 B2
African Row TR14 . . . . 79 B5
Agar Cres TR15 . . . . 139 D6
Agar Ct
  2 Camborne TR15 . . . . 139 C6
  Truro TR1 . . . . 137 D5
Agar Mdws **11** TR3 . . . . . 81 F7
Agar Rd
  Camborne TR15 . . . . 139 D6
  Newquay TR7 . . . . 110 E5
  St Austell PL25 . . . . 114 E6
  Truro TR1 . . . . 137 E5
Agar Terr **12** PL31 . . . . . 109 D5
Agar Way TR15 . . . . 139 C5
Agaton Rd PL5 . . . . 123 E3
Agnes Cl EX23 . . . . 104 F4
Ainslie Terr PL2 . . . . 127 E7
Aire Gdns PL3 . . . . 129 B5
Alamein Ct PL12 . . . . 122 E2
Alamein Rd PL12 . . . . 122 D2
Alan Harvey Ct **14** TR26 . 77 A6
Alan Rd PL28 . . . . 107 D4
Alansmere Ct TR2 . . . . . . 57 A1
Alanta Flats TR7 . . . . 110 E5
Albany Cl
  Redruth TR15 . . . . 140 C3
  Redruth TR15 . . . . 140 C3
  St Agnes TR5 . . . . 68 D8

Albany Ct
  4 Newquay TR7 . . . . . . 110 F6
  Redruth TR15 . . . . 140 D3
Albany Gdns TR15 . . . . . . 140 C3
Albany La TR15 . . . . 140 C4
Albany Pl TR11 . . . . 145 A3
Albany Rd
  Falmouth TR11 . . . . 145 A3
  5 Newquay TR7 . . . . . . 110 F6
  Redruth TR15 . . . . 140 C4
  Truro TR1 . . . . 137 A4
Albany St PL1 . . . . 127 E2
Albany Terr TR26 . . . . 141 B4
ALBASTON 40 E5
Albemarle Villas PL1 . . . . 127 F3
Albert Bldgs **19** TR18 . . . 143 E6
Albert Cotts TR11 . . . . . . 145 B4
Albertha Cl PL4 . . . . 149 B4
Albert Pl
  Camborne TR14 . . . . 138 E3
  21 St Ives TR26 . . . . . . 141 B5
  Truro TR1 . . . . 137 C3
Albert Rd
  Plymouth PL2 . . . . 127 F4
  Saltash PL12 . . . . 123 A2
  St Austell PL25 . . . . 114 D3
  St Ives TR26 . . . . 141 B5
Albert St
  Camborne TR14 . . . . 138 E3
  Penzance TR18 . . . . 143 F6
Albert Terr
  Gunnislake PL18 . . . . . . 40 F5
  Lostwithiel PL22 . . . . . . 112 C2
  18 Penzance TR18 . . . . 143 E6
  26 St Ives TR26 . . . . . . 141 B5
Albertus Dr TR27 . . . . 142 B3
Albertus Gdns TR27 . . . . 142 B3
Albertus Rd TR27 . . . . . . 142 B3
Albert Villas PL2 . . . . 127 E4
Albion Cl PL11 . . . . 127 B3
Albion Dr PL2 . . . . 128 B7
Albion Rd
  Helston TR13 . . . . 146 B4
  Torpoint PL11 . . . . 127 B3
Albion Row TR16 . . . . 80 F8
Alcester Cl PL2 . . . . 127 E4
Alcester St PL2 . . . . 127 F4
Alden Wlk PL6 . . . . 129 B7
Aldercombe La EX23 . . . . 5 A6
Alderney Rd PL6 . . . . 124 F7
Alder Rd PL19 . . . . 147 C3
Aldersley Wlk PL6 . . . . . . 125 A1
Aldreath Cl TR20 . . . . 88 B7

Aldreath Rd TR20 . . . . 88 B7
Alexander Ct
  14 Carnon Downs TR3 . . 81 F7
  Gorran Haven PL26 . . . . . 85 D5
Alexandra Cl
  5 Illogan TR16 . . . . 67 E4
  Plymouth PL9 . . . . 136 B8
  St Ives TR26 . . . . 77 A7
Alexandra Ct TR7 . . . . . . 111 C8
Alexandra Dr PL20 . . . . . . 41 C1
Alexandra Gdns TR18 . . . 143 D4
Alexandra Ho TR18 . . . . . 143 D3
Alexandra Pl
  Penzance TR18 . . . . 143 D4
  5 Plymouth PL4 . . . . . . 128 E4
  St Ives TR26 . . . . 77 A7
Alexandra Rd
  Bodmin PL31 . . . . 109 B5
  Illogan TR16 . . . . 67 D4
  Newquay TR7 . . . . 111 C8
  Penzance TR18 . . . . 143 D4
  Plymouth, Crownhill PL6 . 124 F2
  Plymouth, Ford PL2 . . . . 127 F5
  Plymouth, Mutley PL4 . . 128 E4
  St Austell PL25 . . . . 114 E3
  St Ives TR26 . . . . 77 A7
Alexandra Sq PL12 . . . . . 123 A2
Alexandra Terr
  Mount Hawke TR4 . . . . . 68 C6
  Penzance TR18 . . . . 143 D3
  Plymouth PL2 . . . . 127 F5
  St Ives TR26 . . . . 141 A5
  Tremar PL14 . . . . 38 A4
  2 Truro TR1 . . . . 137 B4
ALFARDISWORTHY 5 E6
Alford Cl EX23 . . . . 104 F5
Alfred Pl PL2 . . . . 127 F5
Alfred Rd PL2 . . . . 127 F5
Alfred St PL1 . . . . 148 C2
Alger Wlk PL6 . . . . 124 E6
Alice La **7** PL1 . . . . 148 B3
Alice St PL1 . . . . 148 A3
Alldritt Cl TR7 . . . . 111 D7
Allenby Rd PL2 . . . . 128 A6
Allendale Cl 58 E8
Allendale Rd PL4 . . . . 149 A4
Allen Pk PL30 . . . . 23 B2
Allen Vale PL14 . . . . 113 A5
Allern La PL5 . . . . 120 D1
Allerton Wlk PL6 . . . . 129 B7
Alley Hill PL20 . . . . 42 A1
Alleyn Gdns PL3 . . . . 128 E8
Allium Ct TR4 . . . . 70 D8

All Saints Pk PL18 . . . . . . 40 E5
Alma Cl TR5 . . . . 68 D8
Alma Cotts PL4 . . . . 149 B2
Alma Pl
  Heamoor TR18 . . . . 143 C7
  Newquay TR7 . . . . 110 D6
  Padstow PL28 . . . . 107 D5
  5 Penzance TR18 . . . . 143 E5
  Redruth TR15 . . . . 140 E5
Alma Rd
  Plymouth PL3 . . . . 128 C4
  Truro TR1 . . . . 69 F3
Alma St PL4 . . . . 149 B2
Alma Terr
  Carharrack TR16 . . . . . . 80 E8
  Gunnislake PL18 . . . . . . 41 A6
  Penzance TR18 . . . . 143 E5
  10 St Ives TR26 . . . . . . 141 B5
Almeria Ct PL7 . . . . 130 D4
Almond Dr PL7 . . . . 131 B6
Almshouse Hill TR13 . . . . 146 D4
ALTARNUN 26 C8
Altarnun Prim Sch PL15 . 26 C7
Alton Pl PL4 . . . . 128 E4
Alton Rd PL4 . . . . 128 E4
Alverne Bldgs **7** TR18 . . 143 D5
ALVERTON 143 C4
Alverton Ct TR1 . . . . 137 E5
Alverton Cty Prim Sch
  TR18 . . . . 143 C4
Alverton Ho TR18 . . . . . . 143 C5
Alverton Rd TR18 . . . . . . 143 D5
Alverton St TR18 . . . . 143 E5
Alverton Terr
  4 Penzance TR18 . . . . 143 D5
  Truro TR1 . . . . 137 D5
Alvington St PL4 . . . . 149 C4
Alwin Pk PL6 . . . . 125 A5
Alwyn Cl TR7 . . . . 111 E6
Amacre Dr PL9 . . . . 135 B6
Amados Cl PL7 . . . . 130 C4
Amados Dr PL7 . . . . 130 C4
Amados Rise PL7 . . . . . . 130 C4
Amal An Avon TR27 . . . . . 142 E7
AMALEBRA 76 F3
AMALVEOR 76 E4
Amanda Way PL14 . . . . . . 38 E4
Amble Rd **26** PL17 . . . . . 39 F4
Ambrose Ct TR15 . . . . . . 140 E7
Amelia Cl TR2 . . . . 71 C6
Amherst Rd PL3 . . . . 148 A4
Amity Pl PL4 . . . . 149 A4
ANDERTON 132 E4

BOSCREEGE 90 C5
Boscundle Ave TR11 144 F1
Boscundle Cl PL25 115 D5
Boscundle Row PL12 123 A2
Bosence Rd TR27 90 C7
Bosillion La TR2 72 A7
Bosinney Rd PL25 114 D3
Bosinver La PL26 59 A1
Boskear La PL31 109 A4
BOSKEDNAN 76 A1
BOSKENNA 97 C4
Boskenna Cross TR19 97 C5
Boskennal Barton TR19 97 B6
Boskennal La TR19 97 B6
Boskenna Rd TR16 80 A5
Boskennel Dr TR27 142 B4
Boskenwyn Prim Sch TR13 92 B3
Boskenza Ct TR26 141 C2
Boskernick Cl TR18 143 B1
Boskernow TR12 100 D6
Boskerris Cres TR26 141 D2
Boskerris Mews TR26 141 D1
Boskerris Rd TR26 141 D2
Boslandew Hill TR19 88 C2
BOSLEAKE 139 C3
Bosleake Row TR15 139 C3
Bosloggas Mews 9 TR11 145 C3
BOSLOWICK 144 F2
Boslowick Cl TR11 144 F3
Boslowick Ct TR11 144 E2
Boslowick Rd TR11 144 E2
Bosmeor Cl TR11 144 E2
Bosmeor Pk TR15 139 D6
Bosmeor Rd TR11 144 E3
Bosnoweth
 Helston TR13 146 D5
 Probus TR2 71 D6
Bosorne Cl TR19 86 E6
Bosorne Rd TR19 86 E6
Bosorne St TR19 86 E6
Bosorne Terr TR19 86 E6
Bosparva La
 Leedstown TR27 78 F2
 Praze-an-Beeble TR14 79 A3
Bospolvans Rd 2 TR9 45 D6
BOSPORTHENNIS 75 F3
Bospowis TR14 138 C3
BOSSINEY 14 D8
Bossiney Rd PL34 14 D7
Bostennack Pl 10 TR26 141 A5
Bostennack Terr 11 TR26 141 A5
Bosuen Rd TR7 111 A7
Bosullow Vean TR20 87 D8
Bos Vean TR12 102 F2
Bosvean Gdns
 11 Illogan TR16 67 E4
 Truro TR1 137 B5
Bosvean Rd TR4 69 F6
Bosvenna View PL31 109 E4
Bosvenna Way TR18 143 B7
Bosvenning Pl TR20 87 E6
Bosvigo Gdns★ TR1 137 A5
Bosvigo La TR1 137 B5
Bosvigo Rd TR1 137 C4
Bosvigo Sch 16 TR1 137 C4
Boswedden Pl TR19 86 E6
Boswedden Rd TR19 86 E6
BOSWEDNACK 76 A4
Boswell Cl PL5 124 B2
Boswergy TR18 143 C5
BOSWINGER 85 B5
Boswithian Rd TR14 138 F6
Bosworgey Cl 3 TR9 45 D6
Bosworgy Rd TR20, TR27 90 B8
BOTALLACK 86 E7
Botallack La TR19 86 E7
Botetoe Hill TR14 79 C4
Botetoe Rd TR14 79 B4
Botha Rd 1 PL27 31 F3
Bothwicks Rd TR7 110 E6
BOTTOMS 96 E5
BOTUSFLEMING 122 B7
Boughthayes Est PL19 147 A5
Boulden Cl PL7 131 C5
Boulter Cl PL6 121 C1
Boundary Cl 21 TR18 143 C1
Boundary Dr EX23 7 B6
Boundary Rd
 Bodmin PL31 109 A4
 Dousland PL20 42 E3
Bounders La TR6 55 B4
Bounder Treath TR12 101 C1
Boundervean La TR14 138 B2
Bounds Cross EX22 8 B4
Bounds Pl PL1 148 B2
Bound The PL10 133 A1
Bounsalls Ct 5 PL15 106 C5
Bounsall's La PL15 106 C5
Bourne Cl PL3 129 D6
Bourneside PL25 114 D3
Boveway Dr PL14 113 E5
Boveway La PL14 113 D5
Boville La PL9 136 C7
Bovisand Ct PL9 134 F2
Bovisand La
 Down Thomas PL9 135 B2
 Staddiscombe PL9 135 D3
Bovisand Pk PL9 135 A1
Bovisand Rd PL9 135 E3
Bowden 14 EX23 4 D1
Bowden Park Rd PL6 125 A1
Bowdens Row TR15 140 A4
Bowers Park Dr PL6 125 E7
Bowers Rd PL2 128 B5
Bowglas Cl TR20 89 A8
Bowhays Wlk 2 PL6 129 C7
Bowjey Ct 9 TR18 143 C1
Bowjey Hill TR18 143 C1
Bowjey Terr 5 TR18 143 C1
Bow La EX23 4 D2
Bowles Rd TR11 145 A6
Bowling Gn
 Menheniot PL14 51 F5
 34 St Ives TR26 141 B6
Bowling Gn The TR2 82 F2
BOWLING GREEN
 Bugle 47 E1
 Redruth 139 D3
Bowling Green Ct
 Hayle TR27 142 D5
 Liskeard PL14 113 B5
Bowling Green Rd TR11 92 F3
Bowling Green Terr 35 TR26 141 B6
Bownder Dowr TR27 142 B3
Bownder Vean PL25 115 A5
Bowood Pk
 Delabole PL33 14 F1
 Helstone PL32 24 B8
Boxhill Cl PL5 124 B3
Boxhill Gdns PL2 128 C8
Box's Shop EX23 7 A4
Boxwell Pk PL31 109 F4
Boyd Ave PL28 107 C5
BOYTON 13 B2
Boyton Com Prim Sch PL15 13 A3
Bracken Cl
 Bodmin PL31 109 E5
 Plymouth PL6 125 D8
Brackenside PL13 62 D1
Bracken Terr TR7 110 E5
Brackwell Pl PL27 108 B5
BRADDOCK 49 F5
Braddock CE Prim Sch PL14 50 B6
Braddock Cl PL26 58 D6
Braddons Hill PL7 130 B7
Bradfield Cl PL6 125 E1
BRADFORD 24 D2
Bradford Cl PL6 129 B7
Bradford Quay Rd PL27 108 C6
Bradley Rd
 Newquay TR7 111 C7
 Plymouth PL4 128 F4
Bradridge Ct PL15 13 A4
Braemar Cl PL7 131 C4
Braeside Pk PL14 50 E8
Braggs Hill PL15 13 B3
Brake La PL10 132 B5
Brake Rd PL5 124 E2
Brake The PL14 37 F4
Bramblebank TR11 145 B7
Bramble Cl
 Newquay TR7 111 A4
 Plymouth PL3 129 B7
 Widemouth Bay EX23 6 F5
Bramble Hill EX23 104 E5
Brambles The
 Liskeard PL14 113 E5
 Lostwithiel PL22 112 C3
Bramble Wlk 1 PL6 129 C7
Bramfield Pl PL6 129 D7
Bramley Cl PL25 114 E4
Bramley Pk PL31 109 F5
Bramley Rd PL3 129 C4
Brancker Rd PL2 128 C6
Brandon Rd PL3 129 C4
Brandon Wlk EX23 6 F5
Brandreth Rd 3 PL3 128 F6
Brandy La TR20 89 F4
BRANE 87 C3
Branksome Dr PL27 108 E5
Brannel Sch The PL26 58 B3
Branscombe Gdns PL5 124 A3
Branson Ct 9 PL7 131 C5
Branson Pk PL19 42 A6
Branwell La TR18 88 E6
Braunton Wlk PL6 129 E8
Bray Cl PL19 147 A5
Brayford Cl PL5 124 B3
Bray Rise TR16 80 A5
BRAY SHOP 28 B1
Bray's Pl PL25 114 F4
Brays Terr 2 TR16 140 F1
BRAZACOTT 12 B2
Brazacott Cross PL15 12 B2
BREA 139 B3
BREA ADDIT 139 B2
Brea Arch TR14 139 A3
Bread St TR18 143 E5
BREAGE 90 F3
Breage CE Sch TR13 90 F3
Break My Neck La TR20 88 B8
Breakwater Hill PL4 149 C1
Breakwater Ind Est PL9 135 C8
Breakwater Rd
 Bude EX23 104 D5
 Plymouth PL9 135 C8
Brean Down Cl PL3 128 E6
Brean Down Rd PL3 128 E7
Brea Rd PL27 21 D2
Breaside TR14 139 A3
Brecon Cl
 Plymouth PL3 129 A7
 1 St Agnes TR5 54 C1
Bredon Ct TR7 110 C6
Bree Shute La 4 PL31 109 E5
BRENT 62 E2
Brentford Ave PL5 124 B5
Brent Knoll Rd 1 PL3 128 E6
Brenton Rd PL11 64 B5
Brentons Pk PL29 22 D6
Brentor Rd
 Mary Tavy PL19 30 F6
 Plymouth PL4 129 B2
Brent Tor★ PL19 30 D7
Brentwartha PL13 62 E2
Brest Rd PL6 125 A3
Brest Way PL6 125 A3
Bretonside PL4 149 A2
Brett Wlk PL7 130 F7
Brewartha TR2 57 E1
Brewers Cl PL30 47 F6
Brewers Hill PL26 58 C8
Brewers Rd TR1 137 F5
Brewery Hill TR26 77 E4
Brewery La TR13 146 B6
Briansway PL12 122 D2
Briardale Rd PL2 127 F6
Briarfield PL23 116 D4
Briarleigh Cl PL6 125 F2
Briar Rd
 Bude EX23 104 E4
 Plymouth PL3 128 F7
Briars Row PL12 122 D4
Briars Ryn PL12 53 B7
Briar Tor PL20 42 D3
Briarwood PL14 113 D5
Brickfields Sp Ctr PL1 127 F2
Brickworks Hill TR16 68 D1
Bridals La PL13 62 E2
BRIDGE 67 E5
Bridge TR9 45 E7
Bridge Cl TR7 111 A4
Bridge Ct PL25 114 F4
Bridge Hill
 Illogan TR16 67 E5
 St Columb Major TR9 45 E6
Bridge Ho
 Delabole PL33 14 E2
 Hayle TR27 142 B6
Bridge Ho The 13 TR18 143 C2
Bridge La PL12 53 A3
Bridgemead Cl PL26 114 C1
Bridgemoor Cross EX22 8 C6
BRIDGEND 112 E3
Bridge Pk EX22 8 A5
Bridge Rd
 Goonhavern TR4 55 D4
 Illogan TR16 67 E4
 Seaton PL11 64 B5
 St Austell PL25 114 B3
 Tideford PL12 52 F2
Bridge Row TR16 67 E5
BRIDGERULE 8 A6
Bridgerule CE Prim Sch EX22 8 A5
Bridgerule Ind Est EX22 7 F4
BRIDGES 59 F8
Bridge St
 Par PL24 60 B6
 7 Stratton EX23 4 D1
Bridges The PL12 122 E1
Bridge The PL1 148 B1
BRIDGETOWN 19 B8
Bridge View PL27 108 C6
Bridge Wlk 2 PL35 9 C2
Bridgwater Cl PL6 125 B1
Bridle Cl PL7 131 B7
Bridle Way
 Quintrell Downs TR8 44 E3
 Saltash PL12 122 D4
Bridwell Cl PL5 127 E8
Bridwell Lane N PL5 127 E8
Bridwell Rd PL5 127 E8
BRIGHTON 57 D5
Brillwater Rd TR11 92 E4
Brimford Cross EX22 3 D4
Brimhill Cl PL7 131 B3
Brisbane Terr PL14 113 C5
Brismar Wlk 3 PL6 129 C7
Briston Orch PL12 53 E7
Britannia Pl PL4 129 B2
Briticheston Cl PL9 136 A5
British Rd TR5 54 D1
Briton's Hill TR18 143 F6
Brixham Wlk PL6 129 E8
BRIXTON 136 F4
Brixton Lodge Gdns PL8 136 F5
Brixton Terr TR13 146 C6
Broad Cl PL22 11 E7
Broadclose Hill EX23 104 E5
Broad La
 Illogan TR15 139 D7
 Trematon PL12 53 E2
Broadland Gdns PL9 136 A8
Broadland La PL9 135 F8
Broadlands Cl PL7 131 A3
BROADLANE 90 E5
Broadley Ct PL6 121 B2
Broadley Ind Pk PL6 121 B2
Broadley Park Rd PL6 121 B2
Broad Mead PL17 39 E5
Broad Park Rd
 Bere Alston PL20 41 B2
 Plymouth PL3 128 D6
Broad Pk
 Launceston PL15 106 B7
 Plymouth PL9 135 C7
 St Keyne PL14 51 B3
Broadshell Cross EX22 8 E5
Broads La TR11 81 F3
Broad St
 12 Launceston PL15 106 C6
 Lifton PL16 19 F4
 Newquay TR7 110 D6
 Padstow PL28 107 D5
 Penryn TR10 144 D7
 7 St Columb Major TR9 45 E6
 Truro TR1 137 E5
Broads Yd PL11 64 C5
Broadview PL19 30 A6
Broad View TR4 56 D1
Broadway The PL9 135 E7
Broad Wlk
 Helston TR13 146 B7
 Saltash PL12 122 E1
Brock Ho 9 PL4 149 A2
Brockhole La PL7 130 E8
Brockley Rd PL3 129 C4
Brocks La PL10 132 F5
Brockstone Rd PL25 115 A5
Brockton Gdns PL6 125 B6
BROCTON 34 A3
Bromfield Cres TR2 57 E1
Bromhead Ct PL6 129 A8
Bromley Ho 6 PL2 128 A4
Bromley Pl 5 PL2 128 A4
Bronescombe Cl TR10 144 D7
Bronte Pl PL5 124 D1
BROOK 147 B2
Brook Cl
 Helston TR13 146 B7
 Plymouth PL7 131 A3
Brook Ct 6 TR11 145 A4
Brookdale Ct 12 PL27 108 B5
Brookdown Terr PL12 122 E3
Brookdown Villas PL12 122 E3
Brook Dr EX23 104 E7
Brooke Cl PL12 123 A2
Brookfield Cl
 Lanjeth PL26 58 E3
 Plymouth PL7 131 B5
Brookfields Cl PL1 127 F1
Brook Green Ctr for Learning PL5 124 B4
Brooking Cl PL6 129 A8
Brookingfield Cl PL7 130 C5
Brooking Way PL12 122 C3
Brook La PL19 147 B2
Brooklands
 New Polzeath PL27 21 D6
 Tavistock PL19 147 D6
Brooklands Ct PL6 124 E3
Brooklyn Flats 18 TR2 95 A6
Brooklyn Terr 17 TR2 95 A6
Brook Pl
 Falmouth TR11 145 A4
 Penryn TR10 144 C7
Brook Rd
 Falmouth TR11 144 F3
 Wadebridge PL27 108 B5
Brooks PL22 49 E3
Brookside
 Chacewater TR4 68 F3
 St Austell PL25 114 F4
Brookside Cl PL15 106 B8
Brook St
 Falmouth TR11 145 A4
 17 Mousehole TR19 88 C1
 Tavistock PL19 147 C6
Brook The PL12 122 E4
Brookward Terr 8 TR18 143 C7
Brookway TR27 142 E7
Brookwood Rd PL9 136 D7
Broomfield Dr
 Bodmin PL31 109 B3
 Plymouth PL9 135 C5
Broomfield Rd PL27 108 D5
Broom Hill PL12 122 D2
Broomhill Cross EX22 5 E3
Broomhill La EX23 4 D2
Broom Pk PL9 135 D5
Broughton Cl PL3 128 F7
Browne Memorial Almshouses PL19 147 A5
Browning Cl 14 TR9 45 D6
Browning Dr PL31 109 C3
Browning Rd PL2 128 A5
Brownlow Pl 5 PL31 109 D5
Brownlow St PL1 148 A2
Browns Hill PL23 116 C4
Brown's Hill TR10 144 C8
Broxton Dr PL9 129 E1
Bruallen Cl PL30 23 E7
Brunel Ave PL2 127 F5
Brunel Prim Sch PL12 122 E2
Brunel Quays PL22 112 D2
Brunel Rd PL12 122 C4
Brunel Terr 3 PL2 127 F5
Brunel Way PL1 148 A2
BRUNNION 77 A3
Brunswick Pl 10 PL2 127 F4
Brunswick Rd PL4 149 B2
Brush End TR26 77 E4
Brynmoor Cl PL3 129 A7
Brynmoor Pk PL3 129 A6
Brynmoor Wlk PL3 129 A6
Bryny Cl PL30 23 E7
Buckett's Hill TR15 140 C2
Buckeys La TR2 95 B6
Buckfast Cl PL2 128 A8
Buckingham Nip TR4 68 F3
Buckingham Pl PL5 123 E2
Buckingham's Cl TR8 56 B7
Buckingham Terr TR16 68 D1
Buckland Abbey★ PL20 41 F1
Buckland Cl PL7 130 D7
BUCKLAND MONACHORUM 42 A3
Buckland St PL1 148 B2
Buckland Terr PL20 42 C2
Bucklawren Rd PL13 63 E7
Bucklers Ho PL25 115 B4
Bucklers La PL25 115 B4
Buckler Village (Mobile Homes Pk) PL25 115 B4
Buckwell St PL1, PL4 149 A2
Buctor Pk PL19 41 D8
Buddle Cl
 Plymouth PL9 136 A5
 Tavistock PL19 147 B6
BUDE 104 E6
Budehaven Com Sch EX23 104 F5
Budehaven L Ctr EX23 104 F5
Bude Ind Est EX23 104 F4
Bude Inf Sch EX23 104 E5
Bude Jun Sch EX23 104 E5
Bude Marshes Nature Reserve★ EX23 104 D4
Bude-Stratton Bsns Pk EX23 7 B8
Bude-Stratton Mus★ EX23 104 D5
Budge Mdws PL15 28 C4
Budleigh Cl PL9 135 F5
Budnic Est TR6 55 B5
Budnic Hill TR6 55 B5
Budock Pl TR11 145 B4
Budock Terr TR11 145 B3
Budock Vean La TR11 93 B2
BUDOCK WATER 144 C2
Budshead Gn PL5 124 C4
Budshead Rd PL5 124 C4
Budshead Way PL5 124 E2
Buena Vista Cl PL6 125 D6
Buena Vista Dr PL6 125 C6
Buena Vista Gdns PL6 125 C6
Buena Vista Way PL6 125 C6
BUGLE 47 D1
Bugle Rural Workshops PL26 47 C1
Bugle Sch PL26 47 C1
Bugle Sta PL26 47 C2
Buildings The TR20 89 A6
Bullan's La TR26 141 A5
Bullans Terr 5 TR26 141 A5
Bulleid Cl PL2 127 F7
Bulleid Way EX23 104 E4
Buller Cl
 Plymouth PL7 130 F4
 Torpoint PL11 127 A3
Buller Hill TR16 80 B6
Buller Ho PL13 117 D3
Buller Pk
 Liskeard PL14 113 D5
 Saltash PL12 122 D3
Buller Rd PL11 127 B3
Buller St PL13 117 C3
Bullers Terr TR15 140 D5
Bull Hill PL23 116 D4
Bullock La
 Helston, Lower Green TR13 146 B5
 Helston, Whitehill TR13 146 C4
Bullock Market Terr 27 TR18 143 E6
Bulmer Rd PL4 149 C3
Bulteel Gdns PL6 124 E7
Bulwark Rd TR13 146 B4
Bungalows The
 Looe PL13 117 D6
 Tintagel PL34 14 D7
Bunkers Hill
 22 St Ives TR26 141 B6
 Townshend TR27 90 C8
Bunyan Cl PL5 124 C2
Burden Cl PL31 109 C4
Burgess Cl EX23 4 D2
BURHOS 79 F2
Burhos Row TR13 79 F1
Buriton Row 32 TR18 143 E5
BURLAWN 108 D1
Burleigh La PL3 128 D7
Burleigh Manor PL3 128 D7
Burleigh Park Rd PL3 128 D6
Burley Cl TR1 137 D3
Burley Ct TR11 145 B4
Burnard Cl PL6 124 E7
Burnards Ct 7 PL31 109 D5
Burnett Cl PL12 122 D2
Burnett Rd PL6 128 F8
Burnham Park Rd PL3 128 D6
Burniston Cl PL7 131 A3
Burnistone Cl PL7 131 A3
Burn La PL19 30 E8
Burns Ave PL5 124 C2
Burns View PL11 65 B5
Burnthouse PL14 37 C1
Burnthouse Cotts TR10 81 C1
Burnthouse La TR27 142 D5
Burn View EX23 104 D6
Burnwithian Terr TR16 68 D1
BURRATON 122 D4
BURRATON COOMBE 122 C2
Burraton Prim Sch PL12 122 C3
Burraton Rd PL12 122 C4
Burrator Rd PL20 42 E3
Burrington Ind Est PL5 124 A1
Burrington Rd PL5 124 A1
Burrington Way PL5 124 B1
Burrow Hill PL9 135 E6
Burrows The TR26 141 A5
BURSDON 3 B6
Bursdon Moor Cross EX39 3 B7
Burthallan La TR26 77 A7
Burton Cl PL6 125 B6
Burton Ho 15 PL25 114 C3
Burwell Cl PL6 125 E4
Bury Cl PL15 11 B1
Bush Hill PL14 36 F2

Chacewater Prim Sch TR4 69 A3
CHADDLEWOOD 131 B6
Chaddlewood Ave PL4 149 B3
Chaddlewood Cl PL7 131 A4
Chaddlewood Ho PL7 131 B5
Chaddlewood Prim Sch PL7 131 A5
Chagford Wlk PL6 129 E8
Chainwalk Dr TR1 137 C6
Chalets The TR18 88 E6
Chalet The PL11 64 C4
Challacombe Gdns TR10 144 C8
Challenger Quay 12 TR11 145 C3
Challgood Cl 1 PL9 135 F5
Challgood Rise PL9 135 F5
Challis Ave TR8 45 A8
Challock Cl PL6 125 D4
Chamberlayne Dr PL7 130 E6
Champion's Ct TR13 146 B6
Chancery Cl TR4 70 D8
Chancery La 23 TR18 143 E5
Chandlers Wlk PL25 115 A3
Chandos Pl 12 PL25 114 C3
Channel Park Ave PL3 129 B5
Channel View
Polruan PL23 116 D2
St Austell PL25 115 A6
St Ives TR26 141 A6
Channel View Terr
Plymouth PL4 149 C4
4 Redruth TR15 140 C4
Channon Rd PL12 122 C4
Chantry Ct PL7 130 B5
Chantry La PL13 117 E4
Chantry Pk 18 PL17 39 E4
CHAPEL
Launceston 106 A5
Quintrell Downs 111 E4
Chapel Cl
Camborne, Kehelland TR14 66 F1
Camborne, Tuckingmill TR14 139 A4
Coad's Green PL15 27 D3
Connor Downs TR27 78 D6
Crantock TR8 110 A3
Gunnislake PL18 40 E5
4 Horrabridge PL20 42 C4
Lanivet PL30 47 E6
St Just in Roseland TR2 82 F2
Chapel Cnr EX22 8 A5
Chapel Cotts EX23 4 C8
Chapel Cres TR4 56 A2
Chapel Ct
Camborne TR14 138 F4
Padstow PL28 107 D5
9 Redruth TR15 140 B5
Chapeldown Rd PL11 127 A2
Chapel Farm TR14 79 E5
Chapel Field PL25 115 B5
Chapel Gn PL26 59 A1
Chapel Ground PL13 117 C3
Chapel Hill
Camborne, Brea TR14 139 A3
Camborne, Tregajorran TR15 139 C4
Gweek TR12 92 C2
Hayle TR27 142 C6
Lanner TR16 80 D6
Launceston PL15 106 B5
Newquay TR7 110 D6
Perranporth TR6 55 B4
Polgooth PL26 59 A1
Ponsanooth TR3 81 B4
Porthtowan TR4 68 A5
Redruth TR16 68 A4
St Erth TR27 142 A1
Sticker PL26 58 F1
Truro TR1 137 B4
Chapel La
Bodmin PL31 109 D5
Goldsithney TR20 89 F5
Hayle TR27 142 D6
Horrabridge PL20 42 C4
Lizard TR12 102 F2
Penryn TR10 144 C7
Polruan PL23 116 D2
St Austell PL25 115 C6
St Mabyn PL30 34 D8
St Teath PL30 23 F6
5 Wadebridge PL27 108 B5
Chapel Mdw
Buckland Monachorum PL20 41 F3
Perranarworthal TR3 81 D6
Chapel Park Terr PL15 106 B5
Chapel Pk PL15 106 B5
Chapel Pl
Pillaton PL12 53 B7
16 Truro TR1 137 D4
Chapel Point La PL26 73 C2
Chapel Rd
Camborne TR14 139 A4
Foxhole PL26 58 D5
Heamoor TR18 143 C8
Indian Queens TR9 45 E1
Leedstown TR27 78 E1
2 Par PL24 60 C4
Roche PL26 46 F3
Saltash PL12 122 B3
St Just TR19 86 E6
St Tudy PL30 23 E3
Chapel Row
Praze-an-Beeble TR14 79 B2
2 Redruth TR15 140 B5
Tremar PL14 38 A3
Chapel Row *continued*
Truro TR1 137 D4
Widegates PL13 63 F8
Chapel Sq
Crowlas TR20 89 B8
Mevagissey PL26 73 C3
Troon TR14 79 E5
Chapel St
4 Bere Alston PL20 41 B1
4 Callington PL17 39 F4
Camborne TR14 138 D2
Camelford PL32 105 C4
Grimscott EX23 5 B2
Gunnislake PL18 40 F6
Lifton PL16 19 F4
Marazion TR17 89 B5
Mevagissey PL26 73 C3
21 Mousehole TR19 88 C1
9 Newlyn TR18 143 C2
Penzance TR18 143 E5
Plymouth, Mount Wise PL1 127 E2
Plymouth PL4 149 A3
Probus TR2 71 C6
Redruth TR15 140 B5
St Day TR16 68 D1
St Ives TR26 141 B5
St Just TR19 86 E6
Tavistock PL19 147 B5
Chapel Terr
Camborne TR15 139 D6
Devoran TR3 81 F6
Falmouth TR11 145 B4
Hayle TR27 142 B5
Par PL24 60 B6
9 Porthleven TR13 98 B8
Portreath TR16 67 C6
Redruth, Carn Brea Village TR15 139 F5
Redruth TR15 140 D2
Ruan Minor TR12 103 A5
St Day TR16 68 E1
10 St Mawes TR2 95 A6
Trewellard TR19 86 F8
CHAPEL TOWN 57 B6
Chapel Town Bsns Pk TR8 57 B7
Chapel Town Cl TR11 93 D4
Chapel Way PL3 129 A6
CHAPLE AMBLE 22 D2
Chapman Ct PL12 122 B3
Chapmans Ope PL1 127 D2
CHAPMAN'S WELL 13 E4
Charaton Cross PL14 38 F4
Chard Barton PL5 124 B3
Chard Rd PL5 123 D2
Chard Terr 6 TR11 145 A3
Charfield Dr PL6 129 A8
Chariot Rd TR15 139 E6
Charles Ave TR11 144 E2
Charles Bassett Cl 6 TR13 146 C5
Charles Cl PL25 114 F3
Charles Cross PL4 149 A3
Charles St
Bugle PL26 47 C1
Newlyn TR18 143 C3
Plymouth PL4 149 A3
Truro TR1 137 C4
Charles Terr PL3 129 A6
CHARLESTOWN 115 B2
Charlestown Prim Sch PL25 115 C3
Charlestown Rd PL25 115 B3
Charlestown Shipwreck & Heritage Ctr★ PL25 115 B2
Charlotte Cl TR4 68 C6
Charlotte St PL2 127 E4
Charlton Cres PL6 125 A2
Charlton Rd PL6 125 A3
Charnhill Cl PL9 136 A6
Charnhill Way PL9 136 A6
Charter Cl TR13 146 C4
Charter Ct TR10 144 D7
Charter Way PL14 113 E6
Chateau Cl PL26 46 D1
Chatsworth Gdns PL5 123 F3
Chatsworth Way PL25 115 C2
Chaucer Rd PL19 147 D5
Chaucer Way PL5 124 C1
Chawleigh Cl PL18 40 F5
Chedworth St PL4 149 A3
Chegwin Gdns TR7 110 E5
Chegwins Hill PL26 58 D5
Chegwyn Gdns 6 TR5 54 C1
Chegwyns PL26 58 D5
Chelfham Senior Sch PL20 40 F3
Chelfham Senior Sch Continuing Ed Department PL19 30 E3
Chellean Vean TR4 81 C7
Chellew Rd TR1 137 F5
Chelmer Cl PL7 131 A5
Chelmsford Pl PL5 124 C4
Chelson Gdns PL6 125 E3
Cheltenham Pl
Newquay TR7 110 D6
Plymouth PL4 149 B4
Chelwood Gr PL7 130 F5
CHENHALLS 142 A2
Chenhalls Cl TR27 77 E2
Chenhalls Rd TR27 142 A2
Chenoweth Cl TR14 138 C4
Chepstow Ave PL6 125 C8
Chequer Tree Ct PL18 40 F5
Chequetts Cl 10 PL17 39 E4
Cheriton Cl PL5 124 A3
Cherrill Gdns EX23 104 E7
Cherrington TR7 110 B5
Cherry Cross EX22 12 B7
Cherry Gdns 14 TR18 143 E5
Cherry Gdn St 15 TR19 88 C1
Cherry Pk PL7 131 A3
Cherry Tree Cl PL31 109 B4
Cherrytree Ho TR18 143 C5
Cherry Tree La PL7 131 A4
Cherry Tree Mews PL25 114 D3
Cheshire Dr PL6 124 D6
Chesnut Cl PL12 122 D4
Chester Ct TR7 111 A6
Chesterfield Rd PL3 129 B4
Chester Pl 4 PL4 128 E4
Chester Rd TR7 111 A6
Chesterton Cl PL5 124 C3
Chesterton Ct PL27 108 A6
Chesterton Pl TR7 111 A7
Chestnut Ave PL9 135 C5
Chestnut Cl
Callington PL17 40 A4
Falmouth TR11 144 F5
Lamerton PL19 30 A4
St Tudy PL30 23 E3
Tavistock PL19 147 D2
Torpoint PL11 126 F3
24 Yelverton PL20 41 B1
Chestnut Gr PL31 109 B4
Chestnut Rd PL3 128 D7
Chestnut Terr PL19 30 A4
Cheviot Rd TR7 110 E4
Chichester Cl PL26 58 E5
Chichester Cres
Newquay TR7 110 F4
Saltash PL12 122 E1
Chichester Ct PL20 42 C4
Chichester Ho PL1 148 B2
Childrey Gdns PL6 125 C1
Childrey Wlk PL6 125 C1
Chili Rd TR15 139 D6
CHILLATON 29 F8
CHILSWORTHY 40 E7
Chilton Cl PL6 129 B7
China Clay Ctry Pk★ PL26 59 A7
Chings Alley 13 PL15 106 C6
Chipponds Dr PL25 114 A3
Chirgwin Ct 22 TR18 143 E5
Chirgwin Rd TR1 137 E4
Chisholme Cl PL25 114 D3
Chisholme Ct PL25 114 D3
Chittleburn Bsns Pk PL8 136 F6
Chittleburn Cross PL8 136 E5
Chittleburn Hill PL8 136 E5
Chivenor Ave PL5 123 D4
Chiverton Cl TR20 89 F4
Chiverton Cross
Blackwater TR4 68 F5
Rosudgeon TR20 89 F4
Chiverton Greenacres TR5 68 D8
Chiverton Way TR20 89 F4
Chollacott Cl PL19 147 C4
Chollacott La PL19 147 D3
Chough Cl
Falmouth TR11 144 E4
Launceston PL15 106 E4
Chough Cres PL25 114 F4
Choughs Cl TR14 138 B3
Christa Ct PL14 38 D7
Christian Mill Bsns Pk PL6 124 E4
Christian Way TR7 111 C7
Chubb Dr PL3 128 B4
Chudleigh Rd PL4 129 A4
Chun Castle★ TR20 87 C8
CHURCHBRIDGE 50 F1
Church Cl
Blisland PL30 35 D8
Lelant TR26 77 E4
Plymouth PL7 130 B7
Trispen TR4 56 D1
CHURCH COMBE 140 A2
CHURCH COVE 103 A2
Church Cove Rd TR12 103 A2
Church Ct PL6 125 A7
Church End PL13 117 D3
Churchfield Cl TR20 89 A8
Churchfield Pl PL24 60 B5
Churchfields Rd TR8 55 D8
Church Gate 3 PL14 113 C5
Church Hill
Calstock PL18 41 A3
Chacewater TR4 68 F2
Golant PL23 61 B6
Helston TR13 146 C7
Herodsfoot PL14 50 E3
Hessenford PL11, PL12 64 B8
Ludgvan TR20 89 A8
Milton Combe PL20 41 F1
Penryn TR10 144 D8
5 Pensilva PL14 38 E4
Plymouth PL6 125 B1
Port Isaac PL29 22 D7
St Day TR16 68 E1
Sticker PL26 58 F1
7 St Mawes TR2 95 A6
Tavistock PL19 147 E2
Tintagel PL34 14 C7
Church Hill Rd PL9 135 A6
Church Ho PL12 123 A2
Churchill Rd PL19 147 D2
Churchill Way
10 Penwithick PL26 59 D7
Plymouth PL3 128 E6
Churchill Wlk PL12 122 E1
Church La
Bodmin PL31 109 E5
Bude EX23 104 D5
Church La *continued*
Calstock PL18 41 A3
Camborne TR14 138 D3
Cargreen PL12 119 A1
Flushing TR11 145 B7
Helston TR13 146 B6
Lelant TR26 77 E4
Lostwithiel PL22 112 C2
Mevagissey PL26 73 C4
Padstow PL28 107 D5
Redruth TR15 140 A3
St Columb Minor TR7 111 E7
St John PL11 132 B8
Tavistock PL19 147 C5
Churchlands PL13 117 D5
Churchlands Cl PL6 125 E7
Churchlands Rd PL6 125 E8
Church Lea
Launceston PL15 106 A7
Tavistock PL19 147 E2
Church Mews
Stithians TR3 80 F3
Week St Mary EX22 11 E8
Church Park Ct PL6 125 E8
Church Park Mews PL27 108 B4
Church Park Rd
Crackington Haven EX23 10 C6
Plymouth PL6 125 E8
Church Path EX23 104 C5
Church Pk
Bodmin PL31 109 F5
Horrabridge PL20 42 C4
Lerryn PL22 61 D8
St Mellion PL12 53 D8
Church Pl
Liskeard PL14 113 C5
18 St Ives TR26 141 B6
Church Rd
Camborne TR15 139 B6
Cury TR12 99 A4
Four Lanes TR16 80 A5
Heamoor TR18 143 C7
Illogan TR16 67 E4
Lanivet PL30 47 E7
Launceston PL15 18 F6
Lelant TR26 77 E4
Mabe Burnthouse TR10 93 C8
Madron TR20 143 A8
Mount Hawke TR4 68 C6
Mylor Bridge TR11 82 B2
Pendeen TR19 75 A1
Penponds TR14 138 B1
Penryn TR10 144 C8
Perranarworthal TR3 81 D5
Plymouth, Plympton PL7 130 F4
Plymouth, Plymstock PL9 135 F7
Saltash PL12 122 D2
Shortlanesend TR4 69 F6
St Austell PL25 115 B3
St Dennis PL26 46 C1
Stithians TR3 80 F4
St Tudy PL30 23 E3
Tideford PL12 52 F2
Church Row
Carharrack TR16 80 F8
Lanner TR16 80 D6
3 Porthleven TR13 98 B8
Sheviock PL11 65 C6
Church Row La PL5 124 C6
Church Sq
8 Bodmin PL31 109 E5
Constantine TR11 92 F4
St Just TR19 86 F6
4 Stratton EX23 4 E1
Church St
Callington PL17 39 E4
Calstock PL18 41 A3
Camborne TR14 138 D3
Carharrack TR16 80 F8
Falmouth TR11 145 B4
Gorran Haven PL26 85 D5
Helston TR13 146 B6
Landrake PL12 53 C3
Launceston PL15 106 C6
Liskeard PL14 113 C5
Looe, East Looe PL13 117 D3
Looe, West Looe PL13 117 C3
Mevagissey PL26 73 C3
15 Newlyn TR18 143 C1
Padstow PL28 107 D5
Par PL24 60 B5
Plymouth PL3 128 A4
Poughill EX23 4 D2
8 St Austell PL25 114 C3
St Columb Minor TR7 111 D7
St Day TR16 68 E1
St Erth TR27 142 A1
St Germans PL12 65 A8
St Just TR19 86 F6
5 Stratton EX23 4 E1
Tywardreath PL24 60 D5
Churchstow Wlk PL6 129 E8
Church Street N PL14 113 C5
Church Street S PL14 113 C5
Church Terr
Devoran TR3 81 F6
Grampound Road TR2 57 E1
St Kew PL30 23 A3
CHURCHTOWN
Bridgerule 8 B6
Camborne 67 E5
Lanivet 47 E7
St Breward 24 B4
CHURCH TOWN 140 A3
Churchtown
Cardinham PL30 35 F3
Gwinear TR27 78 D4
7 Mullion TR12 99 A2
Churchtown *continued*
5 St Agnes TR5 54 C1
St Minver PL27 22 A4
St Newlyn East TR8 56 B7
Church Town TR11 144 D3
Church Town Cotts TR3 81 D5
Churchtown Mdws PL26 58 B4
Churchtown Mews PL30 35 C8
Churchtown Rd
Gwithian TR27 66 B2
Illogan TR16 67 E5
Phillack TR27 142 C7
Portscatho TR2 83 B2
St Stephen PL26 58 B4
Churchtown Terr PL27 32 D6
Churchtown Vale PL12 122 D1
Church View
St Cleer PL14 37 F3
St Dominick PL12 40 D2
St Neot PL14 36 F2
Treburley PL15 28 B5
Walkhampton PL20 42 E4
Church View Cl TR18 143 B6
Church View Rd
Camborne TR14 138 F4
Probus TR2 71 D6
Churchway
Madron TR20 143 A8
11 Marazion TR17 89 C5
Church Way
Falmouth TR11 144 E3
Plymouth PL5 127 E8
St Clether PL15 17 B2
Church Wlk
Redruth TR15 140 A5
South Petherwin PL15 27 E8
12 Truro TR1 137 D5
Chute La PL26 85 D5
Chy-an-Chy 19 TR26 141 B6
Chyanclare TR18 143 D6
Chyandaunce Cl TR18 143 F8
Chyandaunce Terr TR18 143 F8
Chyandor Cl PL24 60 C4
CHYANDOUR 143 F7
Chyandour TR15 140 A4
Chyandour Cl 1 TR26 77 A6
Chyandour Cliff TR18 143 F6
Chyandour La TR18 143 F7
Chy-an-Dour Rd TR20 90 C3
Chyandour Sq TR18 143 F7
Chyandour Terr TR18 143 F7
Chy an Dowr TR27 142 E7
CHY-AN-GWEAL 141 B2
Chy-an-Gweal Est TR20 89 A7
Chy-an-Hall TR18 143 F8
Chy-an-Mor TR20 88 F6
Chy Cober TR27 142 E7
CHYCOOSE 82 A6
Chycoose Parc TR3 82 A5
Chycornick Terr TR18 143 F8
Chygothow TR13 146 B6
Chy Hwel TR1 137 F6
Chy Kensa Cl TR27 142 C5
Chylan Cres TR7 111 E6
Chymeddon TR7 110 E6
Chy Nampara 1 TR11 145 A4
Chynance
Penzance TR18 143 D4
Portreath TR16 67 C6
Chynance Dr TR7 110 D5
CHYNHALE 91 C5
Chynoon Gdns PL25 114 F6
Chynowen La TR8 43 D1
Chynowen Parc TR8 43 D1
Chynoweth PL26 59 C8
Chynoweth Gdns TR18 143 F8
Chynoweth La TR20 89 F6
Chy Pons PL25 114 A4
Chypons Est TR 20 76 F3
Chypons Rd TR12 99 B3
Chypraze Ct TR14 138 B3
Chyreen La
Carnon Downs TR3 81 F8
Playing Place TR3 82 A8
Chyrn Dr PL30 24 B3
Chyrose Rd TR16 68 D1
Chysauster Ancient Village★ TR 20 76 D2
Chytodden Terr TR13 90 F5
Chytroose Cl TR13 146 D8
Chyvelah Ope TR1 69 E3
Chyvelah Rd TR3 69 D4
Chyvelah Vale TR1 69 E3
Chyvellas Cl TR18 143 B1
Chyventon Cl TR19 97 B6
Chyventon Ho TR15 140 B5
Chyverton Cl TR7 110 D4
Chyvogue Mdw TR3 81 D6
Chywoone Ave TR18 143 C1
Chywoone Cres TR18 143 C1
Chywoone Gr TR19 97 F8
Chywoone Hill TR18 143 C1
Chywoone Pl TR18 143 C1
Chywoone Rural Workshops TR19 87 A5
Chywoon Gdns TR15 139 D7
Citadel Ope 13 PL1 149 A2
Citadel Road E PL1 149 A2
Citadel Road W PL1 148 C2
Citadel The★ PL1 149 A1
City Bsns Pk PL3 128 A4
City Coll Plymouth (Kings Road Ctr) PL1 128 A2
City Coll Plymouth (Learning Warehouse) PL1 148 B2

Court Mdw PL13 ... 62 B7
Courtnay Cl PL13 ... 117 D4
Courtney Ho PL5 ... 124 B2
Courtney Rd
  Liskeard PL14 ... 113 D6
  St Austell PL25 ... 114 F5
  Truro TR1 ... 137 B5
Court The
  Camborne TR15 ... 139 C4
  Plymouth PL6 ... 125 C7
  Saltash PL12 ... 122 C2
Court View PL8 ... 136 F4
Courtyard Cotts TR4 ... 70 C6
Courtyard The
  Redruth TR16 ... 139 F2
  Truro TR1 ... 137 D3
Cove Hill
  Perranarworthal TR3 ... 81 D5
  Sennen Cove TR19 ... 96 B7
Cove Mdw PL11 ... 127 A6
Coventry Rd TR11 ... 145 B6
COVERACK ... 101 C1
COVERACK BRIDGES ... 91 E5
Coverack Prim Sch TR12 ... 101 C1
Cove Rd TR19 ... 96 C7
Coverdale Pl PL5 ... 124 C1
Cove The TR4 ... 68 A7
Cowdray Cl PL12 ... 122 E2
Cowdray Terr PL12 ... 122 E1
Cow Lard Cl PL15 ... 106 A4
Cowley Rd PL5 ... 124 D3
Cowling Gdns PL14 ... 51 F6
Cowling Rd 2 TR3 ... 81 F7
COXFORD ... 10 D7
COX HILL ... 68 F2
COXPARK ... 40 D7
Cox Park Terr PL18 ... 40 C6
Cox's Cl PL6 ... 125 B1
COXSIDE ... 149 B1
Coxs Mdw EX22 ... 13 C7
Cox Tor Cl 6 PL20 ... 42 C3
Cox Tor Rd PL19 ... 147 E5
Coypool Rd PL7 ... 130 A6
Crabbs Cl PL15 ... 13 F1
Crabbtree Cl 3 PL14 ... 113 B5
CRABTREE ... 129 E5
Crabtree Cl PL3 ... 129 F5
Crabtree La PL30, PL31 ... 109 D2
Crabtree Villas PL3 ... 129 E5
CRACKINGTON HAVEN ... 10 B7
Crackston Cl PL6 ... 129 B7
CRAFTHOLE ... 65 B5
Craigie Dr PL1 ... 148 A3
Craigmore Ave PL2 ... 127 F5
Craigside PL13 ... 117 D4
Cramber Cl
  Roborough PL6 ... 125 C8
  5 Tavistock PL19 ... 147 B4
Cranberry Rd TR14 ... 138 B3
Cranbourne Ave PL4 ... 149 C4
CRANE ... 138 C2
Crane Manor Ct TR14 ... 138 C2
Crane Rd TR14 ... 138 C2
Cranfield PL7 ... 130 C7
Cranfield Rd TR14 ... 138 B3
Cranmere Rd PL3 ... 129 A6
CRANTOCK ... 43 D3
Crantock St TR7 ... 110 D6
Crantock Terr 7 PL2 ... 128 A5
CRAPSTONE ... 42 B2
Crapstone Terr PL20 ... 42 B2
Crashaw Cl PL5 ... 124 D3
Craven Ave PL4 ... 149 C4
Crawford Rd PL1 ... 148 A4
Creakavose PL26 ... 58 B4
Creakavose Pk PL26 ... 58 A4
Crealy Adventure Park (Cornwall)★ PL27 ... 32 D4
CREAN ... 96 F5
Crease La PL19 ... 147 A4
Creathorne Rd EX23 ... 104 E7
Creative Unit (Krowji)★ TR15 ... 140 A4
Creaz-an-Bre PL26 ... 58 D5
Crediton Wlk PL6 ... 129 E8
CREED ... 72 A6
Creed La TR2 ... 72 A7
Creedy Rd PL3 ... 129 C5
CREEGBRAWSE ... 68 F2
Creekside View TR2 ... 70 F4
Creeping La
  Newlyn TR18 ... 143 C3
  Penzance TR18 ... 143 C4
Crelake Cl PL19 ... 147 C4
Crelake Ind Est 1 PL19 ... 147 B4
Crelake Pk PL19 ... 147 C4
Crellow Fields TR3 ... 80 F3
Crellow Hill TR3 ... 80 F3
Crellow La TR3 ... 80 F3
Crellow Terr TR3 ... 80 F3
Crellow Vale TR3 ... 80 F3
CRELLY ... 91 F7
Crembling Well TR15 ... 139 E6
CREMYLL ... 133 E7
Cremyll Rd PL11 ... 127 B2
Cremyll St PL1 ... 134 A8
Crescent Ave PL1 ... 148 B2
Crescent Avenue Mews PL1 ... 148 B2
Crescent Cl
  Hayle TR27 ... 142 C5
  Widemouth Bay EX23 ... 6 F5
Crescent Gdns TR1 ... 137 B4
Crescent Pl TR19 ... 74 F1
Crescent Rd
  Bugle PL26 ... 47 C1
  Truro TR1 ... 137 B4
Crescent Rise
  Constantine Bay PL28 ... 20 C1
  Truro TR1 ... 137 B4
Crescent The
  Bude EX23 ... 104 D5
  Camborne TR14 ... 138 D4
  Carbis Bay TR26 ... 77 C4
  Common Moor PL14 ... 37 F4
  Crapstone PL20 ... 42 B3
  Gunnislake PL18 ... 41 A6
  Landrake PL12 ... 53 C3
  Lifton PL16 ... 19 F4
  Liskeard PL14 ... 113 C6
  Looe PL13 ... 117 D1
  Newquay TR7 ... 110 E6
  Plymouth PL1 ... 148 B2
  Porthleven TR13 ... 91 B1
  St Austell PL25 ... 115 B5
  St Ives TR26 ... 77 A7
  St Mabyn PL30 ... 34 D8
  Truro TR1 ... 137 B4
  Widemouth Bay EX23 ... 6 F5
Cressbrook Cl PL6 ... 125 F2
Cressbrook Dr PL6 ... 125 F2
Cressbrook Wlk PL6 ... 125 E2
Cresthill Rd PL2 ... 128 B7
Creswell Terr TR19 ... 86 F7
Creykes Ct PL1 ... 148 A3
Cribbage Terr 13 PL31 ... 109 D5
Cricketers Hollow PL27 ... 21 E3
Cricket Pk EX23 ... 7 B6
Crift Cotts PL14 ... 51 F7
Crift La PL12 ... 64 F8
Crill Cnr TR11 ... 144 C1
CRIMP ... 3 A2
Crinnick's Hill PL31 ... 109 E4
Crinnis Cl PL25 ... 115 E3
Crinnis Rd PL25 ... 115 B3
Crinnis Wood PL25 ... 115 E3
Crinnis Wood Ave PL25 ... 115 D3
CRIPPLESEASE ... 77 A3
CROANFORD ... 34 C6
Crocker's Row PL18 ... 41 A6
Crockers Way PL15 ... 13 F1
Crockwell St PL31 ... 109 E5
Croft Comm TR14 ... 79 E5
CROFTHANDY ... 68 E1
Croftlands PL27 ... 21 E3
CROFT MITCHELL ... 79 E4
Croft Parc TR12 ... 102 F2
Croft Pk PL6 ... 125 C7
Croft Rd TR18 ... 143 C4
Croft Row TR16 ... 80 F8
Crofty Cl TR15 ... 139 C5
Cromartie Rd PL4 ... 129 B1
Cromer Cl PL6 ... 125 A7
Cromer Wlk PL6 ... 125 A7
Cromwell Gate PL6 ... 125 C7
Cromwell Rd
  Plymouth PL4 ... 149 C3
  St Austell PL25 ... 114 F3
Crookeder Cl PL9 ... 136 A5
Crookedor La PL11 ... 65 D5
Crooklets EX23 ... 104 C7
Crooklets Rd EX23 ... 104 D6
Cross PL30 ... 47 F1
Cross Cl TR7 ... 111 C7
Cross Comm TR12 ... 102 F2
CROSSGATE ... 19 A7
Cross Gn PL15 ... 19 F7
Cross Hill PL2 ... 127 E4
Cross La
  Bodmin PL31 ... 109 E5
  7 St Austell PL25 ... 114 C3
CROSS LANES ... 99 C4
Cross Lanes
  Chacewater TR4 ... 69 B1
  Cross Lanes TR12 ... 99 C4
  Launceston PL15 ... 106 C8
  Stratton EX23 ... 4 F1
Crossmount TR7 ... 111 D7
Cross Park Ave PL6 ... 124 F1
Cross Park Rd PL6 ... 124 F1
Cross Park Terr PL26 ... 73 C4
Cross Park Way PL6 ... 124 F1
Cross Pk
  Buckland Monachorum PL20 ... 42 A3
  Crafthole PL11 ... 65 B5
Crossroads Cl PL28 ... 31 F8
Cross St
  Camborne TR14 ... 138 D2
  Hayle TR27 ... 142 D6
  Helston TR13 ... 146 B6
  Padstow PL28 ... 107 D5
  13 Penzance TR18 ... 143 E6
  3 Redruth TR15 ... 140 B4
  Wadebridge PL27 ... 108 B5
Cross Terr PL18 ... 40 F5
Cross The
  Camborne TR14 ... 138 D2
  St Dominick PL12 ... 40 D2
  St Newlyn East TR8 ... 56 B7
CROSSTOWN ... 2 B1
Crosswalla Fields TR13 ... 146 C7
Crosswater EX23 ... 2 C1
Crossway PL7 ... 130 D7
Crossway Ave PL4 ... 129 B3
Crossways TR11 ... 144 F2
CROWAN ... 79 C1
Crowan Prim Sch TR14 ... 79 C2
CROWLAS ... 89 C8
Crowlas Ind Est TR20 ... 89 B8
Crown Cl TR7 ... 111 A4
Crown Cres TR8 ... 56 B7
Crowndale Ave PL3 ... 129 A6
Crown Gdns PL6 ... 125 A1
CROWNHILL ... 124 F2
Crownhill Ct PL6 ... 124 F2
Crownhill Fort★ PL6 ... 124 F3
Crownhill Fort Rd PL6 ... 124 F3
Crownhill Rd PL5 ... 124 C3
Crown Rd PL26 ... 58 D8
Crown Terr PL26 ... 58 D8
CROWNTOWN ... 91 B5
Crow Pk PL3 ... 128 F5
Crows-an-Eglos 5 TR26 ... 77 A6
CROWS-AN-WRA ... 96 F8
CROW'S NEST ... 38 B4
Croydon Gdns PL5 ... 123 E4
Crozier Rd 6 PL4 ... 128 F4
CRUGMEER ... 107 A7
CRUMPLEHORN ... 62 D2
Crun-Melyn Parc TR27 ... 142 B4
Crusoe Flats 48 TR26 ... 141 B6
Cryben TR12 ... 92 C1
Cryon View TR1 ... 69 E3
CUBERT ... 55 D8
Cubert Sch TR8 ... 43 D1
Cuby Cl TR2 ... 72 A3
Cuby Rd TR2 ... 71 F4
Cuckoo La TR20 ... 77 A3
Cuddenbeake Terr PL12 ... 65 B8
Cuffe Rd PL3 ... 128 C4
Culbin Gn PL6 ... 129 D7
Culdrose Airfield TR12 ... 146 E1
Culdrose Cl PL5 ... 123 E4
Cullen View TR2 ... 71 C6
Culme Rd PL3 ... 129 A5
Cul-Rian PL26 ... 58 D7
Culroy Flats 12 TR1 ... 137 C4
Culver Cl PL6 ... 129 A8
Culver Ct PL12 ... 122 F2
Culverland Pk PL14 ... 113 C7
Culverland Rd PL14 ... 113 B8
Culver Rd PL12 ... 122 F2
Culvers Mdw PL15 ... 106 B8
Culver Way PL6 ... 129 A7
Culverwood Cl PL7 ... 131 C6
Culvery The PL27 ... 108 B4
Cumberland Rd PL1 ... 127 F1
Cumberland St PL1 ... 127 E2
Cumble Tor La PL12 ... 53 D2
Cundy Cl PL7 ... 130 A7
Cundy's La PL26 ... 58 D4
Cunliffe Ave PL9 ... 135 A6
Cunnack Cl TR13 ... 146 C7
Cunningham Pk TR10 ... 81 C1
Cunningham Rd PL5 ... 124 C8
Cunningham Way PL12 ... 122 D3
CURGURRELL ... 83 C4
Curlew Cl TR7 ... 110 B5
Curlew Mews PL3 ... 129 C4
Curlew Pk Ind Est TR4 ... 69 C3
Curlews TR8 ... 43 B1
Curnow Sch TR15 ... 140 B6
Curnows Rd TR27 ... 142 C5
Currian Hill PL26 ... 58 D8
Currian Rd PL26 ... 58 D7
CURRIAN VALE ... 58 D8
CURRY LANE ... 12 E4
Curtis St PL1 ... 127 E1
Curtis VC Cl TR8 ... 56 B7
CURY ... 99 B4
Cury CE Prim Sch TR12 ... 99 A4
CUSGARNE ... 81 B7
Cusgarne Hill TR4, TR16 ... 81 B8
Cusgarne Prim Sch TR4 ... 81 C7
Custom House Ct TR18 ... 143 F5
Custom House La
  16 Penzance TR18 ... 143 E5
  Plymouth PL1 ... 148 B1
Customs House Hill PL23 ... 116 D4
CUSVEORTH COOMBES ... 69 B2
Cutcrew La PL12 ... 52 E3
Cuth Avallon TR1 ... 137 C4
Cutmere Hill PL12 ... 52 D3
Cutmere La PL12 ... 52 D3
CUTTIVETT ... 53 B5
Cuxhaven Way TR20 ... 88 F6
Cuxton Mdws PL20 ... 41 F3
Cypress Ave PL25 ... 115 F4
Cypress Cl 6 PL7 ... 131 C5
Cyril Rd TR1 ... 137 C5

D

Dabryn Way PL26 ... 58 B4
DADBROOK ... 132 E4
Daglands Hill PL23 ... 116 C4
Daglands Rd PL23 ... 116 C4
DairyLand Farm World★ TR8 ... 44 F1
Daisymount Dr PL28 ... 31 F7
Dale Ave PL6 ... 129 C7
Dale Cl TR7 ... 111 A4
Dale Gdns PL4 ... 128 D4
Dale Rd
  Newquay TR7 ... 111 A4
  Plymouth PL4 ... 128 D4
Daleswood Rd PL19 ... 147 A4
Dalton Gdns PL5 ... 123 E3
Damerel Cl PL1 ... 127 F2
Dandre Apartments TR7 ... 111 A7
Dane Rd TR7 ... 110 D7
Daniel Cl PL25 ... 115 A4
Daniell Ct TR1 ... 137 C3
Daniell Gdns TR1 ... 137 C3
Daniell Rd TR1 ... 137 B3
Daniell St TR1 ... 137 C3
Daniel Pl TR18 ... 143 E4
Daniels La PL25 ... 115 B4
Daniels Sail Loft TR10 ... 144 D7
Danmore Cl PL34 ... 14 C7
Danum Dr PL7 ... 131 B3
DARITE ... 38 B4
Darite Prim Sch PL14 ... 38 A4
Darkey La PL16 ... 19 F4
Dark La
  Camelford PL32 ... 105 C4
  Liskeard PL14 ... 113 D6
  Lostwithiel PL22 ... 112 C1
Darklake Cl PL6 ... 125 E5
Darklake La PL6 ... 125 D8
Darklake View PL6 ... 125 E5
Dark Street La PL7 ... 130 E4
Darlington Rd TR20 ... 88 F6
Darloe La PL13 ... 117 C3
DARRACOTT ... 2 D4
Darracott Hill EX39 ... 2 E4
Dart Cl
  Plymouth PL3 ... 129 D7
  St Giles on the Heath PL15 ... 13 F1
Dartington Wlk PL6 ... 129 E8
Dartmeet Ave PL3 ... 129 B6
Dartmoor View
  Plymouth PL4 ... 129 C3
  Saltash PL12 ... 122 E4
Dartmouth Wlk PL6 ... 129 E8
Darwin Cres PL3 ... 129 D5
Dashwood Ho TR11 ... 145 A6
Daubuz Cl TR1 ... 137 C6
Daubuz Ct TR1 ... 137 D5
Daucus Cl PL19 ... 147 B4
Davenham Cl PL6 ... 125 B6
Davey's Cl TR11 ... 144 E1
David Cl PL7 ... 130 F6
David Penhaligon Way TR1 ... 137 D3
David Southgate Ct PL1 ... 148 A2
DAVIDSTOW ... 16 A6
Davidstow Airfield & Cornwall at War Mus★ Pl32 ... 15 F5
Davy Cl
  Torpoint PL11 ... 126 F3
  Tremar PL14 ... 38 A3
Davy Rd PL6 ... 125 C4
Davys Row PL14 ... 37 E4
Dawe Cres PL31 ... 109 C3
Dawes Cl PL14 ... 50 E7
Dawes La
  Looe PL13 ... 117 D5
  Millbrook PL10 ... 132 E5
  Plymouth PL9 ... 136 D7
Dawlish Wlk PL6 ... 129 E8
Dawney Terr PL11 ... 65 B5
Dawn Rd PL13 ... 117 D2
Daws Ct PL12 ... 123 A2
DAW'S HOUSE ... 18 E1
Daw's Mdw PL32 ... 105 E4
Dawson Cl PL5 ... 123 E1
Daymer La PL27 ... 21 D4
Daymond Rd PL5 ... 123 D2
Dayton Cl PL6 ... 124 E3
Deacon Dr PL12 ... 122 F1
Deacons Gn PL19 ... 147 A3
Dean Cross PL9 ... 135 E7
Dean Cross Rd PL9 ... 135 E7
Dean Hill
  Liskeard PL14 ... 113 B6
  Plymouth PL9 ... 135 E7
Dean La PL14 ... 113 B6
Dean Park Rd PL9 ... 135 D7
Dean Rd PL7 ... 130 D6
Dean St PL14 ... 113 B5
Dean Terr PL14 ... 113 B6
Debden Cl PL5 ... 123 D4
Deeble Cl
  Plymouth PL7 ... 130 E7
  Threemilestone TR3 ... 69 C3
Deeble Dr 20 PL24 ... 60 B4
Deep La PL7 ... 131 C3
Deer Leap PL19 ... 147 D4
Deer Park Cl PL19 ... 147 C5
Deer Park Cres PL19 ... 147 C5
Deer Park Dr PL3 ... 129 D7
Deerpark Forest Trail★ PL14 ... 50 C3
Deer Park La PL19 ... 147 C5
Deer Park Rd PL19 ... 147 C5
Deer Pk
  Newquay TR7 ... 110 D6
  Saltash PL12 ... 122 F3
Defoe Cl PL5 ... 124 C1
Degibna La TR12, TR13 ... 146 C2
DELABOLE ... 14 D3
Delabole Prim Sch PL33 ... 14 D2
Delacombe Cl PL7 ... 130 F7
De-la-Hay Ave PL3 ... 148 A4
Delamere Rd PL6 ... 129 D7
Delavue Terr PL32 ... 105 C3
Delaware Cotts PL18 ... 40 F6
Delaware Ct PL18 ... 40 F5
Delaware Gdns PL2 ... 127 F7
Delaware Prim Sch PL18 ... 40 F5
Delaware Rd PL18 ... 40 F6
Delgany Dr PL6 ... 125 A5
Dell Cl TR18 ... 143 C3
Dell Mdw PL15 ... 18 B8
Dell The
  Plymouth PL7 ... 130 B6
  Tavistock PL19 ... 147 B6
  Truro TR1 ... 137 C5
DEMELZA ... 46 E6
Denas Water TR2 ... 71 A5
Dengie Cl PL7 ... 131 B5
Denham Cl PL5 ... 124 C2
Dennis Cl PL5 ... 127 C7
Dennis Gdns PL15 ... 18 C2
Dennis La PL28 ... 107 D4
Dennison Ave PL25 ... 115 A4
Dennison Rd PL31 ... 109 D5
Dennis Rd
  Liskeard PL14 ... 113 D6
  Padstow PL28 ... 107 D5
Dennybowl La PL12 ... 52 E3
Denyer Ct TR11 ... 145 A6
Denys View TR9 ... 45 F2
De Pass Gdns TR11 ... 145 C3
De Pass Rd TR11 ... 145 C2
Deptford Pl PL4 ... 149 A4
Derby Rd PL5 ... 124 C4
Derby's La PL26 ... 85 C5
Dereham Terr 6 TR1 ... 137 B4
Derowen Dr TR27 ... 142 B3
DERRIFORD ... 125 B4
Derriford Bsns Pk PL6 ... 125 A4
Derriford Health & L Ctr PL6 ... 125 B3
Derriford Hospl PL6 ... 125 B4
Derriford Pk PL6 ... 125 A3
Derriford Rd PL6 ... 125 B4
DERRIL ... 8 D6
Derriton Rd EX22 ... 8 F6
Derry Ave PL4 ... 148 C4
Derry's Cross PL1 ... 148 B2
Derwent Ave PL3 ... 129 C5
Desborough La PL4 ... 149 C3
Desborough Rd PL4 ... 149 C3
Deva Ho TR7 ... 111 A6
DEVERAL ... 78 D2
Deveral Rd TR27 ... 78 D2
Deveron Cl PL7 ... 131 A5
Devington Ct TR11 ... 145 C2
Devington Hall TR1 ... 137 E5
Deviock Hill PL11 ... 64 C5
Devonia Cl PL7 ... 130 E7
DEVONPORT ... 127 D4
Devonport High Sch for Boys PL1 ... 128 A2
Devonport High Sch for Girls PL2 ... 128 C6
Devonport Hill
  Kingsand PL10 ... 133 A2
  Plymouth PL1 ... 127 F1
Devonport Leat PL6 ... 121 B5
Devonport Rd PL3 ... 127 F3
Devonport Sta PL1 ... 127 F3
Devonshire Ct PL11 ... 127 B3
Devonshire Ho
  Plymouth PL1 ... 148 B2
  2 Tavistock PL19 ... 147 B5
Devonshire St PL4 ... 149 A3
Devon Terr PL3 ... 128 E5
Devon Tors PL20 ... 42 D3
Devon Tors Rd 9 PL20 ... 42 C3
DEVORAN ... 81 F6
Devoran La TR3 ... 81 F6
Devoran Sch TR3 ... 81 F6
Diamond Ave PL4 ... 149 B4
Diana Cl TR11 ... 144 E2
Dickens Rd PL5 ... 124 B1
Dickiemoor La PL5 ... 124 C2
Dickna St PL15 ... 13 F1
Dicky La TR3 ... 82 D6
Diddies La EX23 ... 4 E1
Diddies Rd EX23 ... 4 E1
Dieppe Cl PL1 ... 127 F2
Digby Gr PL5 ... 123 F5
Digey Flats 49 TR26 ... 141 B6
Digey The 25 TR26 ... 141 B6
Diggory's Field 4 PL14 ... 38 A3
Dinas Ct PL11 ... 64 C5
Dinas Rd 1 TR9 ... 45 D6
Dingle Cl PL17 ... 28 D1
Dingle Rd
  Plymouth, North Prospect PL2 ... 128 A6
  Plymouth, Plympton PL7 ... 130 C6
Dingles Cl TR3 ... 81 B4
Dingle's Folly PL13 ... 117 C3
Dingles Way PL27 ... 21 E3
Dingwall Ave PL5 ... 124 E3
DINWORTHY ... 3 F2
Dipper Cl EX23 ... 5 A6
Dipper La EX23 ... 5 A7
Dirty La PL12 ... 122 B5
Discovery Wharf 20 PL4 ... 149 A2
Distine Cl PL3 ... 129 B7
Dithmarschen Way PL25 ... 114 B2
Dittisham Wlk PL6 ... 129 E8
Ditton Ct PL6 ... 129 A8
Dixon Pl PL2 ... 127 F4
DIZZARD ... 6 B1
Dobbin Cl PL28 ... 20 F2
Dobbin La PL28 ... 20 F2
Dobbin Rd PL28 ... 20 F2
Dobbs La TR1 ... 137 A4
Dobell Rd PL25 ... 114 E4
DOBWALLS ... 50 E8
Dobwalls Prim Sch PL14 ... 50 E7
Dockacre Rd PL15 ... 106 C6
Dockey 1 PL15 ... 106 C5
Dock La TR18 ... 143 F5
Dockray Cl PL6 ... 125 D4
Dockyard Sta PL2 ... 127 E4
DOCTON ... 2 F8
Doctors Hill
  8 Boscastle PL35 ... 9 C1
  5 St Keverne TR12 ... 101 C4
Doctors La PL12 ... 65 A8
Doctor's La PL14 ... 113 C6
Doddridge Cl PL9 ... 135 F4
Dodson's Gap TR12 ... 99 B7
Doidges Farm Cl PL6 ... 129 B8
Dola La TR20 ... 89 E5

Dolcoath Ave TR14 138 F3
Dolcoath Cl TR14 138 F3
Dolcoath Ind Pk TR14 139 A4
Dolcoath Rd TR14 138 F3
Dolgey Post PL27 32 A4
Dolphin PL29 22 D7
Dolphin Cl PL9 135 F6
Dolphin Court Rd PL9 135 F6
Dolphin Ho 18 PL4 149 A2
Dolphin Sq PL9 135 F6
Dolvin Rd PL19 147 C5
Domellick Cnr PL26 46 B1
Domellick Hill PL26 46 B1
Doniert's Cl 11 PL14 113 B5
Donkey La
  Millbrook PL10 132 C4
  Portwrinkle PL11 65 A4
Donkey Pk PL28 31 F8
Donnington Dr PL3 129 C7
Donnington Rd TR18 143 C3
Donovan Way PL31 109 B4
Dopps Terr TR15 140 C5
Dorchester Ave PL5 124 D4
Dorchester Ct TR14 138 E4
Doreena Rd PL9 136 C7
Dorminack Cl PL26 58 D8
Dormy Ave PL3 128 F5
Dorset Pk PL15 13 A2
Dorsmouth Terr PL7 130 E4
DOUBLEBOIS 50 C8
Doublebois Ind Est PL14 50 D7
Doubletrees PL24 60 B4
Doubletrees Ct 2 PL24 60 B4
Doubletrees Sch 21 PL24 60 B4
Douglas Cl PL26 47 A3
Douglas Dr PL9 136 A6
Douglass Rd PL3 129 C6
Doulton Rd PL25 115 A4
DOUSLAND 42 F3
Dousland Ho PL20 42 E3
Dousland Rd PL20 42 D3
Dousland Terr PL20 42 E3
Dovedale Rd PL2 128 A7
Dove Gdns PL3 129 D7
Dover Rd PL6 125 E3
Dove St 15 TR26 141 B5
Dower's Terr TR16 80 B5
Down Cl PL12 122 C2
DOWNDERRY 64 C5
Downfield Dr PL7 130 F5
Downfield Way PL7 130 F5
Downfield Wlk PL7 130 F5
DOWNGATE
  Kelly Bray 40 A7
  Pensilva 38 D5
Downgate Gdns PL2 128 D8
Downham Gdns PL5 124 C7
Downham Specl Sch PL9 135 F7
Downhorne Pk PL9 135 F6
DOWNINNEY 11 B1
Downlea PL19 147 D4
Down Park Dr PL19 147 D4
Down Parks EX23 5 B7
Down Rd
  Plymouth PL7 131 C5
  Tavistock PL19 147 D4
Downs Cl PL26 58 C8
Downs Hill PL23 61 B5
Downside Ave PL6 129 C7
Downside Cl TR7 111 A4
Downs La PL13 117 B3
Downs Lane Pk PL13 117 B3
Downs Rd PL13 117 C4
Downs The PL13 117 C3
Downstream Cl PL28 107 C5
Downs View
  Bude EX23 104 D7
  Looe PL13 117 C3
Down The PL20 41 C1
DOWN THOMAS 135 C1
Downton Cl PL1 148 A4
Dowren Ho TR27 142 B5
Dozmere TR3 82 C5
Dozmere Cl TR3 82 C5
Dracaena Ave
  Falmouth TR11 144 F5
  Hayle TR27 142 E6
Dracaena Cres TR27 142 E6
Dracaena Pl TR11 144 F4
Dracaena View TR11 144 F5
Dragon L Ctr The PL31 109 F1
Drake Cir PL1, PL4 149 A3
Drakecircus Sh Ctr PL1 149 A3
Drake Ct
  Plymouth, Ernesettle PL5 123 E4
  Plymouth, St Jude's PL4 149 B3
Drakefield Dr PL12 123 A3
Drake Gdns PL19 147 C4
Drake Rd
  Padstow PL28 107 C5
  Tavistock PL19 147 C6
Drakes Cl PL6 124 F4
Drake's Pk 3 PL20 41 B1
Drake Villas PL19 147 A4
Drakewalls Gdns PL18 40 F5
Drakewalls Pl PL18 40 F5
Drake Way PL9 135 E7
Drang The TR9 45 E1
Drannack La TR27 78 D4
Draper Terr 3 PL19 147 B5
DRAWBRIDGE 49 F8
Drax Gdns PL6 128 E8
Draycott Terr TR26 141 C4
Drayton Rd PL5 124 C1
Dreysen Cl TR15 139 C8
DRIFT 87 F3
Drift Cl TR20 87 F3
Drift La PL14 49 C7
Drillfield La 9 TR26 141 B5
Drinnick Terr PL26 58 D6
Drive The
  Helston TR13 146 D7
  Plymouth PL3 128 E7
Driving La PL24 60 C6
Drogeada Cl PL15 27 D3
Droskyn Castle 19 TR6 55 A5
Droskyn Cl 22 TR6 55 A5
Droskyn House Villas TR6 55 A5
Droskyn Way TR6 55 A5
Druckham Pl PL15 106 D5
Druckham Terr PL15 106 D5
Druid's Lodge TR15 139 D5
Druid's Rd
  Camborne TR15 139 D5
  Redruth TR15 139 D6
Drummer's Hill PL26 114 C8
Drummond Cl PL2 127 F7
Drummond Pl PL1 127 F3
Drump Rd TR15 140 C5
Drunken Bridge Hill PL7 130 D4
Dryburgh Cres PL2 128 A8
Dryden Ave PL5 124 C1
DRYM 91 A8
Drym La
  Leedstown TR14 78 F1
  Nancegollan TR14 91 A8
Drym Rd TR13 91 B7
Dualstone Cross EX22 8 D3
Ducane Wlk PL6 125 B1
Duchy Ave TR7 111 C7
Duchy Cl
  Launceston PL15 106 C7
  St Austell PL25 114 F3
Duchy Coll
  Camborne TR14 138 D5
  St Breock PL27 33 C7
  Stoke Climsland PL17 28 D1
Duchy Cotts PL17 28 D1
Duchy Hospl TR1 69 E4
Duchy Terr
  Minions PL14 38 B6
  Upton Cross PL14 38 D7
Duck La PL12 53 E2
Duck St
  9 Mousehole TR19 88 C1
  St Austell PL25 115 B2
Duckworth St 3 PL2 128 A4
Ducky La PL12 53 C3
Ducky Row PL17 40 D4
Dudley Gdns PL6 129 B8
Dudley Rd PL7 130 B5
Dudman Rd TR1 69 F3
Dudnance La TR15 139 B4
Duke's Ct PL26 46 F3
Dukes Dr PL19 41 B4
Dukes Ryde The 1 PL9 135 F7
Duke St
  Launceston PL15 106 A8
  Lostwithiel PL22 112 C2
  Padstow PL28 107 D5
  Plymouth PL1 127 E2
  St Austell PL25 114 C3
  Tavistock PL19 147 C6
  11 Truro TR1 137 D4
Duke's Way TR7 111 A5
DULOE 51 A1
Duloe CE VA Jun & Inf Sch PL14 51 A1
Duloe Gdns PL2 128 C8
Dumbarton Terr 7 TR19 88 C1
Dumfries Ave PL5 124 D3
Duncannon Dr TR11 144 F4
Duncan St PL1 127 E1
Dunclair Pk PL3 129 D5
Duncombe Ave PL5 124 A2
Dundas St 4 PL2 128 A4
Dunders Hill PL27 21 D5
Dundonald St PL2 127 F4
Dungarth Gn PL14 113 D6
Dungarth Rd PL14 113 D6
Dunhead View PL15 28 B6
Dunheved Fields PL15 106 C4
Dunheved Rd
  Launceston PL15 106 C5
  Saltash PL12 122 F2
Dunkeswell Cl PL2 127 F8
Dunley Wlk PL6 125 C1
DUNMERE 34 D2
Dunmere Cl 1 PL24 60 C4
Dunmere Rd PL31 109 B5
Dunnet Rd PL6 124 D7
Dunn St 10 PL35 9 C1
Dunraven Dr PL6 125 A6
Dunsdon Cross EX22 5 F3
DUNSLEY 38 C6
Dunstable Cl PL26 58 D6
Dunstan Cl TR10 144 C8
Dunstan La PL12 40 A1
Dunstanville Terr 12 TR11 145 A5
Dunster Cl PL7 131 C4
Dunston Cl PL26 58 C8
Dunstone Ave PL9 136 A7
Dunstone Cl PL9 135 F7
Dunstone Dr PL9 135 F7
Dunstone La PL9 136 B7
Dunstone Prim Sch PL9 136 A8
Dunstone Rd
  Plymouth, Plymstock PL9 135 F7
  Plymouth, St Budeaux PL5 123 F3
Dunstone View PL9 136 A7
DUNTERTON 28 F6
Duntz Hill PL16 19 F4
Dunvegan Rd TR10 144 B8
Dunveth Rd PL27 108 A5
Dupath La PL17 40 A4
DUPORTH 115 A1
Duporth Bay PL26 115 A1
Duporth Rd PL24, PL26 115 A2
Dural Cross EX22 3 E3
Durban Rd PL3 128 D5
DURGAN 93 D2
Durgan Crossroads TR11 93 D3
Durgan La TR10 144 C8
Durham Ave PL4 149 C4
Durley Dene TR26 77 E4
Durnford St PL1 128 A1
Durnford Street Ope PL1 128 A1
Durning Rd TR5 54 C1
Durrant Cl PL1 127 E3
Durris Cl PL6 125 D4
Durris Gdns PL6 125 D4
Durston Rd EX23 104 E7
Durwent Cl PL9 135 A6
DUTSON 106 E8
Dutson Rd PL15 106 C7
Dutson Terr PL15 106 C7
Dux Cross EX22 8 C6
Duxford Cl PL5 123 E5
Dye House Cotts PL14 36 F2
Dymond Cl PL32 105 B2
Dymond Ct (Kingdom Pl) PL12 122 F2
Dynas-la Rd TR26 141 B4
Dynevor Cl PL3 128 F7

E

Eagle Rd PL7 131 C4
Earle's Retreat TR11 145 B3
Earl's Acre PL3 128 C4
Earl's Dr The
  Cawsand PL10 133 A1
  Kingsand PL10 133 B3
Earls Mill Rd PL7 130 E6
Earls Rise TR7 111 B5
Earls Wood Cl PL6 125 F3
Earls Wood Dr PL6 125 F3
Eastbourne Cl PL25 114 E3
Eastbourne Rd PL25 114 D3
East Bridge 4 TR4 69 A3
Eastbury Ave PL5 124 A2
East Camps Bay PL11 64 D4
East Charles St TR14 138 E2
East Cl TR13 146 D7
East Cliff PL13 117 D3
Eastcliff Ave TR4 68 A7
Eastcliff Avenue No 2 TR4 68 A7
Eastcliffe Rd PL24 60 C5
East Cliff La TR17 89 C5
Eastcote Cl PL6 125 B6
EASTCOTT 3 A3
Eastcott Cross EX23 3 A2
Eastella Rd PL20 42 D2
East End TR15 140 C5
Easterdown Cl PL9 135 F7
Eastern Ave PL14 113 D6
Eastern Gn
  Gulval TR18 88 E6
  Penzance TR18 143 F7
Eastern Green Pk TR18 88 E6
Eastern La TR14 138 D4
Eastern Wood Rd PL7 131 D4
East Fairholme Rd EX23 104 F7
Eastfield Ave PL9 135 C6
Eastfield Cres PL3 129 A6
Eastfield Way PL25 114 F5
East Hill
  Camborne TR14 139 A5
  St Austell PL25 114 D3
Eastlake Ho 5 PL1 149 A2
Eastlake St PL4 148 C3
Eastland Cl TR1 137 F4
EAST LOOE 117 D3
EAST PANSON 13 F3
East Park Ave PL4 148 C4
East Pk
  Pensilva PL14 38 D4
  Redruth TR15 140 D6
East Pool Pk TR15 139 D6
EAST PORTHOLLAND 84 E5
East Quay TR27 142 B6
East Quay Ho PL13 117 D3
East Rd
  Kilkhampton EX23 5 A6
  Menheniot PL14 52 A5
  Quintrell Downs TR8 44 E3
  Stithians TR3 80 F3
East Rise TR11 144 F3
East Rosewin Row 10 TR1 137 D5
East St
  Newquay TR7 110 E6
  Plymouth PL1 148 A2
  Polruan PL23 116 D3
  1 St Columb Major TR9 45 E6
EAST TAPHOUSE 50 B6
East Terr TR27 142 B6
East View PL14 51 F3
East Wharf PL26 73 C3
East Wheel Rose Sta★ TR8 56 C6
Eastwood Park Ind Est TR10 144 D7
Eastwood Rd TR10 144 D7
EAST YOULSTONE 3 C2
East Youlstone Cross EX23 3 C2
Ebenezer Pl 12 TR18 143 C1
Ebrington St PL4 149 A3
Echo Cres PL5 124 D2
Eddystone Cl PL3 129 C6
Eddystone Ct PL13 117 D2
Eddystone Pl 3 PL27 108 B5
Eddystone Rd
  Down Thomas PL9 135 C1
  St Austell PL25 114 E5
  Wadebridge PL27 108 B6
Eddystone Rise PL14 113 D7
Eddystone Road Trad & Ind Est PL27 108 B6
Eddystone Terr
  Plymouth PL1 148 B1
  2 Wadebridge PL27 108 B5
Eden Cl 11 PL24 60 B4
Eden Gdns 14 TR18 143 C1
Eden Project★ PL24, PL26 115 D8
Edenside PL3 128 F6
Eden Terr 13 TR18 143 C1
Edgar Rd
  Jacobstow EX23 11 A6
  Wainhouse Corner EX23 10 F6
Edgar Terr PL4 129 A4
Edgcumbe Ave
  Newquay TR7 110 F5
  Plymouth PL1 148 A3
Edgcumbe Cl PL18 41 A6
Edgcumbe Cres PL10 132 F6
Edgcumbe Ct 3 PL3 128 A3
Edgcumbe Dr PL19 147 B6
Edgcumbe Gdns TR7 110 F6
Edgcumbe Gn PL25 114 A3
Edgcumbe Ho PL1 148 B2
Edgcumbe Park Rd PL3 128 D6
Edgcumbe Rd
  Lostwithiel PL22 112 B1
  Roche PL26 46 F3
  Saltash PL12 122 C5
  St Austell PL25 114 A3
  St Dominick PL12 40 D2
Edgcumbe St PL1 128 A1
Edgcumbe Terr
  Milton Abbot PL19 29 C6
  1 Par PL24 60 B4
Edgecumbe Way PL18 40 E5
Edgecumbe Terr 14 PL20 41 B1
Edgemoor Cl PL14 38 A3
Edinburgh Cl PL25 115 C3
Edinburgh St PL1 127 E1
EDISTONE 2 F8
Edith Ave PL4 149 C4
Edith St PL5 123 D1
EDMONTON 33 B7
Edmund Rd TR15 140 B6
Edna Terr PL4 149 C3
Ednovean La TR20 89 E4
Edward Hain Com Hospl TR26 141 B5
Edwards Cl PL7 131 B4
Edwards Cres PL12 122 C2
Edwards Dr PL7 131 B5
Edwards Rd
  Devoran TR3 81 F6
  St Giles on the Heath PL15 13 F1
Edward St
  Camborne TR14 138 F4
  Truro TR1 137 C4
Edymeade Ct PL15 106 C5
Edymeade Gdn 9 PL15 106 C5
Effingham Cres PL3 128 D7
EFFORD 129 C5
Efford Cres PL3 129 B6
Efford Down Pk EX23 104 C5
Efford Farm Bsns Pk EX23 104 C4
Efford Farm Cotts EX23 104 C4
Efford Fort PL3 129 E6
Efford La PL3 129 B5
Efford Pathway PL3 129 C6
Efford Rd PL3 129 B6
Efford Wlk PL3 129 B6
Egerton Cres PL4 149 C3
Egerton Pl PL4 149 C3
Egerton Rd
  Padstow PL28 107 E4
  Plymouth PL4 149 C3
EGGBEARE 19 A7
EGGBUCKLAND 129 C8
Eggbuckland Rd PL3 129 C7
Eglos Ct PL30 23 E7
Egloshayle Rd
  Hayle TR27 142 E6
  Wadebridge PL27 108 D5
EGLOSKERRY 18 A5
Egloskerry Prim Sch PL15 18 A5
Eglos Mdw TR11 82 A3
Eglos Parc
  Mullion TR12 99 A2
  Wadebridge PL27 108 D5
Eglos Rd
  Ludgvan TR20 89 A7
  Shortlanesend TR4 69 F6
  St Erme TR4 70 D8
Eglos View 2 PL35 9 C1
EGOSHAYLE 108 D6
Egret Cl PL10 133 A6
Eider Wlk TR27 77 E3
Eight Acre Cl 1 PL7 131 C5
Elaine Cl PL7 130 B5
Elbow La PL19 147 C6
ELBURTON 136 B6
Elburton Prim Sch PL9 136 C7
Elburton Rd PL9 136 B8
Eldad Hill PL1 148 A3
Elder Cl 2 PL7 131 B5
Elderfield Cl 7 PL24 60 D5
Eleanor Ho PL1 148 A2
Elerkey Cl TR2 83 F6
Elerkey La TR2 83 F6
Eleven Doors PL25 115 B2
Elford Cres PL7 130 E7
Elford Dr PL9 135 C7
Elford Pk PL20 42 D2
Elgin Cres PL5 124 E3
Elim Ct PL3 128 E5
Elim Terr PL3 128 E5
Eliot Cl PL15 18 C2
Eliot Ct TR7 110 F6
Eliot Dr PL12 65 B8
Eliot Gdns TR7 110 F6
Eliot Rd
  St Austell PL25 114 E4
  Truro TR1 137 C5
Eliot St PL5 127 E8
Elizabeth Cl
  Bodmin PL31 109 D4
  Threemilestone TR3 69 C3
Elizabeth Ct
  Bugle PL26 47 C1
  2 Plymouth PL1 149 A2
Elizabeth House Mus & Arts Gall★ PL4 149 A2
Elizabeth Pl PL4 149 A4
Elizabeth Rd
  Bude EX23 104 E5
  St Austell PL25 114 E3
Elizabeth Terr TR17 89 B5
Ellen Cl TR4 68 C6
Ellenglaze Ct TR8 55 D8
Ellenglaze La TR8 55 D8
Ellenglaze Mdw TR8 55 D8
Elliot Sq PL11 127 B3
Elliot St PL1 148 B1
Elliott Cl PL12 122 D2
Elliot Terr PL1 148 C1
Elliot Terrace La PL1 148 C1
Elliott Rd PL4 129 B1
Elliott's Store★ PL12 123 A2
Ellis Cl TR27 142 C5
Elliston Gdns 3 TR13 98 C8
Ellis Way TR27 142 C5
Elm Cl
  Callington PL17 39 F4
  Camborne TR15 139 D6
  Newquay TR7 110 F4
  Tavistock PL19 147 C3
Elm Cotts PL12 122 C3
Elm Court Gdns TR1 137 D5
Elm Cres PL3, PL4 129 A4
Elm Croft PL2 128 B7
Elm Ct TR1 137 D5
Elm Dr
  Bude EX23 104 F5
  8 St Columb Major TR9 45 D6
Elmgate Crossways PL12 65 E8
Elm Gr
  Feock TR3 82 C5
  Plymouth, Eggbuckland PL6 129 B8
  Plymouth, Plympton PL7 130 E5
Elm Grove Cotts TR10 93 C6
Elmlea EX23 104 F5
Elm Mdw TR3 82 C5
Elm Meadow Dr PL13 117 D4
Elm Pk PL10 133 B6
Elm Rd
  Plymouth, Glenholt PL6 125 D6
  Plymouth, Mannamead PL4 128 F4
Elms Close Terr 25 TR18 143 C2
ELMSCOTT 2 E8
Elmsleigh PL25 114 B3
Elmsleigh Rd PL27 108 B6
Elms The
  Perranuthnoe TR20 89 D4
  Plymouth PL3 128 A3
Elm Terr
  8 Mullion TR12 99 A2
  1 Plymouth PL3 128 F5
  St Austell PL25 114 C4
Elm Tree Rd PL13 117 D4
Elmwood Cl PL6 125 D5
Elowen Cl TR11 144 E2
Elphinstone Rd PL2 128 C7
Elspeth Sitters Ho 11 PL4 149 A2
Elwell Rd PL12 123 A2
Elwick Gdns PL3 129 B5
Embankment La PL4 129 B2
Embankment Rd PL4 129 B2
Embankment Road Lane N PL4 129 B2
Emily Gdns PL4 149 B4
Emlyn Fields PL25 114 F6
Emma Pl PL1 128 A1
Emma Place Ope PL1 128 A1
EMPACOMBE 133 D6
Empire Way TR11 144 E4
Empress Ave 23 TR18 143 E6
Emslie Rd TR11 145 C2
Endeavour Ct PL1 128 A3
Endsleigh Dr PL15, PL19 28 F5
Endsleigh Gdns 2 PL4 149 A4
Endsleigh Gdns Nursery★ PL19 29 B5
Endsleigh Park Rd PL3 128 D6
Endsleigh Pk EX23 7 B6
Endsleigh Pl PL4 149 A4
Endsleigh Rd PL9 135 C7
Endsleigh Terr PL14 113 C6
Eningdale Rd PL19 147 A4
Ennerdale Gdns PL6 124 E5
ENNISCAVEN 46 D2

Holywell Rd continued
Liskeard PL14 113 E6
Newquay TR7 110 F6
Playing Place TR3 82 B8
Home Farm Rd PL9 135 E8
Homefield Pk PL31 109 F3
Home Park Ave PL3 128 E6
Home Park (Plymouth Argyle FC) PL2 128 C5
Home Park Rd PL12 123 A3
Home Pk
Landrake PL12 53 C3
Plymouth PL2 127 F4
Homer Park Lane S PL9 135 C5
Homer Park Rd PL28 20 F2
Homer Pk
Plymouth PL9 135 C5
Saltash PL12 122 D3
Homer Rise PL9 136 B7
Homer Water Pk PL26 58 B4
Homestead Ct TR11 144 F6
Home Sweet Home Terr PL4 149 C2
Homeyard Homes The TR2 83 F6
Honcray PL9 135 D8
Honey's Hill PL30 47 E7
Honey St PL31 109 E4
Honeysuckle Cl
Plymouth PL6 125 E7
Saltash PL12 122 D4
Honeysuckle Gdns PL15 106 E4
HONICKNOWLE 124 B2
Honicknowle PL5 124 B2
Honicknowle Gn PL5 124 B2
Honicknowle La PL5 124 B1
Honicombe Cnr PL17 40 E5
Honicombe Pk PL17 40 E5
Honiton Cl PL5 124 B3
Honiton Wlk PL5 124 B4
Hood Hill TR14 79 A6
HOOE 135 C5
Hooe Hill PL9 135 C5
Hooe La PL9 135 D3
Hooe Manor PL9 135 C5
Hooe Prim Sch PL9 135 B5
Hooe Rd PL9 135 C5
Hooksbury Ave PL7 131 B3
Hooper Ct PL14 113 C8
Hooper La TR14 138 D2
Hoopers Cl PL12 53 C3
Hoopers La PL18 40 F6
Hooper St PL11 127 C3
Hope Terr TR7 110 D6
Hopton Cl
Bude EX23 104 F5
Plymouth PL6 128 F8
Hornapark Cl PL16 19 F3
Hornbrook Gdns PL6 124 D6
Hornby Ct PL1 148 A3
Hornby St 2 PL2 127 F4
Hornchurch La PL5 123 E4
Hornchurch Rd PL5 123 E5
Horn Cross PL9 135 E7
Horn Cross Rd PL9 135 F7
Hornick Hill PL26 58 E4
HORNINGTOPS 51 E3
Horn La
Liskeard PL14 113 B6
Plymouth PL9 135 F7
Horn Lane Flats 4 PL9 135 F7
HORRABRIDGE 42 C5
Horrabridge Com Prim Sch PL20 42 C4
HORSEBRIDGE 29 C1
HORSEDOWNS 78 F1
Horse & Jockey La 2 TR13 146 C5
Horsepool La PL11 65 B6
Horsepool Rd
Connor Downs TR27 78 E6
Sheviock PL11 65 B6
Horseshoe Cl PL26 47 A3
Horsewhim Dr PL17 39 E6
Horse Whim Dr PL25 115 B5
Horsham La
Plymouth, Honicknowle PL5 124 C2
Plymouth, Tamerton Foliot PL5 124 C7
Horsley Rise PL25 114 D3
Horswell Cl PL7 131 B5
Horton Cross EX22 3 F3
Hosford Cl PL9 136 A4
Hosken's Mdw TR19 97 A6
Hosking's Row TR15 140 B4
Hospital Rd
Plymouth PL4 149 B4
Stratton EX23 4 D1
Hotham Pl PL1 148 A4
Houldsworth Rd PL9 135 C7
Houndiscombe Rd PL4 128 E4
Hounster Dr PL10 132 D4
Hounster Hill PL10 132 D4
Housel Bay Rd TR12 102 F2
Housman Cl PL5 124 D3
Howard Cl
Plymouth PL5 123 F2
Saltash PL12 122 D3
Tavistock PL19 147 A5
Howard La EX23 7 C8
Howard Rd PL9 135 E8
Howards Way EX23 104 D5
Howe Downs TR14 79 A2
Howell's Rd 10 EX23 4 E1
Howeson La PL6 125 A4
How St PL4 149 A2
HTP Apartments TR1 137 E4
Hts The PL19 147 A6
HUDDISFORD 3 F6
Hudson Cross EX22 5 E4
Hudson Rd PL27 31 F3
Hughville St TR14 138 D4
Hugus Rd TR3 69 D3
Hull's La TR11 145 C3
Humber Cl PL3 129 D6
Humphrey's Cl PL14 37 F3
Humphry Davy La TR27 142 D5
Humphry Davy Sch TR18 143 E6
Hungerford Rd PL2 128 B5
Hunkin Cl TR1 137 C5
Hunter Cl PL6 124 F2
Huntersfield TR14 138 F7
Hunters's Oak PL20 41 D2
Huntfield Gdns 15 EX23 4 E1
Huntingdon Gdns PL5 124 D4
Huntley Pl PL3 129 C4
Hunts Crossing Sta★ PL15 18 E4
Hurdon Rd PL15 106 D2
Hurdon Way PL15 106 C3
Hurdwick Rd PL19 147 A5
Hurland Rd TR1 137 D3
Hurlers Ct 11 PL14 113 C5
Hurlers The★ PL14 38 A6
Hurlings The TR9 45 E5
Hurrabrook Cl PL6 125 E2
Hurrabrook Gdns PL6 125 E2
Hurrell Cl PL6 124 D6
Hurrell Ct PL3 129 C5
Hursley Bsns Pk PL6 121 D1
Hurst Cl PL9 135 F5
Hustyns PL27 33 D3
Hutchings Cl PL6 124 D6
Huthnance Cl TR1 137 F5
Hutton Hts TR1 69 F3
Huxham Cl PL6 129 A8
Huxley Cl PL7 130 F7
Hyde Park Jun & Inf Schs 1 PL3 128 E5
Hyde Park Rd PL3 128 E5

I

IDLESS 70 B6
Idless La TR4 69 F6
Idless Wood Forest Walk★ TR4 70 B6
Ilbert Cotts PL7 130 E4
Ilbert St PL1 148 B4
ILLOGAN 67 E4
Illogan Downs TR15 139 B8
ILLOGAN HIGHWAY 139 C6
Illogan Pk 8 TR16 67 E4
Illogan Prim Sch TR16 67 D5
Imperial Ct TR11 145 D3
Ince Cl PL11 126 F4
Inchkeith Rd PL6 124 F7
INDIAN QUEENS 45 E1
Indian Queens Ind Est TR9 45 F2
Indian Queens Prim Sch TR9 45 E1
Industrial Est The TR6 55 B4
Infirmary Hill TR1 137 C4
Ingra Rd PL3 129 A6
Ingra Tor Cl 2 PL20 42 C3
Ingra Wlk PL6 125 B8
Innes Ho PL1 148 B3
Inney Cl PL17 39 F4
Inow Terr TR11 93 A2
Institute Hill TR13 98 B8
Instow Wlk PL5 124 A3
Inswell Ct PL19 147 A6
INSWORKE 132 F6
Insworke Cl PL10 133 A6
Insworke Cres PL10 132 F6
Insworke Pl PL10 133 A6
Inverdene PL3 128 D5
Ipswich Cl PL5 124 C4
Iron Mine La PL20 42 E3
Isacombe Oaks PL17 39 F6
Island Cres TR7 110 E6
Island Ct PL13 117 D2
Island Lanes PL31 109 F1
Island Point TR8 44 C6
Island Rd 4 TR26 141 B6
Island Sq 8 TR26 141 B6
Islington Wharf TR10 144 D8
Ivanhoe 6 TR7 110 F6
Ivanhoe Rd PL5 123 D2
Ivey Terr PL14 113 D7
Ivy Cotts PL18 40 F6
Ivydale PL15 106 B6
Ivydale Rd PL4 128 F4
Ivydene Flats TR7 111 D7
Ivy La TR18 143 C5
Ivyleaf Holiday Pk EX23 4 F3

J

Jack Bice Cl PL14 113 E5
Jackett's Steps 6 TR11 145 B5
Jack La TR18 143 C2
Jackman's Mdw PL10 133 A3
Jacks Cl TR10 144 D7
Jack's La PL11 132 B8
Jackson Cl PL5 127 F8
Jackson Pl PL2 127 F4
Jackson Way PL12 122 E3
Jack Stephens Est TR18 143 D6
Jacob's Ladder TR11 145 B4
JACOBSTOW 11 B6
Jacobstow Prim Sch EX23 11 A6
Jago Ave PL11 127 B3
Jago Cl PL31 109 B3
Jago's Slip TR11 145 B5
Jake's La 1 TR4 69 A3
Jamaica Inn Mus★ PL15 25 E3
Jamaica Pl 14 TR18 143 C7
Jamaica Terr 13 TR18 143 C7
James Cl PL9 136 B6
James Pl TR1 137 D4
James Rd PL19 147 E2
James's Cross EX23 2 C2
James St
Plymouth, Mount Wise PL1 127 E1
Plymouth PL4 148 C4
Jane's Ct 9 TR11 145 B5
Jasmine Gdns
Plymouth, Chaddlewood PL7 131 B5
Plymouth, Glenholt PL6 125 E6
Jasmine Way PL28 31 F7
Jasper Parc PL14 37 F3
Jays Cross PL15 19 C6
Jean Cres PL3 129 B6
Jeanne Rees Ct 9 PL14 113 B5
Jedburgh Cres PL2 128 A8
Jeffery Cl PL6 124 D6
Jelbert Way TR18 88 E6
Jellicoe Rd PL5 124 E1
Jenkins Cl PL9 136 A5
Jenkins Ct TR7 110 E6
Jenkins Terr 5 TR15 140 C5
Jenner Parc TR9 45 D6
Jennings Rd TR10 144 A6
Jennings St TR18 143 E5
Jenns Cross EX22 5 F7
Jennycliff La PL9 135 A6
Jennys Combe Cl PL9 135 F4
Jephson Rd PL4 129 B3
Jericho La TR27 142 D1
Jeryon Cl PL25 114 E6
Jessops PL7 130 D7
Jethan Dr TR14 138 B4
Jetty St PL26 73 C3
Jewell's Terr TR16 80 B5
JEWEL'S CROSS 7 F6
Jinkin Ave PL4 149 B4
John Ellis Ct TR27 142 C5
John Kitto Com Coll The PL5 124 B1
John La PL4 148 C4
John's Cnr TR20 89 F5
Johnson Cl 2 PL20 41 B1
Johnson Pk PL18 41 A3
John Sparke Ho 17 PL1 149 A2
Johns Pk TR15 140 B6
John St
Plymouth PL1 127 E3
Truro TR1 137 C4
JOLLY'S BOTTOM 69 A4
Jon Davey Dr TR16 140 C7
Jopes Cl 2 PL14 38 A3
JOPPA
Hayle 142 E4
St Just 87 A4
Jordan La PL20 42 C5
Jorys Mdw PL30 23 E3
Joseph's Ct 27 TR6 55 A5
Joseph's La TR18 143 C8
Jubilee Bglws 20 TR18 143 C1
Jubilee Cl
Cubert TR4 55 D8
Duloe PL14 51 A1
Kilkhampton EX23 5 A6
Saltash PL12 122 D2
Jubilee Cotts
Landrake PL12 53 C3
Saltash PL12 122 C1
Jubilee Ct 15 TR26 77 A6
Jubilee Hill PL13 62 D5
Jubilee Mdw PL25 115 C5
Jubilee Pl
Camborne TR14 138 E3
Plymouth PL3 129 C4
Jubilee Poll TR18 143 F4
Jubilee Rd
Falmouth TR11 145 A5
Pensilva PL14 38 D4
Plymouth PL5 123 F3
Threemilestone TR3 69 C3
Wadebridge PL27 108 C5
Jubilee St TR7 110 D6
Jubilee Terr
Bodmin PL31 109 B5
3 Camborne TR14 138 E2
Goonhavern TR4 55 D5
Helston TR13 146 C4
Plymouth PL4 129 B2
Julian St PL4 149 C2
Julian Wlk PL6 125 E6
Jump Cl PL6 121 C1
Junction Gdns PL4 149 C3
Juniper Way PL7 131 B5

K

Kailem Cl TR9 45 D5
Karenza Ct TR26 141 E2
Kathleaven St PL5 123 D1
Kay Cl PL7 130 F7
Kay Cres PL31 109 B3
Kay Gdns PL27 108 E5
Kays Mews 7 PL34 14 C7
Kea Com Prim Sch TR3 70 A1
Keason Est PL14 39 A2
Keason Hill PL12 53 C8
Keast Cl 2 TR9 45 E1
Keat St PL2 127 E4
Kedlestone Ave PL5 124 A3
Keeble Pk TR3 81 E6
Keep The PL12 122 C2
KEHELLAND 66 F2
Kehelland Village Prim Sch TR14 66 F1
Keigwen Pl TR19 88 C1
Kel Avon Cl TR1 137 F5
Kellaway Pk TR13 146 D6
Kelley Rd TR11 144 E5
Kelliwith TR3 82 B6
Kellow Hill PL13 62 D2
Kellow Pk PL11 65 A7
Kellow Rd PL26 58 C8
KELLY 29 B8
KELLY BRAY 39 F6
Kelly Cl PL5 127 C7
Kelly Coll PL19 147 D7
Kelly Coll Prep Sch PL19 147 D7
Kelly Pk PL30 34 C8
Kelvin Ave PL4 149 C4
Kelwyn Ct TR26 141 C2
KELYNACK 86 F4
Kemp Cl TR1 137 D4
Kempe Cl PL2 127 F6
Kemp's Cl 7 TR5 54 C1
Kempton Terr PL11 127 B2
Kemyell Pl PL2 127 E4
Kendal Gn TR2 57 C1
Kendal Pl PL5 124 E4
Kenidjack Cl TR26 141 E1
Kenilworth Rd PL2 128 B7
Kenilworth Way PL26 58 E5
Kenley Gdns PL5 123 F4
Kenmare Dr PL7 131 A5
Kennall Pk TR3 81 B4
Kennall Vale TR3 81 B4
Kennall Vale Prim Sch TR3 81 B4
Kenna Pk TR1 69 F3
KENNARDS HOUSE 18 B2
Kenn Cl PL5 124 B3
Kennedy Cl TR15 139 B8
KENNEGGY 90 A3
KENNEGGY DOWNS 90 B4
Kennel Hill PL7 130 D4
Kennel Hill Cl PL7 130 C4
Kennerley Terr 16 TR2 95 A6
Kennet Cl PL3 129 B6
Kenneth Launder Ct 10 PL14 113 B5
Kensa Way TR27 78 E6
Kensey Pl 3 PL15 106 C6
Kensey Valley Mdw PL15 106 D6
Kensey View PL15 106 D5
Kensington Pl 8 PL4 128 F4
Kensington Rd PL4 149 B4
Kenstella Rd TR18 143 C2
Kent Ave PL25 115 D3
Kent Cl PL26 58 C8
Kent Rd PL2 127 F5
KENTS 10 F6
KENWYN 137 C6
Kenwyn Church Rd TR1 137 B6
Kenwyn Cl
Bude EX23 104 D7
Truro TR1 137 B6
Kenwyn Hill TR1 137 B6
Kenwyn Mews TR1 137 C4
Kenwyn Pk
St Kew Highway PL30 23 B2
Truro TR1 137 B6
Kenwyn Rd TR1 137 C5
Kenwyn St TR1 137 C4
Kenython La TR19 86 F7
Keppel Pl PL2 127 F4
Keppel St PL2 127 F4
Keppel Terr 8 PL2 127 F4
Kerensa Gdns TR5 68 D8
Kerensa Gn TR11 144 E5
Kergilliack Rd TR11 144 D5
Kerhuon Ct PL31 109 D5
Kerley Gr TR1 69 F3
Kerley Hill TR4 69 A3
Kerley Vale TR4 69 A3
Kernick Bsns Pk TR10 144 A6
Kernick Gdns TR10 144 A6
Kernick Ind Est TR10 144 A7
Kernick Rd TR10 144 B7
Kernick Way TR27 142 E8
Kernow Cl
Bodmin PL31 109 F5
Torpoint PL11 126 E3
Wadebridge PL27 108 B5
Kernow Cres EX23 104 E4
Kernow Ct
Newquay TR7 110 E6
Torpoint PL11 126 E3
Kernow Mill★ PL12 52 E1
Kernyk Lowen TR14 138 F5
KERRIS 97 E8
Kerris Gr TR1 137 B5
KERROW MOOR 59 D8
Ker St Ope PL1 127 E2
Kersbrook Cross PL17 27 F2
Kersey Cl TR11 145 C7
Kersey Rd TR11 145 B7
Ker St PL1 127 E1
Keryor Cl PL25 114 F3
Kestell Pk PL31 109 E2
Kestenenn 16 PL31 109 D5
KESTLE 73 A4
Kestle Ct PL31 109 C5
Kestle Dr TR1 69 F3
KESTLE MILL 111 F1
Kestral Units PL5 124 A1
Kestral Way 10 TR16 67 E4
Kestrel Cl
Plymouth PL6 125 D8
7 Porthleven TR13 98 B8
Kestrel Pk PL19 147 D2
Keswick Cres PL6 125 D2
Keveral Gdns PL11 64 B5
Keveral La PL11 64 B5
Kew Cl TR7 111 A4
Kew Noweth TR14 138 D2
Kew Pendra TR19 97 A6
Kew Pendra Cl TR19 97 A6
Kew Vean TR26 141 C3
KEYBRIDGE 35 B8
Keyes Cl PL1 127 F2
KEYHAM 127 E5
Keyham Ct PL2 127 E6
Keyham Rd PL2 127 E4
Keyham St PL5 127 E8
Keyham Sta PL2 127 E6
Khyber Cl PL11 127 A3
Kibbiscombe Terr PL14 63 A8
Kidwelly Cl PL7 131 C4
Kiel Pl PL3 129 D5
Kilhallon PL24 60 C5
Kilhallon Woodlands PL24 60 C5
KILKHAMPTON 5 A6
Kilkhampton Prim Sch EX23 5 A6
KILLATOWN 37 B1
Killatree Cross EX22 8 F7
Killerton Rd EX23 104 E5
Killicourt TR3 82 A7
Killiers Ct TR15 139 C7
Killiersfield TR15 139 C6
Killigrew Ave PL12 122 D1
Killigrew Gdns TR4 70 D8
Killigrew Pl 9 TR11 145 A4
Killigrew Rd PL14 113 D6
Killigrew St TR11 145 A4
KILLIVOSE 79 C5
Killivose Gdns TR14 138 D1
Killivose Rd TR14 138 D1
Killyvarder Way PL25 115 B6
Kilmar Cl PL14 37 F3
Kilmar Rd PL14 113 E6
Kilmar Way PL14 37 F3
Kilminorth Woods Nature Reserve★ PL13 117 A4
Kilna La PL12 53 A2
Kiln Cl
Cawsand PL10 133 A1
Mevagissey PL26 73 C4
Plymouth PL5 127 C8
Kiln Mdws TR12 92 C1
Kilworthy Hill PL19 147 C6
Kilworthy Rd PL19 147 C6
Kimber Ct TR11 145 B2
Kimberley Ct TR7 110 D6
Kimberley Foster Cl PL11 65 B5
Kimberley Park Rd TR11 145 A4
Kimberley Pk PL14 38 A3
Kimberley Pl TR11 145 A4
Kimberly Cl TR7 110 D6
Kimberly Dr PL6 125 B1
Kiming EX23 104 E4
King Arthurs Terr 5 PL34 14 C7
KINGBEARE 27 A1
King Charles Prim Sch TR11 145 A3
King Edward Cres TR7 110 D7
King Edward Mine Mus★ TR14 79 E5
King Edward Rd PL12 122 F2
Kingfisher Cl
Plymouth PL6 125 E6
Tavistock PL19 147 D2
Kingfisher Dr PL25 115 A4
Kingfisher Way PL9 135 C7
King George V Memorial Wlk TR27 142 C6
KINGSAND 133 A2
King's Ave
Falmouth TR11 144 F4
St Austell PL25 114 D3
Kingsbury Ho TR11 145 A6
Kings Cl PL6 125 E6
Kings Cross EX39 2 E5
Kings Ct PL1 128 A3
King's Hill EX23 104 E3
Kings Hill Cl EX23 104 E4
King's Hill Ind Est EX23 104 F3
Kings Hill Mdw EX23 104 E3
Kingsland Gardens Cl PL3 128 E6
Kingsley Ave PL11 127 B2
Kingsley Cl TR1 69 E3
Kingsley Cove TR4 68 A7
Kingsley Ct TR9 57 E8
Kingsley Meade TR8 111 B5
Kingsley Rd PL4 128 E4
Kingsley Terr TR16 67 C6
Kingsley Way TR13 146 C5
Kingsmill Rd PL12 122 C5
Kings Pippin PL26 58 E5
Kings Rd
Marazion TR17 89 B5
Plymouth, Devonport PL1 127 F2
Plymouth, West Park PL5 123 F3
4 St Mawes TR2 95 A6

Liskey TR6 . . . . 55 A4
Liskey Hill TR6 . . . . 55 A4
Liskey Hill Cres 1 TR6 . . . 55 A4
Liskey Tourist Pk TR3 . . . . 69 C4
Lisson Gr PL4 . . . . 128 F4
Lister Cl PL7 . . . . 130 F6
Lister Hill 10 TR11 . . . . . 145 A4
Lister St TR11 . . . . 145 A3
Listowel Dr PL13 . . . . 117 D4
Listry Rd TR7 . . . . 110 E5
Litchaton Cres PL7 . . . . . 130 B7
Litchaton Way PL7 . . . . . . 130 B7
Litchfield Cl PL7 . . . . 131 B6
Little Ash Gdns PL5 . . . . . 123 B1
Little Ash Rd PL5 . . . . 123 B1
LITTLE BOSULLOW 75 D1
Little Bridge Cross EX22 . . . 8 A5
Littlebridge Mdw EX22 . . . . 8 A5
Little Bridge Pk PL27 . . . . 108 D6
LITTLE BRYNN 46 E5
Little Butts PL9 . . . . 135 E6
Little Castle St 7 TR1 . . . 137 C4
LITTLE COMFORT 28 C7
Little Dean PL14 . . . . 113 A5
Little Dinas PL28 . . . . 107 E4
Little Dock La PL5 . . . . . . 124 B2
Little Down La PL6 . . . . . . 121 E3
Little Down Pk TR7 . . . . . . 111 A4
LITTLE FALMOUTH 145 B7
Little Fancy Cl PL6 . . . . . . 125 C7
Little Gilly Hill 3 TR15 . . 140 C4
Little Gregwartha TR16 . . . 80 A5
Little-in-sight 19 TR26 . . 141 A5
LITTLE KIRLAND 109 C1
Little La
Hayle TR27 . . . . 142 E7
Kingsand PL10 . . . . 133 A2
Staddiscombe PL9 . . . . 135 D3
Little Laney PL13 . . . . 62 D1
Little Mdw
Bodmin PL31 . . . . 109 D5
Pyworthy EX22 . . . . 8 E5
Little Mill La TR27 . . . . 77 E2
Little Oaks TR10 . . . . 144 B6
Little Orch PL12 . . . . 53 C3
LITTLE PETHERICK 32 C6
Little Point Cres PL10 . . . 132 F5
LITTLE PRIDEAUX 60 B7
Little Stark Cl PL26 . . . . . . 58 B4
Littleton Pl PL2 . . . . 127 F4
Little Trelower Pk PL26 . . 58 F1
Little Treloweth TR15 . . . 139 B6
Little Trelyn PL27 . . . . 21 E2
Little Trethewey Est TR19 96 E4
Little Trethiggey TR8 . . . . 111 F2
Little Treverrow PL27 . . . . . 21 E2
Little Western Rly★ TR7 . 110 F5
Little Woburn Cl PL15 . . . 106 C4
Littlewood Cl PL7 . . . . 131 A4
LIZARD 102 F2
Lizard Cl PL6 . . . . 124 F7
Lizard Lighthouse Her Ctr★
TR12 . . . . 102 F1
Lizard Nature Reserve The★
TR12 . . . . 100 F2
Lizard Wlk PL6 . . . . 125 A7
Llantillio Dr PL2 . . . . 128 B8
Llawnroc Cl TR14 . . . . 138 E2
Llewellyn Cl PL32 . . . . 105 C3
Lloyds Rd TR12 . . . . 103 A2
Loatmead Cross EX22 . . . . . . 3 E3
LOCKENGATE 47 E4
Lockeridge Rd PL20 . . . . . . 41 B1
Lockington Ave PL3 . . . . . 128 F7
Locks Wlk PL1 . . . . 127 E1
Lockyer Ct PL1 . . . . 148 C2
Lockyer Mews PL19 . . . . . 147 C6
Lockyer Rd PL3 . . . . 128 E5
Lockyers Quay PL4 . . . . . . 149 B2
Lockyer St PL1 . . . . 148 C2
Lockyer Terr PL12 . . . . 123 A3
Lodenek Ave PL28 . . . . 107 D4
Lodge Dr TR1 . . . . 137 F6
Lodge Gdns PL6 . . . . 124 E3
Lodge Hill PL14 . . . . 113 A3
Lodge La PL8 . . . . 136 F5
Lodge Way TR9 . . . . 45 F2
Loe Bar Rd TR13 . . . . 98 C8
Loe Valley Rd TR13 . . . . . . 146 B7
Lofoten Cl PL1 . . . . 127 E2
Loftus Gdns PL5 . . . . 123 C2
Logans Ct TR26 . . . . 141 D2
Loggans Cl TR27 . . . . 142 E8
Loggans Rd TR27 . . . . 142 F8
Loggans Way TR27 . . . . . . 142 E8
Loggans Wlk TR27 . . . . . . 142 E8
Lollabury Rd PL12 . . . . 122 E3
Lomond Hall TR26 . . . . 141 D1
LONDON APPRENTICE 59 B1
Longacre
Harrowbarrow PL17 . . . . . . 40 C4
Plymouth PL7 . . . . 130 B7
Long Acre PL12 . . . . 122 B4
Long-A-Row Cl EX23 . . . . . 10 C6
Long Barn The TR20 . . . . . . 89 D8
LONGBRIDGE 129 F7
Longbridge Cl PL6 . . . . 129 F6
Longbridge Rd
Plymouth, Laira PL3 . . . . . 129 C4
Plymouth, Longbridge PL6 . 129 E7
Longbrook Barton PL7 . . . 130 D5
Longbrook St PL7 . . . . 130 F4
Longcause PL7 . . . . 130 F4
Longcause Specl Sch
PL7 . . . . 130 F4
Longcoombe La PL13 . . . . . 62 D3
LONGCROSS 29 F6
Long Cross PL29 . . . . 22 C6
Longcross Victorian Gdns★
PL29 . . . . 22 C6
Long Down Gdns PL6 . . . 125 E3
LONGDOWNS 81 A1
Longdowns Trad Est TR10 . 81 A1
Longfield TR11 . . . . 144 E4
Longfield Cl 25 PL17 . . . . . 39 F4
Longfield Dr PL32 . . . . 105 C3
Longfield Pl PL4 . . . . 149 B4
Longfield Rd PL32 . . . . 105 C3
Longfield Villas PL9 . . . . . 135 D8
Longhouse La PL27 . . . . 21 E3
Long La
High Street PL26 . . . . 58 C4
Ludgvan TR20 . . . . 89 A7
St Erth TR20, TR27 . . . . 89 E8
LONGLANDS 122 A1
Longlands PL9 . . . . 135 D8
Longlands La PL12 . . . . . . 122 B1
Long Lanes TR20 . . . . 89 F7
Long Ley PL3 . . . . 129 B6
Longman's La 3 PL17 . . . . 39 E4
Long Mdw PL7 . . . . 130 D7
Long Mdw View PL23 . . . . 116 B5
Longmeadow Cl PL7 . . . . . 130 E7
Longmeadow Rd PL12 . . . 122 E3
Long Moor TR12 . . . . 103 A5
Long Orch PL20 . . . . 41 B1
Long Park Cl PL9 . . . . 135 F5
Longpark Dr EX23 . . . . 6 F5
Long Park Dr PL6 . . . . 125 D7
Long Park Rd PL12 . . . . . . 122 D2
Longpark Way PL25 . . . . . . 114 F5
Long Pk PL15 . . . . 18 D2
Long Rd PL12 . . . . 122 B4
LONGROCK 88 F6
Longrock Bsns Pk TR20 . . 88 F6
Longrock Ind Est TR20 . . . 88 F6
Long Row TR19 . . . . 97 F7
Long Rowden PL3 . . . . 128 E6
Long Steps PL23 . . . . 116 C4
LONGSTONE
Carbis Bay 141 E1
St Mabyn 34 F8
Longstone Ave PL6 . . . . . . 125 A6
Longstone Cl TR26 . . . . . . 141 E1
Longstone Hill TR26 . . . . . 141 E1
Long Terrace Cl 5 PL7 . . 131 C5
Longview Rd PL12 . . . . 122 D3
Longview Terr PL3 . . . . . . 129 B7
Longwood Cl PL7 . . . . 131 A4
Longwool Mdw EX23 . . . . . . 7 B6
LOOE 117 D3
Looe Com Sch PL13 . . . . . 117 D6
Looe Hill
Looe PL13 . . . . 63 F5
Seaton PL13, PL11 . . . . 64 A5
Looe Prim Sch PL13 . . . . . 117 D4
Looe St PL4 . . . . 149 A2
Looe Sta PL13 . . . . 117 C4
Lookout The 7 TR11 . . . . 145 B5
Looseleigh Cl PL6 . . . . 125 A4
Looseleigh La PL6 . . . . 124 F5
Looseleigh Pk PL6 . . . . . . 124 E5
Lopes Dr PL6 . . . . 121 C1
Lopes Rd
Dousland PL20 . . . . 42 E3
Plymouth PL2 . . . . 128 B6
Lopwell Cl PL6 . . . . 124 F5
Lord Louis Cres PL9 . . . . . 134 F6
Lords Mdw TR2 . . . . 71 F3
Lorrimore Ave PL2 . . . . . . 127 F5
Loscombe Ct TR16 . . . . 80 A5
Loscombe La TR16 . . . . 80 A5
Loscombe Rd TR16 . . . . . . 139 E1
Lost Gdns of Heligan The★
PL26 . . . . 73 B5
LOSTWITHIEL 112 E1
Lostwithiel Mus★ PL22 . . 112 C2
Lostwithiel Prim Sch
PL22 . . . . 112 C2
Lostwithiel Rd PL30, PL31 . 48 C7
Lostwithiel St PL23 . . . . . . 116 C4
Lostwithiel Sta PL22 . . . . 112 D2
Lostwood Rd PL25 . . . . . . 114 E4
Lotherton Cl PL7 . . . . 131 B3
Loughboro Rd PL5 . . . . . . 123 C1
LOVATON 42 F1
Love La
Bodmin PL31 . . . . 109 F5
Hayle TR27 . . . . 142 E7
Mousehole TR19 . . . . 88 C1
Penryn TR10 . . . . 144 D8
Penzance TR18 . . . . 143 C4
Saltash PL12 . . . . 122 E2
24 St Ives TR26 . . . . 141 B6
Lovell Rd PL3 . . . . 128 F6
Lovely La PL12 . . . . 65 A8
Loveny Cl PL14 . . . . 36 F2
Loveny Rd PL14 . . . . 36 F2
Lovibond Wlk PL27 . . . . . 108 C5
Lowarth Cl TR13 . . . . 146 B6
Lowarthow Marghas
TR15 . . . . 140 D5
Lowenac Cres TR27 . . . . . . 78 E6
Lowenac Gdns TR14 . . . . . 138 C2
Lowen Ct 7 TR1 . . . . 137 D4
Lowenek Cl TR11 . . . . 144 E5
Lowenna Gdns PL13 . . . . . 117 C4
Lowenna Manor PL27 . . . . 21 E3
Lowen Way TR3 . . . . 69 C3
Lower Anderton Rd PL10 132 F5
Lower Barncoose TR15 . . 139 F6
Lower Biteford Cross EX39 . 3 E6
LOWER BODINNAR 87 E7
Lower Bore St PL31 . . . . . 109 D5
LOWER BOSCASWELL 74 F2
Lower Boscaswell Parc
TR19 . . . . 74 F1
LOWER BREA 139 A3
Lower Broad La TR15,
TR16 . . . . 139 C8
Lower Cardrew La TR15 . 140 B6
Lower Castle Rd TR2 . . . . . 95 A5
Lower Chapel St PL13 . . . 117 D3
Lower Church St TR27 . . . 142 D6
Lower Cleaverfield PL15 . 106 C7
LOWER CLICKER 51 F4
Lower Clicker Rd PL14 . . . . 51 F4
LOWER COMPTON 129 A5
Lower Compton Rd PL3 . 128 F5
Lower Coronation Terr 9
PL17 . . . . 39 F4
Lower Eastcliff TR4 . . . . . . 68 A7
Lower Elms PL27 . . . . 21 F3
Lower Fairfield PL12 . . . . . . 65 A8
Lower Farm Rd PL7 . . . . . 131 A4
Lower Fore St PL12 . . . . . . 123 A2
Lower Glen Pk PL14 . . . . . . 38 D4
Lower Goongumpas La
TR16 . . . . 68 F1
Lower Goonrea PL13 . . . . 117 B4
LOWER GREEN 146 A5
Lower Greenbanks PL27 . . 21 E2
Lower Green St TR18 . . . . 143 D1
Lower Gurnick Rd TR18 . 143 B3
Lower Hill TR13 . . . . 146 C6
Lower Hillcrest
Helston TR13 . . . . 146 C6
9 Perranporth TR6 . . . . . . 55 A4
Lower Hillside PL14 . . . . . . 50 B6
Lower Hugus Rd TR3 . . . . . 69 C3
Lower Kelly PL18 . . . . 41 A3
Lower La
Mawgan TR12 . . . . 99 D7
6 Plymouth PL1 . . . . 149 A2
Lower Lux St 5 PL14 . . . 113 C6
Lower Market St
Looe PL13 . . . . 117 D3
Penryn TR10 . . . . 144 C7
Lower Mdw 5 TR4 . . . . 69 A3
Lower Merritts Hill 22
TR16 . . . . 67 E4
Lower Middle Hill PL14 . . . 38 E4
Lower Molinnis PL26 . . . . . 47 D2
LOWER NINNES 76 B1
Lower Parc TR12 . . . . 92 C2
Lower Park Dr PL9 . . . . . . 135 F4
Lower Pengegon TR14 . . . 138 F3
Lower Peverell Rd TR18 . 143 E7
Lower Pk TR2 . . . . 70 F5
Lower Polstain Rd TR3 . . . 69 D3
LOWER PORTHPEAN 59 E1
Lower Port View PL12 . . . 122 F2
LOWER PROSPIDNICK 91 C6
Lower Pumpfield Row
TR15 . . . . 139 B6
Lower Rd PL11 . . . . 64 C4
Lower Redannick TR1 . . . 137 C4
Lower Ridings PL7 . . . . . . 131 B7
LOWER ROSE 55 D5
LOWER ROSEWARNE 138 C4
Lower Rosewin Row 9
TR1 . . . . 137 D5
Lower Row PL10 . . . . 133 A2
Lower Rowes Terr PL26 . . 58 D5
Lower Saltram PL9 . . . . . . 135 C7
Lower Sheffield TR19 . . . . 97 F7
Lowerside PL2 . . . . 128 A8
Lower Sq EX22 . . . . 11 E8
Lower St
Looe PL13 . . . . 117 D3
Plymouth PL4 . . . . 149 A3
Lower Tamar Terr PL18 . . 41 A7
Lower Terr TR3 . . . . 81 B4
LOWERTOWN
Helston 91 E4
Lostwithiel 48 A4
Lower Town PL17 . . . . 28 E1
Lowertown Cl PL12 . . . . . . 53 C3
Lowertown La TR13 . . . . . 146 C7
LOWER TREBULLETT 28 A4
Lower Tregongeeves
PL26 . . . . 59 A1
Lower Tywarnhayle 18
TR6 . . . . 55 A5
Lower Well La TR13 . . . . . 146 C6
Lower Well Pk PL26 . . . . . . 73 C3
Lower Wesley Terr PL14 . . 38 D4
Lower Woodside PL25 . . . 114 A4
Lowery Cross PL20 . . . . 42 F4
Low Lee Rd TR19 . . . . 88 D1
Lowley Rd PL15 . . . . 18 E2
Lucas Cl PL31 . . . . 109 E3
Lucas La PL7 . . . . 130 D6
Lucas Terr PL4 . . . . 129 B2
LUCKETT 40 B8
Lucknow Rd PL31 . . . . 48 D8
Lucknow Road S 2 PL31 . 48 D8
LUDGVAN 89 A7
Ludgvan Prim Sch TR20 . . 89 B8
Ludlow Rd 2 PL3 . . . . 128 E6
LUFFINCOTT 13 C5
Luffman Cl PL13 . . . . 62 D6
Lugger The TR2 . . . . 83 B2
Lukes Cl TR1 . . . . 137 F5
Luke's La TR20 . . . . 89 F6
Lulworth Dr PL6 . . . . 125 B7
Lundy Cl PL6 . . . . 124 F7
Lundy Dr EX23 . . . . 10 C6
Lundy Rd PL29 . . . . 22 E7
Lusart Dr TR12 . . . . 102 F2
Lusty Glaze Adventure Ctr
TR7 . . . . 111 A8
Lusty Glaze Rd TR7 . . . . . 111 A7
LUTSFORD 3 A6
Lutsford Cross EX39 . . . . . . 3 A6
Lutyens Fold PL19 . . . . 29 C6
Luxmore Cl PL6 . . . . 125 E1
Luxon Dr TR7 . . . . 110 F4
Lux Park L Ctr PL14 . . . . . 113 C7
Luxstowe Dr 1 PL14 . . . . 113 C6
Luxstowe Gdns PL14 . . . . 113 C6
LUXULYAN 48 A1
Luxulyan Rd PL24 . . . . 115 F7
Luxulyan Sch PL30 . . . . 48 A1
Luxulyan Sta PL30 . . . . 47 F1
Lych Cl PL9 . . . . 135 A6
Lychgate Dr TR1 . . . . 137 C6
Lydcott Cl PL13 . . . . 63 F8
Lydcott Cres PL13 . . . . 63 F8
Lydcot Wlk PL6 . . . . 125 A1
Lydford Park Rd PL3 . . . . 128 D5
Lyd Gdns PL19 . . . . 147 D5
Lydia Way PL4 . . . . 149 B4
Lympne Ave PL5 . . . . 123 F5
Lynbridge Ct 5 PL19 . . . . 147 B5
Lyndhurst Ave PL25 . . . . . 115 A4
Lyndhurst Cl PL2 . . . . 128 C6
Lyndhurst Rd PL2 . . . . 128 C6
Lyndon Ct PL12 . . . . 122 D4
Lyndrick Rd PL3 . . . . 128 E7
Lynes Cotts 2 PL14 . . . . . . 51 A7
Lynher Cl PL15 . . . . 27 B3
Lynher Ct PL12 . . . . 122 F1
Lynher Dr PL12 . . . . 122 F1
Lynher St PL5 . . . . 123 D2
Lynher View PL17 . . . . 38 E8
Lynher Way
28 Callington PL17 . . . . . . 39 F4
North Hill PL15 . . . . 27 A4
Lyn-Meynek TR15 . . . . 140 D4
Lynmouth Cl PL7 . . . . 130 C7
LYNSTONE 104 D3
Lynstone Cotts EX23 . . . . 104 D3
Lynstone Rd EX23 . . . . . . 104 D4
Lyn Terr 7 TR18 . . . . 143 C1
Lynwood Ave PL7 . . . . 130 B6
Lynwood Cl PL31 . . . . 109 E4
Lynwood Cotts 1 TR19 . . . 88 C1
Lynwood Flats TR13 . . . . . 91 A1
Lyons Rd PL25 . . . . 115 B4
Lytton Pl PL25 . . . . 114 F4

M

Mabbots Ct TR18 . . . . 143 F6
MABE BURNTHOUSE 93 C8
Mabena Cl PL30 . . . . 34 C8
Mabe Prim Sch TR10 . . . . . . 81 C1
MacAdam Rd PL4 . . . . 149 C1
MacAulay Cres PL5 . . . . . . 124 C1
Macey St PL11 . . . . 127 C3
Mackenzie Pl PL5 . . . . 123 C2
McLean Dr PL26 . . . . 58 D5
Madden Rd PL1 . . . . 127 F2
Maddever Cres PL14 . . . . . 113 C5
Maddock Cl PL7 . . . . 131 A4
Maddock Dr PL7 . . . . 131 B4
Maddocks Cross EX22 . . . . . 3 F2
Madeira Dr EX23 . . . . 6 F5
Madeira Rd
Falmouth TR11 . . . . 145 A1
Plymouth PL1 . . . . 149 A1
Madeira Villas 1 PL20 . . . 42 C5
Madeira Wlk TR11 . . . . . . 145 A2
MADERS 39 D6
Madford La PL15 . . . . 106 C5
Madge Ct 3 PL19 . . . . 147 B6
Madge La PL19 . . . . 147 B6
Madison Terr TR27 . . . . . . 142 E7
Madison Vean TR27 . . . . . 142 E7
MADRON 143 B8
Madron Rd TR18 . . . . 143 C7
MAENPORTH 93 F4
Maenporth Est TR11 . . . . . 93 E4
Maenporth Rd TR11 . . . . . . 93 E4
Maen Valley Pk TR11 . . . . . 93 E5
MAER 104 D8
Maer Down Rd EX23 . . . . 104 C7
Maer La EX23 . . . . 104 D8
Magdalen Gdns PL7 . . . . . 130 F3
Magnificent Music Machines
Mus★ PL14 . . . . 51 C3
Magnolia Cl 3 PL7 . . . . . . 131 B5
Magnolia Ct 3 PL9 . . . . . . 135 F7
Magor Ave TR14 . . . . 79 E5
Maida Vale Terr PL4 . . . . 128 F4
Maiden St 1 EX23 . . . . 4 E1
Maidenwell Rd PL7 . . . . . 130 C5
Maidstone Pl PL5 . . . . 123 E4
Maine Gdns PL2 . . . . 127 F7
Main Rd
Crumplehorn PL13 . . . . 62 D2
Downderry PL11 . . . . 64 C5
Main St TR18 . . . . 143 C7
MAINSTONE 125 F2
Mainstone Ave PL4 . . . . . . 149 C2
Maitland Dr PL3 . . . . 128 F8
Maker La PL10 . . . . 133 B4
Maker Rd PL11 . . . . 127 A2
Maker View PL3 . . . . 128 B4
Malabar Ho TR1 . . . . 69 F3
Malabar Rd TR1 . . . . 69 F3
Mallard Cl PL7 . . . . 130 F5
Mallets Ct PL27 . . . . 108 C6
Malmesbury Cl PL2 . . . . . . 128 B8
Malory Cl PL5 . . . . 124 D2
MALPAS 70 D2
Malpas Ho TR1 . . . . 137 E4
Malpas Rd TR1 . . . . 137 E2
Malt House Ct TR27 . . . . . 142 D6
Malt House Gdns 2
TR18 . . . . 143 C2
Malthouse La TR17 . . . . 89 C5
Malt House The 3 TR18 . 143 C2
MANACCAN 101 A8
Manaccan Prim Sch
TR12 . . . . 101 A8
MANADON 124 D1
Manadon Cl PL5 . . . . 124 E1
Manadon Dr PL5 . . . . 124 E1
Manadon Football Ctr
PL2 . . . . 124 D2
Manadon Hill PL5, PL6 . . . 124 E1
Manadon Vale Prim Sch 1
PL5 . . . . 128 E8
Manaton Cl TR13 . . . . 146 D8
Manby Gdns PL5 . . . . 123 F5
Mandalay Villas 8 TR9 . . . 45 E1
Mandeley Cl PL33 . . . . 14 D2
Manely Way PL17 . . . . 40 C4
Manewas Way TR7 . . . . . . 111 B7
Manfield Way PL25 . . . . . . 115 C4
Manifold Gdns PL3 . . . . . . 129 D5
Manley Cl PL14 . . . . 113 B5
Manley Rd PL14 . . . . 113 B5
Manley Terr 5 PL14 . . . . . 113 B5
MANNAMEAD 128 F5
Mannamead Ave PL3 . . . . 128 F5
Mannamead Ct 9 PL3 . . . 128 F6
Mannamead Rd PL3 . . . . . 128 F6
Man of War View TR12 . . . 102 F2
Manor Bourne Rd PL9 . . . 135 C1
Manor Cl
Blisland PL30 . . . . 35 D8
Crackington Haven EX23 . . . 10 C6
Falmouth TR11 . . . . 144 E5
Heamoor TR18 . . . . 143 D7
Helston TR13 . . . . 146 D8
St Austell PL25 . . . . 114 F5
Tavistock PL19 . . . . 147 A6
Manor Cotts TR11 . . . . 145 D3
Manor Cres TR11 . . . . 144 E5
Manor Ct 1 TR2 . . . . 95 A6
Manor Dr TR26 . . . . 141 C3
Manor Farm PL20 . . . . 42 E3
Manor Farm Cl 7 TR20 . . . 89 E5
Manor Farm Rd PL26 . . . . 115 A1
Manor Gdns
Camelford PL32 . . . . 105 D4
Horrabridge PL20 . . . . 42 B4
Millbrook PL10 . . . . 132 F6
Plymouth PL1 . . . . 148 B2
Redruth TR15 . . . . 140 B6
St Erth TR27 . . . . 142 A1
Truro TR1 . . . . 137 E5
Manor La PL3 . . . . 129 D5
Manor Park Cl PL7 . . . . . . 130 F5
Manor Park Dr PL7 . . . . . . 131 A4
MANOR PARSLEY 68 B5
Manor Pk
Dousland PL20 . . . . 42 E3
Duloe PL14 . . . . 51 A1
Saltash PL12 . . . . 122 D2
Manor Pl TR18 . . . . 143 D7
Manor Rd
Bude EX23 . . . . 104 E4
Camborne TR14 . . . . 138 C2
Carharrack TR16 . . . . 80 E8
Falmouth TR11 . . . . 144 E5
Newquay TR7 . . . . 110 D6
Plymouth PL9 . . . . 135 E8
Tavistock PL19 . . . . 147 B6
Manor St PL1 . . . . 148 A3
Manor View PL24 . . . . 60 B4
Manor Way
Heamoor TR18 . . . . 143 D7
Helston TR13 . . . . 146 D8
Tavistock PL19 . . . . 147 B6
Manse Rd 6 TR3 . . . . 81 F7
Mansion Ho The PL1 . . . . 134 A8
Manson Pl PL26 . . . . 58 C8
Manston Cl PL5 . . . . 123 E5
Mantle Gdns PL5 . . . . 127 D8
Maple Ave
Camelford PL32 . . . . 105 E5
Torpoint PL11 . . . . 127 A3
Maple Cl
Bodmin PL31 . . . . 109 B4
23 Callington PL17 . . . . . . 39 F4
Plymouth PL6 . . . . 125 E6
5 St Columb Major TR9 . . 45 D6
St Dennis PL26 . . . . 58 B8
Tavistock PL19 . . . . 147 C3
Maple Ct 2 PL9 . . . . 135 F7
Maple Gr
Plymouth, Mutley PL4 . . . 128 D4
Plymouth, Plympton PL7 . . 130 B5
Maple Way PL6 . . . . 125 E7
MARAZION 89 B6
Marazion Mus★ TR17 . . . . 89 B5
Marazion Sch TR17 . . . . . . 89 C5
Marchant's Cross PL20 . . . 42 F1
Marchant's Way PL20 . . . . 42 F2
Marconi Centre (Mus)★
TR13 . . . . 98 F2
Marconi Cl TR13 . . . . 146 B6
Marcus Hill TR7 . . . . 110 E6
Marcwheal 6 TR19 . . . . 88 C1
Mardon Cl PL6 . . . . 125 D4
Marett Rd PL5 . . . . 123 F3
Margaret Ave PL25 . . . . . . 114 E3
Margaret Cnr PL31 . . . . . . 109 C4
Margaret Cres PL31 . . . . . 109 C4
Margaret Gdns PL27 . . . . . 108 D5
Margaret Pk PL3 . . . . 128 E8

Parc-an-Dower TR13 ... 146 C6
Parcandowr TR2 ... 57 E1
Parc-an-Forth 6 TR26 ... 77 A6
Parc an Gate TR19 ... 88 C1
Parc-an-Gwarry 7 TR3 ... 81 F7
Parc-an-Ithan TR12 ... 102 F2
Parc-an-Maen 11 TR13 ... 98 C8
Parc an Manns TR11 ... 93 D3
Parc-an-Peath TR19 ... 97 A6
Parc-an-Stamps 4 TR26. 77 A6
Parc an Yorth TR19 ... 86 F8
Parc-Askell Cl TR12 ... 98 E5
Parc Bean Terr TR26 ... 141 A6
Parc Behan Ct TR2 ... 83 F6
Parc Bowen TR13 ... 92 A3
Parc-Bracket St TR14 ... 138 D3
Parc Brawse TR12 ... 102 F2
Parc Briwer TR10 ... 144 D7
Parc Eglos
Helston TR13 ... 146 B6
St Merryn PL28 ... 31 F8
Parc Eglos Sch TR13 ... 146 C6
Parc Enys TR12 ... 99 B4
PARC ERISSEY ... 68 A3
Parc Erissey Ind Est TR16. 68 A3
Parc Fer Cl EX23 ... 4 E1
Parc Godrevy TR7 ... 110 C5
Parc Holland TR13 ... 146 D8
Parc Ledden TR13 ... 146 C6
Parc Ledrak TR13 ... 146 B8
Parc Letta TR18 ... 143 C7
Parc Mellan TR18 ... 143 D7
Parc Merys TR2 ... 83 B2
Parc Monga Rd TR11 ... 92 F3
Parc Morrep TR20 ... 90 B3
Parc Owles TR26 ... 141 D2
Parc Peneglos TR11 ... 82 A3
Parc Pennkarn PL33 ... 14 E3
Parc Rowan TR9 ... 57 E8
Parc Shady TR26 ... 77 C1
Parc Stephney TR11 ... 144 C2
Parc Terr 19 TR18 ... 143 C1
Parc Trenance PL28 ... 31 F7
Parc Trethias PL28 ... 31 F7
Parc Vean PL30 ... 34 C1
Parc Venton Cl 2 TR14 . 138 F2
Parc Villas 17 TR18 ... 143 C1
Parc Wartha Ave TR18 .. 143 D6
Parc Wartha Cres TR18 .. 143 D6
Par Gn PL24 ... 60 C4
Pargolla Rd TR7 ... 110 F6
Park 30 PL15 ... 106 A3
Parka Cl 12 TR9 ... 45 E2
Park-an-Bans TR14 ... 138 E1
Parkancreeg 9 TR3 ... 81 F7
Park an Gonwyn TR26 ... 141 E2
Park an Gorsaf TR14 ... 138 D2
Park an Harvey TR13 ... 146 C6
Park-an-Mengleth TR15 140 D4
Park-an-Pyth TR19 ... 75 A1
Park-an-Tansys TR14 ... 138 F2
Parka Rd
Indian Queens TR9 ... 45 E1
8 St Columb Road TR9 ... 45 E2
Park Ave
Plymouth, Devonport PL1 ... 127 E3
Plymouth, Plymstock PL9 . 135 D7
St Ives TR26 ... 141 B5
PARK BOTTOM ... 139 B8
Park Cl
Illogan TR15 ... 139 B8
Nancegollan TR13 ... 91 B7
Plymouth PL7 ... 130 B7
Park Cnr TR18 ... 143 E5
Park Cres
Falmouth TR11 ... 145 A4
Helston TR13 ... 146 B5
Plymouth PL9 ... 135 C7
Ponsanooth TR3 ... 81 B4
Park Ct
Chillaton PL16 ... 29 F8
28 Penzance TR18 ... 143 E5
Park Dr PL31 ... 109 B4
Parkenbutts TR7 ... 111 D7
Parkengear Vean TR2 ... 71 D6
Parkengue TR10 ... 144 A7
Parkenhead La PL28 ... 20 F2
Park Enskellaw 6 TR12 .. 99 A2
Park en Venton TR12 ... 99 A2
Park-en-Vine PL27 ... 32 D6
Parker Cl PL7 ... 130 B5
Parker Rd PL2 ... 128 B6
Parker's Gn PL18 ... 40 F6
Parkesway PL12 ... 122 D2
Park Fenton PL14 ... 113 D5
PARKFIELD ... 39 A2
Parkfield Dr PL6 ... 125 F1
Park Gwyn PL26 ... 58 B4
Park Hill TR11 ... 145 A4
Park Ho PL25 ... 114 B3
Park Holly TR14 ... 138 B3
Parkins Terr 7 TR1 ... 137 D5
Park La
8 Bere Alston PL20 ... 41 B1
Bugle PL26 ... 47 C1
Camborne TR14 ... 138 E2
Plymouth PL9 ... 135 C7
Parklands PL26 ... 58 C7
Parklands Cl TR7 ... 111 D6
Park Leder TR16 ... 68 C3
Park Leven TR16 ... 139 C8
Park Lowen TR26 ... 141 C2
Parknoweth TR12 ... 99 A4
Parknoweth Cl TR8 ... 56 B6
Park Pl
Grampound Road TR2 ... 57 E1
Wadebridge PL27 ... 108 B5
Park Place La 12 PL3 ... 128 A4
Park Rd
Camborne TR14 ... 138 E4
Fowey PL23 ... 116 C4
Illogan TR15 ... 139 B7
Lifton PL16 ... 19 F3
Liskeard PL14 ... 113 C6
18 Newlyn TR18 ... 143 C1
Plymouth PL3 ... 129 A6
Ponsanooth TR3 ... 81 B4
Redruth TR15 ... 140 C4
St Austell PL25 ... 114 C3
St Dominick PL12 ... 40 D2
Torpoint PL11 ... 127 B3
Wadebridge PL27 ... 108 B5
Whitemoor PL26 ... 58 E8
Park Rd Hos PL22 ... 112 C2
Park Rise TR11 ... 145 A4
Parkryn Rd 4 TR19 ... 88 C1
Parkside PL2 ... 127 F5
Park St PL3 ... 128 A4
Park Stenak TR16 ... 80 F8
Parkstone La PL7 ... 130 F6
Park Street Ope PL3 ... 128 A4
Park Terr
Falmouth TR11 ... 145 A4
Truro TR1 ... 70 D1
Park The
Penryn TR10 ... 144 B7
Tregony TR2 ... 71 F4
Parkvedras Ho 5 TR1 ... 137 B4
Parkvedras Terr 4 TR1 . 137 B4
Parkventon PL26 ... 47 C2
Park View
Lifton PL16 ... 19 F4
Liskeard PL14 ... 113 C6
Perranarworthal TR3 ... 81 E6
Plymouth PL4 ... 149 C3
Summercourt TR8 ... 57 B7
Truro TR1 ... 137 C3
Parkview Apartments TR7 ... 110 F5
Park View Cl TR3 ... 82 A7
Park View Rd TR13 ... 146 B5
Park View Terr PL27 ... 108 B5
Park Villas TR3 ... 81 B4
Park Way PL25 ... 114 F5
Parkway Ct PL6 ... 129 E7
Parkway Ind Est The PL6 ... 129 E7
Parkway The PL3, PL5, PL6 ... 124 B1
Park Wise TR10 ... 144 C8
Parkwood Cl PL6 ... 121 B2
Parkwood Ct PL19 ... 147 D6
Parkwood Rd PL19 ... 147 D6
Park Wood Rise PL16 ... 19 F4
Parkwoon Cl PL26 ... 46 F3
Par La PL24 ... 60 B4
Par Moor Rd
Par PL24, PL25 ... 60 B3
St Austell PL24, PL25 ... 115 F4
PARNACOTT ... 8 E8
Parnell Cl PL6 ... 129 A8
Parr La PL4 ... 149 B2
Parr St PL4 ... 149 B2
Parsonage Ct PL16 ... 19 F4
Parsonage Way PL4 ... 149 B2
Parsons Cl PL9 ... 136 A4
Parsons Ct PL10 ... 132 F6
Parsons Gn PL17 ... 39 E6
Par Sta PL24 ... 60 C5
Partwayes PL19 ... 30 A3
Pascoe Cl TR3 ... 69 D4
Pasley St E PL2 ... 127 F4
Pasley St PL2 ... 127 E4
Passage Hill TR11 ... 82 A3
Passage La PL23 ... 116 B5
Passage St PL23 ... 116 D5
Passmore Cl
Blackwater TR4 ... 68 E5
Liskeard PL14 ... 113 D6
Pathfields EX23 ... 104 E5
Pathway Fields The TR27 ... 142 C5
Patna Pl PL1 ... 148 B4
Pato Point PL11 ... 127 A5
Patterdale Cl PL6 ... 125 D3
Patterdale Wlk PL6 ... 125 D3
Pattinson Cl PL6 ... 125 E2
Pattinson Ct PL6 ... 125 E2
Pattinson Dr PL6 ... 125 F2
PAUL ... 88 C2
Paull Rd PL31 ... 109 B4
Paulls Row 4 TR15 ... 140 C5
PAUL'S GREEN ... 90 E8
Paul's Row TR1 ... 137 D5
Paul's Terr TR1 ... 137 D5
Paviland Grange 6 PL1 . 128 A3
Pavilion Pk TR14 ... 138 F4
Pavlova Cl PL14 ... 113 C5
Pavlova Ct 6 PL14 ... 113 C5
Paynter's Cross PL12 ... 53 E7
Paynter's Cross Cotts PL12 ... 53 E7
Paynters La TR16 ... 67 E4
PAYNTER'S LANE END ... 67 E4
Paynter's Lane End Est TR16 ... 67 D4
Paynter Wlk 5 PL7 ... 131 B5
Peacock Ave PL11 ... 127 A3
Peacock Cl PL7 ... 130 F7
Peacock La PL4 ... 149 A2
Pearce's La 12 TR26 ... 141 A5
Pearce's Row 3 PL24 ... 60 C4
Pearn Cotts 2 PL3 ... 128 F6
Pearn Gdns PL3 ... 129 A7
Pearn Rd PL3 ... 129 A7
Pearn Ridge PL3 ... 129 A7
Pearson Ave 3 PL4 ... 128 F4
Pearson Rd PL4 ... 128 F4
Pebble Ct TR7 ... 111 C7
Pedlars Cl PL15 ... 18 B8
Pedna Carne Mobile Home Pk TR9 ... 57 E8
Pednandrea TR19 ... 86 E6
Pedn-m'n-du TR19 ... 96 A7
Pedn-Moran TR2 ... 95 B6
Pedn-y-ke 1 TR12 ... 99 A1
Peek Moor Cross EX22 ... 13 E4
Peeks Ave PL9 ... 135 F7
Peel St PL1 ... 128 A1
Peguarra Cl PL28 ... 20 E1
Peguarra Ct PL28 ... 20 E1
Pelean Cross TR3 ... 81 B5
Pelham Ct 11 TR11 ... 145 C3
Pellew Cl
7 Falmouth TR11 ... 145 A5
Padstow PL28 ... 107 C5
Pellew Cres TR13 ... 146 C4
Pellew Pl PL2 ... 127 F4
Pellew Rd TR11 ... 145 A5
Pellor Fields TR13 ... 90 F3
PELYNT ... 62 D5
Pelynt Prim Sch PL13 ... 62 D6
Pembrey Wlk PL5 ... 123 E4
Pembroke Cl 7 PL24 ... 60 C4
Pembroke La PL1 ... 127 E1
Pembroke Rd TR7 ... 111 E7
Pembroke St PL1 ... 127 E1
Pemros Rd PL5 ... 123 C1
Penair Cres TR1 ... 137 F6
Penair Sch TR1 ... 70 D4
Penair View TR1 ... 137 F4
Penally Ct PL35 ... 9 D2
Penally Hill PL35 ... 9 D2
Penally Terr PL35 ... 9 C2
Penalverne Ave TR18 ... 143 D5
Penalverne Cres TR18 ... 143 D5
Penalverne Dr TR18 ... 143 D5
Penalverne Pl TR18 ... 143 D5
Penameyne Ct 5 TR26 ... 141 B6
Pen-an-Gwel TR26 ... 141 A4
Penare Gdns 2 TR18 ... 143 E6
Penare Rd TR18 ... 143 E6
Penare Terr TR18 ... 143 E6
Penarrow Cl TR11 ... 144 E2
Penarrow Rd TR11 ... 145 C8
Penarth PL13 ... 117 B3
Penarth Rd TR11 ... 145 A5
Penarwyn Cres TR18 ... 143 B7
Penarwyn Rd PL24 ... 60 B4
Penarwyn Woods 6 PL24 60 B4
PENBEAGLE ... 141 A4
Penbeagle Cl 17 TR26 ... 77 A6
Penbeagle Cres 8 TR26 .. 77 A6
Penbeagle Ind Est TR26 .. 77 A6
Penbeagle La TR26 ... 77 A6
Penbeagle Terr 7 TR26 .. 77 A6
Penbeagle Way TR26 ... 141 A4
PENBERTH ... 97 A3
Penberthy Cross TR27 ... 89 F7
Penberthy Rd
Helston TR13 ... 146 C5
Portreath TR16 ... 67 D6
Penbothidno TR11 ... 92 F3
Pen Brea Cl TR2 ... 95 B6
Penbrea Rd TR18 ... 143 E7
Penbugle La PL31 ... 109 E7
Pencair Ave PL11 ... 126 E2
Pencalenick Specl Sch TR1 ... 70 E4
Pencantol TR4 ... 81 C7
Pencarn Parc TR16 ... 80 A5
Pencarrick Cl TR1 ... 137 B6
PENCARROW ... 105 D1
Pencarrow★ PL30 ... 34 D6
Pencarrow Cl PL17 ... 39 E3
Pencarrow Rd 13 TR16 ... 67 E4
Pencavo Hill PL12 ... 53 A3
Pencoys Prim Sch TR16 .. 80 A5
Pencreber Rd 3 PL20 ... 42 C4
PENCUKE ... 10 D5
Pendale Sq TR1 ... 137 B4
Pendarves
St Merryn PL28 ... 31 F7
Tresillian TR2 ... 70 F5
Pendarves Flats TR18 ... 143 D6
Pendarves Rd
Camborne TR14 ... 138 C1
Falmouth TR11 ... 144 F6
Penzance TR18 ... 143 D6
Truro TR1 ... 137 C6
Pendarves St
Camborne, Beacon TR14 . 138 F1
Troon TR14 ... 79 E4
Pendarves View TR14 ... 138 C1
Pendean Ave PL14 ... 113 B6
Pendean Cl PL14 ... 113 B6
Pendean Ct PL14 ... 113 B6
Pendean Dr PL14 ... 113 B6
PENDEEN ... 75 A1
Pendeen Cl
Plymouth PL6 ... 124 F6
Threemilestone TR3 ... 69 D3
Pendeen Cres
Plymouth PL6 ... 125 A6
Threemilestone TR3 ... 69 D3
Pendeen Ho TR1 ... 69 E4
Pendeen Pk TR13 ... 146 C8
Pendeen Pl TR7 ... 110 F6
Pendeen Prim Sch TR19 .. 75 A1
Pendeen Rd
Porthleven TR13 ... 91 B1
Threemilestone TR3 ... 69 D3
Truro TR1 ... 137 E3
Pendennis Castle★ TR11 145 E2
Pendennis Cl
Penzance TR18 ... 143 E7
Plymouth PL3 ... 128 F8
Torpoint PL11 ... 126 F3
Pendennis Ct TR11 ... 145 D3
Pendennis Pl TR18 ... 143 F7
Pendennis Rd
Falmouth TR11 ... 145 D3
Looe PL13 ... 117 D5
Penzance TR18 ... 143 E7
Pendennis Rise TR11 ... 145 D3
Pender's La TR15 ... 140 B5
Pendilly Ave PL11 ... 126 F2
Pendilly Dr PL25 ... 114 E7
Pendinnes Gdns PL15 ... 106 B8
PENDOGGETT ... 23 A6
Pendola Wlk TR26 ... 141 B5
Pendour Pk PL22 ... 112 E2
Pendower Ct TR2 ... 83 D5
Pendower Rd
Looe PL13 ... 117 E4
Veryan TR2 ... 83 F6
Pendower Terr TR14 ... 138 E1
Pendragon Cres TR7 ... 111 A4
Pendragon Ho TR11 ... 145 D3
Pendragon Rd PL14 ... 113 D6
Pendra Loweth TR11 ... 144 D1
Penday Gdns PL14 ... 50 E7
Pendrea Cl TR18 ... 143 F7
Pendrea Pk TR14 ... 138 F5
Pendrea Pl TR18 ... 143 F7
Pendrea Rd TR18 ... 143 F7
Pendrea Wood TR1 ... 69 F3
PENDRIFT ... 24 B1
Pendrim Rd PL13 ... 117 D4
Pendruccombe Ct PL15 ... 106 D5
Pen-Eglos 8 TR2 ... 95 A6
PENELEWEY ... 82 C7
Penforth TR14 ... 138 E2
Penfound Gdns EX23 ... 104 F5
Penganel Cl TR7 ... 110 D4
Pengarrock Hill TR12 ... 101 D5
Pengarth 1 TR5 ... 54 D1
Pengarth Cl TR1 ... 137 C2
Pengarth Rd TR11 ... 145 A3
Pengarth Rise TR11 ... 145 A3
PENGEGON ... 138 F2
Pengegon Moor TR14 ... 138 F2
Pengegon Parc TR14 ... 138 F2
Pengegon Way TR14 ... 138 F2
PENGELLY ... 14 E2
Pengelly
24 Callington PL17 ... 39 F4
Delabole PL33 ... 14 E2
Pengelly Cl PL11 ... 126 F5
Pengelly Cross
Godolphin Cross TR27 ... 90 F7
Wadebridge PL27 ... 108 C1
Pengelly Hill PL11 ... 127 A5
Pengelly Pk PL11 ... 126 F5
Pengelly Pl TR11 ... 144 E5
Pengellys Row TR14 ... 139 A5
Pengelly Way TR3 ... 69 D3
Pengeron Ave 1 TR14 .. 138 F7
Pengersick Est TR20 ... 90 C3
Pengersick La TR20 ... 90 C3
Pengersick Parc TR20 ... 90 C3
Pengliddon PL27 ... 33 B7
PENGOLD ... 10 A5
Pengover Cl PL14 ... 113 D6
Pengover Gn PL14 ... 51 E8
Pengover Hts PL14 ... 113 D6
Pengover Parc TR15 ... 140 C6
Pengover Pk PL14 ... 113 D6
Pengover Rd PL14 ... 113 E6
Pengrowyn PL26 ... 59 D6
Pengwarras Rd TR14 ... 138 C3
Pengwel 16 TR18 ... 143 C2
PENHALE
Indian Queens ... 57 D8
Millbrook ... 132 D7
Mullion ... 99 D1
Penhale 1 TR6 ... 55 A5
Penhale Cl PL14 ... 37 F3
Penhale Cotts TR3 ... 82 D6
Penhale Est TR15 ... 140 B6
Penhale Gdns TR9 ... 57 D8
Penhale Mdw PL14 ... 37 F3
Penhale Rd
Barripper TR14 ... 79 A4
Carnhell Green TR14 ... 78 F4
Falmouth TR11 ... 144 F1
Penwithick PL26 ... 59 D7
Penhaligon Cl TR15 ... 140 D4
Penhaligon Ct TR1 ... 137 E5
Penhaligon Way PL25 ... 114 F4
PENHALLICK ... 139 C4
Penhall La TR4 ... 68 C6
PENHALLOW ... 55 B2
Penhallow TR15 ... 139 B8
Penhallow Cl
Mount Hawke TR4 ... 68 C6
Veryan TR2 ... 83 C5
Penhallow Ct TR7 ... 111 C7
Penhallow Parc PL33 ... 14 D2
Penhallow Rd TR7 ... 111 C7
Penhalls Way TR3 ... 82 B8
PENHALVEAN ... 80 C4
Penharget Cl PL14 ... 38 D5
Penhaven Cl TR8 ... 56 B7
Penhaven Ct TR7 ... 110 E6
Penhellaz Hill TR13 ... 146 B6
Penhellaz Rd TR13 ... 146 B6
Penhole Cl PL15 ... 27 D3
Penina Ave TR7 ... 110 F4
Peninsula Medical Sch PL6 ... 125 C3
Peninsular Pk PL12 ... 122 C4
Penjerrick Gdns★ TR11 ... 93 D5
Penjerrick Hill
Budock Water TR11 ... 144 C1
Falmouth TR11 ... 93 E5
Penkenna Cl EX23 ... 10 C6
Penkernick Cl TR18 ... 143 B1
Penkernick Way TR9 ... 45 E6
Penknight La PL22 ... 112 A2
Penlean Cl TR15 ... 140 D7
Penlea Rd TR10 ... 144 B8
Penlee Apartments PL23 116 C3
Penlee Cl
13 Callington PL17 ... 39 F4
Praa Sands TR20 ... 90 C3
Tregony TR2 ... 71 F4
Penlee Cotts PL10 ... 64 C2
Penlee Gdns PL3 ... 128 A4
Penlee Ho TR1 ... 69 E4
Penlee House Gall & Mus★ TR18 ... 143 E5
Penlee Manor Dr TR18 .. 143 E4
Penlee Pk PL11 ... 126 E4
Penlee Pl 4 PL4 ... 128 F4
Penlee Rd PL3 ... 128 A4
Penlee St 10 TR18 ... 143 E6
Penlee View Terr 3 TR18 ... 143 E4
Penlee Villas TR3 ... 82 B8
Penlee Way PL3 ... 128 B4
Penlu TR14 ... 138 F5
Penlu Ho TR14 ... 138 F5
Penluke Cl TR16 ... 80 A5
Penmare Cl TR27 ... 142 E7
Penmare Ct TR27 ... 142 E7
Penmare Terr TR27 ... 142 E7
PENMARTH ... 80 C2
PENMAYNE ... 21 E3
Penmayne Parc TR16 ... 140 F1
Penmayne Villas PL27 ... 21 E3
Penmead Rd PL33 ... 14 E2
Penmelen PL32 ... 105 C4
Penmeneth TR13 ... 146 F8
Penmenner Est 7 TR12 . 101 C4
Penmenner Rd TR12 ... 102 F2
Penmere Cl
Helston TR13 ... 146 B7
Penzance TR18 ... 143 E7
Penmere Cres TR11 ... 144 F3
Penmere Ct 4 TR11 ... 145 A3
Penmere Dr TR7 ... 110 C5
Penmere Hill 7 TR11 ... 145 A3
Penmere Pl
3 Falmouth TR11 ... 145 A3
Penzance TR18 ... 143 E7
Penmere Rd
Penzance TR18 ... 143 E7
St Austell PL25 ... 115 A4
Penmere Sta TR11 ... 144 F3
Penmerrin Ct TR7 ... 110 E5
Penmeva View PL26 ... 73 C3
Penmorvah TR11 ... 82 A2
Penmorvah Pl TR14 ... 138 E2
Penmorvah Rd TR1 ... 137 F6
PENNANCE ... 140 F1
Pennance Hill TR11 ... 93 F5
Pennance Ho TR11 ... 145 A2
Pennance La TR16 ... 140 F1
Pennance Parc TR16 ... 140 F1
Pennance Rd
Falmouth TR11 ... 145 A2
Lanner TR16 ... 80 E7
Redruth TR16 ... 140 F1
Pennance Terr TR16 ... 140 F1
Penn an Drea TR13 ... 146 D8
Pennant Farm PL29 ... 22 E6
Pennard Villas PL27 ... 33 B5
Penn Kernow PL15 ... 106 E4
Pennor Dr PL25 ... 114 D3
Pennoweth Prim Sch TR15 ... 140 C5
PENNYCOMEQUICK ... 148 B4
Pennycomequick Hill PL4 ... 148 B4
PENNYCROSS ... 128 C8
Pennycross Cl PL2 ... 128 D8
Pennycross Park Rd PL2 128 C7
Pennycross Prim Sch PL2 ... 128 C8
Pennygillam Ind Est PL15 ... 106 A4
Pennygillam Way PL15 ... 18 E2
Pennys La PL24 ... 115 F5
Penny's La PL9 ... 136 D6
PENNYTINNEY ... 23 A4
Penoweth TR11 ... 82 A2
PENPETHY ... 14 F5
PENPILLICK ... 60 D7
PENPOL ... 82 B6
Penpol Ave TR27 ... 142 C5
Penpol Hill
Crantock TR8 ... 110 B4
Devoran TR3 ... 82 B6
PENPOLL ... 61 D5
Penpol Prim Sch TR27 .. 142 C5
Penpol Rd TR27 ... 142 B5
Penpol Terr TR27 ... 142 B5
Penpol Vean TR27 ... 142 C5
PENPONDS ... 138 B1
Penponds Prim Sch TR14. 79 B5
Penponds Rd TR13 ... 91 A1
Penpons Cl TR18 ... 143 C4
PENPONT ... 24 A1
Penpont Rd TR15 ... 140 D6
Penpont View PL15 ... 26 C7

170 Pen–Pol

Pen Porth Ave TR26 ...... 77 A7
Penquite Dr PL31 .... 109 F5
Penrice Com Coll PL25 .. 115 A3
Penrice Parc PL25 ...... 115 A3
Penrith Cl PL6 .... 125 D3
Penrith Gdns PL6 .... 125 D3
Penrith Wlk PL6 .... 125 D3
PENROSE
St Breward 24 A3
St Eval 31 E5
Penrose Ct
Penzance TR18 .... 143 F6
2 South Tehidy TR14 .... 138 F7
Penrose Parc TR13 .... 91 B1
Penrose Rd
Falmouth TR11 .... 145 A4
Helston TR13 .... 146 C6
Penrose St PL1 .... 148 B3
Penrose Terr TR18 ...... 143 F6
Penrose Villas 5 PL4 ... 128 F4
Penrose Walks★ TR12,
TR13 .... 98 D8
Penruan La TR2 .... 95 B6
PENRYN 144 B7
Penryn Coll TR10 .... 144 B7
Penryn Inf Sch TR10 .... 144 B7
Penryn Jun Sch TR10 .... 144 B8
Penryn Mus★ TR10 .... 144 C7
Penryn St TR15 .... 140 B4
Penryn Sta TR10 .... 144 B8
Pensans Com Prim Sch
TR18 .... 143 D6
Penscombe Cross PL15 ... 28 C6
Penscott La PL26 .... 114 C1
PENSILVA 38 E5
Pensilva TR6 .... 55 A4
Pensilva Ind Est PL14 ... 38 E4
Pensilva Prim Sch PL14 .. 38 E5
Pensilva Rd TR1 .... 137 E6
Penstowe Rd EX23 .... 5 A6
Penstrasse Pl 1 PL24 ... 60 D5
PENSTRAZE 69 A4
Penstraze Bsns Ctr TR4 .. 69 A5
Penstraze La PL26 .... 47 A4
Pensylva PL25 .... 114 E3
Pentalek Rd TR14 .... 138 D1
Pentamar St PL2 .... 127 E4
Pentargon Rd 1 PL35 ...... 9 C1
PENTEWAN 73 C6
Pentewan Hill PL26 ...... 73 D6
Pentewan Rd PL24, PL26 .. 59 C1
Pentidna La TR27 .... 66 B2
Pentillie PL26 .... 73 C4
Pentillie Cl 22 PL20 .... 41 B1
Pentillie Cres PL4 ..... 128 D4
Pentillie Gdns
14 Callington PL17 ...... 39 E4
St Austell PL25 .... 114 F6
Pentillie Rd
Bere Alston PL20 .... 41 B1
Plymouth PL4 .... 128 E4
Pentillie View 23 PL20 .. 41 B1
Pentillie Way PL26 ...... 73 C4
PENTIRE 43 D4
Pentire Ave TR7 .... 110 A5
Pentire Cres TR7 .... 110 B5
Pentire Ct TR7 .... 110 B6
Pentire Gn TR8 .... 43 D3
Pentire Hts TR7 .... 110 A5
Pentire Rd
Newquay TR7 .... 110 C5
Penryn TR10 .... 144 B8
Torpoint PL11 .... 126 F3
Pentland Cl PL6 .... 124 F7
Pen Tor PL30 .... 35 C8
Pentor Ct PL30 .... 35 C8
Pentour 3 PL24 .... 60 B4
Pentowan Ct TR26 .... 141 E2
Pentowan Gdns TR27 ..... 142 E8
Pentowan Rd TR27 .... 142 E8
Pentreath Cl
Fowey PL23 .... 116 B5
Lanner TR16 .... 80 E7
Penzance TR18 .... 143 D7
Pentreath La
Lizard TR12 .... 102 F2
Praa Sands TR20 .... 90 B3
Pentreath Terr TR16 ..... 80 E7
Pentre Ct EX23 .... 4 D4
Pentrevah Ct TR7 .... 110 D6
Pentrevah Rd 8 PL26 .... 59 D7
Pen-Tye TR27 .... 78 E3
Pentyre Ct PL4 .... 149 C4
Pentyre Terr PL4 .... 149 C4
Penvale 4 PL14 .... 38 E4
Penvale Cl TR14 .... 79 B5
Penvale Cres TR10 ...... 144 B8
Penvale Ct 8 TR11 ..... 145 A4
Penvale Dr TR10 .... 144 B8
Penvean Cl TR10 .... 93 C8
Penvean La TR11 .... 144 E5
Penvenen 2 TR6 .... 55 A5
Penventinnie La TR1 ..... 69 E4
Penventinue La PL23 .... 116 B7
Penventon Terr
Four Lanes TR16 .... 80 B6
Redruth TR15 .... 140 A4
Penventon View TR13 ... 146 B5
Penview Cres TR13 ..... 146 B5
Penvorder Cotts PL30 .... 24 B2
Penvorder La PL30 .... 24 B2
Penware Parc TR14 ..... 138 C1
Penwarne Cl TR14 ...... 138 F7
Penwarne La PL26 .... 73 C3
Penwarne Rd TR11 .... 93 D5
Penwartha TR12 .... 101 B2
Penwartha Cl
Constantine TR11 .... 92 F3
St Columb Minor TR7 .... 111 D7
PENWARTHA COOMBE 55 B3
Penwartha Ct TR11 .... 92 F3
Penwartha Rd
15 Illogan TR16 .... 67 E4
Perranporth TR6 .... 55 B4
Penwartha Vean 14 TR16 . 67 E4
PENWEATHERS 69 F2
Penwerris Ct TR11 ...... 145 A6
Penwerris Farm TR11 ... 144 F5
Penwerris La TR11 ..... 145 A6
Penwerris Rd TR1 .... 69 F3
Penwerris Rise TR20 ..... 90 B3
Penwerris Terr 10 TR11 . 145 A5
Penwethers La TR1 .... 69 F3
Penwinnick Cl 9 TR5 .... 54 C1
Penwinnick Parc 4 TR5 .. 54 D1
Penwinnick Rd
St Agnes TR5 .... 68 D8
St Austell PL25 .... 114 B3
Penwith Bsns Ctr TR20 ... 88 F6
Penwith Cl TR26 .... 141 A4
Penwith Coll TR18 ..... 143 D7
Penwithhick Rd PL26 ..... 59 D7
Penwithian Cl TR27 .... 142 E6
PENWITHICK 59 E7
Penwithick Pk 6 PL26 ... 59 D7
Penwith Rd TR26 .... 141 A4
Penwith St 11 TR18 .... 143 E6
Penworth Cl PL15 ...... 106 C5
Penwyth TR12 .... 92 C1
Pen y Bryn PL27 .... 108 D6
PENZANCE 143 F5
Penzance L Ctr TR18 ... 143 D6
Penzance Rd
Helston TR13 .... 146 A6
St Buryan TR19 .... 97 C7
Penzance School of Art
TR18 .... 143 E5
Penzance Sta TR18 ..... 143 F6
Pepo La TR2 .... 72 A7
Pepper Cl PL12 .... 40 C2
Pepper La PL9 .... 136 D7
Peppers Ct PL12 .... 40 C2
Peppers Hill Cl PL15 .... 18 F7
Peppers Park Rd PL14 ... 113 E6
Pepper St PL19 .... 147 C6
Pepys Pl PL5 .... 124 E1
PERCUIL 83 A1
Percuil View TR2 .... 95 B6
Percy Davy Cl TR6 .... 55 A5
Percy St PL5 .... 123 D1
Percy Terr PL4 .... 129 A4
Pergolla Ct 9 TR7 ..... 110 F6
Perhaver Pk PL26 .... 85 D5
Perhaver Way PL26 .... 85 D5
Periwinkle Dr PL7 ..... 131 C5
Per Kithen TR12 .... 102 F2
Permarin Rd TR10 ...... 144 C8
PERRANARWORTHAL 81 D6
Perran-ar-worthal Prim Sch
TR3 .... 81 D6
Perran Cl TR3 .... 81 F6
Perrancombe Garden Ct
TR6 .... 55 A4
PERRANCOOMBE 55 A3
Perran Crossroads TR20 .. 89 E5
PERRAN DOWNS 89 E5
PERRANPORTH 55 B5
Perranporth Cl PL5 .... 123 E4
Perranporth Prim Sch 18
TR6 .... 55 A4
PERRANUTHNOE 89 D4
PERRANWELL
Goonhavern 55 C3
Perranarworthal 81 C6
Perranwell Rd TR4 .... 55 D4
Perranwell Sta TR3 ...... 81 E6
PERRANZABULOE 55 B3
Perranzabuloe Mus★ TR6 . 55 A5
Perry Cl PL19 .... 147 B6
Perryman Cl PL7 .... 130 E7
Perseverance Cotts 1
PL7 .... 130 E7
Peryn Rd PL19 .... 147 A5
Peter Hopper's Hill PL5 . 120 C2
Peter's Cl PL9 .... 136 C7
Petersfield Cl PL3 .... 129 B6
PETER'S FINGER 19 C7
Peters Hill PL26 .... 58 E4
Peters Park Cl PL5 .... 123 E1
Peter's Park La PL5 ... 123 E1
Peters Row TR19 .... 75 A1
PETERVILLE 54 D1
Petes Pl 24 TR26 ...... 141 B5
Petherick Rd EX23 ..... 104 E7
Pethericks Mill EX23 .. 104 E4
PETHERWIN GATE 18 B7
Pethick Cl PL6 .... 124 D6
Pethill Cl PL6 .... 125 F2
Pethybridge Dr PL31 ... 109 B3
Petroc Ct PL18 .... 40 D6
PEVERELL 128 D6
Peverell Park Rd PL3 .. 128 D6
Peverell Rd
Penzance TR18 .... 143 E7
7 Porthleven TR13 ...... 98 C8
Peverell Terr
Plymouth PL3 .... 128 D5
Porthleven TR13 .... 98 B8
Pew Tor Cl
Tavistock PL19 .... 147 E5
3 Yelverton PL20 .... 42 C3
Phernyssick Rd PL25 ... 114 F6
Philgray Cl TR27 ...... 142 E7
Philip Cl PL9 .... 136 A6
Philip Gdns PL9 .... 135 F6
PHILLACK 142 D7
Phillack Hill TR27 .... 142 D7
PHILLEIGH 83 B6
Phillimore St 3 PL2 ... 127 F4
Phoenix Bsns Pk PL6 ... 125 F4
Phoenix Cl 8 PL20 ...... 42 C4
Phoenix L Ctr PL15 .... 106 C4
Phoenix St PL1 .... 148 A2
Piala Pl TR27 .... 142 E7
Piazza 14 TR26 .... 141 B6
Piazza The 5 PL31 ..... 109 E5
Pickard Way EX23 ...... 104 D7
Pickering Villas TR4 .... 69 A3
Picketts Yd TR10 ...... 144 D7
Pick Pie Dr PL6 .... 125 E8
PIECE 139 D2
Pier La PL10 .... 133 A1
Pier St PL1 .... 148 B1
Pigmeadow La PL14 ..... 113 C6
Pike Rd PL3 .... 129 D5
Pikes Hill PL23 .... 116 C4
Pike's Hill TR11 ...... 145 B3
Pike St PL14 .... 113 C6
Pilchard Works The★
TR18 .... 143 C3
Pilgrim Cl PL2 .... 128 B6
Pilgrim Ct 11 PL20 ...... 41 B1
Pilgrim Dr PL20 .... 41 B1
Pilgrim Prim Sch PL1 .. 148 B3
Pilgrims Way TR27 .... 78 C1
Pillars Cl TR8 .... 56 F5
Pillars Rd
Flushing TR11 .... 145 B8
Mylor Bridge TR11 ...... 82 A2
Pillar Wlk PL6 .... 124 E7
PILLATON 53 B6
PILLATONMILL 53 B6
Pill La PL12 .... 122 E4
Pillmere Dr PL12 ...... 122 D4
Pilot Cotts PL28 .... 21 B4
Pinch Hill
Bude EX23 .... 104 F2
Marhamchurch EX23 .... 7 B7
Pinder Ct PL19 .... 147 B5
Pine Cl TR13 .... 146 D5
Pine Ct
Par PL24 .... 115 F6
Perranarworthal TR3 .... 81 D6
Pine Lodge Gdns★ PL25 . 115 D4
Pine Rd TR18 .... 143 B4
Pine Trees on the Lizard★
TR12 .... 99 F5
Pine View
Gunnislake PL18 .... 41 A6
St Dennis PL26 .... 46 D1
Pinewood Cl PL7 ...... 130 F6
Pinewood Dr PL6 ...... 125 E7
Pinewood Flats PL27 .... 21 D5
Pinkhams Cotts PL12 .. 122 B6
Pink Moors TR16 .... 68 D1
Pin La PL1 .... 149 A2
Pinnacle Quay PL4 .... 149 B2
Pinsla Garden & Nursery★
PL30 .... 35 E1
Pinslow Cross PL15 ..... 19 C8
Pintail Ave TR27 .... 77 E3
Pipers Cl PL15 .... 18 E2
PIPERS POOL 17 F3
Piran Cl PL18 .... 40 D6
Piran Hts EX23 .... 104 C2
Pitick Terr TR11 ..... 145 B6
Pitland Cnr PL19 .... 30 D4
Pit Mdw TR11 .... 144 E3
Pits La PL10 .... 64 B2
Pitts Cleave Ind Est PL19 . 30 F3
PITYME 21 F3
Pityme PL27 .... 21 F3
Pityme Bsns Ctr PL27 ... 21 F3
Pityme Farm Rd PL27 .... 21 F3
Pityme Ind Est PL27 .... 21 F3
Pixie's Hall★ TR11 ..... 92 E4
Pixon La PL19 .... 147 B4
Pixon Trad Ctr 2 PL19 . 147 B4
Place de Brest PL1 ... 148 C3
Place Parc TR7 .... 111 D7
Place Rd PL23 .... 116 C4
Place Stables PL23 ... 116 C4
Place View PL23 ...... 116 C4
Place View Rd 15 TR2 ... 95 A6
PLAIDY 117 E5
Plaidy La PL13 .... 117 E4
Plaidy Park Rd PL13 .. 117 E4
PLAIN-AN-GWARRY 140 B6
Plain-an-Gwarry TR15 .. 140 B5
Plaistow Cl PL5 ...... 123 E2
Plaistow Cres PL5 .... 123 E2
Plaistow Hill Inf Sch PL5 123 E2
Planet Pk PL33 .... 14 D2
Plantation La TR27 ... 142 B5
Plantings Sch The PL3 . 128 E6
Plas Newydd Ave PL31 . 109 E3
Platt The PL27 .... 108 C5
Playingfield La TR7 .. 110 D5
PLAYING PLACE 82 B8
Pleasant Pl 15 TR18 .. 143 C7
Pleasure Hill Cl PL9 . 135 D8
Plestin Cl PL15 ...... 106 C7
Pleyber Christ Way PL22 112 C2
Pleydon Cl PL13 ...... 62 E2
Plintona View PL7 .... 130 E7
Plougastel Dr PL12 ... 122 E3
Plough Ct TR10 .... 81 C2
Plough Gn PL12 .... 122 C3
Plumer Rd PL6 .... 124 F2
PLUSHABRIDGE 38 F7
Plymbridge Gdns PL7 .. 130 C7
Plymbridge La PL6 .... 125 B4
Plymbridge Rd
Plymouth, Eggbuckland
PL6 .... 125 C1
Plymouth, Estover PL6 . 125 E5
Plymouth, Mainstone PL6 . 125 F2
Plymouth, Plympton PL7 . 130 C7
Plym Cres PL19 .... 147 D5
PLYMOUTH 148 C1
Plymouth Arts Ctr★ PL4 149 A2
Plymouth Athenaeum &
Theatre★ PL1 .... 148 B2
Plymouth Business Sch
PL4 .... 149 A3
Plymouth City Airport
PL6 .... 125 C5
Plymouth City Mkt PL1 . 148 B3
Plymouth City Mus & Art
Gal★ PL4 .... 149 A3
Plymouth Coll PL4 .... 128 E4
Plymouth Coll Inf Sch 1
PL3 .... 128 F5
Plymouth Coll of Art &
Design PL4 .... 149 A3
Plymouth Coll of Art &
Design (Sutton Annexe)
PL4 .... 149 A3
Plymouth Coll of FE PL2 127 E5
Plymouth Coll Prep Sch
PL1 .... 148 A3
Plymouth Discovery Ctr★
PL3 .... 129 F6
Plymouth Drake Prim Sch
PL2 .... 127 E6
Plymouth Eggbuckland Com
Coll PL6 .... 129 A8
Plymouth Eggbuckland Vale
Prim Sch PL6 .... 129 A8
Plymouth Girls High Sch
PL4 .... 149 A4
Plymouth Keyham Barton RC
Prim Sch PL2 .... 127 E6
Plymouth Knowle Prim Sch
PL5 .... 124 A4
Plymouth Lipson Vale Prim
Sch PL4 .... 129 A4
Plymouth Medical & Tech Pk
PL6 .... 125 A3
Plymouth Pavilions PL1 . 148 B2
Plymouth Rd
Liskeard PL14 .... 113 D5
Plymouth PL7 .... 130 B6
Tavistock PL19 .... 147 B4
Plymouth Road Ind Est
PL19 .... 147 C3
Plymouth St Andrew's CE
Prim Sch PL1 .... 148 B2
Plymouth St Joseph's RC
Prim Sch PL1 .... 127 E2
Plymouth St Paul's RC Prim
Sch PL5 .... 123 D1
Plymouth St Peters CE Prim
Sch PL1 .... 148 B3
Plymouth Ski & Snowboard
Ctr★ PL6 .... 129 E7
Plymouth Sta PL4 ..... 148 C4
Plymouth Thornbury Prim
Sch PL6 .... 125 D4
Plymouth Trade Pk PL4 . 149 C1
Plymouth Whitleigh Prim
Sch PL5 .... 124 D4
PLYMPTON 130 E5
Plympton Hill PL7 .... 130 F3
Plympton Hospl PL7 ... 130 D5
Plympton St Mary CE Inf Sch
PL7 .... 130 D5
PLYMPTON ST
MAURICE 130 E4
Plympton St Maurice Prim
Sch PL7 .... 130 F3
Plym St PL4 .... 149 A3
PLYMSTOCK 135 E6
Plymstock Rd PL9 .... 135 D7
Plymstock Sch PL9 .... 135 F8
Plymstock Sp Ctr PL9 . 135 F8
Plymtree Dr PL7 ...... 130 C7
Plym Valley Rly★ PL7 . 130 A7
Poad's Trust PL14 ...... 51 F5
Pochin Ho PL25 .... 114 F7
Pocklington Rise PL7 . 130 E5
Pocohontas Cres 4 TR9 .. 45 E1
Pode Dr PL7 .... 131 B4
POINT 82 B5
Point Neptune PL23 ... 116 B3
Point Rd TR3 .... 82 A6
Polapit Tamar PL15 ...... 19 A8
POLBATHIC 64 F8
Polbathic Rd TR15 ..... 140 C6
POLBORDER 53 D7
Polbreen Ave TR5 .... 54 C1
Polbreen La TR5 .... 54 C1
POLBROCK 34 A4
Poldark Gdns 7 PL24 .... 60 B4
Poldark Mine★ TR13 ..... 92 A6
Poldark Rd 12 TR16 ..... 67 E4
Poldhu Cl TR26 .... 141 D1
Poldhu Rd
Liskeard PL14 .... 113 D6
Mullion TR12 .... 99 A2
Poldice La TR16 .... 68 E1
Poldice Terr TR16 .... 68 E1
Poldrea PL24 .... 60 D5
Poldrissick Hill PL12 ... 53 C2
Poldrissick La PL12 ..... 53 C2
Poldue Cl TR15 .... 140 D6
Polean La PL13 .... 117 B4
Polean Trad Est PL13 .. 117 B4
Polecoverack La TR12 .. 101 C1
Polgarth
1 Camborne TR15 .... 139 C6
Newlyn TR18 .... 143 B3
Polgarth Cl TR26 ...... 141 D1
Polgaver Ho PL25 ...... 115 E3
POLGIGGA 96 D4
Polgine Cl TR14 .... 79 E5
Polgine La TR14 .... 79 E5
Polglase Wlk TR4 .... 70 D8
Polglaze Cl TR18 ...... 143 D7
Polglist PL26 .... 58 D5
Polgoon Cl TR18 .... 143 C5
POLGOOTH 59 A1
Polgooth Cl TR15 ...... 140 D6
Polgover Way 5 PL24 .... 60 B4
Polgrain Rd TR14 ...... 138 F6
Polgrean Pl PL24 .... 60 B5
Polhigey Terr TR16 ...... 80 C2
Polhorman La TR12 .... 99 A2
Police Ho TR11 .... 145 B4
Polisken Way TR4 .... 56 D1
POLKERRIS 60 E3
Polkerris Pk PL24 .... 60 C4
Polkerris Rd TR16 .... 80 F8
Polkirt Hill
Gorran Haven PL26 ...... 73 B1
Mevagissey PL26 .... 73 C3
Polkirt Hts PL26 .... 73 C3
Polkyth L Ctr PL25 .... 114 E4
Polkyth Par PL25 ...... 114 E4
Polkyth Rd PL25 .... 114 F4
POLLADRAS 90 F5
Pollard Cl
Plymouth PL9 .... 135 B5
Saltash PL12 .... 122 B2
Pollard Rd 7 PL17 ...... 39 F4
Pollards Cl
Goonhavern TR4 .... 55 D4
Pensilva PL14 .... 38 E4
Pollards Way PL12 ..... 122 E3
Polmark Dr PL28 .... 20 D2
Polmarth Cl PL25 ...... 114 F6
POLMASSICK 72 E4
Polmassick Vineyard★
PL26 .... 72 E4
POLMEAR 60 E4
Polmear Ct 9 PL27 .... 108 B5
Polmear Hill PL24 .... 60 E4
Polmear Parc PL24 .... 60 D4
Polmear Rd
St Austell PL25 .... 114 F3
Tywardreath PL24 .... 60 D4
Polmeere Ho TR18 ...... 143 E7
Polmeere Rd TR18 ...... 143 E7
Polmena La PL22 .... 112 E1
Polmennor Dr TR26 ..... 141 D1
Polmennor Rd
Falmouth TR11 .... 144 F1
Heamoor TR18 .... 143 C8
Polmenor Downs N TR14,
TR27 .... 78 F5
Polmenor Downs S TR14 . 78 F4
Polmeor Cl TR26 ...... 141 D1
Polmewan Flats PL26 .... 59 A1
POLMORLA 108 A4
Polmorla Mews 10 PL27 . 108 B5
Polmorla Rd PL27 ..... 108 B5
Polmorla Wlk PL27 .... 108 C5
Polmor Rd TR20 .... 89 B8
POLPEOR 77 B3
Polpeor Row TR27 .... 77 A3
POLPERRO 62 E1
Polperro Heritage Mus of
Smuggling & Fishing★
PL13 .... 62 E2
Polperro Model Village★
PL13 .... 62 D1
Polperro Prim Sch PL13 . 62 E2
Polperro Rd PL13 ..... 117 B4
Polpey La PL24 .... 60 D5
POLRUAN 116 C2
Polruan Cl TR26 .... 77 C4
Polruan Ct TR1 .... 137 E2
Polruan Prim Sch PL23 . 116 D2
Polruan Rd
Redruth TR15 .... 140 D6
Truro TR1 .... 137 E2
Polruan Terr PL1 ..... 148 A3
POLSCOE 112 E3
Polscoe Rd PL22 ...... 112 F3
Polsethow TR10 .... 144 B7
Polstain Cres TR3 .... 69 D3
Polstain Rd TR3 .... 69 D3
Polstain Villas TR3 ..... 69 D3
Polsue Way TR2 .... 70 F5
Poltair Ave PL25 ...... 114 E4
Poltair Cl TR18 .... 143 C7
Poltair Cres PL25 ..... 114 D4
Poltair Ct PL25 .... 114 E4
Poltair Dr TR10 .... 144 B7
Poltair Hospl TR20 ... 143 B8
Poltair Rd
Penryn TR10 .... 144 B7
St Austell PL25 ...... 114 D4
Poltair Sports Coll PL25 114 D4
Poltair Terr 7 TR18 .. 143 C7
Poltamar PL15 .... 106 D5
POLTESCO 103 B5
Poltesco La TR12 ..... 103 B5
Poltisco Cl TR1 ...... 137 E3
Poltisco Wharf TR1 ... 137 E4
Poltisko Rd TR10 ..... 144 B7
Poltisko Terr TR10 ... 144 B7
Poltreen Cl TR26 ..... 141 D1
Polurrian Rd TR12 ...... 99 A1
Polvarth Est TR2 .... 95 B6
Polvarth Rd TR2 .... 95 A6
Polvean Cross PL14 ..... 51 A1

T

Tabernacle St TR1 137 D4
Tackbear Rd EX22, EX23 7 E4
Tailyour Rd PL6 124 F2
Talbot Gdns PL5 127 D7
Talexandra Terr PL15 106 D5
Talgos Cl TR16 140 E8
TALLAND 62 F2
Talland Ct 29 TR26 141 B5
Talland Hill PL13 62 E2
Talland Rd TR26 141 B5
Talland St PL13 62 D1
Talmena Ave PL27 108 A5
TALSKIDDY 45 E8
Talveneth
Camborne TR14 138 F3
Pendeen TR19 75 A1
Redruth TR15 140 C6
Talvenydh Ct PL31 109 D5
Tamar Ave
Plymouth PL2 127 E5
Tavistock PL19 147 D5
Tamar Bridge PL5 123 A2
Tamar Bsns Pk PL15 18 E2
Tamar Cl
18 Bere Alston PL20 41 B1
29 Callington PL17 39 F4
Tamar Ho PL1 127 E1
Tamarisk Cl PL28 31 F7
Tamarisk La TR7 111 A4
Tamar Otter & Wildlife Ctr* PL15 18 B8
Tamar Science Pk PL6 125 C4
Tamarside Com Coll PL5 123 E1
Tamarside Sp Complex PL5 123 F2
Tamar St
Plymouth PL1 127 E3
Saltash PL12 123 A2
Torpoint PL11 127 C3
Tamar Terr
Calstock PL17 41 A3
Horsebridge PL19 29 C1
Launceston PL15 106 D5
Saltash PL12 123 A2
Tamar Valley Ctr* PL18 40 F5
Tamar Valley Discovery Trail* PL20 41 C1
Tamar Valley Donkey Pk* PL18 40 D5
Tamar Valley Sch PL5 123 B1
Tamar View
Launceston PL15 106 D5
Milton Abbot PL19 29 C6
St Dominick PL12 40 D2
Tamar View Ind Est PL12 122 D5
Tamar Villas PL9 135 D7
Tamar Way PL18 41 A6
Tamar Wharf PL1 127 D3
Tamblin Ave PL14 50 E7
Tamerton Ave PL5 123 D1
Tamerton Cl PL5 124 A6
TAMERTON FOLIOT 124 B7
Tamerton Foliot Rd PL6 124 D5
Tamerton Rd PL6 121 B2
Tangmere Ave PL5 123 E5
Tangye Cl TR16 67 E5
Tangye Rd TR15 139 C6
Tanhouse Rd PL22 112 C2
Tanwood View PL31 109 C5
Tanyard La 20 PL17 39 E4
Tapson Dr PL9 135 A6
Taranto Rd TR13 146 D4
Taroveor Rd TR18 143 E6
Taroveor Terr 3 TR18 143 E5
Tarr PL22 49 E3
Tarrandean La TR3 81 E6
Tarten Cross PL12 53 B4
Tate St Ives (Gall)* TR26 141 B6
Taunton Ave PL5 124 B5
Taunton Pl PL5 124 B5
Tavern Barn PL23 116 C5
TAVISTOCK 147 E5
Tavistock Coll PL19 147 A3
Tavistock Com Prim Sch PL19 147 B4
Tavistock Cross PL20 41 C2
Tavistock Hospl PL19 147 B5
Tavistock Mus* PL19 147 C5
Tavistock Pl PL4 149 A3
Tavistock Rd
Callington PL17 39 F4
Launceston PL15 106 D5
Launceston, Stourscombe PL15 106 E3
Plymouth, Manadon PL5 124 E1
Plymouth PL6 125 B5
Yelverton PL20 42 C3
Tavistock St Peter's CE Jun Sch PL19 147 D5
Tavy Pl PL4 128 F4
Tavy Rd
Saltash PL12 123 A3
Tavistock PL19 147 D5
Taw Cl PL3 129 D6
Tayberry Dr TR16 140 F1
Tay Gdns PL3 129 D7
Taylor Cl PL12 122 C3
Taylor Rd PL12 122 C4
Taylor's Cross EX23 5 B7
Taylor Sq PL19 147 B6
Teachers Cl PL9 135 F6
Teats Hill Flats PL4 149 B1
Teats Hill Rd PL4 149 B1
Tedder Rd 4 PL26 59 D7
Tees Cl PL3 129 C7
Teetotal St TR26 141 C6
Tehidy Cl TR14 138 F7
Tehidy Copse TR14 67 B4
Tehidy Country Park* TR14 67 B4
Tehidy Gdns TR14 138 F7
Tehidy Rd
Camborne TR14 138 D4
Tywardreath PL24 60 D5
Tehidy Terr TR11 145 A6
Teign Rd PL3 129 B6
Telcarne Cl TR27 78 D6
Telegraph Hill TR16 68 E1
Telegraph St TR16 68 D1
Telegraph Wharf PL1 134 A8
Telephone La PL26 59 C8
Telford Cres PL5 123 F2
Temeraire Rd PL5 124 D2
TEMPLE 36 B8
Tenacres La PL14 38 E4
Tenby Rd PL5 123 C1
TENCREEK 63 A3
Tencreek Ave TR18 143 E5
Tenderah Ct TR13 146 C7
Tenderah Rd TR13 146 C6
Tennyson Gdns PL5 124 B1
Tern Gdns PL7 130 F5
Terrace The
Chacewater TR4 68 F3
Crafthole PL11 65 B5
Dobwalls PL14 50 D7
Downderry PL11 64 C5
East Portholland PL26 84 E5
Harrowbarrow PL17 40 D5
Penryn TR10 144 C7
Pentewan PL26 73 D6
Port Isaac PL29 22 E7
Portwrinkle PL11 65 A4
Rock PL27 21 D2
St Ives TR26 141 B5
Yeolmbridge PL15 18 E6
Terra Nova Gn PL2 128 B5
TERRAS 58 A4
Terras Hill PL22 112 C3
Terras Rd PL26 58 A4
TETCOTT 13 C7
Tethadene PL30 23 E7
Tewington Pl PL25 114 B4
Tewkesbury Cl PL2 128 A8
Teyla Tor Rd TR26 141 D1
Thackeray Gdns PL5 124 B1
Thames Gdns PL3 129 D5
Thanckes Cl PL11 127 A3
Thanckes Dr PL11 127 A4
Theatre Ope PL1 127 F1
Theatre Royal Plymouth PL1 148 C2
THE BEACON 10 F6
Therlow Rd PL3 129 B6
Thetford Gdns PL6 129 D8
Theydon Rd TR11 144 F3
Third Ave
Plymouth, Billacombe PL9 130 A1
Plymouth, Camels Head PL2 127 E7
Plymouth, Stoke PL1 128 A2
Thirlmere Gdns PL6 124 F4
Thistle Cl PL6 125 E7
Thomas Bullock Cl PL30 48 C2
Thomas Johnson Ct 6 TR1 137 C4
Thomas St 4 TR13 98 C8
Thomas Terr 5 TR13 98 C8
Thornberry Terr TR18 143 F6
Thornbury Park Ave PL3 128 D6
Thornbury Rd PL6 125 E4
Thorn Cl PL15 26 C7
Thorndon Cross EX22 8 F5
Thorne Cross EX23 4 F2
THORNE MOOR 19 F8
Thornhill Rd PL3 128 E6
Thornhill Way PL3 128 E6
Thorn La PL12 122 C3
Thorn Moor Cross PL15 19 F7
Thornpark Rd PL25 114 E5
Thorn Pk PL3 128 F5
Thorn Terr PL14 113 B5
Thornton Ave PL4 149 B4
Thornton Cl PL26 46 F3
Thornville Terr PL9 135 C7
Thornwell La PL12 53 E2
Thornyville Cl PL9 135 C8
Thornyville Dr PL9 135 D8
Thornyville Villas PL9 135 C8
Three Bridges Specl Sch 1 TR10 144 C8
THREE BURROWS 68 F5
Three Corners Cl PL32 105 B2
Three Cross TR13 91 F5
THREE HAMMERS 17 C6
Three Holes Cross PL27 34 A8
THREEMILESTONE 69 D4
Threemilestone Ind Est TR4 69 C3
Threemilestone Prim Sch TR3 69 D3
Threemilestone Ret Pk TR3 69 C4
THREEWATERS 34 C1
THURDON 5 D5
Thurlestone Wlk PL6 129 D8
Tiddy Brook Rd
Tavistock PL19 147 E2
Whitchurch PL19 147 E2
Tiddy Cl
St Germans PL12 65 B8
Tavistock PL19 147 B3
TIDEFORD 52 F2
Tideford Cross La PL12 52 F3
Tideford Dr
Landrake PL12 53 A2
St Germans PL12 65 B8
Tideford Rd PL12 53 C3
Tidemill Ho TR11 145 C3
Tides Reach TR7 111 B7
Tillard Cl PL7 131 C5
Tillie St 5 PL17 39 E4
Tilly Cl PL9 135 F4
Timber Cl PL25 114 B4
Tincombe PL12 122 C2
Tincroft Rd TR15 139 B4
Tin La PL4 149 A2
Tinners Dr PL27 21 D6
Tinners Way
Callington PL17 39 F5
New Polzeath PL27 21 D6
16 St Ives TR26 77 A6
Tinners Wlk TR11 145 D3
Tinney Dr TR1 137 F5
Tinside Lido PL1 148 C1
TINTAGEL 14 D7
Tintagel Castle* PL34 14 B8
Tintagel Cres PL2 128 C8
Tintagel Hts PL34 14 D6
Tintagel Old Post Office* PL34 14 C7
Tintagel Prim Sch PL34 14 C6
Tintagel Rd PL35 9 C1
Tintagel Terr PL29 22 D7
Tintagel Toy Mus* PL34 14 C7
Tintagel Visitor Ctr* PL34 14 C7
Tintern Ave PL4 149 C2
Tiny Mdws
Launceston PL15 18 E1
South Petherwin PL15 27 F8
Tipple Cross PL15 19 C6
Tithe Rd PL7 130 B7
TITSON 7 D4
Tiverton Cl PL6 125 B8
Tobruk Rd PL12 122 E3
Toby Way TR7 110 D7
Toddington Lea PL26 58 E5
TODPOOL 68 F2
TOLBOROUGH 25 E4
TOLCARNE
Camborne 79 D5
Newlyn 143 C3
Tolcarne Cl PL25 114 E3
Tolcarne Mews 7 TR7 110 F6
Tolcarne Rd
Camborne TR14 79 D5
Newquay TR7 110 F6
St Day TR16 68 D1
Tolcarne St TR14 138 D2
Tolcarne Terr TR18 143 C3
Tolcrows Ct TR7 111 C7
TOLDISH 45 F2
Tolgarrick Rd TR14 138 F5
Tolgus Hill TR15 140 A5
TOLGUS MOUNT 139 E8
Tolgus Pl TR15 140 A6
Tolgus Tin* TR16 67 F5
Tolgus Vean TR15 140 A5
Tolgus Wartha TR15 140 A6
Tollgate Cl PL14 113 B4
Tollox Pl PL3 129 B4
Tollyfrank Hill TR2 83 F6
Tolpedn Flats TR26 141 E2
Tolponds Rd TR13 91 A1
Tolroy Rd TR27 142 D1
TOLSKITHY 139 E7
Tolskithy La TR15 139 E6
Tolticken Hill TR16 67 E6
Toltuff Cres TR18 143 C4
Toltuff Rd TR18 143 C4
TOLVADDON 138 F6
TOLVADDON DOWNS 139 A7
Tolvaddon Energy Pk TR14 138 F7
Tolvaddon Rd TR15 139 A5
Tolvan Cross TR12 92 C2
Tolver Pl TR18 143 E6
Tolver Rd TR18 143 E6
Tolverth Terr TR20 88 F6
Tolview Terr TR27 142 B4
Tom Lyon Rd PL14 113 E5
Tom Nicolls Cl 7 PL14 38 A3
Top Hill TR2 57 E1
Top of the Town Ctyd PL12 122 F2
Top Rd PL11 64 C5
Torbridge Cl PL12 122 D2
Torbridge Rd
6 Horrabridge PL20 42 C4
Plymouth PL7 130 E6
Torbryan Cl PL6 129 E8
Tor Cl
Plymouth, Hartley PL3 128 E7
Porthleven TR13 91 B1
Tor Cres PL3 128 E7
Tor La PL12 122 B1
Torland Rd PL3 128 E7
Torleven Rd TR13 91 B2
TORPOINT 127 C3
Torpoint Com Sch PL11 127 A4
Torpoint Inf Sch PL11 127 B3
Tor Rd
Newquay TR7 110 E6
Tor Rd *continued*
Plymouth PL3 128 E7
Torridge Cl PL7 131 A6
Torridge Rd PL7 130 F6
Torridge Way PL3 129 C5
Torr La PL3 128 E7
Torr Rd PL3 128 E7
Torr View Ave PL3 128 D7
Tors View Cl PL17 39 F4
Torver Cl PL6 125 D2
Tor View
Bugle PL26 47 C2
Camelford PL32 105 C2
7 Horrabridge PL20 42 C4
Tregadillett PL15 18 C2
Torwood Cl PL31 109 D4
Tory Brook Ave PL7 130 E6
Tory Brook Ct PL7 130 E6
Tory Way PL7 130 D6
TOSBERRY 3 B8
Tosberry Cross EX39 3 B8
Tothill Ave PL4 149 B3
Tothill Rd PL4 149 B3
Totnes Cl PL7 131 B4
Tovey Cres PL5 124 D2
Towan Blystra Rd TR7 111 A5
TOWAN CROSS 68 B7
Towan Ct PL28 31 E8
Towan Rd
Pentewan PL26 73 D8
Porthtowan TR4 68 A7
Towans The PL28 20 D1
TOWEDNACK 76 E5
Towednack Rd TR26 77 A6
Tower Cl
Pelynt PL13 62 D6
Sennen TR19 96 B6
Tower Ct PL12 122 C2
Towerfield Dr PL6 125 C8
Tower Hill
Looe PL13 117 D3
Wadebridge PL27 108 E5
Tower Hill Rd PL15 13 F1
Tower Mdws TR19 97 A6
Tower Park Est PL13 62 D6
Tower Park Rd PL13 62 C6
Tower Pk
Fowey PL23 116 B3
Lanivet PL30 47 E7
Pelynt PL13 62 D6
Tower Rd
Newquay TR7 110 D6
St Erme TR4 70 D8
Towers Cl PL6 125 F2
Tower St PL15 106 C6
Tower View PL12 122 D1
Town Arms Pas PL31 109 E5
Town End PL31 109 C5
Town Farm TR15 140 C3
Town Farm Cl 5 PL20 42 C4
Townfield TR15 139 C6
Town Hill TR5 54 D1
TOWNLAKE 29 C1
Town Mill Gdns PL19 147 C6
Town Mills Flats PL15 106 B7
Town Quay TR1 137 D4
Townsend
Polruan PL23 116 D2
14 Stratton EX23 4 E1
TOWNSHEND 90 D7
Townshend Ave PL2 127 E5
Townswell Cl PL12 53 E2
Townswell La PL12 53 E2
TRABOE 100 E4
Traboe Cross TR12 100 D3
Tracey Ct PL1 148 B3
Trafalgar Fields TR20 88 B7
Trafalgar Cl PL5 127 D8
Trafalgar Ct TR18 143 F6
Trafalgar Pl 3 PL1 127 F3
Trafalgar Place La PL1 127 F3
Trafalgar Sq TR1 137 D4
Trafalgar St PL4 149 A3
Traine Brake PL9 136 C1
Traine Rd PL9 136 B1
Traly Cl EX23 104 F4
TRAMAGENNA 105 A1
Tram La TR16 140 E1
Tramway Rd PL6 125 E7
TRANNACK 91 D5
Trannack Mill Ind Est TR13 91 E5
Trannack Prim Sch TR13 91 E5
Trannack Terr TR18 143 E7
Tranquil La PL31 109 C5
Transit Way PL5 124 C3
Trasdeves Orch 16 PL17 39 F4
Travers Cl PL14 113 A6
Treago Gdns PL6 125 C8
TREAL 103 A6
Trease TR19 75 A1
Treassowe Rd TR18 143 E6
Treassowe Riding TR20 88 F8
TREATH 93 C1
TREATOR 107 A5
Treator Cotts PL28 107 A5
Trebah Gdns* TR11 93 C2
Treban Rd TR18 143 C4
TREBARBER 44 F5
TREBARTHA 27 A4
Trebartha Cl PL17 39 E3
Trebartha Rd TR1 137 F5
Trebarthen Terr TR4 55 D5
Trebarva Cl TR15 140 A6
TREBARVAH 89 E4
Trebarvah La TR20 89 E4
Trebarvah Rd TR11 92 E4
TREBARWITH 14 C5
Trebarwith Cres TR7 110 E6
Trebarwith Rd PL33 14 D4
TREBEATH 17 F6
Treberran Gdns TR14 138 F6
TREBETHERICK 21 D4
Treboul Cross PL12 64 F8
Treboul Way PL12 65 B8
TREBUDANNON 45 C4
TREBULLETT 28 A5
Treburdon Dr PL26 46 F3
TREBURGETT 23 D6
Treburgie Water PL14 50 D7
TREBURLEY 28 C4
Treburley Cl PL15 28 C4
Treburley Ind Est PL15 28 C4
TREBURRICK 31 D5
TREBYAN 48 C6
Trebyan Bsns Pk PL30 48 C6
Trebyhan Parc TR3 80 F3
Treby Rd PL7 130 F4
Trecarn Cl PL15 106 B5
Trecarne
Falmouth TR11 144 E1
Tremar PL14 38 A3
Trecarne Cl
Polgooth PL26 59 A1
St Austell PL25 115 B5
Truro TR1 137 E5
Trecarne Gdns PL33 14 E3
Trecarne View PL14 37 F3
Trecarrack Rd TR14 138 F3
Trecarrell PL15 106 C4
Trecarrell Cl PL15 106 D4
Trecerus Ind Est PL28 107 B4
Treclago View PL32 105 C2
TRECROGO 27 E7
Tredanek Cl PL31 109 B5
Tredarrup Cross PL15 11 A1
Tredarvah Dr TR18 143 C5
Tredarvah Rd TR18 143 C5
TREDAVOE 143 A2
Tredavoe La TR18 143 B1
Tredenham Cl 4 PL24 60 C4
Tredenham Rd TR2 95 B6
TREDETHY 34 F6
Tredethy Rd PL30 34 F6
TREDINNICK
Looe 63 A8
Penzance 76 A1
St Issey 32 D5
Tredinnick Cotts TR 20 76 A1
Tredinnick La PL12 53 B2
Tredinnick Lane-End PL13 64 A8
Tredinnick Way 12 TR6 55 A4
Tredinnick Wood Cl TR13 146 D8
Tredour Rd TR7 110 E4
Tredova Cres TR11 145 B2
TREDOWN 2 E5
Tredragon Cl TR8 31 C2
Tredragon Rd TR8 31 C2
Tredrea Gdns TR3 81 D5
Tredrea La TR27 77 E2
Tredrea Manor TR3 81 D5
TREDRIZZICK 21 F4
Tredrizzick Cl PL27 21 F3
Tredruston Rd PL27 33 B6
Tredydan Rd PL15 106 B6
Tredynas Rd TR11 145 D3
Tredyson Pl TR11 145 A3
Tre-el-Verne Cl TR1 137 A4
TREEN
Porthcurno 96 F3
Zennor 75 F4
Treen Cotts TR26 75 F4
Treen Flats TR14 138 F3
Treen Hill TR19 96 F4
TREESMILL 60 D6
Treetop Cl PL12 122 D4
Treetops Hill PL13 117 A3
Treeve La TR27 78 C6
Treeve Lane Ind Est TR27 78 C6
TREFANNY HILL 62 D8
Treffry Ct TR7 110 D6
Treffry La PL30 48 C6
Treffry Rd TR1 137 E7
Treffry Way 12 PL24 60 B4
Trefinnick Rd PL17 39 B8
Trefleur Cl 3 PL35 9 C1
Trefloyd Cl PL17 39 E6
TREFOFDA 24 A8
Treforda Rd TR7 110 F4
Treforest Rd PL27 108 A6
Treforthlan 7 TR16 67 E4
Treforthlan Cl 6 TR16 67 E4
TREFREW 105 D6
Trefrew Rd PL32 105 D5
TREFRIZE 27 E3
Trefusis Cl TR1 137 F5
Trefusis Ct TR11 145 A6
Trefusis Gdns PL3 129 A4
Trefusis Rd
Falmouth TR11 144 E2
Flushing TR11 145 C6
Redruth TR15 140 C4
Trefusis Terr
Millbrook PL10 132 E6
Redruth TR15 140 C5
TREGADILLETT 18 C2
Tregadillett Prim Sch PL15 18 C2
Tregaer TR11 145 C3
Tregainlands Pk PL30 34 D3
TREGAJORRAN 139 D4
Tregalister Gdns PL12 65 B8
Tregaller La PL15 18 E1
TREGAMERE 45 F7

Treskilling PL30 59 F8
TRESKINNICK CROSS 6 F1
TRESLOTHAN 79 D4
Treslothan Rd TR14 79 D4
Tresluggan Rd PL5 123 D1
Tresooth Ct TR10 144 D7
Tresooth La TR10 144 C8
Tresooth Terr TR10 144 D7
TRESOWES GREEN 90 D4
TRESOWES HILL 90 E4
Tresowgar La TR2 71 B6
TRESPARRETT 10 B2
TRESPARRETT POSTS 10 C4
Tresprison Ct TR13 146 E5
Tressa Dowr La TR1 137 F5
TRESWITHIAN 138 A3
Treswithian Barns TR14 138 A3
Treswithian Park Rd
TR14 138 B3
Treswithian Rd TR14 138 B3
Tretawn Cl PL30 23 B2
Trethannas Gdns TR14 79 B2
TRETHELLAN 110 C6
Trethellan Hill TR7 110 C5
Trethern Cl TR14 79 E4
Tretherras Cl TR7 111 A6
Tretherras Rd TR7 111 A6
TRETHEVEY 14 F8
Trethevy Cl PL14 37 F3
Trethevy Quoit★ PL14 38 A3
TRETHEWEY 96 E4
Trethewey Cl 10 TR9 45 E6
Trethewey Way TR7 110 D5
Trethew Gdns TR14 138 E4
Trethiggey Cres TR8 111 F3
Trethill La PL11 65 C5
Trethorne Leisure Farm★
PL15 18 B2
Trethorns Ct TR20 89 A8
TRETHOSA 58 A5
Trethosa Rd PL26 58 B4
Trethowan Hts TR1 69 F3
TRETHOWEL 114 C6
Trethurffe Terr TR9 45 E5
Trethurffe Villas TR2 57 C1
TRETHURGY 59 F6
Trethurgy Gdns 17 PL17 39 E4
Tretoil View PL31 109 E2
Tretorvic TR18 143 C8
Tretower Cl PL6 124 F5
TREVADLOCK 27 A6
Trevadlock Hall Pk PL15 27 A6
TREVAIL 43 D1
Trevail Cotts TR8 43 D1
Trevail Way PL25 114 E4
Trevale TR18 143 C5
TREVALGA 9 B1
Trevalga Cl 5 TR6 55 A4
Trevallack Parc 3 TR12 101 C4
Trevallack View 2 TR12 101 C4
Trevallion Pk TR3 82 B5
Trevallyn Rd PL15 106 B4
TREVANCE 32 E6
Trevance TR10 144 A8
Trevance Pk PL24 60 D5
TREVANGER 21 F4
Trevanion Cl PL27 108 B4
Trevanion Ct
Mawnan Smith TR11 93 D3
1 Newquay TR7 110 F6
Truro TR1 69 F3
Trevanion La PL25 59 A3
Trevanion Pk PL27 108 C4
Trevanion Rd
Liskeard PL14 113 D5
St Austell PL25 114 D2
2 Trewoon PL25 59 A3
Wadebridge PL27 108 B4
Trevanion Terr PL27 108 C4
Trevannion Cl PL6 129 A8
TREVANSON 33 C7
Trevanson Rd PL27 108 A6
Trevanson St PL27 108 B6
Trevarner Way PL27 108 D6
Trevarno Cl PL25 59 A3
Trevarno Estate & Gdns★
TR13 91 C5
TREVARNON 78 D6
Trevarnon Cl TR27 78 D6
Trevarnon La TR27 78 D6
Trevarrack Cl TR18 143 F8
Trevarrack La TR18 143 F8
Trevarrack Pl TR18 143 F8
Trevarrack Rd TR18 143 F8
Trevarrack Row TR18 88 E6
TREVARREN 45 E3
Trevarren Ave TR16 80 A5
TREVARRIAN 31 C1
Trevarrian Hill TR8 44 D8
TREVARRICK 72 F2
Trevarrick Ct TR26 141 C1
Trevarrick Dr PL25 114 B4
Trevarrick Rd PL25 114 B3
TREVARTH 80 E7
Trevarth Est PL26 73 C4
Trevarthian Ho TR17 89 B5
Trevarthian Rd PL25 114 C4
Trevarth Rd TR11 144 F5
Trevarth Terr TR16 80 E7
Trevarweneth Rd 8 PL24 60 B4
Trevassack Ct TR27 142 D6
Trevassack Hill TR27 142 E6
Trevassack Parc TR27 142 E6
Trevaunance Cl TR5 54 C2
Trevaunance Cove★ TR5 54 D2
Trevaunance Rd TR5 54 C2
Trevaylor Cl TR1 137 E6
Trevaylor Rd TR11 144 F5
Trevean Cl TR14 138 B3
Trevean Gdns 3 TR18 143 D5
Trevean La TR20 89 F4
Trevean Rd
Penzance TR18 143 D5
Truro TR1 69 F3
Trevean Way
Newquay TR7 110 C5
Rosudgeon TR20 89 F4
Trevear Cl PL25 114 D3
Trevear Rd PL26 58 B4
Trevecca Cotts PL14 113 C8
Treveglos TR27 142 B6
Treveglos Rd TR11 144 E1
TREVEIGHAN 23 F6
Trevelga Ct TR7 111 A7
Trevelgue Ct TR8 44 C6
Trevelgue Rd TR7, TR8 44 C6
Trevellan Rd TR11 82 A3
Trevella Rd EX23 104 E7
TREVELLAS 54 F2
Trevella Vean TR4 70 D8
TREVELMOND 50 D6
Trevelthan Rd 18 TR16 67 E4
Trevelva Rd TR1 137 E2
Trevelveth Rd TR8 110 B3
Trevelyan Cl 10 TR20 89 E5
Trevelyan Rd TR15, TR16 67 E4
Trevelyan Way 5 TR20 89 E5
TREVEMPER 110 E2
Trevemper Rd TR7, TR8 110 F3
TREVEN 14 C6
Trevena Cl TR18 143 C4
Trevena Cross TR13 90 F3
Trevena Dr 8 PL34 14 C7
Trevena Gdns TR11 93 D3
Trevena Lodge 6 PL34 14 C7
Trevena Rd TR18 143 C4
Trevena Terr TR7 110 D6
Trevendon PL17 28 D1
Treveneague Gdns PL2 128 D8
Trevenen Rd TR13 146 C5
Treveneth Cres TR18 143 C1
Treveneth Pl 1 TR18 143 C1
Treven La TR27 78 B1
Trevenna Cross TR8 45 A8
Trevenner Ho 8 TR15 140 B5
Trevenner La TR17 89 C5
Trevenner Mews 6
TR15 140 B5
Trevenner Sq TR17 89 C5
TREVENNING 23 F5
Treven Noweth TR16 68 C3
Trevenson Ct TR15 139 B6
Trevenson La
Camborne, Pool TR15 139 A6
Camborne TR14 138 D2
Trevenson Rd
Camborne TR15 139 B5
Newquay TR7 111 B6
Trevenson St TR14 138 D2
Treventon Cl
Falmouth TR11 144 E4
Portscatho TR2 83 B2
Treventon Rd TR2 83 B2
Treventon Rise 11 TR9 45 E6
TREVERBYN
Penwithick 59 C7
St Cleer 37 B2
Treverbyn Cl
Liskeard PL14 113 E6
Plymouth PL7 130 D6
Treverbyn Com Prim Sch
PL26 59 C8
Treverbyn Gdns PL25 114 F4
Treverbyn Rd
Falmouth TR11 144 E1
Padstow PL28 107 E4
Plymouth PL7 130 D6
St Austell PL25 114 E7
Stenalees PL26 59 C8
St Ives TR26 141 A5
Truro TR1 137 E6
Treverbyn Rise TR10 144 A8
Trevere Cl TR27 78 E6
Treverno Rd TR14 138 E6
TREVERVA 93 B6
Treveryn Parc TR11 144 C2
TREVESCAN 96 B5
Trevessa Cl PL2 128 D8
Trevethan Cl TR11 145 A4
Trevethan Ct 2 TR11 145 A5
Trevethan Gdns 2 TR11 145 A4
Trevethan Hill 1 TR11 145 B5
Trevethan Pk PL20 119 F4
Trevethan Rd TR11 145 A4
Trevethan Rise TR11 145 A4
Trevethenick Rd TR1 137 E3
Treveth La TR13 146 D8
TREVETHOE 77 D3
Treveth Tean TR9 57 E8
Treveth Ylyn TR14 138 F5
TREVIA 105 B4
TREVIADES 93 A3
Trevia La PL32 105 B4
Trevian Cl 6 TR6 55 A4
Trevia Pk Terr PL32 105 C3
Treviglas Cl TR7 111 D7
Treviglas Com Coll TR7 111 D7
Treviglas La TR2 71 C6
Treviglas Rise TR2 71 C6
TREVIGRO 39 C4
TREVILLA 82 C6
Trevilley La PL30, PL33 23 E8
Trevillick La PL30 23 F6
Trevilling Rd PL27 108 B6
Trevillis Pk PL14 113 B4
TREVILSON 56 D6
Trevilson Cl TR8 56 C7
Trevince Parc TR16 80 F8
Trevingey Cl TR15 140 A3
Trevingey Cres TR15 140 A3
Trevingey Parc TR15 140 A4
Trevingey Rd TR15 140 A3
TREVISCOE 58 B7
Trevisker Prim Sch PL27 31 F3
Treviskey Hill TR2 84 B3
Trevissome Ct TR11 144 F6
Trevithick PL28 31 F8
Trevithick Ave PL11 126 F4
Trevithick Cl
Newquay TR7 110 F4
St Merryn PL28 31 F8
Truro TR1 137 E6
Trevithick Cres TR27 142 D5
Trevithick Ct
3 Camborne, Illogan Highway
TR15 139 C6
Camborne TR14 138 C3
Truro TR1 137 E6
Trevithick Jun & Inf Sch
TR14 138 D1
Trevithick Rd
Camborne, Illogan Highway
TR15 139 C6
Camborne TR14 138 D3
Chacewater TR4 69 A3
Falmouth TR11 144 E5
Plymouth PL5 123 E2
St Austell PL25 114 E3
Truro TR1 137 E5
Trevoarn TR27 142 B5
Trevol Bsns Pk PL11 126 D3
TREVOLLARD 53 D1
Trevollard PL13 61 F7
Trevollard La PL12 53 D1
Trevol Pl PL11 126 E3
Trevol Rd PL11 126 E3
TREVONE 20 E2
Trevone Cres PL25 114 A4
Trevone Gdns PL2 128 D8
Trevone Rd PL28 20 F2
Trevoney TR11 144 C2
Trevor Cl PL28 20 C1
Trevorder Cl PL11 126 F2
Trevorder Dr PL25 114 E7
Trevorder Rd PL11 126 F2
Trevorgans Cross TR19 96 F8
TREVORRICK 107 E1
Trevose Ave TR7 110 C6
Trevose Cl TR5 54 C1
Trevose Ho TR1 69 E4
Trevose Rd TR1 69 F4
Trevose Way PL3 129 C6
Trevowah Mdws TR8 110 A3
Trevowah Rd TR8 43 D3
TREVOWHAN 75 C2
Trevozah Cross PL15 28 B8
Trevu Ho TR14 138 E1
Trevu Rd TR14 138 E2
Trevurvas La TR13 90 C3
TREW 90 F4
TREWALDER 14 E1
Trewall Hill PL11 64 D5
Trewan Hall TR9 45 E7
Trewans Terr TR15 140 A6
Trewardreva Cross TR11 92 E4
Trewarlett Cross PL15 28 A7
TREWARMETT 14 D5
Trewarne La TR8 111 F3
Trewartha Cl TR26 141 D1
Trewartha Ct 4 PL14 113 C6
Trewartha Est TR26 141 D1
Trewartha Flats TR26 141 D1
Trewartha Rd TR20 90 C3
Trewartha Terr 12 TR18 143 E6
Trewarton Rd TR10 81 D2
Trewarveneth Farm Cotts
TR18 88 C2
Trewarveneth St TR18 143 C2
TREWASSA 15 F5
Trewassa Flats PL32 15 F5
Trewavas Cres TR13 146 C5
Trewavas Rd TR18 143 C1
Treweath Rd TR18 143 D7
Treweege Row TR3 80 E4
Treweeks Rd TR19 75 A1
Treweese Cross PL14 52 B7
Treweese Rd
Menheniot PL14 52 B7
Quethiock PL14 52 B8
TREWELLARD 86 F8
Trewellard Hill TR19 87 A8
Trewellard Ind Est TR19 86 F8
Trewellard Rd TR19 86 F8
Trewelloe Rd TR20 90 C3
Trewelm La TR16 68 E1
TREWEN 17 E2
TREWENNACK 146 F8
TREWENNAN 23 E8
Trewen Rd TR11 144 C2
Trewen Terr TR11 144 C2
Trewern La TR20 87 E6
TREWETHA 22 E7
Trewetha Farm Lodges
PL29 22 E7
Trewetha La PL29 22 D7
TREWETHERN 22 E3
TREWEY 76 B5
Trewey Hill TR 26 76 B4
Trewhella La TR20 89 F7
Trewhella Terr TR20 90 A6
Trewhiddle Rd PL25 114 C2
Trewidden Cl TR1 137 E5
Trewidden Ct TR1 137 E5
Trewidden Gdn★ TR20 88 A4
Trewidden Rd TR26 141 B5
TREWIDLAND 51 C2
Trewidland Prim Sch
PL14 51 C3
Trewince TR11 93 B3
Trewince La
Grampound Road TR2 57 E1
Lostwithiel PL22 112 C3
Porth Navas TR11 93 B3
Trewince Manor TR2 95 C6
Trewince Terr 2 TR18 143 C1
Trewince Villas PL27 32 E6
Trewinnard Ct TR1 137 B6
Trewinnard Gr TR1 137 B6
Trewinnard La TR27 77 E1
Trewinnard Rd TR3 81 D5
Trewinnick Council Hos
PL27 32 A5
Trewinnick Rd PL27 32 A5
Trewinnow Cross PL15 27 D6
TREWINT 10 F8
Trewint Cres PL13 117 D4
Trewint Est PL14 52 A5
Trewint La
Landrake PL12 53 B2
Rock PL27 21 D3
Trewint Rd PL14 52 A6
Trewirgie Cty Jun Sch
TR15 140 B4
Trewirgie Gdns TR15 140 B4
Trewirgie Hill TR15 140 B3
Trewirgie Rd TR15 140 B3
Trewirgie Vean TR15 140 B4
Trewiston La PL27 21 E3
Trewithan Parc PL22 112 D2
Trewithen Gdns★ TR2 71 E6
Trewithen Parc TR8 56 B7
Trewithen Rd TR18 143 D5
Trewithen Terr TR13 90 D5
TREWITHIAN 83 B4
Trewithy Ct PL6 124 F1
Trewithy Dr PL6 124 F1
TREWOLD 9 E1
Trewollock Cl PL26 85 C5
Trewollock La PL26 85 C5
TREWOODLOE 39 B6
Trewoolsta Terr 6 PL14 38 E4
TREWOON
Mullion 99 B2
St Austell 59 A3
Trewoon Rd TR12 99 B2
Treworden Cl EX23 4 E1
Treworder La PL27 108 F5
Treworder Rd TR1 137 B3
TREWORGA 83 D7
Treworgan Ct TR4 56 D1
Treworgan View TR4 56 D1
TREWORLAS 83 D5
Treworlis Cl TR13 146 D8
TREWORNAN 22 C1
TREWORRICK 37 E3
TREWORTHAL 83 C5
Treworthal Rd TR3 81 D5
Treworvenneth Dr 9
TR17 89 C5
Trewrickle La PL11 65 A5
Trewyn Flats 41 TR26 141 B6
Treyew Pl TR16 80 F8
Treyew Prim Sch TR1 137 A4
Treyew Rd TR1 137 B3
TREZAISE 47 A2
Trezaise Ave PL26 47 A2
Trezaise Cl PL26 47 A2
Trezaise Rd PL26 46 F2
Trezaise Sq PL26 47 A2
Treza Rd TR13 91 A1
Trezela Rd TR18 143 D6
Trinity Cl
Bere Alston PL20 41 B1
Carnkie TR16 80 C2
Trinity Praze TR16 80 C2
Trinity St PL25 114 C3
Trinity Way PL19 147 A4
Tripp Hill PL14 36 F2
TRISPEN 56 D1
Trispen Hill TR4 56 D1
Tristan Rd TR1 137 F5
Triumphal Cres PL7 130 A6
TROAN 57 C8
Trolver Hill TR3 82 B6
Trolvus Vean TR10 81 A1
TROON 79 E5
Troon Moor TR14 79 E4
Troon Prim Sch TR14 79 E4
Troon Row TR13 90 F3
Troubridge Rd TR13 146 C4
Trowbridge Cl PL5 124 C4
Troy Ct PL23 116 C4
Truck Hill TR2 71 B6
Trunglemoor Cotts TR19 88 C2
Trungle Parc TR19 88 C2
Trungle Terr TR19 88 C2
TRURO 137 E3
Truro Bsns Pk TR3 69 C3
Truro Coll 22 TR1 137 D4
Truro Coll (Tregye Campus)
TR3 82 A7
Truro Dr PL5 124 A5
Truro High Sch for Girls
TR1 137 C3
Truro Hill TR10 144 C8
Truro La TR10 144 C8
Truro L Ctr TR1 69 E3
Truro Prep Sch TR1 69 F4
Truro Rd
Lanivet PL30 47 F7
St Austell PL25 114 A2
Truro Sch TR1 137 E3
Truro Sta TR1 137 B4
Truro Vean Terr TR1 137 D5
TRUSCOTT 18 D4
TRUTHAN 56 C2
TRUTHWALL
Marazion 89 D7
St Just 86 E7
Truthwall La TR19 86 F7
Tryelyn PL31 109 F2
Tryhornek TR26 77 D4
Trythall Prim Sch TR 20 76 B1
TRYTHOGGA 143 F8
Trythogga Hill TR18 143 F8
Trythogga Rd TR18 143 F8
Tubbon Hill TR3 81 A4
TUBBS MILL 72 D2
Tucker Cl PL5 127 F8
TUCKERMARSH 41 B2
Tuckers Cl TR8 111 B4
TUCKINGMILL
Camborne 139 A4
St Breward 24 B4
Tuckingmill Terr TR13 91 E4
Tudor Cl PL9 135 E5
Tudor Ct PL12 123 A2
Tuke Cl TR11 144 E5
Tunnels Through Time★
TR7 110 D5
Turbill Gdns 4 PL7 131 B5
TURFDOWN 48 E8
Turfdown Rd PL30 48 E8
Turf St PL31 109 E5
Turnavean Rd PL25 114 A5
Turnaware Rd TR11 144 E2
TURNCHAPEL 135 B7
Turnpike
Gunnislake/Calstock PL18 40 E5
Helston TR13 146 C7
Turnpike Hill 2 TR17 89 C5
Turnpike Pl PL14 113 B4
Turnpike Rd
Connor Downs TR27 78 D6
Marazion TR17 89 C5
Turnpike The TR19 86 F6
Turnquay PL9 135 C7
Turret Gr PL4 128 F4
TUTWELL 29 A2
Tuxton Cl PL7 131 C3
TWELVEHEADS 69 B1
Twelvewoods Cl PL14 50 E8
Twelvewoods Pl PL14 50 E8
Twinbrook Pk TR11 93 B3
TWO BURROWS 68 E5
Two Hills Pk PL12 122 C2
Two Trees PL27 108 B4
Two Trees Rd PL22 112 F1
Tyacke Rd TR13 146 B5
Tybesta TR2 72 A7
Tye Hill Cl PL25 59 A3
Tyland Rd PL32 105 F4
Tylney Cl PL6 125 B6
Tynance Ct PL26 58 C8
Tyndale Cl PL5 124 B1
Tyringham Pl TR26 77 E4
Tyringham Rd TR26 77 E4
Tyringham Row TR26 77 E4
Tyshute La PL26 59 A1
Tything Wlk 4 PL3 128 E6
TYWARDREATH 60 E5
Tywardreath Highway
PL24 60 C6
Tywardreath Hill PL24 60 D4
Tywardreath Prim Sch
PL24 60 D5
Tywarnhale Way TR4 68 A6
Tywarnhayle Rd TR6 55 A5
Tywarnhayle Sq 23 TR6 55 A5

U

Uglow Cl TR14 138 C3
Ulalia Rd TR7 110 F6
Ullswater Cres PL6 124 E4
Umfulla Pl 13 TR26 141 B5
Under Chapel Yd TR18 143 F4
Undercliff TR27 142 D7
Undercliff Rd PL9 135 B7
Underhayes La PL15 106 A8
Underhill Rd PL3 128 A4
Underhill Villas 1 PL3 128 A3
Under La PL15 18 C3
Underlane
Boyton PL15 13 A3
Marhamchurch EX23 7 B6
Plymouth, Plympton PL7 130 C5
Plymouth, Plymstock PL9 135 E6
Under Rd
Boscastle PL35 9 C1
Bridgerule EX22 8 A5
Gunnislake PL18 41 A6
Underways PL20 41 B1
UNDERWOOD 130 C5
Underwood Rd PL7 130 D4
Unicorn Cl PL7 130 B6
Union Cnr TR11 144 D5
Union Hill
St Columb Major TR9 45 E6
6 Stratton EX23 4 D1
Truro TR1 70 D5
Union Pl
Fowey PL23 116 D4
Plymouth PL1 148 A2
Truro TR1 137 D5

Union Rd TR11 . . . . 144 D6
Union Sq TR9 . . . . 45 E6
Union St
Camborne TR14 . . . . 138 D2
27 Penzance TR18 . . . . . . 143 E5
Plymouth PL1 . . . . 148 A2
Truro TR1 . . . . 137 C5
UNITED DOWNS 81 A8
United Downs Ind Pk
TR16 . . . . 81 A8
United Rd TR16 . . . . 80 F8
Unit Hos PL27 . . . . 33 B5
Unity Cl PL6 . . . . 125 D5
Unity Rd TR13 . . . . 98 C8
University College Falmouth (Annexe) TR11 . . . . 145 B4
University College Falmouth (Tremough Campus)
TR10 . . . . 144 A8
University College Falmouth (Woodlane Campus)
TR11 . . . . 145 B3
University of Plymouth Bsns Sch PL4 . . . . 148 C4
University of Plymouth (Cookworthy Bldg)
PL4 . . . . 149 A3
UPCOTT 2 F4
Upcott Cross EX39 . . . . 2 F5
Upland Cl TR1 . . . . 137 F6
Upland Cres TR1 . . . . 137 E6
Upland Dr PL6 . . . . 125 A5
Uplands
Lostwithiel PL22 . . . . 112 B2
Saltash PL12 . . . . 122 E1
Tavistock PL19 . . . . 147 A4
Uplands Vean TR1 . . . . 137 F5
Upper Castle Rd TR2 . . . . . 95 A6
Upper Chapel PL15 . . . . . . 106 A4
Upper Dobbin Cl PL28 . . . . . 20 F2
Upper Dobbin La PL28 . . . . 20 F2
Upper Eastcliffe Rd PL24 . . 60 D4
Upper Hillcrest 8 TR6 . . . . 55 A4
Upper Knollys Terrace La
PL3 . . . . 128 C4
Upper Lemon Villas TR1 . . 137 C3
Upper Ridings PL7 . . . . . . 131 B7
Upper School La TR1 . . . . 137 C3
Upperton La PL6 . . . . 121 F3
Upper Tredrea TR3 . . . . . . 81 D5
UPTON
Bude 104 C2
Upton Cross 38 C7
Upton Cl PL3 . . . . 129 B7
UPTON CROSS 38 D6
Upton Cross EX23 . . . . 104 C2
Upton Cross Prim Sch
PL14 . . . . 38 C7
Upton Mdws EX23 . . . . 104 C3
Upton Terr EX23 . . . . 104 C2
UPTON TOWANS 78 B6
Upton Twrs Nature Reserve★
TR27 . . . . 78 B6
Urban Terr PL17 . . . . 39 F5
Uxbridge Dr PL5 . . . . 123 E4
Uzella Pk PL22 . . . . 112 C2

V

Vaagso Cl PL1 . . . . 127 E2
Valency Row PL35 . . . . 9 C2
Valentine Row 4 PL17 . . . . 39 E4
Valiant Ave PL5 . . . . 124 A4
Vallard's La PL12 . . . . 53 E4
Valletort Flats PL1 . . . . . . 128 A2
Valletort Ho PL1 . . . . 148 C3
Valletort La PL1 . . . . 128 A3
Valletort Pl PL1 . . . . 128 A2
Valletort Rd PL1, PL3 . . . . 128 A3
Valletort Terr PL1 . . . . 148 A4
Valley Bglws PL13 . . . . 117 F5
Valley Cl
Goonhavern TR4 . . . . 55 C3
Truro TR1 . . . . 69 F3
Valley Gdns 20 TR16 . . . . . 67 E4
Valley La TR3 . . . . 81 F7
Valley Park La PL26 . . . . . 73 C3
Valley Rd
Bude EX23 . . . . 104 E5
Carbis Bay TR26 . . . . 141 C2
Mevagissey PL26 . . . . 73 C4
Plymouth PL7 . . . . 130 B5
Saltash PL12 . . . . 122 E2
Valley The TR19 . . . . 96 E3
VALLEY TRUCKLE 105 C2
Valley View
Bodmin PL31 . . . . 109 E3
19 Illogan TR16 . . . . 67 E4
Plymouth PL6 . . . . 125 D7
Redruth TR16 . . . . 140 E1
St Keyne PL14 . . . . 51 A4
St Teath PL30 . . . . 23 E7
Wadebridge PL27 . . . . 108 C4
Valley View Cl PL3 . . . . . . 129 B6
Valley View Dr TR1 . . . . 69 F3
Valley View Pk
Bodmin PL31 . . . . 34 D2
St Austell PL26 . . . . 47 C2
Valley View Rd PL3 . . . . . 129 B7
Valley View Terr TR3 . . . . . 81 B5
Valley Wlk PL6 . . . . 125 E6
Vanguard Cl PL5 . . . . 124 D1
Vapron Rd PL3 . . . . 128 F6
Varfell La TR20 . . . . 89 A7
Varley La PL14 . . . . 113 B5
Varley Terr 1 PL14 . . . . . . 113 B5
Vauban Pl PL2 . . . . 127 F4
Vaughan Cl PL2 . . . . 128 C7
Vauxhall Ct 10 PL4 . . . . . . 149 A2
Vauxhall Quay PL4 . . . . . . 149 A2
Vauxhall St PL4 . . . . 149 A2
Vauxhall Street Flats 19
PL4 . . . . 149 A2
Vean Rd TR14 . . . . 138 E2
Vean Terr TR14 . . . . 138 E2
Vear Ho TR14 . . . . 138 D2
Vellan Cl TR14 . . . . 79 B5
Vellandrucia TR3 . . . . 80 F3
Vellanhoggan Mews TR18 88 E6
VELLANOWETH 89 A8
Vellan Parc Ave TR27 . . . . 78 C5
Vellan Vrane TR27 . . . . 78 C5
Venetian Views TR9 . . . . . . 57 D8
Venland Cl 9 PL14 . . . . 38 A3
Venn Cl 6 PL3 . . . . 128 E6
Venn Cres PL3 . . . . 128 E6
Venn Ct PL3 . . . . 128 E6
Venn Gdns PL3 . . . . 128 E7
Venn Gr PL3 . . . . 128 E6
Venn Hill PL19 . . . . 29 C6
Venn La PL2, PL3 . . . . 128 C6
Venn Way PL3 . . . . 128 E7
Venslooe Hill PL14 . . . . . . 113 B7
VENTERDON 28 D2
Ventnor Terr TR26 . . . . . . 141 A6
Venton Cl PL15 . . . . 18 B8
Venton East Sq TR19 . . . . . 86 F6
VENTONGIMPS 55 C2
Venton Lace Rd TR2 . . . . . 57 E1
VENTONLEAGUE 142 F7
Ventonleague Hill TR27 . . 142 E7
Ventonleague Row TR27 142 E7
Ventonraze TR16 . . . . 67 E4
Ventonraze Terr 2 TR16 . . 67 E4
Venton Rd
Falmouth TR11 . . . . 144 E4
St Ives TR26 . . . . 141 C3
Ventonvaise 5 TR6 . . . . . . 55 A5
Venton Vision Rise TR26 . . 77 A7
Veor Rd TR7 . . . . 111 C7
Verden Cl PL3 . . . . 128 E5
Verdun Terr PL14 . . . . 113 B5
Vermont Gdns PL2 . . . . . . 127 F7
Verna Pl PL5 . . . . 123 D2
Verna Rd PL5 . . . . 123 E2
Vernigo Cross PL12 . . . . . . 40 B1
Vernon Pl TR11 . . . . 145 B4
Vernon Villas PL24 . . . . . . 60 B4
Vernon Way TR10 . . . . 144 B7
VERYAN 83 F6
Veryan CE Prim Sch TR2 . . 83 F6
VERYAN GREEN 83 F7
Viaduct Hill TR27 . . . . 142 E6
Viaduct La TR14 . . . . 138 A1
Vicarage Cl
Budock Water TR11 . . . . . 144 C3
Menheniot PL14 . . . . 51 F5
Vicarage Gdns
Milton Abbot PL19 . . . . . . 29 C6
Plymouth PL5 . . . . 123 B1
Vicarage Hill
Budock Water TR11 . . . . . 144 C3
Mevagissey PL26 . . . . 73 C4
10 St Austell PL25 . . . . . . 114 C3
St Day TR16 . . . . 68 E1
9 Tintagel PL34 . . . . 14 C7
Vicarage La
Lelant TR26 . . . . 77 E4
Manaccan TR12 . . . . 101 A8
Poundstock EX23 . . . . 6 F2
Vicarage Mdw PL23 . . . . . 116 C4
Vicarage Rd
Bude EX23 . . . . 104 D5
Plymouth PL7 . . . . 130 C6
Porthleven TR13 . . . . 91 A1
St Agnes TR5 . . . . 54 D1
Torpoint PL11 . . . . 127 B2
Tywardreath PL24 . . . . 60 D5
Vicarage Row TR13 . . . . . . 90 F3
Vicarage Terr TR11 . . . . . . 92 F4
VICTORIA
Lostwithiel 112 B2
Roche 46 F4
Victoria Ave PL1 . . . . 148 A4
Victoria Bsns Pk PL26 . . . . 47 A4
Victoria Cl PL14 . . . . 113 C6
Victoria Cotts
Budock Water TR11 . . . . . 144 C3
Falmouth TR11 . . . . 145 B3
Plymouth PL6 . . . . 129 B8
Victoria Ct 15 TR18 . . . . . 143 E6
Victoria Gdns
2 St Columb Road TR9 . . . . 45 E2
Threemilestone TR3 . . . . . . 69 D3
Victoria La PL12 . . . . 122 F2
Victoria Mews 17 TR18 . . 143 E6
Victoria Pk PL27 . . . . 108 D6
Victoria Pl
31 Penzance TR18 . . . . . . 143 E5
Plymouth, Devonport PL2 . 127 F4
Plymouth PL1 . . . . 148 A2
Ponsanooth TR3 . . . . 81 B4
8 St Austell PL25 . . . . . . 114 C3
12 St Ives TR26 . . . . 141 B6
Victoria Quay
5 Falmouth TR11 . . . . 145 B5
Truro TR1 . . . . 70 D1
Victoria Rd
Bude EX23 . . . . 104 D7
Camelford PL32 . . . . 105 E4
Plymouth PL5 . . . . 123 D2
Roche PL26 . . . . 46 F3
Saltash PL12 . . . . 122 F2
St Austell PL25 . . . . 114 F3
11 St Ives TR26 . . . . 141 B6
Victoria Rd *continued*
Threemilestone TR3 . . . . . . 69 D3
Victoria Road Prim Sch 1
PL5 . . . . 123 D1
Victoria Row TR19 . . . . 86 E6
Victoria Sq
Bodmin PL31 . . . . 109 F3
16 Penzance TR18 . . . . . . 143 E6
Truro TR1 . . . . 137 C4
Victoria St
Camborne TR14 . . . . 138 D2
St Columb Major TR9 . . . . . 45 E6
Torpoint PL11 . . . . 127 B3
Victoria Terr
4 Liskeard PL14 . . . . 113 B5
Nanpean PL26 . . . . 58 D6
Plymouth PL4 . . . . 148 C4
Portscatho TR2 . . . . 83 B2
St Breward PL30 . . . . 24 B3
Victory Rd EX22 . . . . 13 A8
Victory St PL2 . . . . 127 E6
Vigo Bridge Rd PL19 . . . . 147 C6
Vigo Mews PL19 . . . . 147 C6
Village Dr PL6 . . . . 121 C1
Village Farm Cl EX23 . . . . . . 7 B6
Village The
Buckland Monachorum
PL20 . . . . 41 F3
Duloe PL14 . . . . 51 A1
Villa Marina TR17 . . . . 89 B5
Villiers Cl PL9 . . . . 135 D7
Vincent Way PL12 . . . . 122 F2
Vine Cres PL2 . . . . 128 B6
Vinefield Ct TR11 . . . . 145 B7
Vine Gdns PL2 . . . . 128 B6
Vine Pl 10 PL24 . . . . 60 D5
Vinery La PL7, PL9 . . . . . . 130 E1
Vineyard The TR3 . . . . 80 F3
Vingoe's La TR20 . . . . 88 B7
Vinstone Way PL5 . . . . . . 123 D1
Violet Dr PL6 . . . . 125 E8
Violet La PL19 . . . . 147 E6
Virgin Hill TR17 . . . . 89 C6
Virginia Gdns PL2 . . . . 127 F7
Virgin Pl 16 TR19 . . . . 88 C1
Virgin St 26 TR26 . . . . . . 141 B6
Visicks Works TR3 . . . . 81 E6
Vivian Cl TR7 . . . . 110 E5
Vivian Ct TR1 . . . . 137 D3
Vivian Pk TR14 . . . . 138 F2
Vivian Rd PL31 . . . . 109 B4
Vixen Tor Cl PL20 . . . . 42 C3
VOGUE 68 D1
Vogue Hill TR16 . . . . 68 D1
Vogue Terr TR16 . . . . 68 D1
Vorfield Cl TR15 . . . . 140 B6
Vosporth Hill TR8 . . . . 110 A3
Voss Rd PL12 . . . . 53 E1
Vounder Glaze TR19 . . . . . 86 E6
Voundervour La 20 TR18 . 143 E5
Vyvyan Dr TR8 . . . . 44 E3
Vyvyan Pl TR13 . . . . 146 C5
Vyvyan St TR14 . . . . 138 D3
Vyvyan's Terr TR14 . . . . . . 79 B2

W

Waddon Cl PL7 . . . . 130 E7
WADEBRIDGE 108 A6
Wadebridge Com Prim Sch
PL27 . . . . 108 C6
Wadebridge L Ctr PL27 . . 108 C7
Wadebridge Rd
St Mabyn PL30 . . . . 34 C8
St Tudy PL30 . . . . 23 E3
Wadebridge Sch PL27 . . . 108 D6
Wadeland Terr 3 PL14 . . . 51 A7
Wadham Cl 4 PL14 . . . . . 113 C5
Wadham Dr PL14 . . . . 113 D5
Wadham Ho 5 PL14 . . . . . 113 C5
Wadham Rd PL14 . . . . 113 D5
Wadham Terr 6 PL2 . . . . 128 A5
Wagg La TR2 . . . . 71 C6
Waggon Hill PL7 . . . . 131 A4
WAINHOUSE CORNER 10 E6
Wain Pk PL7 . . . . 130 F4
Wainsway TR6 . . . . 55 A4
Wainways EX23 . . . . 10 F6
Wakefield Ave PL5 . . . . . . 123 E1
Wake St PL4 . . . . 148 B4
Walcot Cl PL6 . . . . 125 E3
Waldon Cl PL7 . . . . 131 B6
Walker Lines Ind Est 3
PL31 . . . . 48 D8
Walker Terr PL1 . . . . 148 B1
Walkham Bsns Pk PL5 . . . 124 B1
Walkham Cl PL19 . . . . 147 D5
Walkham Mdws PL20 . . . . . 42 C4
WALKHAMPTON 42 D4
Walkhampton Rd PL20 . . . . 42 C4
Walkhampton Wlk PL6 . . . 125 E1
Walkham Terr 4 PL20 . . . . 42 C5
Walk Terr PL23 . . . . 116 C2
Walk The PL15 . . . . 106 C6
WALL 78 E3
Wallace Mews 1 PL31 . . . 109 D5
Wallace Rd
Bodmin PL31 . . . . 109 D5
Plymouth PL7 . . . . 131 A4
Walled Gdn The TR10 . . . 144 A6
Wall Gdns TR27 . . . . 78 E3
Wallpark Cl PL7 . . . . 130 F7
Wall Rd TR27 . . . . 78 E3
Wallsend Ind Est PL4 . . . 149 C1
Wall Vean TR27 . . . . 78 E3
Walnut Cl PL7 . . . . 131 B5
Walnut Dr PL7 . . . . 131 C5
Walnut Gdns PL7 . . . . 131 C5
Walreddon Cl PL19 . . . . . 147 B4
Walsingham Ct PL7 . . . . . 131 B6
Walsingham Pl 15 TR1 . . 137 D4
Walters La PL15 . . . . 18 D5
Walters Rd PL5 . . . . 123 C2
Waltham Pl PL2 . . . . 128 A8
Walton Cres PL5 . . . . 124 C1
Wandle Pl PL3 . . . . 129 D5
Wansford Mdws PL26 . . . . 85 C5
WANSON 6 F3
Wanstead Gr PL5 . . . . 124 A2
Wantage Gdns PL1 . . . . . . 148 A3
WARBSTOW 11 B1
Warbstow Com Sch PL15 . 11 B1
WARBSTOW CROSS 11 B2
Warburton Gdns PL5 . . . . 123 C1
Ward Cl 4 EX23 . . . . 4 D1
Wardlow Cl PL6 . . . . 128 F8
Wardlow Gdns PL6 . . . . . . 128 F8
Wardour Wlk PL6 . . . . 125 B7
Ward Pl PL3 . . . . 129 B5
Warfelton Cres PL12 . . . . 122 E2
Warfelton Gdns PL12 . . . . 122 E2
Warfelton Terr PL12 . . . . 122 E2
Waring Rd PL6 . . . . 124 D7
WARLEGGAN 36 C4
Warleigh Ave PL2 . . . . 127 E5
WARLEIGH BARTON 123 F8
Warleigh Cres PL6 . . . . . . 124 F5
Warleigh La PL2 . . . . 127 E5
Warleigh Rd 2 PL4 . . . . . . 128 E4
Warmwell Rd PL5 . . . . 123 E4
Warne Cl TR2 . . . . 71 F3
Warran La PL19 . . . . 147 C3
Warraton Cl PL12 . . . . . . 122 D3
Warraton Gn PL12 . . . . . . 122 D3
Warraton La PL12 . . . . . . 122 D3
Warraton Rd PL12 . . . . . . 122 D3
Warren TR26 . . . . 141 B5
Warren Cl 18 TR13 . . . . . . 98 C8
Warren La PL5 . . . . 124 A8
Warren Pk PL6 . . . . 125 D7
Warren Rd TR9 . . . . 45 F2
Warrens Field PL32 . . . . . 105 D5
Warren St PL2 . . . . 127 E4
Warren The PL13 . . . . 62 E1
Warspite Gdns PL5 . . . . . . 124 D2
Warton Cl PL5 . . . . 124 D3
Warwick Ave
Illogan TR16 . . . . 67 D4
Plymouth PL5 . . . . 124 D3
Warwick Cl PL28 . . . . 31 F8
Warwick Cres 5 PL27 . . . . 31 F3
Warwick Dr PL25 . . . . 115 B5
Warwick Orchard Cl PL5 124 B3
Warwick Rd EX23 . . . . 104 E4
Wasdale Cl PL6 . . . . 125 D2
Wasdale Gdns PL6 . . . . . . 125 D2
WASHAWAY 34 C4
Washbourne Cl PL1 . . . . . 127 E3
WATERGATE 24 E8
Watergate La PL30 . . . . . . 34 C8
Watergate Rd TR8 . . . . 44 C6
Watering Hill Cl PL25 . . . 114 E3
Waterings Rd TR11 . . . . . . 82 A2
Water La
Crantock TR8 . . . . 110 A3
Delabole PL33 . . . . 14 E3
Golant PL23 . . . . 61 B5
Hayle TR27 . . . . 142 B3
St Agnes TR5 . . . . 54 D1
WATERLOO 35 D7
Waterloo TR1 . . . . 137 E4
Waterloo Cl
Plymouth PL1 . . . . 128 A2
St Mawes TR2 . . . . 95 A6
Waterloo Ct PL1 . . . . 128 A2
Waterloo Pl TR11 . . . . 145 B4
Waterloo Rd TR11 . . . . . . 145 B4
Waterloo St
Plymouth PL4 . . . . 149 A4
Plymouth, Stoke PL1 . . . . 128 A3
Waterloo Yard Flats PL1 128 A2
Water-ma-Trout TR13 . . . 146 C8
Water-ma-Trout Ind Est
TR13 . . . . 146 C8
Waters Ct TR15 . . . . 140 E7
Waters Edge
Newquay TR7 . . . . 110 A6
Tavistock PL19 . . . . 147 D6
Water's Edge PL28 . . . . . . 107 E6
Watersedge Cl PL25 . . . . . 114 B4
Waterside Lane PL30 . . . . . 47 E7
Waterside Mews PL1 . . . . 127 D3
Watersmead Parc TR11 . . 144 C3
Watery La
Bodmin PL31 . . . . 109 D5
Milton Combe PL6 . . . . . . 120 D6
Watson Gdns PL4 . . . . 149 B3
Watson Pl PL4 . . . . 149 B2
Watts Park Rd PL2 . . . . . . 128 C7
Watts Rd PL19 . . . . 147 B5
Watts' Rd PL4 . . . . 149 C3
Waveney Gdns PL5 . . . . . . 124 C3
Waverley Rd PL5 . . . . 123 D2
Wavish Pk PL11 . . . . 126 E3
Waycott Wlk PL6 . . . . 124 D6
Way Cross PL15 . . . . 27 B3
Wayfield Rd TR11 . . . . 82 B2
Wayside Ct TR7 . . . . 111 A4
Wayside Folk Mus★ TR
26 . . . . 76 B5
WEARDE 122 F2
Wearde Rd PL12 . . . . 122 E1
Webber Hill TR11 . . . . 145 B4
Webber St TR11 . . . . 145 B4
Webbs Ct 9 PL14 . . . . 113 C6
Webb St PL23 . . . . 116 D4
Wedgewood Rd PL25 . . . . 115 A4
WEEK GREEN 11 E8
WEEK ST MARY 11 E8
Weeks Rise PL32 . . . . 105 B2
Weeks Row PL18 . . . . 41 A6
Weekstone Cross EX22 . . . . 8 C8
Weeth Cl TR14 . . . . 138 C3
Weethes Cotts 6 TR18 . . 143 D5
Weeth La TR14 . . . . 138 C3
Weeth Prim Sch TR14 . . . 138 C4
Weeth Rd TR14 . . . . 138 C4
Weir Cl PL6 . . . . 125 F2
Weir Gdns PL6 . . . . 125 F2
Weir Rd PL6 . . . . 125 F2
Welbeck Ave PL4 . . . . 148 C4
WELCOMBE 2 D5
Welcombe Cross EX39 . . . . 3 B4
Welcome Cl TR4 . . . . 56 D1
Welland Gdns PL3 . . . . . . 129 C5
Weller Ct TR11 . . . . 145 B3
Wellfield Cl
Coad's Green PL15 . . . . . . 27 D3
Plymouth PL7 . . . . 131 C5
Well Gdns PL1 . . . . 148 B3
Wellhay Cl PL9 . . . . 136 C6
Wellhouse The 8 PL14 . . . 113 C6
Wellington Cl TR14 . . . . . 138 C3
Wellington Gdns TR11 . . . 145 B4
Wellington Pl
Falmouth TR11 . . . . 145 B4
Penzance TR18 . . . . 143 D5
Wadebridge PL27 . . . . 108 C4
Wellington Plantation
TR3 . . . . 82 B7
Wellington Rd
Camborne TR14 . . . . 138 D3
Porthleven TR13 . . . . 91 B1
St Dennis PL26 . . . . 58 C8
2 St Eval PL27 . . . . 31 F3
Wellington St
Plymouth PL4 . . . . 149 A4
Plymouth, Stoke PL1 . . . . 128 A3
Torpoint PL11 . . . . 127 B3
Wellington Terr
Falmouth TR11 . . . . 145 B4
Porthleven TR13 . . . . 91 B1
Portscatho TR2 . . . . 83 B2
2 Truro TR1 . . . . 137 C4
Well La
Constantine TR11 . . . . 92 F4
Falmouth TR11 . . . . 145 B4
Goldsithney TR20 . . . . 89 F5
Lamorna TR19 . . . . 97 E5
Liskeard PL14 . . . . 113 C6
St Cleer PL14 . . . . 37 F3
St Keverne TR12 . . . . 101 D4
Tregony TR2 . . . . 71 F3
Tremar PL14 . . . . 38 A3
Welcombe EX39 . . . . 2 E5
Well Mdw PL15 . . . . 18 A5
Wellpark Rd PL18 . . . . 40 F5
Well Park Rd PL11 . . . . . . 127 B3
Wellsbourne Pk PL3 . . . . . 129 A6
Wells Ct PL10 . . . . 132 E4
Well St
Callington PL17 . . . . 39 E4
Delabole PL33 . . . . 14 E3
Tregony TR2 . . . . 71 F3
Tywardreath PL24 . . . . 60 D5
Well Way TR7 . . . . 111 C7
Welman Rd PL10 . . . . 132 F6
Welsby Terr PL14 . . . . 37 F3
WELSFORD 3 C8
Welsford Ave PL2 . . . . 127 F5
Welway TR6 . . . . 55 A4
WEMBURY 136 B1
Wembury Park Rd PL3 . . . 128 D6
Wembury Rd PL9 . . . . 136 A4
WENDRON 91 F6
Wendron CE Prim Sch
TR13 . . . . 91 F5
Wendron St TR13 . . . . 146 C6
WENFORDBRIDGE 24 A2
Wenlock Gdns PL2 . . . . . . 128 B8
WENMOUTH CROSS 37 A3
Wensum Cl PL7 . . . . 131 A4
Wentwood Gdns PL6 . . . . . 125 E3
Wentwood Pl PL6 . . . . 125 E3
Wentworth Cl
Lynstone EX23 . . . . 104 C3
Polzeath PL27 . . . . 21 D5
Redruth TR15 . . . . 140 C3
Wentworth Pl PL4 . . . . 129 B2
Wentworth Way PL12 . . . . 122 C2
WERRINGTON 18 F6
Werrington Dr PL17 . . . . . . 39 E4
Werrington Prim Sch
PL15 . . . . 18 F7
Wesley Ave PL3 . . . . 128 E5
Wesley Cl
Kelly Bray PL17 . . . . 39 F6
Stenalees PL26 . . . . 59 C8
Wesley Cottage Mus★
PL15 . . . . 26 B7
Wesley Ct
Penryn TR10 . . . . 144 C8
Pensilva PL14 . . . . 38 D4
25 Porthleven TR13 . . . . . . 98 C8
Torpoint PL11 . . . . 127 C3
Wesley La PL12 . . . . 122 F2
Wesley Pl
5 Newlyn TR18 . . . . 143 C2
Plymouth, Mutley PL3 . . . . 128 E5
1 Plymouth, Stoke PL2 . . 128 A4